Platform Ecosystems

Aligning Architecture, Governance, and Strategy

Platform Ecosystems
Aligning Architecture, Governance, and Strategy

Amrit Tiwana

AMSTERDAM • BOSTON • HEIDELBERG • LONDON
NEW YORK • OXFORD • PARIS • SAN DIEGO
SAN FRANCISCO • SINGAPORE • SYDNEY • TOKYO

Morgan Kaufmann is an imprint of Elsevier

Acquiring Editor: *Andrea Dierna*
Editorial Project Manager: *Lindsay Lawrence*
Project Manager: *Malathi Samayan*
Designer: *Russell Purdy*

Morgan Kaufmann is an imprint of Elsevier
225 Wyman Street, Waltham, MA 02451, USA

Library of Congress Cataloging-in-Publication Data

Tiwana, Amrit
  Platform ecosystems: aligning architecture, governance, and strategy / Amrit Tiwana.
    pages cm
  Includes bibliographical references and index.
  ISBN 978-0-12-408066-9 (alk. paper)
  1. Computer software industry. 2. New products. I. Title.
  HD9696.63.A2T59 2014
  338.4'7004–dc23

                                                                    2013037658

British Library Cataloguing-in-Publication Data
A catalogue record for this book is available from the British Library

ISBN: 978-0-12-408066-9

Printed and bound in the United States of America
14 15 16   13 12 11 10 9 8 7 6 5 4 3 2 1

For information on all MK publications, visit our website at www.mkp.com or www.elsevierdirect.com

To my Dad.

Brief Contents

Contents

PART IV ORCHESTRATING EVOLUTION

Introduction

Platform Ecosystems provides a strategic roadmap for designing and orchestrating software platform ecosystems. The book is based on two assumptions. First, there are no cheap tickets to mastering platforms. If there were, we'd have a hundred Facebooks and Apples today. Second, nurturing platforms requires thinking at the *nexus* of software design and business strategy.

This book was motivated by the disproportionate attention in the popular press to a few superstar platforms, such as Amazon, Apple, Google, and Facebook, and the alarming overuse of phrases such as "competitive advantage" and "disruptive innovation." "Be more like them," urge the pundits. Advising companies to follow the examples of such companies is like advising me to emulate Tom Cruise! Good in theory, but utterly unrealistic and impractical. Attempting to emulate superstar platforms put on a pedestal by the business press is a futile exercise for most companies that lack their heft and resources, and because popular press admonitions overlook their humble and scrappy beginnings. Such anecdotes make enjoyable reading but are a hazardous basis for running a business. Instead of attempting to generalize lessons from a few outlier superstar platforms, this book distills a few enduring principles for developing and sustaining platform businesses designed and run by mere mortals like you and I. The book targets an unfilled void for an actionable managerial guide to orchestrating the evolution of software-based platform ecosystems.

Think of this book as a map, not a global positioning system. As luddite as it sounds for a software-centric book, a map remains valuable long after the GPS has run out of batteries. However, with a map you have to get your bearings first and then do the driving yourself. This book will simply provide you the tools, but how you use them is up to you. This is neither a technology book nor a management book; rather, it is about how their nuanced *interplay* shapes a platform ecosystem's evolution. It offers an actionable, graspable introduction to this interplay, backed by original research, tangible metrics, rich historical data, and real-world cases.

Four properties that differentiate platform markets from other markets—the figurative baby in the bathwater—are fundamental to the platform thinking introduced in this book:

1. *Compressed evolution.* Dynamics visible only over 30–40 years in most industries can be observed in 5–7 years in platform businesses. As a growing variety of nontechnology industries become more software-centric, they increasingly acquire properties that were historically unique to the software business.
2. *Evolution predicts survival.* A successful product or service that meets the needs of existing customers will fail if it does not evolve. Platforms must be designed to be evolvable, and evolutionary metrics—not software or business metrics—are needed to chart their evolutionary trajectory.
3. *Harnessing external disruptions.* All major disruptive innovations in almost every industry have always come from outsiders. Platform industries simply allow such disruption to be harnessed productively by industry insiders, offering them the opportunity to be some part of the new order. Understanding the dynamics of platform markets, irrespective of your industry, is increasingly critical to avoid becoming the next Borders, Circuit City, or Pony Express.
4. *Architecture–governance alignment shapes evolution.* The architecture of a platform is inseparable from how it ought to be governed. This requires codesigning and coevolving them as a platform

ecosystem progresses through different stages in its lifecycle. How alignment of platform governance with its architecture shapes the evolutionary trajectory of platform ecosystems is therefore the overarching theme of this book.

Preview of this book's message

The key message of this book can be summarized on an index card (see Figure 1) as follows:

1. Platform ecosystems are replacing traditional models in and beyond the software industry, driven largely by the digitization of products, services, and business processes. They can expand the pie for everyone but require a fundamental shift in strategic mindset.
2. Survival and prosperity of platform ecosystems require a platform owner to deliberately *orchestrate* their evolution.
3. Orchestrating their evolution requires that their architecture and governance interlock and subsequently coevolve, which is biologically inspired business design.

How this book is organized

The jigsaw in Figure 2 summarizes the organization of this book. The book is organized in four parts. In spite of the hyperlinked world in which we dwell, I recommend that you go against the grain and read this book linearly. The reason: Each part builds on ideas introduced in the preceding parts. Therefore, ideas in Part II will make more sense if you read them after you read Part I. A Lessons Learned section

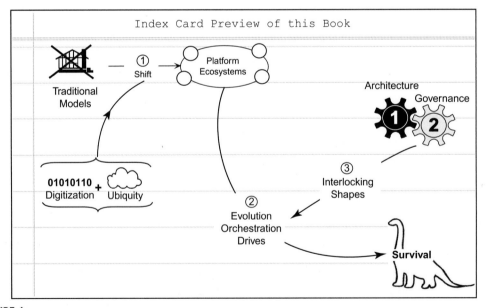

FIGURE 1

An index card–sized preview of the book.

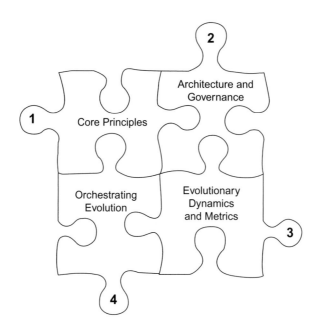

FIGURE 2

Organization of this book.

summarizes the key ideas at the end of each chapter. Hopefully, this will be more useful as a tickler than as a cure for insomnia.

Part I of the book describes the rise of platform ecosystems (Chapter 1) and then describes their core concepts and nine principles (Chapter 2). I then describe what makes platform businesses different from product and service businesses (Chapter 3), and their value proposition from the perspective of a platform owner, app developers, and end-users (Chapter 4). This part also provides a four-lens framework for spotting opportunities for transforming products and services into platforms.

Part II tackles the two gears of the motor of platform evolution: platform architecture and governance. It first explains the role of architecture in partitioning and integration of innovation work among the platform owner and app developers (Chapter 5). The architecture of a platform and the microarchitecture of its apps, however, must be appropriately governed to realize their innovation potential. The multifaceted notion of platform governance encompassing pricing, control, and decision rights is described in Chapter 6.

Part III provides a foundation for understanding evolution in platform markets. It begins with operational and strategic metrics of evolution that span the different time horizons (Chapter 7), followed by real options thinking for coping with technological and market uncertainty (Chapter 8). I then describe five discrete operations that provide the alphabet for evolving platforms and apps (Chapter 9).

Part IV puts the two gears of ecosystem evolution—architecture and governance—together. It describes how the interplay of technical architecture and governance guides the evolution of the platform, its apps, and entire ecosystems. It describes how platforms (Chapter 10) and apps (Chapter 11) evolve to develop and sustain a competitive advantage over time. We delve into how such architecture–governance alignment shapes their resilience, scalability, and composability in the short term;

stickiness, platform synergy, and plasticity in the medium term; and envelopment, durability, and mutation in the long term. The emphasis is on helping readers—both platform owners and app developers—make informed, practical decisions with an appreciation of their short-term and long-term evolutionary consequences.

Part V—the book's conclusion—summarizes and extends the core ideas developed in this book beyond software platform ecosystems to business ecosystems across a variety of nontechnology industries. It also provides a Monday morning agenda for preparing managers to spot opportunities to nurture biologically inspired platform-like business ecosystems in nontechnology product and service industries.

Assumptions about you

I make three assumptions about you as a reader of this book. I hope that at least two of these are true if this book is going to help you. First, that you are either an IT professional who appreciates that great technology with bad business strategy often fails in the market or you are a business manager who appreciates that bad technology can stall even the most brilliant business strategy. Second, that you appreciate that evolution of technology matters a great deal to its competitive survival and prosperity. Third, that you lack the deep pockets of the likes of Amazon and Facebook yet want to understand how platform thinking can be *applied* to your own work. If you are an app developer, you probably already understand modularity, systems integration, and the role of SDKs, APIs, and toolkits but not how economic principles, governance, and technical design choices preordain business strategy and evolution. This book provides you insights into the business consequences of technical decisions. If you are a business manager and those words are Greek to you but you do understand concepts such as returns to scale, lock-in, and competitive advantage, this book will provide you new insights into how they are inseparable from technology architectures in competitive markets. The ideas in Part III and beyond, which originate in evolutionary biology, are likely to be less familiar to either group.

What this book is *not* about

Let me also explain what this book is *not* about and what distinguishes this book's approach. This book is:

- *Not about my opinion.* I enjoy watching David Letterman as much as my next-door neighbor, but I would not bet my livelihood on his opinion. Opinions can be flawed, sometimes totally wrong. If Peter Drucker's opinion can be wrong, so can your $1,200-an-hour Gucci-clad consultant's. This book is not built on cherry-picked "best practices" of a few superstar platforms or the epiphany that I had in the shower this morning on how *you* should run *your* business. Those are a dime a dozen. Instead, this book is based on years of research spanning 139 studies by precisely 105 researchers (including some of my own research) in hundreds of big and small companies in dozens of countries. This research—cited at the end of this book—spans business strategy, software architecture, economics, and evolutionary biology. The book is based on research, but is not a theory book. It is designed to be an enduring, practical toolkit.
- *Not about trends.* Trends fade but principles endure. Today's poster child becomes tomorrow's has-been. The cycle repeats. iOS took over Blackberry, which took over Palm, which took over the

paper organizer. The pattern is surprisingly predictable; in every case, the incumbent realized too late that the rules of the game had changed. Rather than being trendy, this book will help you benefit from trends. Think of ice harvesters in Minnesota in the 1800s, the cotton gin, the horse buggy, the Pony Express, residential telephones, and video rental stores. Their albatross was their failure to evolve, which is why platform evolution that has historically escaped the radar screens of both managers and technologists is a pervasive theme in this book. The frameworks here provide ropes and anchors to navigate progress into the unknown.

- *Not about a silver bullet*. This book offers no "methodology" that promises the world but often cannot even deliver a village. A methodology assumes that there *is* a formula. Like an airplane, a methodology gets you and 273 other companies following it to exactly the same destination—hardly a good way to create a unique competitive advantage.
- *Not about business common sense and execution*. Rumors of the demise of basic economic principles have been greatly exaggerated. Basic business common sense (e.g., the need to make more money than you spend) is alive and kicking, and no insight in this book will trump that. Similarly, solid execution is what keeps a good idea from degenerating into cheap talk. However, this book will spend little time on execution as there are many other excellent books on software implementation.

Think of this book as a conversation between you and me. I would love to hear your comments, suggestions, reactions, and criticisms. Feel free to email me at tiwana@uga.edu.

Amrit Tiwana
Athens, Georgia

Supplemental Materials

Supplemental materials can be downloaded from https://store.elsevier.com/product.jsp?isbn=9780124080669&_requestid=291788

The Rise of Platforms

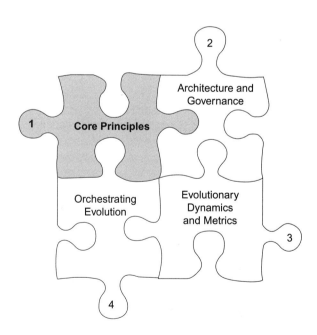

2

Architecture and
Governance

1   **Core Principles**

Orchestrating
Evolution

Evolutionary
Dynamics
and Metrics

3

4

The Rise of Platform Ecosystems

1

May you live in interesting times.
Ancient Chinese curse

IN THIS CHAPTER

- What platforms are and what they are not
- Core components of platform ecosystems
- Drivers of the migration toward platforms in diverse industries

1.1 THE WAR OF ECOSYSTEMS

Blackberry had everything going right. It had fanatically loyal customers and its products were innovative, well engineered, durable, and got raving reviews from critics. After years of commanding a lion's share (about 50%) of the smartphone market that it largely created, it had trouble breaking past a 1% market share with its newest products by 2012, leading to its subsequent downfall Blackberry assumed that the problem was Apple and then Google—both industry outsiders—who had since entered the fray. So, it did what made sense: Price more competitively, invest more in developing new products, upgrade its operating system, and step up marketing. Nothing worked. Its error was failing to realize that the basis for competition had changed: It was no longer Blackberry against Apple smartphones. Instead, it was the Blackberry ecosystem against the iOS ecosystem. It was not one product against another but Blackberry's army of 8000 external innovators against Apple's 200,000. Blackberry's mistake was failing to realize the ecosystem on which its continued success depended. All three companies made good products, but the lack of enough innovative apps muted Blackberry's market potential. It was already too late to catch up by the time Blackberry realized that the competitive blueprint had shifted. The *Red Queen* effect[1]—the need to run faster just to stay in the same place—had taken over.

Platforms are creating an entirely new blueprint for competition—one that puts ecosystems in head-to-head competition. The ongoing migration from product and service competition to platform-based competition in many industries and markets is driven by forces—packetization of products, services, and activities; software embedding and ubiquitous networking of everyday objects; and the increased need for specialization—that are increasingly infusing characteristics of the software industry into

---

☆"To view the full reference list for the book, click here or see page 283."
[1]As the next chapter explains, one competitor successfully adopting a platform-centric approach can compress an entire industry's innovation clockspeed, requiring much greater effort just to stay in the same place.

many nontechnology industries. What served firms well in product-based markets can become their Achilles heel in platform-based markets. Managing platform-based businesses requires an entirely different mindset for strategy. Most of the old rules of business are alive and well, but many of the assumptions behind them do not hold in such environments. However, few observers have moved beyond individual superstar anecdotes of Apple, Facebook, and Amazon to analyze the broader principles and mechanisms that generalize beyond them. How should platforms be designed? How should they be governed, controlled, and priced? How can the work of so many be coordinated in the absence of familiar organizational structures? How do these choices shape their evolvability, their competitive durability, and their survival? How can their design create win–win propositions for app developers and users? How does a product or service even become a platform? The objective of this book is to provide you with actionable tools to arrive at your own answers about platform design strategies, and for platforms beyond the idiosyncrasies of the few poster children of the popular press.

This book is based on two premises. First, that the migration of competition from products to platforms—in technology and nontechnology industries alike—requires a different mindset for managing them. Second, evolvability in unforeseeable ways is key to thriving in platform markets but is rarely the dominant emphasis in complex software systems. Architecture and strategy are the two gears of a platform's evolutionary motor that must interlock and align. Evolution[2] is therefore predicated in the *interplay* between its irreversible architecture and how it is governed. Platforms that thrive are ones whose *ecosystems* outpace rival ones in the evolutionary race. They orchestrate their ecosystems to leverage the drive and expertise of many outsiders without compromising ecosystem-wide integration. But not all platforms are created equal; the seeds of effective orchestration are sown in their early architecture. This is also where the landmines that lead to their collapse are hidden.

This chapter lays a foundation for introducing these ideas. It begins with an overview of software platforms and how they are changing the rules of competition. It then identifies the central elements of platform ecosystems and their competitive environment. It also clarifies what is *not* a platform. It then describes the five drivers of the migration toward software platforms in a variety of technology and nontechnology industries ranging from smartphones, appliances, fast food, craft machines, automobiles, medicine, and professional services. These include (1) the need for deepening specialization as firms struggle to deliver increasingly complex products and services; (2) the "packetization" of products, services, business processes, and activities; (3) the baking of routine business activities into software across a plethora of industries; (4) the emergence of the Internet of Things; and (5) the growing ubiquity of cheap, fast, and untethered digital networks. The *confluence* of these drivers can infuse properties of software platforms into products and services in mundane activities in nontechnology industries, making this book's content surprisingly industry agnostic. This transformation can change how firms make money, retain customers, organize, and survive.

1.2 PLATFORM ECOSYSTEMS

Platform-based software ecosystems such as the iOS and its 800,000 "apps" produced by 200,000 firms or Facebook and its 9 million apps are increasingly becoming the dominant model for the software

[2]Evolution is multifaceted, as described in Part III, encompassing ideas such as durability of competitive advantage, stickiness, enveloping adjacent market, innovation at the app and platform level, and creating derivative and "nested" platforms.

industry and digital services.[3] The utility of almost any platform is increasingly shaped by the ecosystem that surrounds it. Take Apple's record-breaking iOS platform that includes the iPhone, iPod, and iPad. Its value to its 365 million users comes largely from the 800,000 complementary apps over which Apple has little ownership. Unlike traditional software development, platforms are designed to leverage the expertise of a diverse developer community—with ingenuity, hunger, skills, and an appreciation of user needs that platform owners might not possess. The emergence of such platform ecosystems (simply, systems composed of diverse smaller systems) is relocating the locus of innovation from the firm to a massive network of outside firms. The goal is to rapidly develop new capabilities and foster innovations unforeseeable by the platform's original designers. The idea of a platform as a foundation on which one builds is not new. Product families have existed in the tooling industry for decades, automotive platforms underpinned General Motors' dominance over Ford in the 1920s, operating systems are the engines in the IT industry, and "two-sided markets" that bring together buyers and sellers have existed since medieval times (Eisenmann et al., 2006; Fichman, 2004; Katz and Shapiro, 1994). But software infuses unique but poorly understood properties into platforms.

Our focus in this book is on *software-based platforms*, which create distinctively more complex opportunities and challenges than other types of platforms. They also function on a scale that is unprecedented in the industrial age because they allow literally hundreds of thousands of small companies to collectively do things that a traditional network of partners or intricate supply chains could not even dream of accomplishing. The potential power of platform ecosystems comes from leveraging the unique expertise of many, diverse independent app developers driven by market incentives on a scale that is impossible to replicate within a single organization. The platform model essentially outsources to thousands of outside partners innovation that used to be done inhouse, who bear all the cost and risk of innovating and then share the proceeds with the platform owner. The platform model throws the brainpower of thousands of small firms, mixes it with their hunger to succeed in the market, and lets the market determine the winners and losers. This potent mix of specialized expertise with the disciplining power of markets can foster innovation at a rate that exceeds by orders of magnitude conventional business models. Products that became platforms from 1990 until 2004 enjoyed a 500% increase in innovation, most of which came from outside developers (Boudreau, 2010). A platform's success therefore depends not only on the platform owner, but also on a multitude of ecosystem partners' ability to deliver (Adner, 2012, p. 1).

1.2.1 Elements of a software platform ecosystem

A platform-based ecosystem consists of two major elements—a platform and complementary apps—as Figure 1.1 illustrates. A software *platform* is a software-based product or service that serves as a foundation on which outside parties can build complementary products or services. A software platform is therefore an extensible software-based system that provides the core functionality shared by "apps" that interoperate with it, and the interfaces through which they interoperate (Baldwin and Woodard, 2009; Tiwana et al., 2010). We refer to the lead firm primarily responsible for the platform as the *platform owner*, sometimes also called the ecosystem's keystone firm (Iansiti and Levien, 2004) or the economic catalyst (Evans and Schmalensee, 2007). Platform ownership can be shared by multiple firms and a platform need not be proprietary or for-profit. An *app* refers to an add-on software

---

[3]Sources: http://148apps.biz/app-store-metrics/ and http://newsroom.fb.com/Platform.

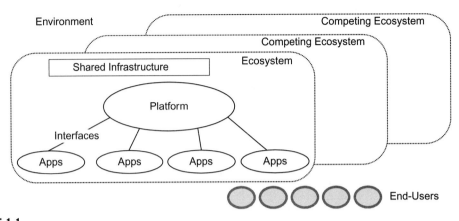

FIGURE 1.1

Elements of a platform ecosystem.

subsystem or software service that connects to the platform to extend its functionality. Although such complementary subsystems are often also called add-ons, plug-ins, modules, and extensions, here we refer to such platform complements simply as apps and their developers as app developers. Apps are complementary goods for platforms; platforms are functionally more desirable when there are a wide variety of complements available to them. (Two products are complements when one increases the attractiveness of the other; think of cookies and milk or a laptop and a Web browser.) For example, Internet streaming boxes are more desirable when streaming content is widely available; smartphones are more valuable when networks supporting them exist; Amazon's Kindle is more valuable when publishers produce e-books. The platform therefore consists of the enabling core technologies and shared infrastructure that apps can leverage. Apps access and build on the functionality of the platform through a set of *interfaces* that allow them to communicate, interact, and interoperate with the platform. The metaphor that science fiction fans can relate to is that the platform is like the *Starship Enterprise* and apps are like the little shuttlecrafts that dock into its myriad ports. The collection of the platform and apps that interoperate with it represents the platform's *ecosystem*. A platform ecosystem therefore meets the criteria for defining a complex system; one comprised of numerous interacting subsystems (Simon, 1962). Table 1.1 summarizes these core elements of a platform ecosystem.

Outside of these central elements of a platform ecosystem are three other contextual features: end-users, rival platform ecosystems, and the competitive environment in which they exist. End-users are the collection of existing and prospective adopters of the platform. The characteristics and diversity of this market evolves over time and as industries converge and split. A platform ecosystem exists within a larger competitive environment, often competing with other rival platform ecosystems. Such rival platform ecosystems constantly compete for both users and app developers. For example, Apple's iOS competes with Google's Android, Blackberry, Nokia's Symbian, and Microsoft's mobile platforms. The competition within this environment is rarely directly among the platforms themselves but rather among competing ecosystems. The more intense this competition, the more important a platform's evolution becomes for surviving and thriving. A vibrant and dynamic ecosystem is therefore key to the survival of any software platform, and increasingly of products and services as they morph into platforms or become subservient complements of another platform.

Table 1.1 Core Elements of a Platform Ecosystem

Element	Definition	Example
Platform	The extensible codebase of a software-based system that provides core functionality shared by apps that interoperate with it, and the interfaces through which they interoperate	iOS, Android Dropbox, Twitter AWS Firefox, Chrome
App	An add-on software subsystem or service that connects to the platform to add functionality to it. Also referred to as a module, extension, plug-in, or add-on	Apps Apps Apps Extensions
Ecosystem	The collection of the platform and the apps specific to it	
Interfaces	Specifications that describe how the platform and apps interact and exchange information	APIs Protocols
Architecture	A conceptual blueprint that describes how the ecosystem is partitioned into a relatively stable platform and a complementary set of apps that are encouraged to vary, and the design rules binding on both	–

An ecosystem can also be divided into its upstream and downstream parts of a value chain, as illustrated in Figure 1.2. The *upstream* part of the value chain is what goes into producing the platform itself (component and hardware suppliers, software licensors, manufacturing partners, network connectivity providers). The *downstream* part of the value chain includes platform complement producers (primarily app developers and complementary service providers), end-users who adopt it, and other intermediaries between the platform owner and end-users such as retailers and carriers (Adner and Kapoor, 2010). Apps are therefore *downstream complements* to a platform. Table 1.2 provides examples of various contemporary platform ecosystems and their downstream complements. Downstream complements are bundled *by a platform's end-users* to customize the platform to their unique needs (Adner and Kapoor, 2010). Other downstream complements are necessary but insufficient to sustain differentiation of a platform vis-à-vis rival platforms. The platform itself therefore serves as only one part of the larger bundled system from which the platform's end-users derive value. The attractiveness of a platform to end-users comes not from the platform itself but from what they can do with it. The fate and survival of a platform then critically hinges on the diversity and vibrancy of its downstream ecosystem. The evolutionary battles of platform dominance and survival are fought primarily downstream, where formidable competitive barriers for rival platforms can be created. That does not mean that the upstream is unimportant; it just does not differentiate platforms in their evolutionary trajectory to the same degree as long as they manage the upstream task of executing the platform assembly process comparably efficiently. Our focus in this book is therefore exclusively on the downstream part of the platform value chain.

1.2.2 What a platform is not

We must also draw a sharp boundary of what a platform is *not*, particularly given the colloquial use of the label in ways that can mean many different things to different people. The common denominator of all platforms is that they facilitate interactions between two *distinct* groups (the two

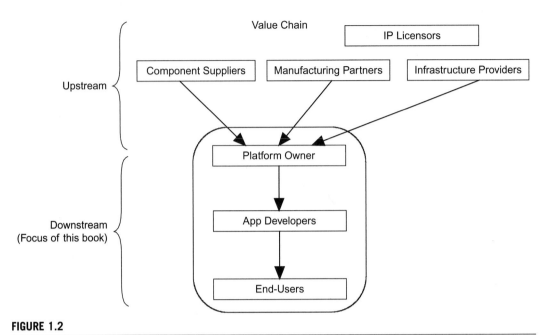

FIGURE 1.2

Upstream and downstream parts of platform value chains.

Table 1.2 Examples of Software Platforms		
Industry	**Platform**	**"Apps"**
Mobile computing	Blackberry OS	Apps
	Apple's iOS	
	Google's Android	
	Palm OS/HP TouchOS (defunct)	
Browser	Firefox	Extensions
	Google Chrome	Add-ins, Web apps
Social networks	Dropbox	Apps
	Twitter	
	Facebook	
Publishing	Amazon's Kindle	e-Books
	iTunes	Music
Specialized software tools	R (statistical analysis platform)	Modules
Operating systems	Ubuntu Linux	Applications
Search engines	Users	Advertisers
Video games	Gamers	Game developers

"sides") that want to interact with and need each other (Evans and Schmalensee, 2007, p. 38). The platform's value to a user depends on the number of adopters on the other side. Our focus here is on multisided platforms rather than one-sided platforms, which we do not consider true platforms at all. Instead, they are products or services often confused or mislabeled as platforms. A platform by definition is at least two-sided (Eisenmann et al., 2006). Almost every example of successful platforms touted in the press—iPhone, Windows, Facebook, Skype, Amazon, eBay, Google, Firefox, and Dropbox—started out not as platforms but as standalone products or services that were valuable to end-users. Only after end-users widely adopted these products and services did they add a second side—developers—and transform into a platform. In one-sided platforms, the platform owner does not directly interact with two groups that might want to interact with each other; rather, it interacts primarily with one. Oracle, for example, provides enterprise systems to firms such as Target and Wal-Mart to enhance their business processes; however, it does not directly interact with their customers. Apple's iOS, Google's Chrome and Android, Mozilla's Firefox, Ubuntu, Dropbox, Twitter, and Amazon Web Services (AWS) are examples of platforms. Platforms are not more complex versions of supply chains either. Supply chains are often one-sided markets rather than multisided markets, and therefore obey a different, simpler, and more predictable set of principles. We focus in this book on platforms in competitive consumer markets and exclude internal IT "platforms" that organizations build primarily for their own use. We also focus less on trading platforms that solely exist to match buyers and sellers of commodities (e.g., eBay and Amazon) in favor of software-based platforms where complementors actually contribute to the functionality and capabilities of the platform.

1.3 DRIVERS OF THE MIGRATION TOWARD PLATFORMS

Recent advances in technology are increasingly making it possible to reconfigure traditional industries along the lines of software-centric platforms abundant in ecosystem-creation opportunities. Much of this shift is facilitated by five drivers. These drivers, accelerating the migration from product and service competition to platform-based competition in a variety of diverse industries, are summarized in Figure 1.3 and their consequences in Table 1.3. These drivers include (1) deepening specialization within industries; (2) the "packetization" of products, services, business processes, and activities; (3) the baking of routine business activities into software; (4) the emergence of the "Internet of Things"; and (5) the growing ubiquity of mobile Internet protocol-based data networks. It is the confluence of these drivers that is transforming platforms into the de facto engines of new economic activity.

The graveyard of fallen giants is littered with once-dominant companies that failed to recognize these shifts in their own industry. They can make proven business models obsolete, alter the foundational assumptions of the industry, and require a different mindset to compete in an industry. It is not just the technology industries but any information-intensive industry that is likely to be affected by these drivers. And, as we explain in the subsequent chapters, some of these drivers can transform a low-skill, non-information-intensive industry into an information- and skill-intensive industry that then begins to behave like any other platform-centric industry. These drivers become even more forceful when they coexist, and their joint effects often exceed the sum of their parts.

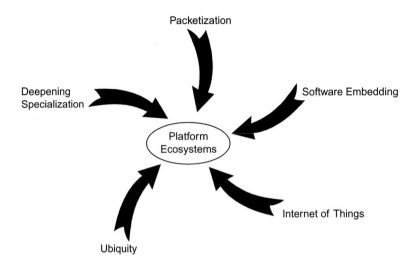

FIGURE 1.3

The five drivers of the migration toward platform-centric business models.

Table 1.3 Consequences of the Five Drivers Toward Platform-Centric Business Models		
Driver	**Description**	**Consequences**
Deepening specialization	Increased need for deep expertise due to growing complexity of products and services	• Simultaneously shrinking and expanding firm boundaries • Red Queen effect from clockspeed compression • Increased interdependence among firms
Packetization	Digitization of "something"—an activity, a process, a product, or a service—that was previously not digitized	• Location-independent distribution ability of work • Deepening specialization
Software embedding	Baking a routine business activity into software	• Products-to-services transformation • Morphing physical–digital boundary • Convergence of adjacent industries
Internet of Things	Everyday objects inexpensively gaining the ability to directly talk using an Internet protocol	• Deluge of data streams from networked objects • Context awareness
Ubiquity	The growing omnipresence of cheap and fast wireless Internet data networks	• Loosely coupled networks rival efficiencies of firms • Alters who can participate from where • Alters where services can be delivered • Scale without ownership

1.3.1 Driver #1: Deepening specialization

Customers are increasingly demanding more customization instead of homogenous products and services delivered in volume (Williamson and De Meyer, 2012). At the same time, the complexity of products and services across diverse industries is also increasing. In software products in particular, the number of lines of code is estimated to double every 2 years (Evans et al., 2006, p. 303). For every line of software code in a typical software product in 2010, extrapolating this pattern for the following 20 years, as shown in Figure 1.4, suggests a dramatic growth in complexity over time. As products and services grow in complexity, it is increasingly difficult for one company—no matter how large—to specialize simultaneously in all domains that go into producing it (Evans et al., 2006, p. 53; Williamson and De Meyer, 2012). As knowledge needed to deliver increasingly complex products and services becomes more dispersed across many firms and many markets, no single firm or small network of firms can innovate alone (Dougherty and Dunne, 2011; Williamson and De Meyer, 2012). This creates a greater pressure for companies to more deeply specialize in their core competence and leave the rest to capable partners. This has increasingly led to the disaggregation of firms into complex supply chain networks involving many partners, and now into even larger ecosystems of smaller firms that specialize narrowly and deeply. These outsiders can potentially bring a breadth of deep insights about specialized domains, different application markets, and geographies that one company would struggle to maintain inhouse. Manufacturing, IT services, financial services, engineering, and even medical services industries are beginning to see this trend.

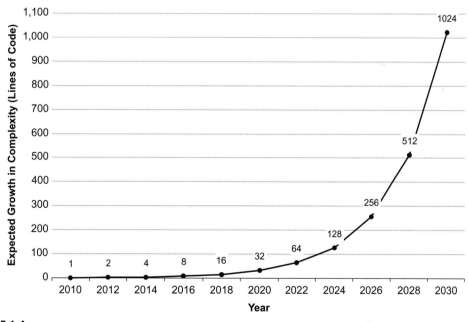

FIGURE 1.4

Extrapolating the increase in complexity for a single line of code in 2010 indicates a thousand-fold growth in complexity in two decades.

Location-dependence and coordination costs have often been the constraints that keep firms from disaggregating further, but the other four drivers—packetization, embedding of processes in software, the emergence of the Internet of Things, and ubiquity—are beginning to change that. A platform-centric approach enables pooling of multiple firms' knowledge bases that are more valuable in combination than in isolation.

1.3.1.1 Consequences

Deepening specialization has three consequences: (1) simultaneously shrinking and expanding firm boundaries, (2) the *Red Queen* effect, and (3) increased need for integration of distributed expertise. First, deeper specialization around their core competence means that companies are under pressure to do more of what they are really good at and less of everything else. The boundaries of the firm are therefore simultaneously contracting and expanding. They are contracting in the sense that the firm is focusing on a narrowing sliver of the value chain in Figure 1.2—the sliver where it focuses exclusively on its core capabilities. It is expanding in the sense that it relies on a broader community of outsiders to perform the complementary activities that go into delivering an attractive product or service. This is reducing the core activities that are done inhouse but simultaneously expanding the boundaries of the firm to include a greater assortment of outside partners. Ecosystems are an approach for dealing with such growing complexity without losing focus on what a firm does well. Platform-based businesses can potentially leverage the diversity and deep domain knowledge of a large pool of outside innovators, who are driven by market incentives. If managed right, the sheer pursuit of self-interest by these outsiders can accelerate the company's innovation around its core specialty far beyond what a lone corporation can possibly accomplish.

Second, one competitor successfully adopting a platform-centric approach can compress the clock-speed of innovation in the entire industry. It puts intense pressure on other firms in that industry to continuously innovate to keep their products and services differentiated, or else face the march of commoditization or outright irrelevance in a competitive marketplace. Firms in that industry cannot afford to ignore it; if their rivals are deepening specialization, they must too because staying in the same place is likely to require even more effort (see the *Red Queen effect* in Chapter 2). For example, Apple's iPad progressed through four generations within two years after its introduction, while Blackberry's Playbook struggled with its first generation. It did not matter that Blackberry once dominated the smartphone industry; the bar to keep up had been raised dramatically. This problem is not unique to the technology industries, as the examples throughout the book illustrate.

Third, this increased interdependence—across domains, markets, and geographies—between the firms needs to be managed. They need to be able to coordinate and integrate their dispersed contributions to deliver a valuable offering in the market. The mechanisms of authority, command-and-control, and contracts that underpin the very success of conventional firms rarely exist in ecosystem markets. Much of what makes traditional organizations efficient is precisely what can stifle innovation in large-scale ecosystems comprised of many independent firms. Modern business strategy focuses on "the firm," not ecosystems; it emphasizes planning rather than serendipitous emergence, equilibrium rather than disequilibrium (Dougherty and Dunne, 2011). Not understanding how to manage such interdependence can keep companies from taking advantage of the very real opportunities that platform-based business models can offer. This requires managers to go back to the drawing board and rethink how to manage this increased interdependence between the firm and its complementors.

1.3.2 Driver #2: Packetization

The second driver behind the rise of platforms is packetization. *Packetization* is the ability to digitize "something"—an activity, a process, a product, or a service—that was previously not digitized. Anything that can be digitized can be broken into Internet data "packets" and transported quite literally at the speed of light and at near zero cost across large distances. A digitized packet can be sent at nearly zero cost to someone a thousand miles away to work with, and then be sent back after processing all within fractions of a second. Digitization of music, books, and software is old news. The more interesting trends in digitization are in business activities that were previously thought as being location-dependent and localized.

Consider placing an order for a Big Mac in a McDonald's drive-through window in your neighborhood. Taking those orders had to be done by an hourly employee who heard the customer through the drive-through microphone and punched in the order for the cooks in the kitchen, who then promptly delivered the Big Mac to the customer a minute or two later. Historically, this was considered a job impossible to outsource. It had to be done at the store by employees working right there. That was until McDonald's figured out that a drive-through order was nothing more than a voice-based interaction—no different from a Skype conversation—and that the entire interaction could be packetized. This realization transformed McDonald's order-taking processes. Today, when a customer pulls into the drive-through, rarely does she realize that the order taker on the other end of the speakerphone in Atlanta is several thousand miles away in Honolulu, Hawaii. The entire interaction occurs through voice packets that are digitized and sent to Hawaii, where a professional order taker enters the order into a computer that displays the output back at the customer's store. The few seconds shaved from each order add up, the professionalization of order taking means a more consistent experience for customers and deeper specialization among McDonald's employees. Packetization can therefore create specialization in even the most mundane activities that until recently could not be separated from their location.

Digitization need not occur on a large scale in a product or service industry to inject more platform-like attributes into it. Any product or service, or the business processes and activities that go into producing it, can be visualized along three dimensions that can be physical or digital: (1) the product or service itself, (2) how it is transacted or purchased, and (3) how it is delivered. A shift from physical to digital in even one of the three facets can open up platform opportunities. Figure 1.5 illustrates this packetization cube framework with examples of digitization shifts in each of the three dimensions in a variety of industries such as retail, white goods manufacturing, entertainment, music, fast food, and healthcare. Think of your own industry to envision emerging opportunities; advances in technology are making it possible to accomplish packetization where it was not possible until recently. For example, additive manufacturing (also known as three-dimensional printing) is beginning to allow digital delivery of physical products. Additive manufacturing has the potential for transforming manufacturing just as the Internet transformed information, further blurring the boundary where the physical world ends and the digital realm begins.

1.3.2.1 Consequences

Packetization has two consequences: (1) it breaks the constraint of location-dependence and (2) it leads to deepening specialization. First, by digitizing even one aspect of an activity or process, it removes its location-dependence. The packetized activity can be completed anywhere that the packet can be sent. This opens up entirely new possibilities for division of labor—among humans and among machines—that goes into completing it. It can begin at the location where it originated, then its bits and pieces can

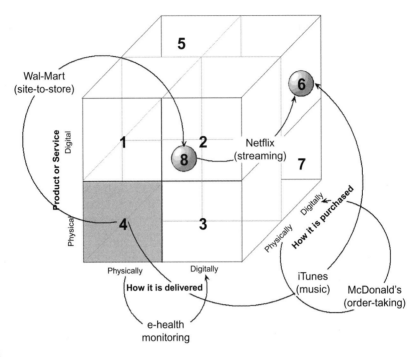

FIGURE 1.5

The packetization cube framework.

be distributed to workers in five different cities, and the completed output is delivered back at its point of origin. This means that even the most rote business activity can potentially be decomposed into pieces that can be executed in different places, by different parties, and then be reaggregated almost instantaneously. The Internet's near zero costs of communication and increasing speeds make it feasible to fundamentally rethink how the work to accomplish a packetized activity is partitioned and where it is done. Firms can now divvy up parts of the activity wherever the best cost/expertise combination is available in ways that were unimaginable until recently. Such packetization is creating a vast but largely invisible parallel economy that is on a trajectory to outgrow the physical economy in a couple of decades (Arthur, 2011). Business processes that once occurred among humans are now being executed among self-organizing machines, constantly leaving and reentering the physical world. Complexity theorist Brian Arthur describes this as the economy "growing a neural system" that is magnitudes of order faster, more predictable, and more productive than what it's replacing. By breaking free from geographical constraints, packetization of a product or service also vastly expands its potential market (Andreessen, 2011). Put another way, packetization is enabling entirely new business models that would have been the realm of fiction a decade ago.

Second, packetization is deepening specialization across all industries and professions. Part of the job of the jack-of-all-trades hourly employee at McDonald's has shifted to a specialist order taker, who just does more of the same activity. Similar trends of further decomposition of specialized activities are occurring across myriad professions including medicine, higher education, software development, engineering design, accounting, financial services, customer support, and marketing. Consider a cardiologist in Richmond, Virginia, whose private practice sends packetized X-ray images to specialized technicians in Bangalore for interpretation and annotation overnight. The cardiologist can see more patients per hour because he is spending less time on lower value-added activities and more on his area of core competence. Therefore, professional work is becoming narrower and more specialized, and some of it is increasingly possible to delegate to machines that demand neither employee benefits nor breaks. This increased specialization and automation of rote work allows local specialists to focus on higher value-added tasks and on more creative work. The same consequence arises at the firm level as well. Packetization allows firms to increase their focus on even narrower aspects of their core competence where they can add most value, and potentially use a diverse ecosystem of specialist partner firms to provide the other pieces.

1.3.3 Driver #3: Software embedding

Software embedding refers to baking routine business processes or activity in software. Software systems are increasingly the invisible engine running many businesses (Evans and Schmalensee, 2007, p. 5). Routine business processes and day-to-day activities are becoming increasingly ingrained in networked software applications. Andreessen (2011), founder of Netscape, warns that software is "eating the world," implying that it is taking over a growing percentage of the value chain of industries that are inhabitants of the physical world. Products and services across all types of industries have steadily growing software content, either directly in them or in their production value chain. Even a burger at your neighborhood McDonald's. When you pay for a meal at a McDonald's cash register, the order processing, payment processing, coupon validation, and kitchen notification is all embedded in software. Instead of a human performing the right sequence of tasks, the store's software system manages it. An activity can therefore seamlessly move between the physical and digital realms, creating Brian-Arthur's (2011) so-called "parallel invisible economy." Such software applications are increasingly networked, which means data across business processes can be aggregated instantaneously across stores, across firms, and across national boundaries. As such software embedding grows across product and service businesses in almost every industry, the performance of products and competitive delivery of services is increasingly dependent on software. As products and services become more software-intensive, software disproportionately shapes construction, delivery, and the end-user experience. Virtually every business is a software business to some degree, and software is increasingly gaining the power to make or break businesses and business models. Pricing and revenue models of traditional industries then begin to resemble the software industry, and an appreciation of platforms becomes increasingly vital to their sustained competitive advantage. The embedding of software is also transforming products into more platform-like services. For example, a major source of revenue for embroidery machines sold by Bernina and craft cutting machines by Silhouette is from selling digital patterns and designs that customers load onto the machines. Most of these digital designs are produced by independent third parties, mostly mom-and-pop design firms. This is effectively turning something as unexpected as a craft toolmaker into a platform owner. The perils of not fully appreciating the growing software-intensity of nonsoftware products are illustrated by Toyota's 2009–2011 recall of 9 million cars that cost the company several billion dollars, attributable almost exclusively to software glitches. As the software content of almost every industry—automobiles, insurance, retail, manufacturing, aviation, even fast food—increases, the difference between them and a software company is blurring.

Although even the most complex products have largely been self-contained, they are now becoming a part of something larger (de Weck et al., 2011, p. 7), morphing into what can be described as "systems of systems" (de Weck et al., 2011, p. 13). At that point, a nontechnology company's products and services inescapably acquire some properties of software platforms and become increasingly subject to their evolutionary dynamics.

1.3.3.1 Consequences

Software embedding has three consequences: (1) transformation of products into services, (2) morphing of the digital–physical boundary, and (3) convergence across industries. First, as a greater proportion of products are embedded in software, the opportunities to transform them into services increases. This trend is widely observed in the IT industry, where software such as mail clients have been replaced by services such as Gmail; licenses for databases have been replaced by utility-like storage services; and costly enterprise systems are increasingly being replaced by Web-based services. Kraft's Tassimo coffee machines, for example, can report what is being brewed by its users and when, turning it into a platform—at least from Kraft's perspective—for real-time intelligence gathering about consumer behavior and trends. In the automotive industry, cars increasingly offer subscription-based conveniences such as traffic monitoring, live navigation, and driving-based maintenance scheduling; this is an indication of their growing service content. The upside of this transformation is that services, unlike products, offer the potential for lock-in and a revenue stream as opposed to a one-time sale of a product. Firms that can make this transition can fundamentally alter their revenue model. However, the combination of the other four drivers also means that firms are increasingly going to be reliant on a vast network of specialized outside firms to be able to deliver on their own promises.

Second, increased embeddedness of business processes and activities in networked software further blurs the boundary between the digital and physical world. This requires firms in just about any nontechnology industry to take the intertwined software content of their own work as seriously at their bread-and-butter domain. Third, it simultaneously opens up opportunities and threats of convergence. Convergence means that two industries that were formerly independent are becoming mutually competitive and overlapping (Messerschmitt and Szyperski, 2003, p. 207). As two adjacent industries begin to bleed into each other, it creates opportunities for one to swallow the other by offering the incumbent firm's product functionality or service as part of its own. (Also see envelopment in Chapter 2.) Platforms are powerful vehicles for converging markets. Apple, for example, has used its iOS platform to begin swallowing the adjacent online gaming console industry. Amazon has used its Kindle platform to become a book publisher and its AWS platform to begin swallowing segments of the IT services industry.

1.3.4 Driver #4: The internet of things

The fourth shaping force is the emerging Internet of Things, which allows everyday objects embedded with inexpensive sensors—pacemakers, shoes, tires, coffee machines, thermostats, billboards, and washers and dryers—to directly communicate using the same protocol that connects the Internet. The declining cost and increasing speed of semiconductors increasingly allow computing and communication capabilities to inexpensively be embedded in everyday objects. The number of devices connected to the Internet outgrew the number of humans in 2008; 50 billion "devices" will be connected to the Internet by 2020 (Jackson, 2011). Payments using mobile devices had crossed the $1 trillion threshold by the beginning of 2014. Smart meters that optimize electricity usage, vending machines that adjust prices based on weather, health monitors that report anomalies to physicians; CT scanners that beam diagnostic scan images; coffeemakers and washing machines that sense user behavior; and cows whose sensors transmit 200 megabytes of health data each year (Jackson, 2011; Thompson, 2010) all mark the beginnings of this shift. You might skeptically ask how such objects will be powered. Won't we start running out of IP addresses if everything gets networked? Such devices require little power to run, which can feasibly be extracted from thin air by tapping into ambient electromagnetic radiation (the cell phone signals and Wifi signals around you) (Economist, 2010b). And Internet addresses are not likely to run out with the adoption of an upgraded Internet protocol (IPv6), which allows 100 unique addresses for every atom on Earth (i.e., 340 trillion, trillion, trillion devices and objects can have their own Internet addresses). This book therefore refers to these artifacts as networked devices rather than machines or computers.

1.3.4.1 Consequences

The emergence of the Internet of Things has two consequences: (1) the generation of a deluge of data streams from networked objects and (2) increased context awareness. First, today's business models are based on largely static stocks of information. Businesses collect data on sales, clean it, analyze it, and use the analysis to inform business decisions. Some do it better than others, but the data is assumed to be a *stock* of data. The Internet of Things changes it to a constant deluge of data *streams* rather than data points that businesses are used to. An apt metaphor is a comparison between Niagara Falls and a pond; knowing how to swim in the latter won't get you very far in the former.

Second, networked objects can also communicate contextual information such as location, surroundings, and temperature in real time. The pathways of information are therefore changing, making objects in the physical world parts of an information system (Chui et al., 2010). Their ability to "talk" to other objects and systems in real time is making them smarter, autonomous, and more cooperative. Such contextual awareness makes entirely new business models and pricing strategies feasible. Whether it is tracking pallets in supply chains, monitoring driver behavior to determine insurance premiums, monitoring wear and tear on a car's tires to assess safety, or monitoring window-shopping behavior of potential customers in a store to determine optimal pricing that will lead to a sale, the commonality is the increased information intensity of doing business and the greater context awareness. This is increasingly fusing processes and objects in ways that make physical things parts of business processes. Turning these advances into a more dynamic, sense-and-respond capability demands new ways of handling the deluge of real-time data streams and even more specialized skills to turn it into a competitive advantage. It is almost impossible for one firm to do all of this, in turn requiring turning to ecosystem partners to contribute complementary capabilities. As some firms in an industry begin to exploit this emerging trend, it will further compress the timeframe within which other firms can exploit this data.

1.3.5 Driver #5: Ubiquity

The fifth driver of the rise of platforms is the omnipresence—or ubiquity—of increasingly cheaper (see Figure 1.6) and faster (see Figure 1.7) wireless data networks built around the Internet protocol. The ability to packetize something would be worthless if the packets were expensive to rapidly move over networks, or if the recipient had to be tethered to a desktop or physical location to receive them. The growing ubiquity—the property of being present everywhere—of Internet-based data networks

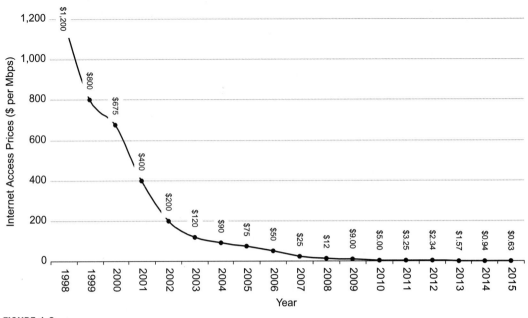

FIGURE 1.6

Internet access costs have been declining by a third every year.

Raw data source: http://drpeering.net/white-papers/Internet-Transit-Pricing-Historical-And-Projected.php.

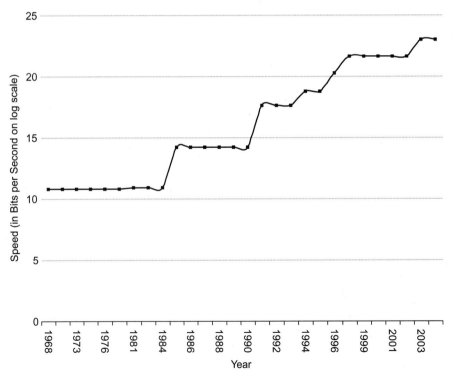

FIGURE 1.7

Internet backbone speeds increase by an order of magnitude every decade.

Raw data source: www.singularity.com/charts/page81.html.

is changing that. Furthermore, data communication costs are declining and network speeds have increased dramatically in the past decade. The speed of data networks on smartphones and mobile tablets far exceed those of land-based broadband connections a decade ago, and cost a fraction. Most of these networks all speak the same language—TCP/IP—the Internet protocol. This means that anything that can be packetized can potentially be delivered to end-users just about anywhere: at home, at work, in a store, in a car, in the air, or on a job site. Similarly, packetized activities can inexpensively be performed by geographically dispersed individuals. But, where will so much wireless bandwidth come from if trillions of things were to be networked? The freeing-up on the spectrum used for the now-defunct analog television broadcasts is helping create even longer-range networks capable of wirelessly moving Internet data at blazing speeds (400–800 mbps) (Economist, 2010a), further accelerating ubiquitous connectivity. The costs of entry of a new startup using digital infrastructure have declined a hundredfold in the last decade; a basic Internet application that used to cost $150,000 a month 10 years ago now costs $1500 (Andreessen, 2011). We are at a very nascent stage of truly ubiquitous connectivity, but we are progressing toward it in leaps and bounds.

1.3.5.1 *Consequences*

The primary consequence of ubiquity is that it will allow loosely coupled networks of small firms to rival the efficiencies of large firms. By banding together and helping coordinate distributed resources and participants in producing products and services, it turns the conventional model of scale through ownership to one of scale without ownership. Coupled with the trends toward packetization (driver #2), it alters who can participate in producing products and services and from where. It also alters where they can be delivered and from where. Location will matter less because companies can compete from anywhere, with rapidly eroding local advantages. Just as Kenmore can troubleshoot networked washing machines in an owners' home in Atlanta from a thousand miles away (Prentice, 2010), it can do the same 10,000 miles away in a customer's home in Japan or Australia. They also allow companies to crowd-source and "unsource" activities to their consumers, who help each other solve problems and do the work that was previously done by inhouse employees (Economist, 2012a,b). Furthermore, companies that were locationally disadvantaged can now compete without that handicap. Amazon, for example, has exploited ubiquity using smartphone apps that allow consumers to do price comparisons by scanning product barcodes in their competitors' stores. Using GPS data sent with every price scan, Amazon can crowd-source pricing intelligence-gathering to its own customers. Ubiquity allows specialization to coexist with collaboration; mass collaboration and crowd-sourcing become feasible and cost-effective; and expertise distributed across a company's locations no longer needs to remain in silos. A customer interaction can instantaneously and cost-effectively bring together specialized contributors dispersed across multiple continents. For example, American Express uses this shift to be able to seamlessly shuttle customer support calls between specialized agents in India and Florida in real time. However, exploiting growing ubiquity in sustainable ways that continue to competitively differentiate firms requires putting on a platform thinking cap.

1.3.6 **The perfect storm**

It is tempting but flawed to think that software-based platforms apply only to the IT industry. Platform markets are rapidly emerging in a variety of non-IT industries because these five drivers do not exist in isolation. It is the *combination* of these drivers that is creating unprecedented opportunities to transform products and services across a wide variety of industries into software-centric platforms. The presence of one driver can make another driver more forceful, leading to a joint effect that exceeds the sum of their parts. Platform ideas are industry agonistic and the ecosystem dynamics that this book explores are applicable to a growing number of diverse industries. Innovation ecosystems like the ones on which this book focuses are increasingly emerging in the mortgage, finance, drug development, microprocessor, software, automotive, healthcare, banking, food services, and energy industries (Dougherty and Dunne, 2011). While it might be decades before this potential is fully realized in many industries, they will nevertheless begin exhibiting platform-like properties before then. It is therefore important for managers in just about every industry to understand the blueprints of platform-based markets to recognize and adapt to these shifts.

1.4 LESSONS LEARNED

Platforms are challenging conventional models that served us well in the industrial era. The confluences of five forces is creating the perfect storm fertile in opportunities to transform diverse industries into software-centric platforms. This transformation can alter how a firm makes money, retains customers, organizes everything from mundane tasks to innovation, and ensures its own survival. A brief summary of the core ideas described in this chapter appears below.

- *Platforms are changing the rules of competition.* Competition is migrating to rival platform ecosystems competing against one another, replacing competition among rival products and services. The potent mix of specialized expertise with the disciplining power of platform markets can foster innovation at a pace that can trump even the mightiest product and service business. Companies that fail to recognize this shift in their own industries are on a death march, on the waiting list of fallen giants like the Pony Express, Kodak, Blackberry, Palm, and Sony. The slower managers are in recognizing this, the more likely their companies are to become victims of the Red Queen effect, unable to catch up.
- *Platform ecosystems are composed of externally produced complements that augment the capabilities of the platform.* A software platform is an extensible software product or service that serves as a foundation on which independent outside parties can build complementary products or services ("apps") that interoperate through the platform's interfaces. The collection of the platform and apps that interoperate with it represents the platform's ecosystem.
- *Innovations that differentiate platforms often emerge in the downstream part of the platform's value chain.* A platform ecosystem's value chain has upstream and downstream parts. The upstream part of the value chain is what goes into producing the platform itself. The downstream part includes app developers who produce capability-augmenting extensions to the platform. End-users can uniquely mix-and-match which of these downstream complements they include in their own instantiation of the platform ecosystem.
- *A platform without at least two distinct groups or "sides" is not a platform.* A true platform must be at least two-sided and span at least two distinct groups such as app developers and end-users that interact with each other using the platform. Platforms should not be confused with one-sided products and services, or with supply chains, all of which obey a different, simpler, and more predictable set of principles.

- *Most successful platforms began as standalone products or services.* Many successful platform examples touted in the press—iOS, Windows, Facebook, Skype, Amazon, eBay, Google, Firefox, Salesforce, and Dropbox—started out as standalone products or services that subsequently transformed into platforms by adding a second distinct group.
- *The confluence of five drivers is accelerating the migration toward platforms in a variety of industries.* These drivers include the need for deepening specialization within industries as they struggle to deliver increasingly complex products and services; "packetization" of products, services, business processes, and activities into digital bits; baking of routine business activities into software in industries as diverse as fast food, medicine, healthcare, automotive, education, engineering, accounting, financial services, and marketing; the emergence of the Internet of Things that allows everyday objects to communicate using the Internet; and finally the growing ubiquity of cheap, fast, and untethered Internet protocol-based networks.
- *Platform ecosystem ideas in this book are industry agnostic.* As the five drivers described in this book begin to affect various nontechnology industries, they infuse properties of software platforms into their products and services. Managers—independent of their industry—should therefore grasp the ideas described in this book so they are able to recognize and are ready to embrace platform opportunities and threats in their industries. As the old saying goes, fortune favors the prepared mind.

The next chapter introduces 10 core platform concepts that will provide us a shared vocabulary for the subsequent chapters in this book. These include the multifaceted notion of platform lifecycles and distinctive properties of software platforms such as network effects, multisidedness, different types of lock-ins, multihoming, tipping, and envelopment. It also explains nine guiding principles that we build on in later chapters on platform architecture, governance, and evolution. Some of these principles relate to getting platforms off the ground (e.g., the chicken-or-egg problem and the penguin problem), others relate to their design (e.g., the seesaw problem, the Humpty Dumpty problem, and the mirroring principle), and the last set guides their evolution (the Red Queen effect, emergence, the Goldilocks rule, and coevolution).

Core Concepts and Principles

Now, here, you see, it takes all the running you can do, to keep in the same place.
Red Queen to Alice in Lewis Carroll's *Through the Looking-Glass*

IN THIS CHAPTER

- Core concepts
  - Understanding platform lifecycles using dominant designs, S-curves, and diffusion curves
  - Platform properties: multisidedness, network effects, multihoming, architecture, and governance
  - Platform dynamics: tipping, lock-in, competitive durability, and envelopment
- Guiding principles
  - Platform startup principles: the chicken-or-egg problem and the penguin problem
  - Platform design principles: the seesaw problem, the Humpty Dumpty problem, and the mirroring principle
  - Platform evolution principles: the Red Queen effect, emergence, the Goldilocks rule, and coevolution

2.1 INTRODUCTION

As a foundation for delving into platform architectures, governance, and evolution, this chapter introduces some core concepts and principles that we will subsequently build on. Among the core concepts, we first describe the notion of platform lifecycles with three facets to characterize where a platform is in its lifecycle. The strategies for orchestrating the evolution of a platform ecosystem from a platform owner's perspective and the app developers' approach for managing their own work varies markedly depending on the platform's stage in its lifecycle. We then describe the notions of multisidedness, network effects, multihoming, tipping, lock-in, and envelopment that will help us grasp how software platform ecosystems begin and evolve. We also briefly introduce the concepts of architecture and governance that are the focus of the subsequent section of this book. We then describe nine principles guiding the initial development and subsequent evolution of platform ecosystems. The intent is for us to have a shared vocabulary that can serve as a foundation for the subsequent chapters of this book.

2.2 CORE CONCEPTS

Platform ecosystems build on several fundamental ideas that must be grasped to understand how they are designed and how they evolved. These ideas make platform-centric businesses substantively

---

☆"To view the full reference list for the book, click here or see page 283."

different from most conventional business models and also from much of traditional software development. These foundational concepts are central to appreciating the ideas developed in the rest of the book. Because many of these concepts apply to platforms, apps, and ecosystems, we generically refer to all three in this chapter as technology solutions.

Table 2.1 briefly summarizes these concepts and identifies whether each of them is directly relevant to the platform, its apps, and the ecosystem as a whole.

The first set of core concepts relate to the platform lifecycle, which is a multifaceted characterization of whether a technology solution is in its pre- or post-*dominant design* stage; its current stage along the *S-curve*; and the proportion of prospective users that have already adopted it (the *diffusion curve*). The next set includes the notion of *multisidedness*, which is a central property of a technology solution for it to qualify as a proper platform; the notion of *network effects* of various kinds that give most of the invincible properties such as *lock-in* that dominant platforms appear to possess; and the challenges associated with adopters who simultaneously commit to multiple rival platforms (*multihoming*). Finally, we briefly describe the notion of competitive durability and envelopment, and also provide a layperson's introduction to the concepts of architecture and governance that the subsequent section of this book explores in depth.

2.2.1 The platform lifecycle

The lifecycle of most technology innovations has three parts: the emergence of the ideal technology solution itself, its progression along a technology maturity curve, and its penetration in its pool of prospective end-users. These lifecycle characterizations apply both to platforms and apps, so we generically refer to both as technology solutions in describing platform lifecycles. Figure 2.1 illustrates these three dimensions.

2.2.1.1 Emergence of a dominant design

The emergence of the technology solution itself goes through two distinct phases, the shift between which is marked by the emergence of a so-called *dominant design* (Anderson and Tushman, 1990; Utterback, 1996). Figure 2.2 illustrates this. When a technology solution first emerges, multiple firms will enter the fray with competing alternative designs. In the early phases of a platform market, a variety of firms experiment with different types of features, capabilities, and designs to assess the market's response. The predominant design phase is therefore marked by mass entry of competitors and multiple competing solutions to address the same market needs. As these competing designs continue to improve, at some point one design will eventually become widely accepted—implicitly or explicitly—as the winning standard. This happens when both customers and producers eventually arrive at some consensus about the optimal solution attributes that best meets customers' needs out of all competing designs. This then becomes the industry's dominant design and is usually associated with mass exit of competitors—a shakeout—from the market or switching over to the dominant design. The dominant design does not mean that every competitor will use the same technology per se but that it defines the expected norms for meeting users' needs. The dominant design is often not necessarily the technologically superior solution. It also invariably involves compromises because it is designed to appeal to a broad range of users.

An example of the emergence of a dominant design in the smartphone platform market is the iPhone. Its design characteristics increasingly define industry norms for competing in that market: a touch-based interface, a baseline set of internal functions (email, browser, text messaging), the

Table 2.1 Core Concepts and Where They Directly Apply in Software Ecosystems

Concept	Relevance			Description
	Platform	App	Ecosystem	
Platform lifecycle	●	●	●	A multifaceted characterization of whether a technology solution—a platform, an app, or the entire ecosystem—is in its pre- or post-dominant design stage; its current stage along the S-curve; and the proportion of the prospective user base that has already adopted it
Dominant design	●	●		A technology solution that implicitly or explicitly becomes the gold standard among competing designs that defines the design attributes that are widely accepted as meeting users' needs
S-curve	●	●	●	A technology's lifecycle that describes its progression from introduction, ascent, maturity, and decline phases
Leapfrogging	●	●	●	Embracing a disruptive technology solution and using it as the foundation for the firm's market offering in lieu of an incumbent solution in the decline phase of its S-curve
Diffusion curve	●	●		A description of whether a technology solution—a platform or an app—is in the stage of having attracted the geeks, early majority, late majority, or laggards to its user base
Multisidedness				The need to attract at least two distinct mutually attracted groups (such as app developers and end-users) who can potentially interact more efficiently through a platform than without it
Network effects	●	●		A property of a technology solution where every additional user makes it more valuable to every other user on the same side (same-side network effects) or the other side (cross-side network effects)
Multihoming	●			When a participant on either side participates in more than one platform ecosystem
Tipping	●	●		The point at which a critical mass of adopters makes positive network effects take off
Lock-in	●	●	●	The ways in which a platform can make it more desirable for existing adopters to not jump ship to a rival
Competitive durability	●	●	●	The degree to which the adopters of a technology solution continue to regularly use it long after its initial adoption
Envelopment	●	●		When a platform swallows the market of another platform in an adjacent market by adding its functionality to its existing bundle of functionality
Architecture	●	●		A conceptual blueprint that describes components of a technology solution, what they do, and how they interact
Governance	●		●	Broadly, who decides what in a platform's ecosystem. This encompasses partitioning of decision-making authority between platform owners and app developers, control mechanisms, and pricing and pie-sharing structures

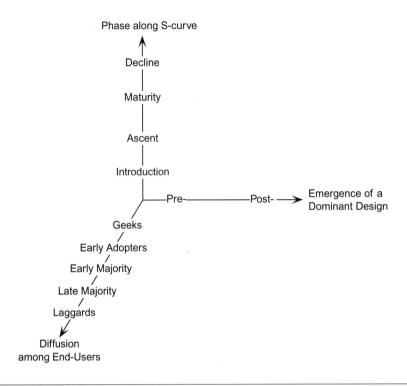

FIGURE 2.1

The three dimensions of the platform lifecycle.

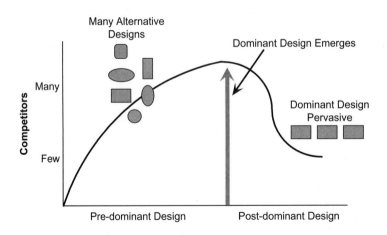

FIGURE 2.2

Pre- and post-dominant design phases in a software platform.

pocket-size form factor, software upgradability, and a virtual keyboard. Until a dominant design emerges, there is little consensus on the definition of an ideal solution for the same market and this remains the focus of competition among rival designs.

After a dominant design emerges, the few surviving competitors increasingly model their own solutions on the dominant design and compete by making incremental improvements on it. The emergence of iOS as the dominant design in 2010 led Google's Android and Blackberry's platforms to begin following Apple's lead in their own competing platforms. The basis of competition shifted away from trying dramatically different approaches to meeting customer needs and instead on trying to improve on each other's designs. However, these were simply variants of the same dominant design. In the post-emergence phase of the platform's lifecycle, the focus also increasingly shifts toward price-based competition. The same dynamics have repeatedly occurred in the markets for almost every new category of applications for these platforms as they progressed from their inception to going mainstream. However, even after a dominant design emerges, many rival systems (platforms or apps) can persist without one clear winner. But they usually share strong commonalities with the dominant design. This can lead to legal problems that are particularly acute in software platforms vis-à-vis other technology industries, as dominant designs often define key elements of user interfaces' look and feel and human–machine interactions that intellectual property laws cannot yet fully contend with. The majority of a platform's adopters arrive after the emergence of a dominant design, where the technology adoption curve dramatically takes off.

THE RULE OF ONE

Why do platform industries settle on one dominant design instead of continuing to offer a variety of solutions? The primary reason is that many platform industries exhibit increasing returns to adoption (i.e., the more a technology is adopted, the more valuable it becomes). The more a dominant design is used, the more they are improved. Another reason is that as a dominant design is more widely adopted, more specialized complements (such as apps) emerge that are designed specifically to work with that dominant design. This results in a self-reinforcing feedback loop that makes the dominant design increasingly more dominant independent of whether the competing designs are technologically superior or inferior.

2.2.1.2 S-curves and leapfrogging

We can also analyze the phase of a technology solution's lifecycle based on whether it is in (1) the introductory stage, which immediately follows its development and R&D stages; (2) the ascent stage, where it had reached breakeven and is beginning to gather steam; (3) the maturity stage; or (4) the decline phase, where it is becoming less useful than it used to be. This trajectory resembles an S-shaped curve (hence the term *S-curve*; Figure 2.3).

As a technology solution crosses the mature phase and enters the decline phase, the focus of competition shifts from product innovation to process innovation (see Figure 2.4) (Adner and Levinthal, 2001). In other words, instead of trying to improve the solution itself, competitors shift their attention to improving how it is produced and how it is delivered. Participants in platform markets must remember what causes the decline phase to set in and what can be done about it. It is usually because of a competing technology solution that at least does what the preceding technology solution did, but better or cheaper.

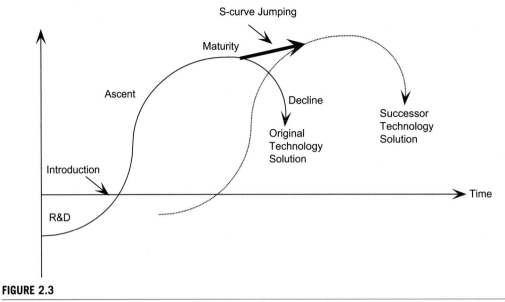

FIGURE 2.3

S-curves in the technology lifecycle.

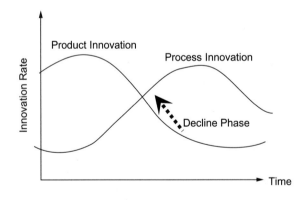

FIGURE 2.4

Process innovation replaces product innovation as a technology solution matures.

The death march of most technology solutions begins at the outset of the decline phase of the S-curve. The ideal choice for the incumbent technology—and for those who depend on it for their bread-and-butter—is to "leapfrog" to the next S-curve. This means embracing the disruptive technology solution and using it as the foundation over the incumbent technology solution for its product or service offering in the marketplace. Most firms that attempt it fail miserably. Their entire businesses are based on the outgoing technology, and they have usually invested sweat and tears into honing their business models and capabilities around it. It is therefore difficult for incumbents to rationalize walking away from it and switching to what might appear to be a fledgling technology solution with uncertain prospects.

Think of how Kodak first responded when its chemical photography business was threatened by digital photography; Remington typewriters when word processors were first introduced; traditional book publishers when e-books first emerged; the Pony Express when the telegraph was invented; and Canon's successful digital cameras when smartphones threatened the business. Perhaps recalling the story of Minnesota's flourishing ice harvesting industry (see the sidebar and Figure 2.5) will help you remember the point that this, unfortunately, is a mistake that gets repeated, forgotten, and repeated over and over again. Figure 2.5 illustrates how the ice harvesting industry reacted in the 1800s to the emergence of the refrigerator. The pattern can readily be applied to many recent replacement technology solutions such as e-books vis-à-vis books, digital music distribution vis-à-vis CDs, and voice-over-Internet vis-à-vis telephones. The first reaction from the incumbent firm is to ignore the potentially threatening alternative technology, then to dismiss it as irrelevant and low quality, then ferociously engage in process innovation to deliver the existing technology more cost effectively, then to price cut aggressively, and finally to give up (Figure 2.6).

FIGURE 2.5

Ice harvesters, circa 1889.

Source: Sketch by Joseph Becker in Frank Leslie's illustrated newspaper, March 16, 1889, p. 96; reproduced from the Library of Congress wood engraving LC-USZ62-104051. Digitized by Library of Congress at www.loc.gov/pictures/item/91787147.

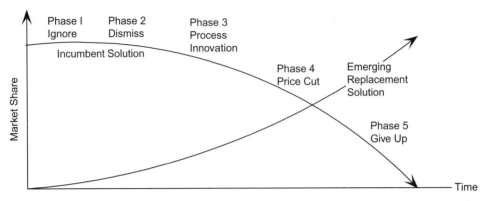

FIGURE 2.6

How incumbent technology solutions react to potential replacement technologies.

THE PARABLE OF THE MINNESOTA ICE HARVESTING INDUSTRY

Waseca, Minnesota, was flourishing in 1809. Three in four residents were prosperous ice harvesters. This town, like many others in Minnesota, Wisconsin, and New England, had a burgeoning industry harvesting blocks of ice from deep frozen lakes to ship not just to meat-packing plants and breweries in New Orleans but also to customers in China, South America, and Western Europe. A milestone was when a hundred tons of ice survived a 16,000-mile journey to Calcutta, India. By 1900, the ice harvesters could barely whet the global appetite for ice, which had an annual market for 10 million tons in the United States alone.

By 1928, the entire industry vanished without a trace. The culprit was Apalachicola, Florida-based physician John Gorrie's 1850 invention, an artificial gas-compression ice machine that blended together a neglected 1834 British patent for artificial vaporization and a technique developed 2 years earlier by Ferdinand Carre for processing water into ice using ammonia. As the disruptive threat of an artificial ice machine loomed larger, the ice harvesters did precisely what the US auto industry tried after 1991 and the US airline industry after 2001: They systematically attempted to improve what they did best. Better ice-cutting saws, better-insulated storage sheds, more efficient distribution, and lower prices. But squeezing more efficiency out of a leapfrogged business model mattered little.

The death knell of the Waseca ice harvester was not someone who could do it better, but differently. Neither was it a breakthrough innovation. Instead, it was a novel assemblage of existing technologies that simply rendered the traditional business model irrelevant. Parallels can easily be drawn in many flourishing industries today. Some react like the ice harvesters but far too many are too dismissive of individual emerging technologies. But miss the forest for the trees, and it's hard to be prepared when you don't know *what* you're watching out for. The lesson for managers from the parable of the ice harvesters is to continuously connect the dots even when there aren't enough dots yet; imagine possible assemblages of existing and emerging technologies, no matter how far-fetched.

To keep from becoming the next ice harvester parable, managers must fear most someone who pieces together seemingly unrelated innovations to introduce a different way to satisfy existing market needs, not someone who just does it better, faster, or cheaper. The fatal disruptive threat is rarely a single innovation or technology but a novel reconfiguration of existing technologies that entirely circumvents the industry's dominant business model. Rather than letting their fears of cannibalizing existing business overpower the need to actively seek and invest in real options on even absurdly peripheral innovations, managers must constantly imagine ways to cannibalize it. When business is good, humble managers must not forget the ice harvesters. The ones that are condemned to repeat history are the ones that forget it.

However, it is possible to make the leap using "real options" thinking before the next S-curve fully takes shape. (Chapter 8 focuses on real options theory.) Leaping from one S-curve to the next requires embedding different types of real options in architectures, envelopment of adjacent markets, shifting focal target markets, and using the six modular operators. This requires thinking of architecture in software platforms and their governance. These tools are described in detail in Part IV of this book, where the term *leapfrogging* is used to refer to this idea of jumping across successive S-curves.

2.2.1.3 The technology diffusion curve on the end-user side

The adoption lifecycle of a technology solution by its end-users can be described using Rogers's (1995) diffusion curve, just as dominant designs and S-curves describe lifecycles on the supplier side. As Figure 2.7 illustrates, the diffusion of a technology solution begins with a very small minority that adopts it for technology's sake more than its widespread utility. These are the geeks and influencers who get it off the ground. The geeks are followed by a wave of early adopters, who add up to about a sixth of the total potential user base. This is where the technology innovation hits what Geoffrey Moore calls "the chasm." Only after this chasm is crossed does the first big wave of early adopters and then the next big wave of late adopters arrive. At this point, 85% of the potential adopters are on board. The last sixth of the eventual user base are the laggards. Since platforms have at least two distinct groups of adopters, this model can be used to describe adoption of a platform both by end-users and by app developers. In managing the evolution of a technology lifecycle, different evolutionary properties should be the focus of attention, depending on which of the five phases of the diffusion curve a technology solution is in. Similarly, the emphasis of governance also must shift to match a technology solution's progression along the diffusion curve. The diffusion curve will therefore resurface when we subsequently delve into governance and evolution.

2.2.2 Multisidedness

A key property of platforms is their multisidedness, where each "side" refers to a *distinct* group of stakeholders that the platform brings together. For example, the iOS platform brings together app developers (one side) and end users (the other side). These two sides would ordinarily face much

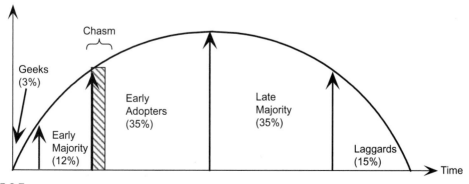

FIGURE 2.7

The technology diffusion lifecycle on the end-user side.

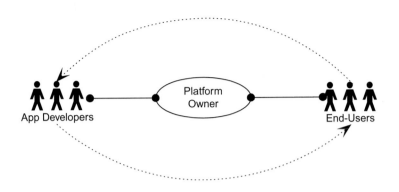

FIGURE 2.8

Two sides in a multisided platform.

higher costs in finding and transacting with each other without the platform than with it. The platform creates value by facilitating participants on one side finding those on the other side, or *mediating* their interactions. Figure 2.8 illustrates this. In theory, both sides can find and trade with each other directly and without the platform, and this must be costlier for a platform to be viable. The platform is therefore valuable to either side when interacting. Like platforms, apps can also evolve into standalone platforms or platforms within another platform (nested platforms) by evolving them to become multisided.

Multisided markets have long existed outside of the technology industries.

Table 2.1 provides examples of such markets, where a firm acts as a market-maker that facilitates interactions between two distinct groups that need each other but would find it costlier to find and then transact with each other. A software platform can act as a market-maker between two such sides, but brings unique capabilities and opportunities that rarely exist outside of software-based platform markets. A software platform is multisided if two or more distinct *types* of participant groups use the platform to *directly* interact with each other. These distinct groups want to interact with each other but need the platform to be able to. Most multisided platforms are two-sided. For example, app developers and end-users are the two sides in iOS's app store platform. Similarly, third-party sellers and customers directly interact with each other on Amazon, and buyers and sellers on eBay.

It is important not to confuse one-sided services with multisided ones; we do not even consider one-sided platforms as true platforms. Rather, they are services that have the *potential* to evolve into a multisided platform. For example, the file-sharing service Dropbox primarily has one distinct participant group, its end-users. They do not directly interact with another distinct participant group on the other side, just with other users of Dropbox. In contrast, two distinct groups of participants exist in day-to-day two-sided networks such as credit cards (cardholders and merchants), video gaming (gamers and game producers), and movie theaters (studios and moviegoers). Three-sided platforms are also becoming more prevalent. (See Table 2.2 for examples outside the software industry.) For example, Apple increasingly connects three distinct types of groups with the free apps distributed in the iOS App Store: end-users, app developers, and advertisers. Multisidedness is therefore a critical requirement for the more sophisticated platform dynamics to arise.

Table 2.2 Examples of Multisided Market Makers Outside the Software Industry

Two-Sided Market-Maker	First Side	Second Side
Credit cards	Cardholders	Merchants
HMOs	Patients	Physicians
Operating systems	End-users	Application developers
Travel sites	Travelers	Airlines
e-healthcare	Physicians	Medical services firms
Agoras in ancient Greece, shopping malls	Buyers	Merchants
Business schools	Future managers	Employers
Cable television networks	Subscribers	Content providers and studios
Professional services firms	Professional specialists	Clients
Flea markets	Bargain shoppers	Sellers

HOW MANY SIDES TO BEGIN WITH?

A difficult question that a startup platform usually faces is how many sides it should try to attract at the outset and which side it should subsidize to reach critical mass. Although it might appear on first glance that attracting as many sides as possible is a good strategy, upstart platform owners must be cautious for two reasons. First, attempting to attract many sides at the same time can spread the platform owner thin and keep it from dedicating enough resources to solve the chicken-or-egg problem of getting both sides onboard. It is easier to solve that problem by starting with fewer sides, usually just one. (The various strategies for doing this are discussed in Chapter 4.) Second, it can accidentally trigger negative network effects instead of positive ones, or a deadly mix of both where the negative network effects overwhelm the positive ones.

2.2.3 Network effects

Network effects refer to the degree to which every additional user of a platform or app makes it more valuable to every other existing user. Economists call these network externalities (Katz and Shapiro, 1994; Saloner and Shepard, 1995) or Metcalfe's law. Consider the very first user of Facebook. The value of Facebook to her was zero since there was no other user to network with. The second user increased the value of Facebook to the first user. The millionth user dramatically increased the value of Facebook to herself and to every other user before her. This means that the value of adding another user to a platform dramatically increases its potential value to every other user. The logic is simple: Every additional user dramatically increases the number of other users that he or she can interact with. For example, Facebook's billion users make it much more attractive for the next user after them to join Facebook, illustrated in Figure 2.9. The value of the system increases almost exponentially rather than linearly (as the square of the number of users or number of users times their logarithm, depending on which version of Metcalfe's law one considers); thus each additional user potentially increases the value of the system to other users dramatically rather than gradually (Figure 2.10). Once such network effects are triggered, the platform can enter a self-reinforcing cycle. While network effects create high barriers to entry into platform markets, they also create a hard-to-assail position once they are in place.

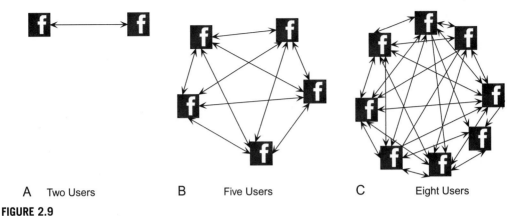

A   Two Users   B   Five Users   C   Eight Users

FIGURE 2.9

Networks effects leverage the number of users that any user can communicate with.

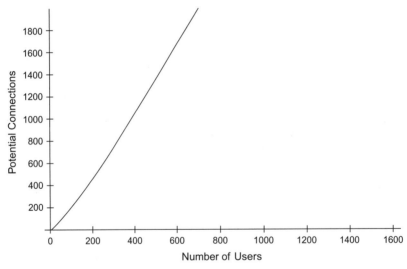

FIGURE 2.10

Network effects exponentially increase the platform's value.

Although network effects in commonplace usage of the concept refer to *positive* network effects, there are two more nuanced properties of network effects: direction and sidedness. Direction can be positive or negative. Unlike the positive network effects just described, a negative network effect exists when every additional user of a system makes it *less* valuable to other users. Think of a highway: Every additional driver on the highway potentially makes it more difficult for other drivers to navigate speedily through the traffic, thus decreasing its appeal to existing drivers. Similarly, every additional user on a cable Internet network in your neighborhood potentially reduces the bandwidth available to you, reducing its value from your perspective. It is possible for a platform to simultaneously exhibit negative and positive network effects after it reaches a threshold user base. Ensuring that the net of these is still positive requires careful attention to architecture (Chapter 5) much before this conflict is noticeably manifested.

The second property of network effects is whether they are same-side or cross-side (see Figure 2.11). *Same-side* network effects arise when adding an additional participant (e.g., end-user) to one side of the platform changes its value to all other participants on the same side. For example, adding an additional Skype user increases its value to other Skype users (a positive same-side network effect); adding another driver to a busy highway decreases its appeal to other users (a negative, same-side network effect). *Cross-side* network effects arise when adding an additional participant (e.g., end-user) to one side of the platform increases or decreases its value to all other participants on the *other* side. For example, the more people buy iPads, the more developers want to write apps for iPads. This is a positive cross-side network effect.

Each combination of direction and sidedness of network effects can put a platform in one of four cells in Figure 2.12. As we will see in subsequent chapters, the nature and direction of network effects has a lot to do with the underlying architecture of the platform and the way in which it is governed. In other words, network effects can thoughtfully be designed into a platform, and this has powerful strategic consequences as a platform evolves. Architecture and governance can be mutually reinforcing or mutually destructive. Together, their effects—both good and bad—can exceed the sum of their parts. A well-designed platform should deliberately harness this interaction in the evolution of its ecosystem.

Network effects of a second kind arise when the demand for one platform complement with strong network effects increases the demand for the platform itself. Independent of whether the positive network effects are same-side or cross-side at the platform level or even at the app level, the platform stands to gain from them. For example, the presence on a platform of a popular app with strong network effects (e.g., Skype) increases the demand for the platform as well (e.g., iOS devices).

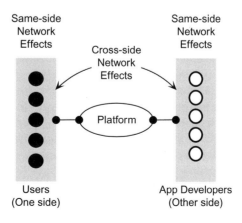

FIGURE 2.11

Same-side versus cross-side network effects.

	Same Side	Cross-side
Negative	Adding someone **decreases** appeal to all existing users on the **same** side	Adding someone decreases appeal to all existing users on the **other** side
Positive	Adding someone **increases** appeal to all existing users on the **same** side	Adding someone increases appeal to all existing users on the **other** side

FIGURE 2.12

Four types of network effects in platforms.

2.2.4 Multihoming

The simplest example of multihoming is likely in your wallet. You likely have more than one credit card, perhaps an American Express and a Visa. Yet you likely use one predominantly and keep the other as a backup. In this example, you are multihoming across two rival platforms. *Multihoming* in platforms refers to when a platform participant on either side participates in more than one platform ecosystem (Armstrong, 2006; Armstrong and Wright, 2007). An app developer who simultaneously develops her app for Android and iOS is multihoming on those platforms. An end-user who owns both a Blackberry and an iPhone is similarly multihoming on these platforms. An adopter can multihome in ownership, usage, or both. The software industry has historically relied on exclusivity contracts and intentional incompatibility to coerce developers to single-home. However, intense market competition, particularly in platform markets where a clear winner is yet to emerge, increases the likelihood that developers will multihome. It is also a rational approach because they can place their bets on multiple competing platforms and avoid the downsides of being stranded on a losing platform. For end-users, the ongoing costs of establishing and maintaining multiple platform affiliations is usually a deterrent to multihoming. The higher these costs, the lower the likelihood that an app developer or end-user will multihome. Platform owners can discourage multihoming by decreasing the costs of homing on their platform vis-à-vis rival platforms. The costs of multihoming are therefore distinct from switching costs associated with platform lock-ins. How can platform owners cope with the reality of multihoming yet differentiate their platform from its rivals? When should a platform owner or app developer aggressively deter multihoming and when should he or she encourage it? The answer lies in how platform governance is matched with platform lifecycles, which we discuss in detail in Chapter 6.

2.2.5 Tipping

Network effects kick in only after a minimum number of users have adopted the technology solution. This minimum number of adopters after which network effects are manifested is known as the platform's *critical mass* or tipping point. Once a platform reaches this critical mass, network effects become noticeable and a potentially self-reinforcing positive feedback loop. For new platforms, reaching this critical mass with the first distinct side of adopters is perhaps the biggest hurdle that platform owners face. For existing platforms, harnessing them to nudge the platform's evolutionary trajectory is the key challenge. Therefore a platform requires vastly different strategies before and after it reaches a tipping point.

2.2.6 Lock-in

Achieving critical mass introduces a different set of challenges for platforms: Competing platforms now know for sure that there is viable market. A successful platform is therefore likely to face intense competition both from copycat platforms as well as truly differentiated platforms. While this competition increases the variety of alternatives available to consumers and is usually good for consumers, it can often create conditions of a zero profit industry for platform owners and app developers. Severe price competition means that pricing of rival platforms can devolve into a race to the bottom. The challenge then is retaining both users and app developers who might be tempted to switch to a competing platform. The ways in which a platform can make it more desirable for existing users to stay put and not jump ship to a rival platform broadly refers to *lock-in*. Lock-in can occur both in consumer-grade platforms (e.g., iOS, Android) and in enterprise-grade platforms (e.g., SAP, Peoplesoft).

Lock-in can either be coercive or value-driven. Although lock-in often carries a negative connotation, evoking images of a powerful platform owner making it costly or impossible for existing users to switch to a competing platform (e.g., Monteverde and Teece, 1982), that heavy-handed approach eventually fails. *Coercive lock-in*, as we subsequently describe, is potentially breakable (using technologies such as middleware, adapters, and protocol translators). This approach relies on creating high switching costs: Costs associated with terminating the existing use of a technology solution to migrate to a rival one. An alternative way of creating lock-in is by making the platform increasingly more valuable to its users so that the choice to switch to a competing platform simply becomes unappealing vis-à-vis staying with the incumbent platform. The strategies for creating such platform lock-ins are potentially more bountiful in software-based platforms relative to nonsoftware platforms. The effective strategies for *value-driven* lock-in that platform owners can use over end-users and over app developers also vary based on the stage of the platform's lifecycle, as we describe in Part IV of this book.

2.2.7 Competitive durability

A technology solution is competitively durable when its adopters continue to use it long after the initial adoption (Tiwana et al., 2010). For example, the majority of apps see intensive usage after their initial adoption but eventually decline in their usage. In contrast, a competitively durable app continues to be regularly used. Usage (e.g., hours per week), nonabandonment (a stable or increasing usage pattern after initial adoption), and the ratio of regular users to adopters are proxies for competitive durability at the app level. Maintaining competitive durability usually requires making a technology solution sticky by strengthening network effects or aggressively adding functionality that its users value.

2.2.8 Envelopment

When a platform begins to offer the functionality of another platform in an adjacent market in addition to its existing bundle of functionality, it is said to have enveloped—or swallowed—the latter (Eisenmann et al., 2006). Figure 2.13 illustrates envelopment. For example, the iOS platform successfully added gaming functionality to its platform, effectively swallowing the functionality of hand-held

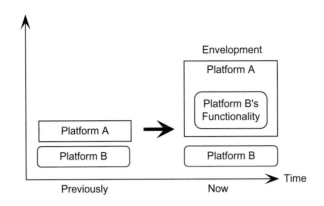

FIGURE 2.13

Envelopment of one platform (B) by a platform (A) in an adjacent market.

gaming platforms such as Nintendo DS and Sony's Playstation Vita. Similarly, by adding digital photography capabilities, smartphones have enveloped the adjacent digital camera market. Envelopment is usually viable when the two adjacent platforms have a considerable overlap in their user bases, and when the enveloping platform offers a bundle of functionality that is perceived as being a better value proposition by end-users of the enveloped platform. We subsequently describe strategies for how a platform facing a threat of envelopment can respond. Envelopment is a distinct concept from convergence; envelopment latter occurs at the platform or app level and convergence former across industries.

2.2.9 Architecture

Architecture is the conceptual blueprint that describes the structure of a technology solution. Architecture describes the components of a complex system, what they do, and how they interact (van Schewick, 2012, p. 21). This high-level description specifies the components of a system, the externally visible properties of these components, and the relationships among them (Sanchez, 1995; van Schewick, 2012, p. 21). The architecture of a platform or an app is therefore a high-level description of its building blocks and how they are related to each other, not a working implementation. Broadly, architectures can vary between the two extremes of being perfectly modular (plug-and-play) and perfectly monolithic. Most architectures fall somewhere along this continuum.

Architectures are a defining property of individual apps and how they interact with other apps and the platform (Tiwana et al., 2010). They are also a defining property of the platform itself. The architectural properties of the apps in a platform's ecosystem and of the platform aggregate to describe the overall architecture of a platform's ecosystem. Most architectural decisions by ecosystem participants are therefore made at the app and platform level rather than the ecosystem level. Architecture imprints the evolution of a platform ecosystem because it defines how innovation work is partitioned among the app developers and the platform owner and also how their outputs are reintegrated into a coherent whole. Architectures therefore reduce complexity that any ecosystem participant must contend with, and allows them to benefit from valuable ignorance of each other's work without compromising ecosystem-wide integration. The evolvable architectures that this book emphasizes are Lego-like modular architectures. Architectures are largely technical decisions with enormous strategic consequences. Their technical nature and strategic implications make them especially messy for technologists and managers because they span both realms, of which one is usually outside the domain of expertise of either type of individuals. Architectural choices are also largely irreversible in practice, and the constraints imposed by them become apparent long after such choices have been made. Technical architectures are inseparably intertwined with governance of the platform ecosystems, which is often also described as its business architecture.

2.2.10 Governance

Governance broadly refers to who decides what in a platform's ecosystem. This encompasses three facets: (1) how decision rights are divvied up between the platform owner and app developers, (2) what types of formal and informal control mechanisms are used by the platform owner (e.g., gatekeeping, performance metrics, processes that app developers are expected to follow, and informal clannish pressure), and (3) pricing structures, including decisions about which side gets subsidized. (Chapter 6 focuses on governance.) Governance impacts the evolutionary dynamics in platform ecosystems, and the competitive advantage generated by governance choices can strengthen or diminish with the choice of architecture for the platform (Chapter 10) and for apps (Chapter 11).

2.3 GUIDING PRINCIPLES

Nine guiding principles underpin the emergence and evolution of platform ecosystems. The first four are related to the initial development of platform ecosystems. These include the idea that a platform ecosystem must evolve at least as rapidly as its rivals in order to survive (the *Red Queen effect*); it must simultaneously attract two distinct groups to the platform but neither will join unless a critical mass exists on the other side (the *chicken-or-egg problem*); uncertainty about whether other users on either side will adopt a platform can stall initial adoption altogether (the *penguin problem*); and the majority of innovations in such platforms cannot be planned but instead spontaneously emerge from relentless pursuit of selfish interests by various ecosystem participants (*emergence*). The next set of principles relate to how a platform ecosystem can be orchestrated to evolve. These include the idea that a platform owner must strike a delicate balance between autonomy granted to app developers and the integration of their work with the platform (the *seesaw problem*); the platform ecosystem must be designed so its parts can be separated for independent development and then seamlessly reintegrated (the *Humpty Dumpty problem*). However, this requires the organizational structure of the platform's ecosystem to mirror its architecture down to the app level (the *mirroring principle*); and its governance and architecture must be codesigned and coevolved (*coevolution*). The final principle is to always offer a set of three ordered choices at the app level, with the expectation that the majority of users will gravitate toward the middle choice that appears "just right" (the *Goldilocks rule*). These guiding principles are summarized in Table 2.3 and described next.

2.3.1 The Red Queen effect

The Red Queen effect, referring to the increased pressure to adapt faster just to survive, is driven by an increase in the evolutionary pace of rival technology solutions (Barnett and Hansen, 1996). It is an evolutionary idea to explain the coevolution of competing platforms and the demise of ones that do not adapt fast enough relative to rivals. It is based on the anecdote in Lewis Carroll's *Through the Looking-Glass*, where two characters (Alice and the Red Queen; Figure 2.14) were constantly running

Table 2.3 Summary of the Nine Guiding Principles in Platform Markets

Principle	Key Idea
Red Queen effect	The increased pressure to adapt faster just to survive is driven by an increase in the evolutionary pace of rival technology solutions
Chicken-or-egg problem	The dilemma that neither side will find a two-sided technology solution with potential network effects attractive enough to join without a large presence of the other side
The penguin problem	When potential adopters of a platform with potentially strong network effects stall in adopting it because they are unsure whether others will adopt it as well
Emergence	Properties of a platform that arise spontaneously as its participants pursue their own interests based on their own expertise but adapt to what other ecosystem participants are doing
Seesaw problem	The challenge of managing the delicate balance between app developers' autonomy to freely innovate and ensuring that apps seamlessly interoperate with the platform
Humpty Dumpty problem	When separating an app from the platform makes it difficult to subsequently reintegrate them
Mirroring principle	The organizational structure of a platform's ecosystem must mirror its architecture
Coevolution	Simultaneously adjusting architecture and governance of a platform or an app to maintain alignment between them
Goldilocks rule	Humans gravitate toward the middle over the two extreme choices given any three ordered choices

FIGURE 2.14

Alice (middle) and the Red Queen (left).

Source: Charles Sylvester, Journeys Through Bookland, *Bellows-Reeve Company, Chicago, 1909.*

yet remaining in the same place relative to each other. In platform markets, this means that in order to survive, a technology solution must evolve faster just to match the rate at which competing solutions are evolving. If the pace of adaptation of one competing solution increases, it puts much greater pressure for its rivals to increase their pace of adaption just to remain in the game. The consequence of the Red Queen effect is that the harder a rival platform tries to get ahead of the dominant platform, the further behind it appears to fall. It is easy to miss the nuance that the bar itself is rising. Intensification of a rival platform's efforts to get ahead of others leads to intensification of effort by rivals, gradually raising the bar for them all. (This behavior is also called escalation in systems thinking; Meadows, 2008, p. 124.)

2.3.2 The chicken-or-egg problem

A platform cannot attract app developers unless it has a large base of end-users, and a large base of users is unlikely to join unless a platform has a large variety of apps available that end-users perceive as valuable. Neither side will join the platform without the other. This dilemma that neither side will find a platform or app with network effects potentially attractive enough to join without a large presence of the other side is the chicken-or-egg problem (Caillaud and Jullien, 2003). Consider why either side will find it more attractive only after a large adopter base has formed on the other side of a platform. End-users derive a large part of their value of a platform from the apps that they can use on it. This means that the absence of available apps will decrease the perceived attractiveness of a platform. The reason app developers are going to perceive a platform as valuable only if it has a large installed base of end-users is simple: An app has large upfront fixed costs but low variable costs. Producing the first copy can be a costly endeavor, but making additional copies is almost costless. Therefore, app developers can realize considerable economies of scale only if they can reach a large number of adopters/users. Not addressing the chicken-or-egg problem is guaranteed to break a platform even before it has a chance of taking off.

2.3.3 The penguin problem

The "penguin problem" arises when a new platform is introduced that has strong potential for network effects, but no end-users adopt it because they are unsure whether others will adopt it as well (Farrell and Saloner, 1986). Early adopters who buy into the promise of strong network effects might be stuck with a dud investment if a critical mass of other users does not follow. This waiting game can potentially stall a critical mass of users from adopting an otherwise promising platform. The metaphor is based on a group of hungry penguins waiting for each other to dive into waters where they know they can find food, but are unsure about whether there is also a predator lurking. The lingering doubt in a penguin's mind is whether jumping in for food is worth becoming someone else's food! This excessive inertia is also the flip side of excess momentum, where some early users adopting a new platform lead a disproportionately large number of others to adopt the same platform. Economists also call this the "bandwagon effect" (Rohfls, 2003, p. 195). The penguin problem is partly why a superior platform that cannot break the adoption inertia barrier often loses out to an inferior platform that does overcome the problem. The penguin problem is particularly acute when the prospective user base for a new platform is the installed base for an existing—perhaps inferior—platform (Farrell and Saloner, 1986). It is less acute for a new platform that needs to attract new users but does have a potentially rivalrous older technology solution that it indirectly competes with. Overcoming the penguin problem requires careful attention to governance, particularly which side the platform owner subsidizes in pricing to break the logjam. A second approach that we discuss subsequently is one of strategically vacillating between compatibility and incompatibility with potentially rival solutions (platforms, apps, or ecosystems) over different phases of their lifecycle.

2.3.4 Emergence

Emergence is a self-organizing, ecosystem-wide order that arises not from the imposition of a master plan by the platform owner but from the actions of interdependent app developers and platform owners who are selfishly pursuing their own interests based on their own expertise but continuously adapting to feedback based on what the others in the ecosystem are doing (Dougherty and Dunne, 2011). Emergent properties of a technology solution are those that arise spontaneously in response to the aggregate behavior of apps within the ecosystem or are triggered by technological or regulatory changes in the environment (as described in Part IV of this book). Emergent innovations that advance the platform ecosystem will not arise unless emergence is enabled and shaped effectively by platform owners (Dougherty and Dunne, 2011). Because emergence cannot be predicted and planned, the best the platform owner can do is to not quash it. Platform owners can shape emergence primarily by providing a guiding vision and by facilitating coordination (which is messier than it appears on first glance), but then getting out of the way. In other words, the big picture goals for "what" app developers should accomplish can be set to some degree by the platform owner, but not how they are accomplished.

2.3.5 The seesaw problem

The biggest strength of a platform ecosystem—its diversity—can also be the root of chaos. Apps must seamlessly integrate and interoperate with the platform, but the very things conducive to app–platform integration can also be intrusive to the autonomy of app developers in ways that discourage emergent innovation around the platform. Too much autonomy can compromise integration; overemphasis on integration can compromise app developers' autonomy (see Figure 2.15). The key challenge for platform owners is therefore to manage the delicate tension between developer autonomy on one hand and ecosystem-wide integration on the other. A platform that thrives will neither be like a democracy nor a centrally planned regime. Instead, it must be like a benevolent dictatorship, as Chapter 6 elaborates. Managing this delicate balance between autonomy and integration is what we refer to as the seesaw problem. The seesaw problem can be managed by aligning architecture and governance at the app level.

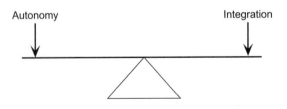

FIGURE 2.15

The platform owner must manage the delicate balance between app developers' autonomy and app–platform integration.

2.3.6 The Humpty Dumpty problem

The Humpty Dumpty problem is one where separating an app from its platform in order to upgrade can make it difficult to put them back together again. The term originates from the eighteenth-century riddle of Humpty Dumpty, who broke after a fall and no one could figure out how to put him together again (Figure 2.16).

Subsystems within complex software systems composed of many such subsystems often have intricate dependencies among each other (Simon, 1962). This means that a change in one app can potentially have a ripple effect on the platform or other apps. Similarly, a small change in the platform can have a ripple effect that can break previously functioning apps (Tiwana et al., 2010). This is like a domino effect—a chain reaction—where one change in a part of the ecosystem can cause other elements of it to behave

FIGURE 2.16

The Humpty Dumpty problem originates in the fable of the character who broke and no one could put him back together again.

Source: The Editorial Board of the University Society, Boys and Girls Bookshelf, *The University Society, New York, 1920.*

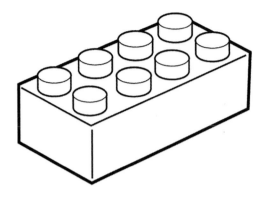

FIGURE 2.17

The Humpty Dumpty problem is solved through Lego-like software platform architectures.

unpredictably in ways that cannot be anticipated. The sole responsibility of managing the Humpty Dumpty problem lies in software architecture (Chapter 5), both at the platform level and at the app level.

A well-designed platform ecosystem should ideally be like a set of Lego blocks. Lego blocks come in all shapes and sizes, with just one thing in common: their connection points (see Figure 2.17). As long as a Lego block obeys the size and placement of the connection points between blocks, its shape and size do not matter and each individual block can be assured that it will fit with just about any imaginable mix of other Lego blocks. This allows complex structures to be composed from simple collections of Lego blocks. In software platforms, the aspiration to be Lego-like means that it should be possible for an app developer to:

- Readily separate an app from the platform
- Independently update, revise, refine, and extend the app without needing to directly interact with the platform owner or other app developers
- Readily plug the revised app back into the platform and be confident that it will interoperate

By the same token, it should be possible for the platform owner to make any changes internal to the platform without having to ask, interact, or coordinate with app developers. Lego-like architectures are what we call modular architectures, which is the focus of Chapter 5.

2.3.7 The mirroring principle

The mirroring principle is an idea used to align governance and architecture in modular complex systems. The crux of the mirroring principle is that the organizational structure of a platform's ecosystem must mirror its architecture (Hoetker, 2006; Sanchez and Mahoney, 1996). This means that the way in which a platform is governed and the way in which it is architected must be mirror images of each other in order to be mutually reinforcing. If apps are loosely coupled with the platform, their developers must have considerable autonomy from the platform owner. If they are tightly integrated with the platform, the platform owner and app developers should be tightly integrated in their work as well. Figure 2.18 illustrates the idea. We develop this idea in depth in Chapters 10 and 11, after we delve into architecture and governance in Chapters 5 and 6.

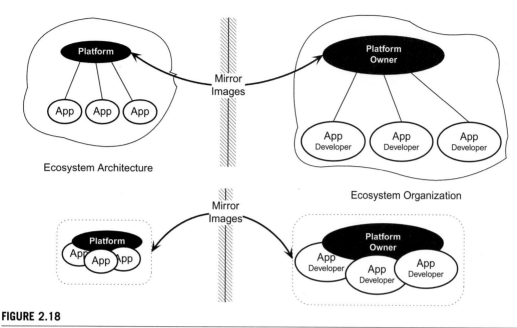

FIGURE 2.18

The mirroring principle.

2.3.8 Coevolution

The viable governance strategies for platform ecosystems are bounded by their architecture, and the evolvability of architectures can be accentuated or attenuated by how they are governed. If the two are codesigned, they can be mutually reinforcing in ways that exceed the evolutionary advantages that either an evolvable architecture or good governance can provide in isolation (Tiwana and Konsynski, 2010). This book therefore emphasizes the importance of aligning the technical architecture of a technology solution with its governance. The subsequent chapters develop the idea that architecture and governance work as two gears of the motor of ecosystem evolution, which must be aligned with each other (Figure 2.19).

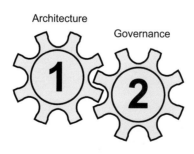

FIGURE 2.19

Architecture and governance are the two gears of evolution of a platform ecosystem.

However, such alignment is not a one-time activity. Rather, as the competitive environment of a technology solution changes, its user base expands or contracts, or emerging technology innovations require tweaking either architecture or governance, the other also needs to be adapted to maintain their initial alignment. Our premise is that the architectures of complex systems influence and are influenced by the economic systems in which complex systems are designed, evolved, and consumed. We refer to this notion of evolving architecture and governance of a technology together as coevolution (Tiwana et al., 2010). Parts III and IV of this book delve into the evolutionary consequences of such coevolution of architecture and governance for platforms and their apps.

2.3.9 The Goldilocks rule

The Goldilocks rule is the idea that given any three ordered choices, humans will gravitate toward the middle over the two extreme choices. (The Goldilocks label originates from the 1837 fairy tale (Figure 2.20) by Robert Southey in which the central character Goldilocks enters the home of three bears. Feeling sleepy, she rejects one bed because it was too big, a second one because it was too small, and chooses the third one because it was "just right.")

FIGURE 2.20

Goldilocks and the Three Bears is a lesson in how we gravitate toward the middle choice, which we often view as "just right."

Source: Arthur Mee and Holland Thompson, The Book of Knowledge, *The Grolier Society, New York, 1912.*

Starbucks, for example, offers three choices for most drink sizes with the expectation that customers will (and often do) pick the middle one. The two extremes are perceived either too small or too big, with the middle one "just right." The two extreme choices in this ordered set of three choices therefore serve primarily to nudge a customer toward the intended middle choice. If the middle option is priced to generate the highest profit, the anchoring effect of the other two extreme options can be sufficiently strong in nudging customers toward the middle, which can be priced to sell at a lower profit margin yet generate the highest aggregate revenue and profits. The bottom line is to be able to use this strategy to sell a greater volume of the middle option. As a corollary, offering more than three versions is suboptimal because choice clutter creates confusion. There are therefore diminishing returns in offering too much choice (Evans and Schmalensee, 2007, p. 33). This rule can be used to version apps and platforms. For example, instead of offering a free version and a paid version of an app, an app developer might generate higher aggregate margins by offering three versions using a variety of versioning criteria, described in detail in Chapter 11.

2.4 LESSONS LEARNED

Software platform ecosystems must be orchestrated rather than managed. This is because their strength is the diversity of external innovators; but their work must also be integrated with the platform if the advantages of this diversity are to be realized in practice. Some of the underlying principles and concepts are unusual enough both for managers and for software developers that it is important for us to be on the same page about what they mean throughout the book. We generically used the term *technology solution* to refer to both platforms and apps because many of the ideas apply to both, and some to the entire ecosystem (Table 2.1). A brief summary of the core ideas described in this chapter appears below.

- *Strategies that are appropriate for managing platforms and apps vary with where they are in the evolutionary lifecycle.* The lifecycle of a technology solution is a three-dimensional property that encompasses whether it is in the pre- or post-dominant design stage, where it falls in the technology maturity trajectory (the S-curve), and what proportion of the total prospective user base has already adopted it.
- *Software platforms have intrinsically different properties compared to other types of platforms.* Their multisidedness offers fertile opportunities to create both same-side and cross-side network effects, lock-ins that can be both coercive and value-driven, and the prospects of swallowing adjacent platforms as well as the dangers of being swallowed by one.
- *Architectures of technology solutions provide the blueprint for mass coordination.* The conventional coordination and control mechanisms that work well in conventional organizations and supply chains are prohibitively costly and implausible to use in large ecosystems. Architecture instead provides the blueprint for both partitioning innovation work across the many participants in a platform ecosystem and for integrating it.
- *Governance can amplify or diminish the advantages of good architecture.* Governance and architecture must be codesigned and coevolved because they act as the two gears of a platform's evolutionary motor. A misfit between the two can lead to evolutionary penalties and the eventual demise of a previously successful technology solution.

- *Evolutionary pace of a platform is relative to its rivals.* A platform must evolve at least as rapidly as its rivals to remain viable (the Red Queen effect).
- *Emergent innovation can only be facilitated, not planned by a platform owner.* Most innovations around platforms are emergent in the sense that they spontaneously arise from the selfish pursuit of self-interest by individual ecosystem participants. A platform owner must make the ecosystem conducive to such emergent innovation to fully realize the potential of platform ecosystems.
- *New platforms must overcome the chicken-or-egg problem and the penguin problem to get off the ground.* The multisided nature of platforms makes it unattractive for either side to join unless there is a critical mass on the other side. App developers, for example, will find a platform attractive only if it has a large pool of prospective users; users will find a platform attractive only if there is a large variety of apps to complement the platform. Uncertainty about whether others will join the platform ecosystem can stall initial adoption, creating the penguin problem. Governance tuned to different phases of a platform's lifecycle (Figure 2.1) can help overcome these startup problems.
- *Platforms must be designed to overcome three problems that can impede their evolution.* First, platform owners must balance the need to grant sufficient autonomy to app developers to innovate freely without compromising integration of their work into the platform's ecosystem (the seesaw problem). Second, apps must be separable from the platform to freely evolve, but it must also be easy to subsequently reintegrate them with the platform (the Humpty Dumpty problem). Third, how innovation work is organized should mirror the architecture of the platform and the "microarchitecture" (see Chapter 5) of individual apps (the mirroring principle).

In the next chapter, we describe how platform businesses differ from product and service businesses, how these differences catapult most managers and technologists out of their comfort zone, and the five necessary changes in managers' mindsets and assumptions in platform markets.

Why Platform Businesses Are Unlike Product or Service Businesses

3

It's not that we need new ideas, but we need to stop having old ideas.
Edwin Land

IN THIS CHAPTER

- How platform businesses differ from product and service businesses
- Why platforms need a mindset different from products and services
- How products and services can evolve into platforms
- Four lenses for spotting platform opportunities

3.1 INTRODUCTION

To appreciate the distinctive challenges and opportunities that platforms bring, it is important to first recognize precisely how they differ from the two dominant models of industrial organization: product and service industries. The significance of platform thinking lies in the distinctive ways in which the market potential, structure, and management of platform businesses diverge from traditional product and service businesses. These differences nullify the ingrained assumptions and the managerial mindset that works well in product and service businesses. The mindset needed for managing platform businesses is sufficiently different that it throws most managers and technology professionals out of their comfort zone.

This chapter explores these differences and explains how managers' mindsets, assumptions, and mental models must evolve to be cognizant of them. Unlike product and service businesses, platform businesses can cost-effectively target microsegments of their markets, potentially create durable revenue streams, and offer opportunities to sustain higher margins than products or services in equally competitive markets. However, their structure with potentially vast armies of ecosystem partners rather than a smaller network of supply chain partners resembles no familiar product or service business. Their unique cost structures allow highly asymmetric pricing across their different sides and disperse the locus of where innovation is generated, as well as the costs and risks associated with innovation generation around the platform. Therefore, platform businesses must be managed differently from product and service businesses, with architecture rather than authority and contracts providing coordination, orchestration foreshadowing conventional notions of management, and the need for platform owners to walk the tightrope between granting sufficient autonomy to app developers and ensuring integration of the outputs of diverse ecosystem participants. These differences require a shift in the

---

☆"To view the full reference list for the book, click here or see page 283."

49

managerial mindset, which an appreciation of the inseparability of the success of platform owners from the success of app developers, an emphasis on designing for evolvability to survive Darwinian marketplace competition, and understanding how the two gears of a platform's evolutionary motor—architecture and governance—must interlock for it to move forward. We conclude the chapter with a four-lens framework to help managers in product and service businesses spot opportunities to transform them into platform businesses.

We begin by contrasting platform businesses with product and service businesses. Table 3.1 briefly summarizes the commonalities and differences among them.

3.1.1 Market potential differences

A key difference between products and platforms is that platforms are multisided while products are rarely so. This dramatically expands the market potential of platforms. Platforms offer the potential for economies of scale for platform owners and app developers that far exceed that in products and services. By tapping into both mass markets and long-tails of those markets through extensive customization by end-users, they can capture a larger extent of the market than even mass-produced products. Finally, they offer distinctive ways of locking in customers and potentially transforming a one-time lump-sum sale model for products into a service-like revenue stream. Lock-in coupled with the potential for strong network effects (where more users make a platform more valuable to all other users; see Chapter 2) allows successful platforms to enjoy potentially high margins in highly competitive markets compared to products and services in equally competitive markets. These features mean that the economic returns from successfully transforming a product or service to a platform significantly grow its revenue potential.

3.1.2 Structural differences

The market potential of platforms comes from their distinctive difference in how they are structurally organized vis-à-vis products and services. Although both products and services increasingly use complex supply chains spanning the globe, their size pales in comparison to the bigger platform ecosystems. Interfirm networks such as supply chains and production networks are an important source of value creation in most product and services industries. But such networks in platform ecosystems are much larger, more diverse, and more fluid (Williamson and De Meyer, 2012). They are like partner networks on steroids. Ecosystems can therefore be orders of magnitude more complex than supply chains used for products and services (Williamson and De Meyer, 2012). Contrast the 50 firms that collaborated to develop Boeing's Dreamliner or the 37 firms that contribute to producing the iPhone device to the half million app developers who develop apps for the iOS and Android platforms. But platform markets offer less concentrated control than product or service markets. A platform is only partially under the platform owner's control (Gawer and Cusumano, 2008). The ownership of a platform ecosystem and the associated intellectual property is also highly fragmented among the platform owner and app developers, unlike products and services where one firm often maintains proprietary control over its core products or services. Unlike products or services that must attract customers, platforms are inherently "multisided" (see Chapter 2); they need to simultaneously attract at least two distinct groups of participants with very different needs and motivations (e.g., end-users and app developers). But unlike products or services, the risks and costs of most innovation are borne by outsiders who are also the locus of innovation generation.

Table 3.1 How Platforms Differ from Products and Services

Attribute	Product	Service	Platform
Market potential differences			
Scale economies potential	High	Low	Very high
Customization by end-users	Limited	Potentially extensive	Extensive
Market	Segments	Segments	Microsegments
Long-tail potential	Low	High	Very high
Lock-in potential	Low to medium	High	Very high
Network effects potential	Low	High	Very high
Revenue model	Lump-sum sale	Revenue stream	Revenue stream
Margins in competitive markets	Low	Low	Potentially high
Structural differences			
Production network contributors	Small network of firms	Small network of firms	Ecosystem; potentially hundreds of thousands of partners
Dominant costs	Fixed costs	Variable costs	High fixed costs for platform owner; low fixed costs for app developers; declining variable costs for both
Multisidedness (Chapter 2)	Rare	Occasional	Often
IP ownership	Firm	Firm	Dispersed
Pricing	Cost-plus	Value-driven	Asymmetric across two sides
End-user value creation locus	Firm	Firm	Ecosystem
Locus of control	Firm	Firm	Distributed among firms
Ownership	Firm	Firm	Diffused across ecosystem
Dominant innovator	Firm	Firm or service chain	Largely app developers
Dominant risk taker	Firm	Firm	Largely app developers
Management-style differences			
Innovation mode	Planned	Planned	Emergent
Management model	Command-and-control	Coproduction with customers	Orchestration
Critical success factor	Good management	Process rigor	Orchestration
Key tension	Predicting and anticipating consumer preferences	Customization to idiosyncratic consumer needs	Ecosystem partners' autonomy versus ecosystem-wide integration
Startup bottleneck	Attracting customers	Attracting customers	Attracting both sides

3.1.3 Management style differences

The diversity of ecosystem participants is the biggest strength of platform-based thinking, but it is also its biggest challenge. Specialization requires each participant in a platform's ecosystem to focus narrowly and deeply on their own unique capabilities and on leveraging those of others. This requires the platform owner to walk a delicate balance between granting app developers unfettered autonomy to innovate without compromising ecosystem-wide integration of their outputs. The fundamental structural differences in how platforms are organized vis-à-vis products and services means that several assumptions in how products and services are managed no longer hold. It requires control without ownership, orchestration without authority, and direction without enough expertise by the platform owner. The closest analogy that we develop extensively in Chapter 6 on governance is the notion of orchestration, where the platform owner provides just enough guidance to the platform's app developers to gently but invisibly nudge the evolutionary trajectory of the platform in a desirable direction. In platforms, emergent innovation therefore foreshadows centrally planned innovation (Dougherty and Dunne, 2011); orchestration of ecosystem partners replaces coordination through command-and-control and authority over employees and contractors. Solid execution and good management intuition still have a place, but secondary to ecosystem orchestration.

3.2 WHY PLATFORMS NEED A DIFFERENT MINDSET

Platforms require a significant shift in the prevailing mindset among managers in the software industry as well as just about high other industry with any information content. The differences violate the assumptions that most managers are trained to make, particularly about ownership and control. And they take away the tools and frameworks that help conventional firms prosper. The five reasons for this are summarized in Table 3.2.

1. *Product competition is migrating to platform competition.* Competition in many industries is increasingly shifting away from product against product toward platform against platform. This means that having a superior standalone product does not guarantee market success against an inferior product with a more powerful ecosystem. This trend is pervasive in browsers (e.g., Firefox, Chrome, and Opera), smartphone operating systems (iPhone, Android, MS Mobile), Web services (Google Payments, Amazon Elastic Cloud, Hadoop), social media (Facebook, Twitter), marketplaces (SABRE, eBay), and gaming (Xbox, Apple's Touch, Sony Playstation). As software is embedded in more products—washers, refrigerators, cars, shoes—and business processes in more service businesses—hourly-wage jobs, healthcare, finance, marketing, accounting—are embedded in software, this migration toward platform competition is beginning to reach far beyond the IT industry from which it originated. In such environments, the success of a platform offering is inseparable from the platform's ecosystem partners' ability to deliver. The platform owner and complementors depend on each other and share a common fate. Innovations are not generated by a single firm, but the entire ecosystem (Dougherty and Dunne, 2011). Systems competition is therefore replacing product competition. But this requires managers to think in terms of ecosystems and manage the delicate balance between their own firms' interests and those of their partners. And it requires recognizing that their fates are intertwined. An ecosystem is not a zero-sum game: Instead of thinking in terms of how the pie can be

Table 3.2 How Platform Thinking Requires a Different Mindset Toward Business Strategy

Driver	Traditional Product/Service Markets	Platform Markets
Migration from product competition to platform competition	A good product that offers a valuable value proposition to customers has a fair shot in the market	Rival platforms' ecosystems compete with each other; a good product without a compelling ecosystem has no shot in the market
Organizational boundaries blur	Coordination is achieved through authority and command-and-control structures	Conventional coordination mechanisms cannot scale to large platforms; alternative coordination mechanisms must be created
Architecture matters	Architecture rarely enters strategic thinking beyond centralized and decentralized organizational design choices	Architecture provides the blueprint for coordination across thousands of ecosystem partners where conventional coordination mechanisms fall apart
Evolutionary fit—not just efficiency—determines a platform's fate	Focus on operational efficiency and maximizing predictability	Platforms that evolve faster outlast their rivals
Coevolution of architecture and governance	Architecture of products and services are designed separately from the governance of the organization that produces them	Architecture and governance are the two gears of a platform's evolutionary motor; the two must be mutually reinforcing, interlock, and coevolve

more favorably split between a platform owner and its myriad partners, it requires thinking in terms of how the pie can be expanded.

2. *Organizational boundaries are blurring.* The conventional notion of organizational boundaries expands and becomes more porous in platform markets. It is increasingly difficult to draw a line where the platform owner's boundary ends and the ecosystem partners' organizational boundaries begin. Conventional coordination mechanisms and command-and-control hierarchies that make conventional organizations work are neither scalable to thousands of interdependent ecosystem partners, nor does the platform owner have the legitimate authority to dictate their work as it can in conventional organizations and supply chains. Yet the need for effective coordination is paramount for maintaining coherence and delivering value to the end-user. Nuanced and more sophisticated governance is then key to coordinating the ecosystem without stifling ecosystem partners' autonomy to innovate. Governing platforms therefore requires a delicate balance of control by a platform owner and autonomy among independent app developers. Orchestration rather than management becomes key. Orchestration entails control without the tried-and-tested coordination mechanisms of ownership and authority. Platform managers must therefore shift their mindset to emphasize orchestration over management, evolvability over stability, autonomy to innovate over control, and integration over efficiency.

3. *Architecture matters.* As innovation moves out of the realm of a single firm and emerges from the orchestrated effort of a multitude of specialized, independent firms, the capability to both partition

and integrate the work of many independent firms in the ecosystem becomes essential to creating and sustaining a competitive advantage. Managing these dependencies is the crux of coordination. Unfortunately, all known coordination mechanisms that have served firms well in the industrial age—authority, hierarchies, multinationalization, performance metrics, ownership, contracting—are unscalable to networks of firms as potentially large as platform ecosystems. Coordination in platforms is achieved instead by their architecture—a concept largely absent in business strategy—which provides a blueprint for coordination and integration of the work of many organizations. Architecture is central for both partitioning innovation work across many firms and for integrating their work into a coherent product or service offering. Platform architecture is the DNA that—and much like our own—sets a platform on a largely unchangeable evolutionary trajectory. The graveyard of once-dominant platforms (think: Palm and Blackberry) is a poignant reminder that they were not designed to evolve. Early architectural choices by a platform owner are almost impossible to reverse later on, but influence who can participate in the ecosystem, how aggressively they invest, and their incentives to participate. Architecture is no longer just a technical decision but one with irreversible strategic consequences, both in the short term and in the long term. Architecture must therefore earn a place in the nucleus of strategy in platform markets. This requires understanding what architectural choices exist, when and how they facilitate coordination, and their longer-term business consequences. Architecture, however, is often the realm of IT departments and is outside the comfort zone of most managers. Good managers are trained to make sure that every little thing that goes into a product or service fits well. The problem is that such thinking obsesses over the upstream but forgets the downstream, where the bulk of platforms' ecosystems reside. That might be the recipe for making a good product, but not one that can prosper in a platform marketplace. Similarly, great software designers can code technical marvels but be oblivious to how their technical choices can cripple strategic options. (Chapter 5 focuses on platform architecture.) Effective platform orchestration therefore requires a nuanced appreciation at the *intersection* of traditionally disparate perspectives of software design and business strategy.

4. *Survival requires guided evolution.* Business strategy generally emphasizes predictability and efficiency. These are necessary but insufficient for a platform to thrive in a dynamic competitive environment (Katz and Shapiro, 1994; Schilling, 2000). Successful platform ecosystems don't just materialize and sustain; they need a carefully thought-out roadmap to evolve. The roadmap must be flexible enough to not be overly constraining yet be sufficiently defined to provide an overarching vision. Therefore, the focus must shift to understanding evolutionary dynamics and guiding the evolution of platforms and their ecosystems. Much like biological species, platforms that outlast their rivals are ones whose ecosystems evolve more rapidly. It is the *alignment* between platform architecture and platform governance that jointly determines their evolutionary trajectories, and in turn platform differentiation. But different subsystems in an ecosystem might evolve at different rates, and coping with these differential rates of change within an ecosystem is a challenge for managers. (Part III of this book focuses on evolution and its metrics and drivers in software platforms.)

5. *Evolution requires the platform's two gears—architecture and governance—to interlock.* Architecture and governance are like the gears in a platform's evolutionary motor: one must interlock with the other for it to move the evolutionary motor forward (see Figure 3.1). Realizing the potential of thoughtfully designed architectures requires ensuring that a platform is governed to take advantage of its architecture. (Governance simply means who makes what decisions and how

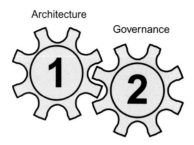

FIGURE 3.1

Architecture and governance are the two gears of a platform's evolutionary motor.

the pie is split among the platform owner and app developers.) The two can be perfect in isolation but will underdeliver on their potential if one does not align well with the other. Traditional software businesses pay close attention to the architecture of software products, but little to governance. Traditional business strategy pays close attention to governance, but little to architecture. The unique characteristic of platforms is the need for the two to be codesigned to interlock, and more importantly to coevolve. Technological developments might lead to incremental changes in architecture; shifts in the competitive environment can require changes in how the platform is governed. Changes in either can result in mislocking of architecture and governance, with evolutionary penalties. Managers in platform businesses must simultaneously tackle both technology and strategy decisions, which are inseparably intertwined. The two must be constantly realigned and coevolve to ensure that they interlock. This interlocking determines how well a platform responds to dynamics in the competitive environment, evolving user bases, and emergent market opportunities. This is often outside the comfort zone of most managers because it requires understanding the interplay between technology and strategy. Most managers specialized in one are rarely immersed in the other. (Platform governance is discussed in Chapter 6, and their interlocking in Parts III and IV of this book.)

3.3 HOW PRODUCTS AND SERVICES CAN EVOLVE INTO PLATFORMS

Most successful platforms start out as successful standalone products, and some as services or one-sided platforms. Most unsuccessful platforms that you have never heard of *started out* as platforms. History is replete with promising platforms that should have made history but never took off because they forgot that it takes two to tango. The biggest challenge to getting a platform off the ground is simultaneously attracting two distinct sides to the platform (see the chicken-or-egg problem in Chapter 2) (Rysman, 2009). There are ways around the problem in textbook theory (such as price subsidies), but they are costly and prone to failure in practice. The safest approach is to get one side onboard first by offering a product or service that is valuable and attractive by itself. In real options lingo (Chapter 8), this would be investing in a future option to create a platform. The iPhone did not become successful on the coattails of the iOS ecosystem; rather, the ecosystem became successful on the coattails of a successful product that was innovative, well made, valuable to buyers, and backed by good support and service. The most successful software platforms started out as stellarly successful products that subsequently evolved into platforms. The iPhone (the precursor to iOS) began life as a standalone product—not as a multisided platform—as did Microsoft Windows; so did Facebook, Skype, Amazon, eBay, Google, Firefox, and Dropbox. Only after one side—the consumers—adopted it in droves did each of these add a second side to evolve into a real platform. The iPhone added the App Store a year later, Windows added APIs, Facebook and Google added advertising, Skype and Firefox added extensions, and Dropbox added apps and API services. The very reason the second side—the complement producers—found these platforms attractive was that there was already a large group on the first side (the end-users). If your bread-and-butter is a successful product or service, you're already past the first hurdle that stymies most fledgling platforms: Attracting the first side.

3.3.1 The four lenses for spotting platform opportunities

Many products and services have the potential to morph into a platform. But how does one recognize a potential platform opportunity? Four simple questions can get you started. These four questions are like the lenses of a telescope; you'll spot fertile platform opportunities better if you use all four simultaneously. The four-lens platform opportunity spotting framework is summarized in Figure 3.2.

1. *Can you identify at least two distinct groups who want to—but cannot cost-effectively—interact with each other?* The potential for platforms is greatest where two distinct groups—say innovators and consumers—want to interact with each other more easily but cannot do it on their own (Evans and Schmalensee, 2007; Evans et al., 2006, p. 3). Each side would benefit if someone helped them find each other and transact cost-effectively—the role that a potential platform serves. It need not be impossible for the transaction to occur without a platform; it should just become

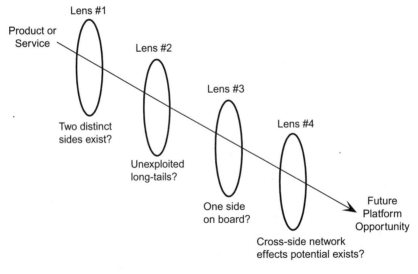

FIGURE 3.2

The four lenses for spotting platform opportunities.

easier or more cost-effective if a prospective platform can connect them in ways that they directly cannot. The platform therefore serves as a catalyst that facilitates value-creating interactions between two groups (Evans and Schmalensee, 2007). One of these two sides should be the *existing* core customer group of your product or service.

2. *Are there long-tails in your markets that are unattractive to directly pursue but potentially attractive to smaller players in your industry?* Think of the core and the niche groups of customers in your product or service's customer pool. Pursuing the niche group—the so-called long-tails of your core market—with needs sufficiently different from your core group compromises scale economies. Would this niche group be attractive to smaller players in your industry, which is the side other than your core group in a potential platform? Here are a few questions to help identify this other side. Are the five drivers discussed in Chapter 1 creating new opportunities to digitize and unbundle activities or services that are currently done inhouse? Are these necessary to deliver your product or service but not a core competence of your company? Would you be better off if they were handled by an outside firm with a core competence in their domain? The ideal scenario is if this other side can build on your own capabilities as a starting point for their own work and would not be able to cost-effectively replicate the scale of the complementary capabilities that you can bring to the platform. In other words, your potential platform should solve at least one core problem that is common to and widespread in your product or service's industry (Gawer and Cusumano, 2008). Can you envision ways in which these smaller firms can build their work on your own product or service capabilities? If your answers to these questions are affirmative, think of how you can create a convincing, win–win, pie-expanding proposition for this other side that you would need to attract.

3. *Do you already have one of two sides on board?* If you already have a successful product or service, you likely have one side already on board to evolve into a two-sided platform. Having a successful product or service is the first step toward solving the chicken-or-egg problem. The challenge then is one of crafting an attractive value proposition for getting the other side on board. (Chapter 6 describes strategies for accomplishing this.)

4. *Can you envision ways to generate positive cross-side network effects?* Network effects can be same-side or cross-side. Same-side network effects mean that adding more adopters of your product or service will increase its value to all your existing customers. But such network effects primarily increase the value of the product or service to existing customers and do not turn it into a platform. Cross-side network effects are when adding the second distinct group of adopters increases the value of your product or service to your existing and prospective core group of current customers. Cross-side network effects often arise when the second side you're thinking of produces downstream complements that your core customer group (the first side) can use to enhance what they can do with your product or service. A clearly identified second side with strong cross-side network-effects potential is necessary to survive copycat competitors, noncoercively lock in both sides into a prospective platform, and create a success-begets-more-success type of self-reinforcing feedback loop dynamic in a platform. If you can identify more than one "other side," narrow down your platform thinking hat toward the group with the clearest cross-side network-effects potential.

If you can affirmatively answer at least two of these four questions, your product or service has the potential to evolve into a platform.

3.4 LESSONS LEARNED

Platform businesses differ markedly in their market potential, structure, and management approaches from product and service businesses. This requires managers to change their mindset and ingrained assumptions in how they manage a platform business vis-à-vis a product or service business. A brief summary of the core ideas described in this chapter appears below.

- *Platforms have greater intrinsic market potential relative to products or services.* Platform businesses offer much higher potential for generating economies of scale. Extensive user-driven customization of platforms with diverse ecosystem complements allows them to penetrate microsegments and long-tails of markets that are usually inaccessible to product and service businesses. They also offer a higher potential for noncoercively locking in customers. Like services, they can generate revenue streams rather than lump-sum sales. Products that can make the leap from product to platform can therefore dramatically alter their revenue model. Finally, the intrinsic properties unique to software platforms allow the successful ones to produce higher margins for platform owners and app developers than products or services can in equally competitive markets.
- *Platform businesses are structurally different from product or service businesses.* Unlike products and services that rely on a small network of supply chain partners, platform businesses rely on potentially vast ecosystems of outside innovators. Platforms are always multisided, with ownership of assets and intellectual property as well as control dispersed among members of the ecosystem. Because of their unique cost structure where the platform owner faces higher fixed costs than app developers, and the potential for self-reinforcing network effects and lock-in over app developers and end-users, pricing across the two sides of a platform business can often be asymmetric (with one side often heavily subsidized). Unlike product and service businesses where the focal firm is the dominant innovator and risk taker, the dominant innovators and risk takers in platform businesses are often the app developers. App developers are therefore often the primary locus of innovation generation in platforms. In return, they also have greater prospects for more handsome payoffs in the marketplace than do suppliers in conventional supply chains of product and service firms.
- *Platform businesses must be managed differently from product or service businesses.* Unlike product and service businesses where innovation is an outcome of careful planning, innovation in platform businesses is often emergent. The platform owner lacks legitimate authority over app developers to command and control them like employees or contractually bound supply chain partners in a product or service business. Orchestration therefore foreshadows traditional management and process control in platform businesses. The initial challenge of attracting at least two distinct sides to the platforms is therefore as prominent as the need to anticipate and predict customer needs that predominates product and service businesses. The biggest ongoing challenge for platform owners is to balance the delicate tension between respecting the autonomy of its ecosystem partners without compromising the seamless integration of their outputs back into the platform's ecosystem.
- *Platforms need a different managerial mindset.* Four assumptions that are reasonable in product and service businesses need to be altered to adapt the mindset with which managers approach platform businesses. First, platform businesses pit a platform's ecosystem against a rival ecosystem. The success of a platform is inseparable from the success of app developers. It is as important for the

platform owner to help the app developers deliver on their promises as it is for it to deliver on its own promises. Second, conventional coordination and control mechanisms that fare well in product and service businesses are unscalable to growing platform ecosystems. Architecture must then assume the dominant coordination and control role. Architecture is usually outside the realm of most managers and strategy is outside the realm of most software architects. This chasm must be bridged for architectural choices to be strategically sound, and platform strategies to be evolvable. Third, platforms that evolve faster are more likely to survive evolutionary competition. Unlike product and service businesses that are designed with short-term efficiency and effectiveness, platform businesses must also emphasize designing for evolvability. Finally, architecture and governance are the two gears of a platform's evolutionary motor. This requires managers to understand how they can be codesigned to be mutually reinforcing and interlocking, and subsequently how to coevolve them.

• *The potential opportunities for evolving products and services into platforms can be spotted using the four lens framework (Figure* 3.2*).* The four thought experiments to recognize this potential for morphing using this framework are: (1) identifying at least two *distinct* groups who want to but cannot cost effectively interact, (2) recognizing long-tails in your markets unattractive to you but attractive to other smaller players in your industry, (3) having one of these two sides as the core customer group of your product or service, and (4) identifying ways to generate positive cross-side network effects.

In the next chapter, we delve into how platforms offer a distinctive value proposition to three types of participants—platform owners, app developers, and end-users—with different needs and motivations for joining a platform. We also describe how a platform-centric model can potentially deliver compelling value to these three groups in ways that a product or service without a platform rarely can.

The Value Proposition of Platforms

I conceive that the great part of the miseries of mankind are brought upon them by false estimates they have made of the value of things.
Benjamin Franklin

IN THIS CHAPTER

- The value proposition of software platforms for:
  - Platform owners
  - Complementors (app developers)
  - End-users

The three groups of participants in a platform ecosystem—platform owners, app developers, and end-users—have unique needs and motivations for participating in it. Therefore, a platform must uniquely appeal to each group in how it aligns with their interests relative to a product or service. To be sustainable, a platform-based business model must also satisfy their needs better than alternative business models. This chapter focuses on the distinctive value proposition that software platforms offer to platform owners, app developers, and end-users.

For platform owners, platforms enable massively distributed innovation on a scale that exceeds conventional product or service supply chains, transfer of the majority of costs and risks associated with innovating around the platform, allowing the platform owner to focus on doing more of what it does best and leaving the rest to its ecosystem partners, using self-interest and market incentives to align the interests of app developers with the platform's interests, and increasing the prospects of surviving shifts, collisions, and disruptions in its markets. For app developers, platforms lower entry barriers by providing a shared foundation to use as a starting point for their own work. They also provide access to a prospective customer pool, which can find and transact with the app developers more easily through the platform than they could without it. For end-users, platforms can allow extreme levels of customization to their unique needs by enabling them to themselves mix-and-match apps that increase their personal utility of the platform. They are also the primary beneficiaries of competition among platforms and among app developers with the platform, potential usefulness-enhancing same-side network effects, and from the faster pace of innovation that can increase the usefulness of their initial investment in a platform over time. These value promotions are summarized in Table 4.1 and are discussed next.

☆"To view the full reference list for the book, click here or see page 283."

Table 4.1 The Value Proposition of Platforms for Platform Owners, App Developers, and End-Users

Stakeholder Group	Value Proposition
Platform owner	• Massively distributed innovation • Risk transfer • Capturing the long-tail • Competitive sustainability
App developers	• Technological foundations that sharpen focus on app development • Market access
Users	• Mix-and-match customization • Faster innovation • Competition among rivals • Lower search and transaction costs

4.1 PLATFORM OWNERS

The value proposition of a platform for the platform owner is fourfold: (1) massively distributed innovation, (2) risk transfer, (3) capturing the market's long-tail, and (4) increased competitive sustainability.

4.1.1 Massively distributed innovation

The primary value proposition of platforms for platform owners is the potential to innovate on a scale and scope around the platform that are inconceivable in a traditional firm. Platforms allow the platform owner to infuse the power of competitive markets into traditional organizations. Instead of itself attempting to innovate in diverse markets and domains where the platform has potential applications, the platform owner can massively distribute innovation work to large numbers of app developers. Applications are where the real value in differentiating a platform from the end-users' perspective comes. Such app developers are often closer to the pulse of their market, can bring deep and nuanced understanding of their customer segments and application domains to the table, and can collectively generate a constant stream of innovations that complement the platform. Mobilizing local insights of its complementors allows a platform to potentially penetrate diverse market domains, industries, and geographies, often far beyond what the platform owner might have been able to envision. Theoretically, all of this could be done inhouse by a single firm. But realistically, the economics of attempting it and the distraction from the firm's core competence associated with it make it almost unfeasible.

As the old adage goes, producing good ideas requires producing more ideas. And the best way to produce more innovative ideas is to have many minds independently attack a problem space with diverse approaches. Platform-based ecosystems therefore have the potential capability to create entirely new platform capabilities through partitioning of innovation activities and their integration (Dougherty and Dunne, 2011). As long as the platform owner can successfully foster competition among application developers in the same space, it is likely that different developers will experiment using a variety of approaches, designs, and solutions to meet the needs of their own markets. This parallel approach to innovation and problem solving that rewards the survival of the fittest solution is a far cry from a single firm that typically can select only one approach for addressing a customer problem or emerging need. This increases the likelihood that some innovative solutions out of multiple competing ones will stick and help maintain the platform's differentiation in the market. At the same time, it allows the platform owner to specialize in its core activities even more narrowly and deeply. The pursuit of innovation around the platform by many complementors can also accelerate the rate at which innovations are realized across the platform's ecosystem. This acceleration of the innovation clock speed raises the bar for rival platforms and products.

4.1.2 Risk transfer

App developers bear most of the financial risk in pursuing their own ideas for apps for a platform. Therefore, unlike traditional product development, the costs and risks of developing new platform-specific innovations shift from the platform owner to app developers. These app developers are driven by the hunger to succeed, with the prospects of large payoffs if they do. App developers can therefore bolster the platform's competitive advantage purely by pursuing their selfish self-interest (but only if governance is gotten right). Therefore market success and failure functions as a built-in disciplining device for app developers in platform markets. The platform owner's fixed costs of developing and maintaining the platform also can be spread across many app developers and users.

4.1.3 Capturing the long-tail

Platform markets have two pieces: a mass market that characterizes its average consumer and a niche market that demands functionality, which is so different from the typical consumer that relatively small incremental quantities of a product or service can be sold if the platform catered to that market (see Figure 4.1). Therefore, firms often must focus on the needs of the mass market in conceiving new products and services, which they can deliver with economies of scale and sell in large volumes. However, the long part of the tail—the niche markets with highly specialized and uncommon

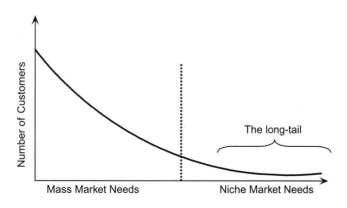

FIGURE 4.1

Platform owners can use ecosystems to capture their market's long-tail.

needs—are often more than one homogenous group of niche customers. There are often *many* small niche groups of customers with fairly unique needs that would be economically unfeasible for one firm to try to please. The many niche markets that are economically impractical for a firm to cater to can collectively add up to a substantial lost opportunity, sometimes adding up to exceed the size of the mass market. Companies like Amazon understand this, and have successfully addressed the long-tails of the markets that their real-world rivals such as Barnes and Noble cannot justify satisfying. Think of the likelihood of your local bookstore carrying a book on logistic regression that maybe two customers will buy in a year. This would take away from the space used to stock a popular bestseller that might sell a thousand copies a year.

A platform strategy potentially allows the platform owner to capture such niche markets without having to attempt to create products and services for them. Instead, app developers might find the niche markets lucrative enough to pursue using the platform as a foundation. The platform owner can therefore penetrate many market niches without bearing the direct costs or risks of dabbling in them (Meyer and Selinger, 1998). By mobilizing a diverse army of complementary resources and expertise to tackle the long-tails of the platform's market, the platform owner can remain focused in its core activities and on the mass market while bolstering the prospects that the platform will meet complex and diverse demands for specialized, customized solutions from customers in their market's long-tail (Williamson and De Meyer, 2012). This allows mass customization taken to an extreme because it allows the platform's end-users in microscopic segments of the long-tail to mix-and-match apps from the ecosystem to meet their unique needs.

A platform that successfully captures the long-tail of its markets using its ecosystem can create a win–win, pie-expanding payoff for everyone involved. Amazon, for example, had 300,000 outside developers and 2 million third-party sellers using its platform extensions, collectively accounting for 36% of its $18 billion revenue in 2012. Apple similarly has paid about $10 billion in royalties to its iOS developers—far exceeding what the entire U.S. book publishing industry annually pays in royalties to all of its authors combined.

4.1.4 Competitive sustainability

A platform-based strategy also has the potential to increase a platform's competitive sustainability. Platforms can become exponentially more popular as they grow in popularity; success begets more success, at least in the short term. Rapid access to a diverse variety of complements increases the value of the platform to both existing and prospective end-users. Attracting a diversity of outsiders with deep domain expertise and intrinsic hunger to innovate around a platform can create a self-positive cycle: The more end-users can do using a platform, the more attractive it will be for them. The more users a platform has, the more attractive app developers are likely to find it. Platforms can therefore catalyze a virtuous cycle once the bedeviling problem of attracting both sides is overcome (Eisenmann et al., 2006). Once established, platforms can also be notoriously difficult to dislodge because a rival would not only have to deliver a better price–performance ratio but would also have to rally app developers around it. This ensures that once the positive cycle begins, the platform will be better able to evolve and dynamically reconfigure to shifting user bases and emerging needs. But this is just one of the many ways explored in this book that a platform can bolster its competitive sustainability. Many other design and governance tools can strengthen such network effects and create noncoercive, value-driven lock-ins for users.

4.2 APP DEVELOPERS

The value proposition of platforms for app developers and external complementors are twofold: (1) a technological foundation that provides app developers the advantages of scale without ownership and (2) market access.

4.2.1 Technological foundations

A software application has two broad functional elements: (1) those unique to the market niche of an individual app and (2) those that it shares in common with at least some other apps. The value of the app is mostly created from the unique functional elements, but the common, somewhat generic functional elements are necessary for the unique elements to function. A platform can aggregate the common elements of functionality and provide them as the foundation on which app developers can build unique elements. This is often accomplished in software platforms by services and interfaces through which apps can access the common functionality. In software platforms, the platform owner therefore contributes value by provisioning the base functionality on which app developers can build their work. For example, in video gaming and hand-held gaming systems, audio, graphic processing, and networking functionality is often provisioned by the platform (for example Valve Corporation's Steam game development platform). In contemporary smartphone platforms, network access, processing, and notification functionality is often provided by the platform. This allows thousands of developers to use that common functionality as the starting point for their own work. The scalable, investment-intensive shared assets, functionality, and services provided by the platform can be leveraged by many apps. This shift in moving from a standalone product model to a platform model is illustrated in Figure 4.2.

The implications of this are twofold. First, as the duplicated elements of app functionality are collapsed into the platform, app developers can afford to specialize more exclusively on producing the unique functional elements of their apps where their expertise presumably lies and where they can create more distinctive value. The costs of the shared platform are spread across many app developers, so potentially massive scale economies can be created in the shared functionality. The primary value of

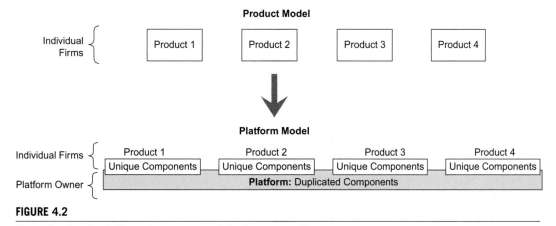

FIGURE 4.2

How migration to platforms increases specialization among firms.

platform-based development for app developers is therefore the elimination of non-value-adding duplication and reduction of development costs through large-scale sharing, all without the need to overtly coordinate with other app developers (Evans and Schmalensee, 2007; Evans et al., 2006, p. 17). Individual app developers no longer need to replicate the common functionality elements that do not directly differentiate them in the market, and also frees them from the responsibility and costs of provisioning this baseline infrastructure needed for their apps to function. This lowers the entry barriers for app developers, who no longer need to be able to make irreversible investments in creating that functionality on a large scale. An app developer can develop a new app without starting from scratch and without reinventing the wheel in creating shared functionality that does not directly differentiate or provide utility for *its* end-users. The emphasis therefore shifts toward greater specialization among app developers (Iansiti and Levien, 2004, p. 149). However, creating and maintaining a competitive advantage requires attention to evolving platforms and apps in the face of rivals and copycats—the focus of Part III and beyond in this book.

Second, the reduction in initial financial outlays by app developers makes it financially feasible to attack long-tails of markets that would have otherwise been economically unviable. This potentially creates a win–win proposition for platform owners who often cannot economically target niche user bases in their market's long-tail and for app developers who can have some assurance that the platform owner will not invade their niche. (When it does happen, how platform owners and app developers can tackle it is subsequently discussed in Part IV of this book.) The true potential of the platform therefore comes not just from its native capabilities but from the many serendipitous applications that end-users can put it to. This is driven largely by the diversity of apps that end-users can mix-and-match in use. The attractiveness of a platform to prospective end-users is therefore influenced by the availability and diversity of apps that complement it. This creates a natural alignment between the vested self-interests of app developers and the platform owner.

4.2.2 Market access

Platforms potentially offer app developers access to existing markets that would have been inaccessible to an app developer working in isolation. App developers are often like mom-and-pop stores, but the market potential that platforms can open up to them is unprecedented as the popular ones sell millions, if not billions, of copies. Platforms can do this by making it easier for prospective consumers of the app to find it and to cost-effectively acquire and deploy it in their own instantiations of the ecosystem. Platforms can make it easier for a potentially large set of platform users to find complementary apps. Software production involves sharp economies of scale: The initial copy of an app requires a substantial investment to produce but subsequent copies can be costlessly created and distributed. Therefore, an app developer has strong incentives to make the investment only when there exists a prospective pool of buyers that is sufficiently large for the app developer to break even. Therefore, copies of an app sold after the breakeven point (i.e., where revenues from copy sales balance out the app developer's cost of producing the app) largely represent profits. Without the platform providing access to a prescreened pool of prospective customers, it would be much harder for an app developer to be found by the same customers. As a platform's user base grows in sheer numbers, across geographical markets, and across industry segments, so does the pool of prospective customers accessible to the app. The net effect of using a platform is the potential for expanding demand for the app developer's work (Evans et al., 2006, p. 79). (Economists call these *search* costs.) However, once a willing customer finds the app, the app developer also incurs costs of actually selling and delivering the app. Economists call these *transaction costs* (Rochet and Tirole, 2006; Williamson, 1991), which are incurred during the transaction after a search by the customer has been completed. Platforms can potentially reduce such transaction costs. The most common among such mechanisms are a payment mechanism infrastructure, which are shared by all participants on both sides of the platform. The platform infrastructure can also lower app developers' distribution costs.

4.3 END-USERS

The value proposition of platforms for end-users is fourfold: (1) almost-perfect customization, (2) faster innovation with network benefits, (3) benefits of rivalry on the supply side of platforms, and (4) lower search costs and transaction costs.

4.3.1 Mix-and-match customization

Most products are designed with a mass market in mind, where the focus is on meeting the needs common to the average user. Any idiosyncratic needs of an end-user that are not shared with the average user are likely to go unmet. For example, most users would use email on a smartphone but very few users would need a bibliography management tool. Software-based platforms that have a large variety of complements available allow immense levels of customization to end-users' unique needs from a platform. Mixing-and-matching apps deployed by an end-user on a platform allows for large-scale customization of the ecosystem to individual users' diverse and unique needs. Platforms therefore can offer end-users the ability to get complex, highly customized bundles of product or service functionality from a platform. This user-driven bundling of apps with the platform to create a unique portfolio is different from a one-size-fits-all approach that has been mainstream in the software industry. (If a platform has a variety of apps available that users can readily integrate with it, the platform can be described as having high *composability*.)

4.3.2 Faster innovation and network benefits

Unlike buying a product whose features are likely to remain much like they were when an end-user purchased it, a platform can grow in its capabilities and functionality long after the end-user has adopted it. Like wine, a platform can appreciate in value in a competitive market after it has been adopted. Intraplatform competition among apps and interplatform competition among competing platforms delivers a faster rate of innovation that is likely to benefit the end-user most. This innovation dynamic can increase the value of adopting a platform dramatically over time. Both platform owners and app developers have strong incentives to increase the value of the platform to prospective end-users by exploiting network effects. The end-user is one of the primary beneficiaries of the consequences of this incentive. As platforms evolve through different stages of its lifecycle, as discussed in Chapter 2, the focus of competition can shift toward a race-to-the-bottom, price-based competition, which usually benefits end-users the most by lowering their out-of-pocket platform adoption costs.

4.3.3 **Competition among rivals**

Rival apps compete for end-users' attention. Similarly, rival platforms compete with each other for end-users. This competition eventually rewards survival of the fittest. End-users benefit directly from this competition because it provides access to apps that survive the value that they offer vis-à-vis competing apps. End-users also benefit from competition among rival platforms, which rewards platforms that deliver the most value for money to end-users in the long run. Once a platform reaches a more mature stage of its evolutionary lifecycle (the post-dominant design phase), the focus of competition shifts toward price-based competition. This eventually lowers the ongoing costs of using the platform and increases their affordability to end-users.

4.3.4 **Lower search and transaction costs**

Platforms can potentially reduce end-users' search costs—costs incurred by them prior to transacting with platform complementors. For example, end-users might need to ascertain the trustworthiness of an app supplier and the quality of an app. A platform can provide mechanisms for reducing such costs, for example, by aggregating reviews of past purchasers, screening and certifying apps, and by establishing itself as a trusted intermediary. Generally, reducing search costs involves the platform owner providing information about each side to the other side to facilitate screening. They can also reduce the costs incurred by the users during their transactions with app developers through platform-based transaction and exchange mechanisms.

4.4 **LESSONS LEARNED**

Software platforms offer distinctive value propositions for platform owners, app developers, and end-users. Each of these have distinctively different needs and motivations for participating in a platform ecosystem. Therefore, a platform-based business model must not only meet these distinctive needs but must also do so in a more compelling manner than a standalone product or service business model. A brief summary of the key points described in this chapter appears below.

*   *The value proposition for platform owners.* Platforms enable platform owners to innovate on a scale that they could not by themselves. They do this by massively distributing innovation activities that would otherwise have to be done inhouse across a diverse pool of outsiders with strong market-based incentives, drive, and deeper expertise in narrow domains and market segments. This simultaneously allows the platform owner to do more of what it does best and sharpening its focus around what it perceives as its core competence. Doing this allows capturing of the underexploited long-tails of its core market, transferring the costs and risks of developing new innovations to app developers, and increasing the likelihood that the platform can evolve to competitively sustain in shifting market environments.
*   *The value proposition for app developers.* Platforms enable app developers to use the baseline capabilities of the platform as the foundation for their own work. Instead of replicating the functionality that their apps share with other apps, their upfront investment is therefore limited to functionality that their apps do not share with others. This makes it economically viable to target long-tail markets that would otherwise have been difficult to justify targeting, and gives

them the advantages of scale without the cost of ownership by piggybacking on the platform. Platforms also provide access to an existing pool of customers, who can more easily find the app developer's work and more efficiently transact with them. Therefore, they reduce both search costs and transaction costs between app developers and their prospective customers.

- *The value proposition for end-users.* The primary value proposition of platforms for end-users is that they can more uniquely customize their instantiation of a platform to their idiosyncratic needs by mixing-and-matching from a diverse pool of apps that augment the utility of a platform. This resembles mass customization of a product or service with a customer segment of one customer. End-users also benefit from the accelerated pace of innovation around their investment in the platform, with the prospects of increasing value over time as well as network effects that are also in the best interests of platform owners and app developers in competitive platform markets. Finally, platforms lower search costs and transaction costs associated with finding and acquiring apps relative to doing the same without a platform in the middle.

In the next chapter, we delve into architecture in platform ecosystems. We explore the architecture of the core platform and the micro architecture of individual apps that complement it. We also explore how such architectural choices affect the dependencies between the platform and apps, and how they facilitate partitioning and integration of innovation activity in platform ecosystems.

Architecture and Governance

II

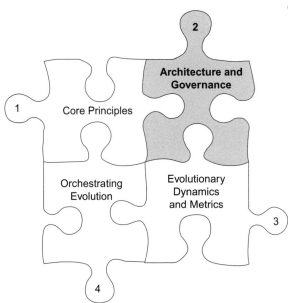

Platform Architecture

5

Each person making ... four thousand eight hundred pins in a day. But if they had all wrought separately and independently ... not each of them have made twenty, perhaps not one pin in a day.
Adam Smith in *The Wealth of Nations* (1776)

IN THIS CHAPTER

- How complexity paralyzes innovation in ecosystems
- How architectures reduce complexity
- Two functions of architecture: partitioning and reintegration
- Two facets of ecosystem architecture: platform architecture and app microarchitecture
- Four desirable properties of platform architectures
- Modularization
- Two mechanisms for modularizing architectures: decoupling and interface standardization
- Simple rules for what goes into the platform and what stays out
- Tradeoffs in architectural choices

5.1 HOW UNEMPLOYED HAIRDRESSERS BECAME FRANCE'S MATHEMATICAL CHAMPIONS

The inspiration for solving an innovation problem too complex for anyone to grasp comes from an unlikely source: unemployed hairdressers in 18th-century France. Gaspard de Prony (Figure 5.2) was a civil engineer who the French revolutionary government charged with a most unenviable task in 1790: create the largest, most precise set of trigonometric tables ever created (Langlois and Garzarelli, 2008). Baffled by this seemingly impossible task, de Prony was absent-mindedly flipping through Adam Smith's *Wealth of Nations* (Figure 5.1) in a bookstore when he was hit by an epiphany. He could "manufacture" trigonometric tables like Adam Smith's workers manufactured pins in a pin factory, by division of labor. Except, it was going to be division of cognitive labor rather than physical labor. So de Prony began in earnest. He first recruited four of the most eminent French mathematicians—Legendre, Prieur, Cote d'Or, and Carnot—to devise formulae that could be numerically calculated. He then passed along these formulae to about a dozen average mathematicians, who

---
☆"To view the full reference list for the book, click here or see page 283."

AN

INQUIRY

INTO THE

NATURE AND CAUSES

OF THE

WEALTH OF NATIONS.

By ADAM SMITH, LL. D.

WITH A LIFE OF THE AUTHOR,

AN INTRODUCTORY DISCOURSE, NOTES, AND

SUPPLEMENTAL DISSERTATIONS.

By J. R. M^cCULLOCH, Esq.

PROFESSOR OF POLITICAL ECONOMY IN THE UNIVERSITY OF LONDON.

IN FOUR VOLUMES.

VOL. I.

EDINBURGH:

PRINTED FOR ADAM BLACK, AND WILLIAM TAIT;

AND LONGMAN, REES, ORME, BROWN, AND GREEN,

LONDON.

M.DCCC.XXVIII.

FIGURE 5.1

Adam Smith's *Wealth of Nations* inspired de Prony's creation of trigonometric tables in 1790.

DE PRONY,
(Gaspard-Clair-François-Marie-Riche)
Chevalier de l'Ordre du Roi, Officier de la Légion d'honneur,
Inspecteur g.ᵃˡ et directeur de l'école royale des Ponts et Chaussées

Né à Chamelet, (Rhône) le 22 Juillet 1755, élu en 1795.

FIGURE 5.2

Gaspard de Prony (1755–1839).

turned them into simple algorithms and created templates of tables to be filled by hand. Filling these tables required little knowledge of math beyond addition and subtraction. Each table could be filled without any knowledge of the other tables. It was simple grunt work at this point.

France in the late 1700s was like the United States after 2008: excesses were frowned upon, a recession was in full swing, and austerity was expected in high society. This gave de Prony the perfect cadre of workers to do the grunt work: about a hundred unemployed French hairdressers. There was no communication from the hairdressers to the mathematicians, and no feedback from the mathematicians to the hairdressers. In four years, this team of hairdressers was producing close to a thousand results a day.

de Prony took an innovation problem too complex for one person to wrap his head around and made it solvable by partitioning it into smaller, independent problems that required little knowledge of the other pieces. Doing this required little central coordination and little ongoing communication, and the individual hairdressers' output could be plugged back into the slowly forming book of tables. de Prony's ingeniousness was in how he partitioned the complex innovation problem into small, independent problems. The magic was in how they could then be reassembled to form the whole. The same approach can also work in organizing innovation in platform ecosystems. The key to this is platform architecture, the focus of this chapter.

Platform architecture is the first gear in a platform ecosystem's evolutionary motor (Figure 5.3). A platform requires an "architecture of participation" to grow its ecosystem (Baldwin and Clark, 2006). Outside app developers must simultaneously be *able* to and be *motivated* to innovate around it. Ability without motivation is as worthless as motivation without ability. Creating the ability is the realm of platform architecture. Platform architecture determines the divisibility of innovation work among app developers and the platform owner. It also influences its subsequent reintegration. Platform architecture is the blueprint. Creating motivation is the realm of platform governance (Chapter 6). Evolution of a platform's ecosystem is therefore predicated in the interplay of its architecture with how it is governed.

This chapter provides a foundation for understanding platform architectures. It begins by explaining how complexity stymies innovation and leads to an unrealistic optimism bias in platform ecosystems. It then describes how a platform's architecture can make growing complexity manageable by serving two functions: partitioning innovation tasks and facilitating reintegration of an ecosystem's parts. It explains how architecture is a platform's DNA that preordains viable organizing logics and irreversibly imprints its evolutionary trajectory. What appears to be a technical decision has huge strategic consequences. A platform's properties are inherited by apps in their own architectures, but imperfectly.

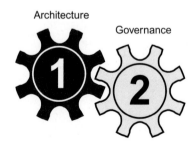

FIGURE 5.3

Architecture is the first gear in a platform ecosystem's evolutionary motor.

We explain the connections between a platform's architecture and the "microarchitecture" of apps (a microscopic view) as well as ecosystem architecture (a telescopic view).

A good architecture must exhibit four simple properties that it shares with the architecture of modern cities: simplicity, resilience, maintainability, and evolvability. We also explain the two mechanisms for modularizing architectures along with practical guidelines to implement them. We also revisit Goldilocks, who cautions that you neither want too little nor too much modularity but something in the middle. We explain this by putting ourselves in the shoes of a platform owner and an app developer, and offer guidelines to help you figure out how much modularity is *just right*. Finally, we segue into platform governance (the topic of the next chapter), which influences the degree to which the potential advantages of thoughtful platform architecture are realized in practice.

5.2 COMPLEXITY: THE ACHILLES HEEL OF PLATFORMS

A platform ecosystem can be envisioned as a complex system. Broadly, a complex system is one comprised of a number of parts that have many unpredictable interactions (Simon, 1962). It is comprised of smaller subsystems whose interactions and interdependencies are difficult to describe and manage (de Weck et al., 2011, p. 186). An ecosystem's complexity is a function of the number of unique subsystems present in it. The more numerous such subsystems, the greater its complexity. In a platform ecosystem, these subsystems are the platform and the apps that interoperate with it. Complex systems that were complex to begin with can become even more complex over time as they evolve.

Complexity is the Achilles heel—a potentially deadly weakness—of platforms. Complexity creates two challenges that worsen over time: incomprehensibility and a gridlock. First, platform ecosystems become increasingly difficult to be comprehensible in their entirety to one person (Baldwin and Clark, 2000, p. 5; de Weck et al., 2011, p. 27). They often stretch the ability of a human mind to grasp their complexity. Platform architects therefore quickly become unable to comprehend the technology that they invent. App developers face a similar challenge because they become increasingly unable to comprehend the complexity of the ecosystem in which their apps must function. Second, it creates a gridlock problem. Managing such complexity can become so daunting that it can paralyze any one ecosystem participant's ability to change a subsystem for which she is responsible. This is because a slight change in one app or in the platform can have unpredictable ripple effects that can potentially break the ecosystem. Like in a house of cards, moving one might do nothing bad or it might bring the entire structure down. The solution to the challenges created by growing complexity is to reduce it.

Remember the old fable of the elephant and the eight blind men (Figure 5.4A). Each was asked, "What do you see here?" Each touched the elephant and drew different conclusions. One concluded that it was a rope, another said it was a wall, another thought it was a fan and another concluded that it was a spear. A platform ecosystem often faces the same problem: Each app developer sees a different image of the ecosystem when looking at the whole from her own perspective. Now look at a different picture (Figure 5.4B). Would the eight blind men be any closer in their interpretations of that object? Likely. The bottom line is that more complex a man-made object gets, the harder it becomes to comprehend for any one individual. This incomprehensibility can become the showstopper in a platform's evolvability.

FIGURE 5.4

What do you see in these pictures (A) and (B)?

5.2.1 Two types of complexity

Complexity can be of two types: structural complexity and behavioral complexity. An ecosystem can be both structurally complex (interconnections between its parts are difficult to describe) and behaviorally complex (its aggregate behavior is difficult to predict or control) (de Weck et al., 2011, p. 185). The two types of complexities are often (but not always) correlated: Systems that are structurally complex are also often behaviorally complex. We believe that architecture is the lever to tackle structural complexity and governance (Chapter 6) is the lever to tackle behavioral complexity. Architecture is therefore a tool for simplifying and precisely describing the interconnections between parts of an ecosystem—potentially reducing structural complexity. It does this by reconfiguring the structure of dependencies between the platform and its apps within an ecosystem.

5.2.1.1 How complexity amplifies innovation risk in platforms

Structural complexity matters for innovation in ecosystems because it magnifies what Ron Adner (2012, p. 49) calls co-innovation risk. A useful way to think of dependencies is to compare the difference between joint and independent probabilities (Adner, 2012, p. 48). Consider a simple example in Figure 5.5 where two app developers and the platform owner must contribute to, say, creating a novel smartphone app. If each has an 80% chance of being able to deliver their part, the likelihood of successfully implementing the app is far lower than 80%. This is because realizing an innovation with dependencies among the three parties is governed by joint, not independent, probabilities. The likelihood that the app will succeed is a pitiful 51% (80% × 80% × 80%). This means that although the three partners are fairly likely to be able to deliver on their promises, the odds of success in their joint endeavor are about 50–50. It is easy for each partner to be confident about the success of the project, when the reality is bleaker than any one of them might realize. As the number of parties involved increases, so does co-innovation risk. But co-innovation risk

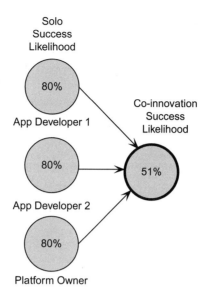

FIGURE 5.5

Co-innovation risk is magnified by complexity.

exists only if the work of one developer relies on the successful completion of the work of the other two in Figure 5.5. A powerful way to reduce this risk is by lowering the dependencies between the contributions of the three parties in this example. Reducing dependencies reduces interactions among them, hence reducing the structural complexity of the system in Figure 5.5. Architecture is a way to reduce such dependencies among subsystems that constitute a complex system. Thoughtful architectures however are not a silver bullet: They cannot eliminate complexity but can make it more manageable.

5.3 THE TWO FUNCTIONS OF ECOSYSTEM ARCHITECTURE

The biggest potential strength—and the biggest weakness—of platform ecosystems is their diversity, both in apps that constitute them and the app developers that develop such apps. Architectural choices by platform owners that quash the autonomy of app developers kill innovation potential. On the other hand, the same architectural choices can also fail to leverage this diversity into a cohesive platform, resulting in unfettered chaos. Platform ecosystems must therefore manage the delicate balance between coordination and autonomy (Iansiti and Levien, 2004, p. 5). Architecture is a tool for balancing the need for autonomy among app developers without compromising the capacity to integrate their work into a cohesive ecosystem.

Architecture, however, lurks in the blind spot of most strategy thinking, largely because it is perceived as the outcome of a technical decision-making process. Two types of costs directly stemming from platform architecture and with strategic consequences enter the picture: (1) the costs incurred by app developers of doing business with platform owners ("transaction costs")[1] and (2) the costs incurred by them to manage the dependencies between apps and the platform ("coordination costs"). If both parties were part of the same organization as was historically the case in traditional software development teams, these costs would have been lower. However, the moment app developers and platform owners become standalone organizations, these costs can overwhelm any prospect of cost-effective collaboration among them. (They tend to be higher across organizations than inside organizations.) Transaction costs and coordination costs among a platform owner and app developers determine whether a multi-organization ecosystem is even viable around a platform. A well-designed architecture can minimize both types of costs (Baldwin and Woodard, 2009). Architecture in a platform ecosystem ought to serve two overarching functions: partitioning and systems integration.

5.3.1 Partitioning

Partitioning refers to a decomposition of the ecosystem such that each subsystem in it is relatively autonomous from others (Figure 5.6). The primary function of architecture is to provide a framework to decompose a complex ecosystem into relatively independent subsystems. When designers envision a complex system, they quickly hit human cognitive limits due to its complexity. One way to reduce this complexity and make it cognitively manageable is to decompose the complex system into smaller pieces—platform and apps—that can work together to deliver the desired functionality. So, a complex system can be broken down into a collection of black boxes that do specific things. Such decomposition can continue ad infinitum where a complex ecosystem is decomposed into smaller and smaller subsystems. However, it is useful to stop this decomposition exercise when further decomposition no longer aids comprehensibility or no longer enhances autonomy among contributors to a platform ecosystem. When an element in a subsystem can no longer be decomposed meaningfully, it is said to have reached an *atomic* level of decomposition.

A well-partitioned architecture describes how these little black boxes behave and talk to each other, but not how they work. What happens inside a black box remains inside that black box. Once this collection of black boxes is envisioned, each of them can be designed and implemented individually with the hope that when they are all pieced together the much larger complex system will emerge. Unless the

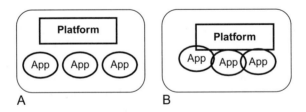

A

B

FIGURE 5.6

A well-partitioned architecture decomposes the platform and apps into relatively autonomous subsystems (A, not B).

---

[1]Transaction costs are simply the overhead costs of doing a trade in the open market between two parties that might not have the same interests. They have a long tradition in the history of economics (see Baldwin, 2008; Williamson, 1987, 1991, 1999, 2010) and technology strategy (see Ang and Straub, 1998; Tiwana and Bush, 2007; Young-Ybarra and Wiersema, 1999).

platform and apps can be readily separated, it is increasingly impossible for them to be developed by independent parties. Partitioning of subsystems through architecture can therefore allow innovation partitioning among organizations that develop them. A "good" architecture should respect this black-boxing because it can pay off handsomely: Ideally, each black box can be implemented by completely independent organizations, motivated by different things, driven by different expertise.

In theory, that's the promise of platform thinking; instead of one company having to implement all the black boxes, hundreds of thousands of different companies (as in the case of iOS and Android) can create the black boxes. The power of the market then takes over—the valuable black boxes survive and the rest fade away in a competitive marketplace for black boxes. In platform ecosystems, almost all these black boxes are the apps developed by independent entrepreneurs, who take over the innovation role from the platform owner and collectively expand it to a scale that the platform owner cannot even imagine replicating inhouse. Architectures that effectively partition complexity allow these numerous outside organizations to provide the pieces of a larger ecosystem while also ensuring that the parts coherently fit together. Software architecture can therefore enable a divide-and-conquer approach in which a complex ecosystem is divvied into manageable components—the platform and its many apps—that can be developed independently and subsequently brought together. (This decomposition is what we subsequently call *modularization*.)

Partitioning affects the work of both the platform owner and app developers. For the platform owner, effective partitioning has consequences for viable organizational structures around a platform. Effective partitioning largely determines whether the development of complementary apps is best done inhouse by the platform owner (as has traditionally been done for complex software) or by a distributed, multiorganizational ecosystem. Platform architectures therefore mold viable business models (Meyer and Selinger, 1998), both opening and constraining possibilities for platform owners. It also allows outsiders to engage in parallel competing efforts to solve the same problems using a variety of different approaches. Therefore partitioning created by a platform's architecture permits variety in the apps that can complement the platform. The greater the uncertainty a platform faces about end-users' needs, the more valuable is such diversity; a greater variety of competing attempts to meet end-users' needs increases the odds that some attempt will work. Partitioning also reduces complexity: If a complex ecosystem can be divided into separate parts such as each part can be developed by different people, the limitation of complexity disappears (Baldwin and Clark, 2000, p. 5).

Consider how partitioning affects the work of app developers. The architecture of a platform ecosystem specifies how the ecosystem is decomposed into the platform and apps that interoperate with it, and how the two types of subsystems interoperate to provide the overall functionality of the platform ecosystem. Their architecture therefore influences which parts of the ecosystem (e.g., the platform or other apps) must be tweaked to implement a new version of an app, and in turn influences the costs incurred by the app developer for changing the app. If the architecture of an app is less independent of other subsystems in the ecosystem (Figure 5.6B), it is not possible to make changes to an app without also having to make parallel changes in the platform and possibility in other apps. As a platform ecosystem's complexity grows, interdependencies between the platform and apps can become so numerous that integrated development efforts become impossible (Ethiraj and Levinthal, 2004b). Such a platform can grow into an immensely complicated tangle of interconnections, with each part potentially dependent on every other part. The app developer would need to know beforehand what these dependencies are and which can be prohibitively difficult to understand and keep track of as a platform gets more complex. Therefore, even small changes can have an unpredictable cascade of ripple effects on other parts of the ecosystem. The greater the number of other subsystems that must be tweaked in order to successfully alter an app, the greater are the coordination costs faced by an app's developer (Adner and Kapoor, 2010). If apps are to be successfully produced by outsiders, these costs must be contained.[2] Architectural differences across platforms can therefore explain partly why the costs of innovating can be starkly different even for the same app across comparable rival platforms. Architectural differences can also explain not just the frequency of innovations feasible by app developers but also the types of innovations that do and do not occur in an ecosystem.

Partitioning through architecture influences how much app developers need to understand the insides of the platform and need to be aware of other apps that their own app might interact with. A well-partitioned architecture can provide app developers the benefit of *valuable ignorance*: In doing their own work, they need not know how a platform does what it does. Nor do they need to understand the intricacies of the platform native functionalities on which their app draws. This form of ignorance is valuable because it allows app developers to focus largely on their own work yet be able to subsequently integrate their completed app with the platform. It allows them to sharpen focus on their distinctive knowledge and capabilities for creating and implementing novel ideas that they can pursue relatively autonomously. A well-partitioned architecture can therefore reduce the costs faced by both app developers and platform owners to coordinate their work with each other. This is what economists call *transaction costs* (Baldwin, 2008; Williamson and De Meyer, 2012). Therefore, by simultaneously enabling and constraining individual participants in a platform's ecosystem, architectures influence innovation generation both by the platform owner and app developers. Architectural differences can therefore affect the intensity, quality, and type of app innovation that are critical determinants of the vibrancy of the platform's ecosystem.

5.3.2 Systems integration

The second function of architecture is to enable systems integration. Systems integration refers to coordination of development activities among app developers and the platform owner. Systems integration capability of a platform is a platform's capacity to combine the different competencies of app developers with those of the platform. Although partitioning of apps and platforms allows app developers to pursue their development work building on their own strengths, these apps must eventually interoperate with the platform to deliver value to end-users. Apps mixed-and-matched by an end-user must coherently work together in individual end-user instantiations of the ecosystem (Boudreau, 2010). Integration between a platform and apps is therefore critical to realizing the potential of apps by app developers participating in a platform's ecosystem. If apps seamlessly interoperate with the platform and augment its own capabilities in creative ways, the ecosystem can become a powerful mechanism for a platform to acquire a steady stream of new capabilities from its ecosystem partners.

App developers face two broad types of costs in their ongoing work: (1) *app innovation costs* and (2) *systems integration costs*. App innovation costs are an app developer's costs of actually designing and implementing the changes over the lifecycle of an app. For example, if Skype wants to add new functionality to its iOS app, these are the costs of conceptualizing, designing, and

---

[2]Generally, costs of coordinating across interorganizational boundaries of different organizations are much greater than they are among groups within the same organization (Rysman, 2009).

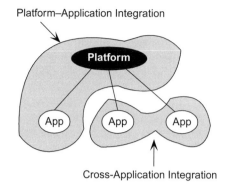

FIGURE 5.7

The two types of systems integration costs faced by app developers.

implementing a revised app with that functionality. Systems integration costs are the effort required by Skype developers to ensure that the revised Skype app will function as intended when installed on an iOS device.

Systems integration costs then refer to the effort required to manage the dependencies among a platform and apps in an ecosystem. The potential advantages of a large ecosystem can easily be wiped out if systems integration costs are high. App developers directly face two types of systems integration costs, illustrated in Figure 5.7: (1) those of integrating an app with the platform (application–platform integration costs) and (2) those of integrating an app with other potentially interacting apps in the ecosystem (cross-application integration costs). The second type of systems integration costs can be reduced by a platform's architecture, but the first type is more challenging for two reasons. First, different apps might evolve at different rates (Baldwin and Clark, 2000, p. 297). This means that app integration with the platform is lumpy rather than predictable. Second, changes in the platform itself can require an app to be changed to maintain its integrity and interoperability. Therefore, it is more useful to think of system integration costs as ongoing rather than a one-shot integration activity. Different platform architectures, however, impose different levels of system integration costs for apps, and in turn can change the rate of investment by app developers in app innovation. Architecture influences the initial and subsequent releases' systems integration costs faced by app developers by altering modifiability of an app. This in turn affects app developers' incentives to innovate rapidly and the extent to which they will be willing to bear the risk of app innovation. High systems integration costs faced by an app developer can therefore discourage innovation by app developers.

The common systems integration approach in the software industry is overt communication between the parties. The two parties communicate, interact, and coordinate their own work to ensure that their subsystems will work together. In platforms, such ongoing interaction between the platform owner and an app developer is one mechanism for ensuring successful systems integration. This approach, however, becomes increasingly infeasible in complex ecosystems involving thousands of app developers, where different apps might also be evolving at a different pace.

An alternative solution is not to maximize communication among them but rather minimize the *need* for it. Platform architecture can potentially reconfigure the structure of dependencies among a platform and apps. It can provide the blueprint that stitches together apps and the platform on a scale where communication-based coordination mechanisms of traditional organizations are simply infeasible. Architecture—by specifying dependencies and interactions between apps and the platform—can then become an invisible coordination mechanism that can substitute for such overt communication-based coordination in platforms ecosystems. Early architectural choices by a platform owner—by influencing the costs of realizing innovations at every level—can therefore either catalyze or discourage experimentation within a platform's ecosystem.

5.4 ECOSYSTEM ARCHITECTURE

Platforms are *purposefully designed* complex systems with an underlying structure that influences how they behave, function, and evolve over time. Like any other complex system, a platform ecosystem can be envisioned as composed of many interacting subsystems. How these subsystems interact is determined by the platform ecosystem's architecture. Two broad types of subsystems here are the platform itself and the portfolio of apps that augment it. Just as the architecture of a building is different from the building itself, the architecture of a platform ecosystem is at a higher level of abstraction than either the platform or the apps. Architecture is to a platform ecosystem what a blueprint is to a building. Rather than a working system, it is a description of the building blocks of an ecosystem and how they relate to each other, what they do, and how they interact (van Schewick, 2012, p. 21). This high-level description specifies the components of the ecosystem, the externally visible properties of these components, and the relationships among them (van Schewick, 2012, p. 21). Ecosystem architecture ideally partitions the ecosystem into two types of subsystems: (1) a highly reusable core platform that remains relatively stable and (2) a set of complementary apps that are encouraged to vary (Baldwin and Woodard, 2009). Architecture therefore describes the early design decisions about the decomposition of a platform ecosystem into a platform and apps. These choices have considerable evolutionary consequences because they are largely unchangeable, as we describe in the next section.

Architecture is meaningful only in relation to other parts that together constitute the whole ecosystem. Architecture is a hierarchal concept: Ecosystems can be decomposed into interrelated subsystems such as apps, which also have architectures (Baldwin and Clark, 2000, p. 413). Ecosystem architecture can be thought of as comprised of two levels: (1) the architecture of the platform itself (*platform architecture*) and (2) that of an app, which we refer to as that app's *microarchitecture*. Platform architecture is like viewing a platform ecosystem through a telescope and app microarchitecture is like viewing architecture through a microscope. This distinction is illustrated in Figure 5.8. Platform architecture includes the core platform *and its interfaces*. Recall that a platform is a set foundational functionality and shared assets made available to apps through a set of interfaces. Platform architecture should tell apps both what the platform does and how to use the platform (Parnas et al., 1985). The latter is a role directly played by the platform's interfaces, which therefore must be treated as an integral part of a platform's architecture.

Although the platform has a specific architecture that all apps see, the architecture of individual apps within the same platform can vary from one app to another. Platform architecture imposes constraints on all apps in a platform's ecosystem; therefore many properties of app architectures are correlated with the architecture of the platform. However, the two are rarely identical because there can be considerable variance among apps developed for the same platform. Therefore, an app's "microarchitecture" will define how each individual app interacts, communicates, and interoperates

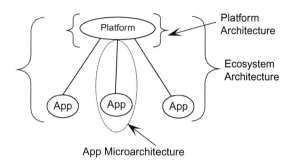

FIGURE 5.8

Ecosystem architecture is comprised of platform architecture and app microarchitecture.

with the platform. Even if the platform owner attempts to impose architectural guidelines on app developers, the extent of compliance by individual app developers with such guidelines can result in different app microarchitectures. A useful way to think of the distinction is to distinguish between envisioned versus realized architecture. Platform architecture is architecture for apps as envisioned by a platform owner; app microarchitecture is the same architecture as realized in the implementation of an individual app by its developer. This inheritance of properties of platform architecture by apps gives them their evolutionary properties.

Such decomposition can continue until the lowest atomistic level is reached. For example, an app can be further divided into subsystems, and subsystems within those subsystems, *ad infinitum*. However, for practical purposes, it is meaningful to stop at the level after which further decomposition no longer aids comprehension. Zooming out—the opposite of architectural decomposition—results in a more aggregate view of a platform ecosystem. For example, individual ecosystems themselves might be embedded within a larger architecture, which can be aggregated to the highest level of the Internet as a whole. They also coexist, compete, and cooperate with rival ecosystems.

5.4.1 App microarchitecture

Each app can have its own internal structure that represents its *internal* microarchitecture. The internal microarchitecture of the app influences its *external* architecture (i.e., how it connects to the platform).

5.4.1.1 The four functional elements inside an app

Any software app's internal functionality can be decomposed into four functional elements shown in Figure 5.9. These four pieces are:

1. *Presentation logic.* An app's presentation logic is where almost all of the interaction with the end-user occurs. It is the part of the application that handles receiving inputs from the end-user and presenting the application's output to the end-user.
2. *Application logic.* The second function is the core work performed by the application that is distinctive to it. This encompasses the functionality of the app that makes it uniquely valuable to its end-users. For example, a video conferencing app's core application logic is the video streaming between two client devices.

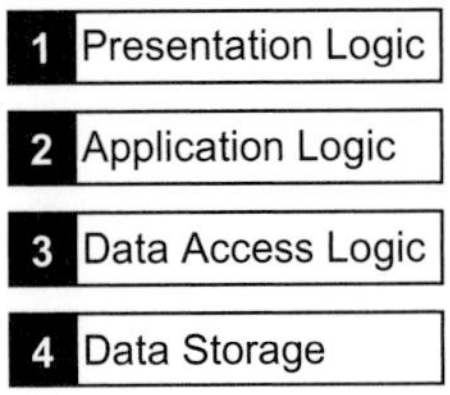

FIGURE 5.9

The four pieces of an app's internal functionality.

3. *Data access logic.* The third function is the processing required to access and retrieve data. This often equates with database queries through which user-specified data is retrieved from data storage. Examples of data access can include tag searches to retrieve emails, flight pricing data used by a travel reservation app, retrieving a media file such as a music file, or specific images from a larger database of images.[3]

4. *Data storage.* The last function is data storage. Most apps require data to be stored somewhere in order to be retrieved. This can be a small text file written by a word-processing app, map data in a navigation app, PDFs in an annotation app, images in a note-taking app, pictures in a camera app, or messages in an email app.

These four functional elements constitute the entirety of the *internal* microarchitecture of any app. These four elements can be placed on either the client side or the server side in several plausible arrangements.

An app's internal microarchitecture (also known as its network architecture) is simply a description of how these four functional elements are distributed between a client and a server connected by the Internet. Note that the client and the server need not be actual computers but can be any device (e.g., smartphone, tablet, object, or appliance) that is connected to the Internet. The five common arrangements that spread the four pieces across a network result in four different types of app microarchitectures: (1) standalone, (2) cloud, (3) client-based, (4) client–server, and (5) peer-to-peer. These five app microarchitectures apply to any networked application.

5.4.1.2 Unique properties of platform-based app functional partitioning

The unique aspect of these app architectures in platform settings, however, is that each individual functional element can be flexibly partitioned between the app and the platform, as Figure 5.10 illustrates. An app developer can rely entirely on the platform itself to build each part of the app, or choose to build part of the client-side and part of the server-side functionality itself and rely on the platform for the remainder. (An app can also invoke third-party Web services using Web service APIs (application programming interfaces) to implement some of its functionality.) The modularity of the connections—defined by decoupling and interface standards compliance—between the app and a platform in such divvying-up of client- and server-side functionality then represents its *external* microarchitecture. For example, 50% of the presentation logic of an app might be implemented within the app and the other 50% might be implemented in the platform. The app then invokes the capabilities of the platform to execute its own presentation logic. The choice of how much of each functional element

---

[3]The accessed data can be either user-owned or provided by a third-party supplier.

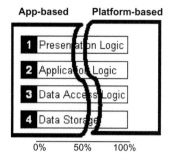

FIGURE 5.10

Each of the four functional elements of an app can be flexibly partitioned between an app and the platform.

is app-based and how much of it is platform-based is largely a decision made by app developers. The connections between the two big blocks in Figure 5.9 that are split between an app and a platform defines its external microarchitecture.

An app's designer has considerable freedom in choosing how much of an app's functionality to pull from the platform and how much to build herself (Figure 5.10). The division of functionality between the app and the platform in app microarchitecture is therefore not a given but rather a choice. This choice influences how much of the app development work is done by the app developer and to what extent the app leverages and invokes the capabilities of a platform in order to function. This results in different app microarchitectures for similar apps even within the same platform. This choice also has nonobvious consequences that can enable and constrain the future evolution of the app in nuanced ways. As the next section of this book explains, such choices have considerable consequences on the evolutionary trajectories open to and closed to individual apps. This type of partitioning of each functional element between the app and platform allows the app developer to avoid duplication of the core functionality of the platform and instead focus on building capabilities unique to the app. In platform-based apps, some part of the functionality for one or more of the functional elements will *always* reside on the platform than in the app. This is the premise of platform-centric models and also the reason for the importance of platform governance (the focus of the next chapter).

5.4.1.3 Standalone microarchitecture

The first app microarchitecture is standalone architecture (Figure 5.11). Here all four functional elements are on the client side and nothing resides on the server side. Internet connectivity is therefore unnecessary for the app to function. This is the model for applications that dominated in the era that preceded Internet-enabled computing beginning in the 1990s. However, these four functional elements themselves can be divvied up between the platform and the app, with varying proportions of each implemented in the app and invoked by the app from the platform. Examples of such apps include a PDF reader or a flashlight app.

5.4.1.4 Cloud microarchitecture

The second app microarchitecture is cloud architecture (Figure 5.12). All four functional elements reside on the server side. The client device then simply becomes a "dumb" terminal that serves only to accept user inputs and display outputs. Although some of the presentation or data storage

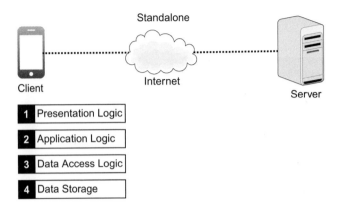

FIGURE 5.11

All four functional elements reside on the client device in the standalone app microarchitecture.

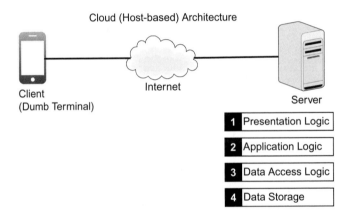

FIGURE 5.12

All four functional elements reside on the client device in the cloud app microarchitecture.

functionality might also reside on the client side, most of it is on the server side. This model mirrors host-based computing architectures from the mainframe era and contemporary "thin client" architectures. Examples of apps using such architectures are most search engines, where almost all of the work of the search application is done on the server side and the client is usually a browser that serves little purpose other than accepting user inputs and displaying outputs. Other examples include Web-based email apps such as Gmail.

Cloud microarchitectures have three advantages. The key advantage of this arrangement is economies of scale: All of the functionality of the app is managed in one centralized location. A second advantage is that rolling out new features and functionality is easier because little or no upgrades are required on the client side. Instead, rolling them out simply requires changes on the server side. This benefit holds only in theory. In practice, however, the server-side functionality that is platform-based is not under the direct control of the app developer. This makes it challenging to roll out new functionality to the app's users as readily as it might appear on paper. Third, cloud microarchitectures are potentially more secure because all of the app's functionality is centralized on the server side. There is only one major point of vulnerability relative to other microarchitectures: the server. Such architectures are particularly attractive in platform apps where the device on the client side does not have much processing power. This is often the case with networked objects that are used as part of the emerging Internet of Things.

This microarchitecture has two big downsides. First, all of the work of the app must be done on the server side. As user demand and usage intensity grows, the server side can become overloaded and slow to respond to requests from the client side. This can potentially result in sluggish response times. Put another way, the app has greater network usage intensity. Second, capacity upgrades on the server side cannot be incremental. Instead, they are large and potentially expensive. In other words, cloud-based architectures are not cost-effectively scalable. And the more the app leverages the platform, the more dependent the app developer becomes on the platform.

5.4.1.5 Client-based microarchitecture

The third app microarchitecture is client-based architecture (Figure 5.13). This arrangement is similar to standalone architectures with the exception that the data storage function is placed on the server side. The key driver of the advent of these architectures is an increase in the processing power of client devices (such as smartphones and tablets) and the advent of high-speed ubiquitous connectivity. This allows the majority of the functionality of the app to reside on the client device. This microarchitecture makes sense if storage capacity is a constraint on the client device. The upside of this arrangement is that the data resides in a centralized location, which makes it easier to secure. The key downside of this architecture is network congestion: All data must travel over the Internet from the server to the client each time the application is used. This includes data that might not be needed by the user, which cannot be separated from the data the user actually needs because the data access logic is on the client side. This can result in larger than necessary bandwidth consumption and can result in sluggish application performance. If the app is data intensive, this microarchitecture also suffers from lack of cost-effective scalability since part of the app's functionality is derived from servers (usually run by the app developer or run by the platform owner but paid for by the app developer). Scaling up can therefore be costly.

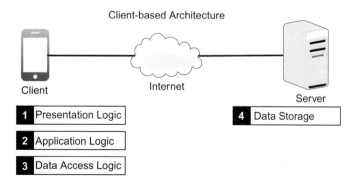

FIGURE 5.13

Only data storage resides on the server side in client-based app microarchitecture.

5.4.1.6 Client–server microarchitecture

The fourth widely used app microarchitecture is client–server architecture (Figure 5.14). This arrangement evenly splits the four functional elements of an app between clients and servers. While data access logic and data storage reside on the server side, presentation and application logic reside on the client side. In practice, the application logic is often split between the client and server, although it predominantly resides on the client. This design balances processing demands on the server by having the client do the bulk of application logic and presentation. It also reduces the network intensity of an app by limiting the data flowing over the Internet to only that which is needed by the user. Placing the data access logic on the server side accomplishes this; the queries from the client are initiated from the client but executed by the server, which only sends back the results of those queries rather than the entire raw data as client-based microarchitectures do. The downside of client–server app microarchitectures is that different types of client devices must be designed to invoke the data access logic on the server side in compatible ways. Depending on how the server-side functionality is split between an app and the platform, this arrangement can potentially free up app developers' attention to focus their attention on developing the core functionality of the app (where most end-user value is generated) and fret less about the data management aspects of the app.

5.4.1.7 Peer-to-peer microarchitecture

The final app microarchitecture is peer-to-peer architecture (Figure 5.15). The same device acts as a client and as a server in this arrangement, with significant elements of each of the four functions of the app present on it. Because each device serves simultaneously as a client and a server, the consolidated device is often referred to as a *servlet*. In its pure form, there is no separate server or centralized point of control. This means that every client also simultaneously acts as a server. Therefore all devices connected to peer-to-peer architecture can simultaneously initiate requests and fulfill requests from each other. The key advantage of this approach is immense scalability: The addition of every new client simultaneously adds server capacity to the network. Scaling the capacity of any other architecture usually requires additional capacity on the server side, the need for which is eliminated by the use of peer-to-peer microarchitectures. Skype is an example of such architecture; it allows tens of millions of users to simultaneously use the service and can readily and automatically scale to meet rising demand. The incremental cost of adding another use is therefore pennies, and adding more users improves app performance unlike all other app microarchitectures where adding more users degrades performance.

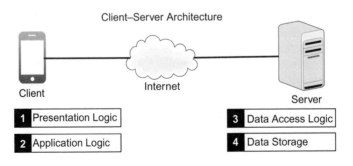

FIGURE 5.14

Client–server app microarchitectures evenly split application functionality among clients and servers.

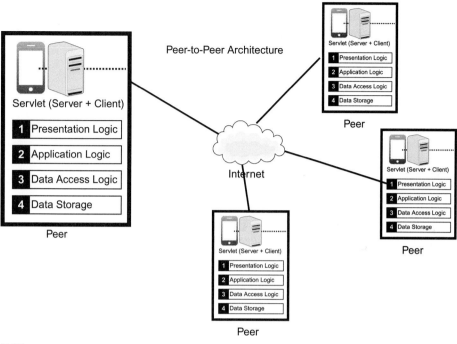

FIGURE 5.15

Peer-to-peer app microarchitecture.

However, this microarchitecture has two caveats. First, there is little or no control that the app developer has over the users of such apps. This limits the utility of this arrangement to only a few types of applications where central coordination and control are not needed and need for scalability is extremely high. Second, this architecture rarely exists in its purely decentralized form. Some centralized control is often needed and accomplished by retaining some of the server-side functionality on a separate server. This hybrid form of peer-to-peer architecture infuses some elements of the other microarchitectures (e.g., adding a central server) into the completely decentralized pure-form peer-to-peer arrangement.

Client–server and cloud-based architectures dominate contemporary platforms. Hybrid microarchitectures that mix-and-match properties of these five are increasingly in use; nevertheless, one architectural approach dominates even in such hybrids. For example, Skype has a predominantly peer-to-peer architecture, with some elements of the client–server model incorporated into it (e.g., monitoring user availability and initiating calls).

5.4.1.8 Tiering in app microarchitectures

The preceding app microarchitectures split the functional elements of an app between two devices: a client and a server. They are therefore called two-tier architectures. This logic can be extended to splitting this functionality among one client but more than one server. As this splitting is done using three devices, it becomes a three-tier architecture (see Figure 5.16); more than three devices makes it an

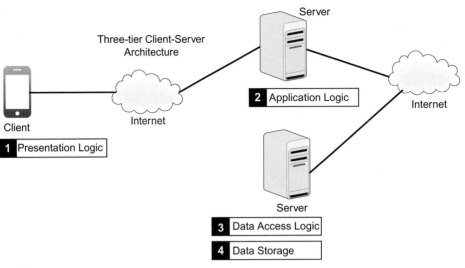

FIGURE 5.16

Tiering.

n-tier architecture. In any such multi-tiered architectures, there is always only one client. (Tiering is conceptually distinct from layering.[4])

The upside of tiering is that it increases scalability of the app. Separating the functional elements of an app into more than two tiers allows just one device associated with specific functionality to be replaced or upgraded. If the demand for, say, application logic increases, just the servers hosting that functional element need to be replaced or upgraded. In platform-based apps, three-tier architectures are often used when an app draws on different servers for part of its functionality. Tiering also provides app developers the future flexibility to more easily move one tier of the app from being app developer-owned to being platform-based or vice versa. This phenomenon was widely observed when Apple introduced its cloud-based data storage service in its iOS platform, which many app developers deployed for the data storage tier. The downside of tiering is that because the data now must travel along more paths, the network bandwidth intensity and the risk of sluggish performance both increase with tiering. The remainder of this book will use a two-tier architecture for simplicity; the logic can readily be extrapolated to multi-tier architectures.

An ongoing evolution in app microarchitectures is that the networks connecting various devices have increasingly migrated to Internet protocol (IP). Independent of the type of network (Wifi, 3G, LTE), the common language spoken by them is IP. This protocol delivers just about any type of information (e.g., voice, video, text) formatted as small IP packets—of fixed-size blocks of data—with a standardized structure between any two devices designed to speak the language, and it does so robustly, error-free, inexpensively, and over long distances using the Internet. This allows increasingly heterogeneous devices and networked "things"—including ones that do not yet exist—to interoperate with each other from the client and server side.

---

[4]Layering is a special extension of modular design that constrains permissible interactions among modules. A subsystem assigned to a specific layer can use only the subsystems in the lower layers or in the same layer, but not in the layers above it.

5.4.1.9 *Strategic and evolutionary consequences of app microarchitectures*

An important question for app developers is therefore how to partition an application across the Internet (internal microarchitecture) and across the app and the platform (external microarchitecture). These choices are made early in their lifecycle and are almost impossible to subsequently reverse. Several properties of an app are affected by the microarchitectural choices made by their developers during their initial implementation. Some of these qualities are immediately visible in the short term: speed, security, reliability, scalability, testability, and usability. Performance of an app depends on the complexity of interaction and the amount of communication between the app and the platform ecosystem (including other apps). The amount of communication in turn depends on how the four pieces of functionality are distributed between an app and the platform by its developer's architectural choices.

However, other evolvability-related qualities are visible only in the longer term: maintainability, extensibility, evolvability, and the capacity to mutate and envelop adjacent app market segments. (For example, changes to an app can be made faster and more cost-effectively if few systems outside of the app require tweaking when the internal functionality of an app is changed.) App microarchitecture also enables versioning of apps, as described in Chapter 11. App microarchitecture also has direct strategic consequences for same-side and cross-side network effects, and for how inextricably an app can get locked into one platform. Therefore, evolvability of an app is preordained by its microarchitecture. Unfortunately, architectural choices always involve tradeoffs; maximizing one attribute usually requires compromising on another. The consequences for the app's visible performance are immediate, but the more profound evolvability consequences surface much later. App designers must be cognizant of these tradeoffs so they can make them consciously rather than recognizing them after the fact. (Chapter 11 tackles these issues in detail.)

5.5 FOUR DESIRABLE PROPERTIES OF PLATFORM ARCHITECTURES

Platform architecture is an enduring—often irreversible—choice with profound evolutionary and strategic consequences. Good platform architecture has four desirable properties. These architectural properties always invoke tradeoffs such that dramatically increasing one property will reduce another. It is therefore impossible for any architecture to simultaneously have high levels of all of these properties. On the other hand, some of these properties are correlated; increasing one can help nudge another property upward. A platform architect should aspire for "satisficing" (a mix of satisfactory and sufficient) levels of a mix of these properties. We focus primarily on the architectural properties of the platform rather than of apps. Apps can potentially inherit a platform's architectural strengths, but this usually requires that the platform first have them! Performance is visibly missing on this list, largely because an acceptable level of performance is taken to be a precondition for a platform to be viable in the immediate future. By taking performance off the list, we focus on the core properties of architecture that influence the *evolution* of a platform. The four desirable properties are:

1. *Simple.* The architecture of a platform should be simple enough to be comprehensible at least at a high level of abstraction. This means that the platform should be conceptually decomposable into its major subsystems, the platform's functionality reused by many apps should be identifiable, and interactions between the platform and apps should be well defined and explicit. In short, simplicity pays off.

2. *Resilient*. One defective app should not cause the entire ecosystem to malfunction. The key to such resilience is to ensure that apps are weakly coupled with the platform through interfaces that do not change over time. This approach of keeping platform–app dependencies to a minimum also makes the entire ecosystem more stable in its performance.

3. *Maintainable*. It should be possible to cost-effectively make any changes within the platform without inadvertently "breaking" apps that depend on it. Conversely, changes in an app should not require parallel tweaking in the platform. This is accomplished through partitioning it into standalone subsystems (described elsewhere in this chapter) and then linking them using standardized interfaces. Designing for maintainability also increases a platform's composability (i.e., capacity to integrate with new apps).

4. *Evolvable*. Evolvability means the capacity to do things in the future that it was never originally designed to do. For this, the architecture—particularly the interfaces—of a platform must endure over time. This property allows a platform to be extensible in the near term and exhibit emergent behavior in the longer term. The key to evolvability is stable yet versatile platform interfaces that ensure autonomy between the platform and apps, make the architecture rich in "real options" (Chapter 8), and permit its mutation into derivative platforms (see Chapters 7 and 9).

5.5.1 Architectural lessons from cities

The architecture of platform ecosystems has several interesting parallels with the architecture of modern cities with long histories such as Atlanta or Paris (Table 5.1). Although this chapter focuses primarily on similarities in their structure, we revisit the parallels in their governance and evolution in subsequent chapters.

Table 5.1 Parallels Between the Architecture of Modern Cities and Platform Ecosystems

City	Platform Ecosystem
Structure	
Mix of preserved old buildings and new buildings	Mix of stable platform and new apps
Variety of buildings	Variety of apps
Stable roads and utilities (e.g., water, electricity, and sewage)	Stable interface infrastructure
Shared public facilities and infrastructure	Shared platform services and functionality reused by many apps
Discrete neighborhoods with unique character and purpose (e.g., residential vs. commercial)	Partitioning of functions with commonality and reusability into the platform, and unique functionality with low reusability into apps
Multiple stakeholders (businesses, residents)	Multisidedness (app developers, end-users)
Long lifespan of streets	Long lifespan of platform interfaces
Varied building designs	Varied app microarchitectures

Table 5.1 Parallels Between the Architecture of Modern Cities and Platform Ecosystems—cont'd

City	Platform Ecosystem
Governance	
City ordinances	Platform design rules
City taxes	Pricing policies and revenue-splitting arrangements between platform owner and app developers
Citizens' right to vote	Shared governance (decision-rights partitioning)
Law enforcement by the city	Interface standards enforcement by the platform owner
Autonomy of citizens within the constraints of city laws	Autonomy of app developers, with the constraints of the platform's rules
Evolution	
Retirement of old assets	Retirement of legacy functionality
Expansion into outskirts	Expansion with new interfaces and APIs
Gentrification of neighborhoods	Widespread adoption of once-unique services and functionality by many apps
Renovation of historic buildings	Expansion of platform core functionality over time
Capacity to absorb new migrants	Capacity to scale
Modernization while preserving its character	Emergent properties of the platform

5.6 MODULARITY OF ARCHITECTURES

Modularity is the general property of any complex system. Any complex system can be decomposed into smaller subsystems that are always going to be interdependent to some extent and independent to some extent (Simon, 1962). Modularization then refers to the extent to which the interdependence among these subsystems is intentionally reduced by design (Parnas, 1972; Parnas et al., 1985). Reduced interdependence simply means that changes in one subsystem do not create a ripple effect on the rest of the complex system. When viewed as a complex system, the two distinct types of subsystems in a platform ecosystem are the platform and apps. An ecosystem exhibits modularity if the platform and apps can be designed independently but will work together to constitute the ecosystem (Sanchez and Mahoney, 1996). Modular designs are therefore more Lego-like. An ecosystem can be intentionally *designed* to be more modular, although a less modular design can accomplish the same function. We therefore distinguish the process of *modularization* from the property of modularity. Modularization is the *deliberate activity* of increasing modularity of a system whereas modularity is a system's descriptive property of being more modular.

Consider a simple illustration of two different designs of a screwdriver in Figure 5.17. The first design (A) is a non-modular ("monolithic") design and the second design (B) is a modular design. Both designs provide the same functionality. However, the more modular design can be produced differently vis-à-vis the monolithic design. The monolithic design has to be produced as a single unit by one organization. (The smallest subsystem is the whole screwdriver.) The modular design has four parts (the four subsystems that constitute the whole screwdriver), each of which can be produced by four independent

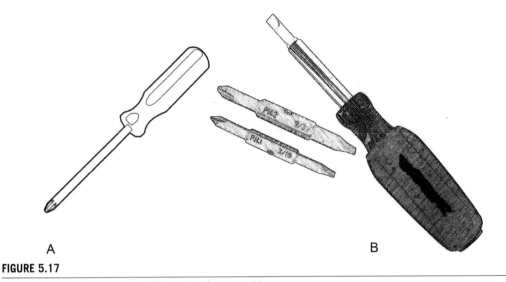

FIGURE 5.17

Monolithic (A) versus modular (B) design of a screwdriver.

organizations. The only information that each of these organizations needs to know is the size and shape of interface for the part for which they are responsible. As long as each of them complies with the specification for their part, fit between the four parts is guaranteed without the need for any additional coordination among them. A modular architecture of the screwdriver (B) therefore allows its production to be distributed among multiple organizations. Put another way, modularization of the screwdriver's architecture makes viable a different organizational design for producing it. The design philosophy is minimizing dependence across the four parts but maximizing it within them. These organizations need not know any internal details of other parts or how they are constructed, just how to connect to them. They can work in blissful ignorance of the other three parts of the screwdriver and focus exclusively on the one part for which they are responsible. The only requirement for compatibility is compliance with the appropriate physical dimensions of the interfaces. This allows each organization to specialize more deeply in improving its own part, engendering a laser-like focus on honing its core competence. If the same set of organizations attempted to jointly produce the monolithic design, they would require intense supervision, iteration, and coordination to produce it. A potential tradeoff is that the monolithic design might initially outperform the modular design. However, the modular design offers one advantage: Any new shape or size for a screwdriver tip can readily be added to the modular design in the future, even if it was not foreseeable by its original designer. This property is what we described in Chapter 2 as emergence. Changes in the architecture of the product can therefore open up new possibilities for who can participate in producing it and whether partitioned production can be accomplished cost-effectively. The process of converting a monolithic design into a more modular design is called *modularization*.

We can draw five useful lessons about design modularization from this example. Modularization of the screwdriver's architecture:

1. Makes its production divisible among many organizations (partitioning)
2. Restricts their interdependence to its connection points (interfaces)

3. Relies solely on compliance with interface specifications to integrate the four organizations' outputs (systems integration)
4. Sacrifices some performance for future flexibility (the so-called modularity tax)
5. Allows unforeseeable capabilities to be added in the future (emergent properties)

5.6.1 Software modularity

The same logic applies to the design of software-based platform ecosystems. Modularity of a platform ecosystem refers to the degree to which the platform and apps can be designed, implemented, operated, and altered independent of each other (de Weck et al., 2011, p. 188). Modularity in software systems is a property that can reside anywhere along a continuum ranging from perfectly monolithic to perfectly modular. A perfectly monolithic system is one where every app is highly interdependent with the platform. An example of a monolithic architecture is one where a platform and an app are integrated into a single system (e.g., the Mail app in iOS). A complex system like this can achieve high levels of integration across the subsystems that constitute it, and can exhibit high levels of performance and an assemblage of components that fit each other like a glove. The iPad would be an example of a monolithic hardware system. The other extreme would be a highly modular complex system such as a desktop PC. Each component connects to others using highly standardized interfaces, and can be replaced with a different component that adheres to the same interface specifications. This sort of plug-and-play architecture is an example of a modular system. Most complex systems fall in between these two extremes of monolithic and modular architectures.

Although the merits of either approach have been debated for years, industry battles have been fought over the philosophies (e.g., the PC vs. Mac dynamics in the 1990s); we will refrain from even attempting to settle that debate in this book. Instead, the important point to remember is that the *degree* of modularization of platform architectures has strategic and evolutionary consequences. Depending on a platform's strategy, different types of architectural choices will lead a platform ecosystem down different forks in the evolutionary road. Some architectures are more conducive to fostering the inventions of these "black boxes" than others. Therefore architectural choices by platform owners, and also by app developers, have decisive consequences for whether one ecosystem out-innovates another. But understanding these dynamics requires first understanding various elements of architecture with a degree of nuance that is not yet common practice among software developers and managers.

5.6.2 Platform architecture: an ecosystem's DNA

Architecture is to a platform ecosystem what your DNA is to you: You cannot change it after the fact. Even though it is possible to change it in theory, it is almost impossible to change it in practice. It puts you on a future trajectory that you cannot completely escape. Likewise, platform architecture preordains the realm of what a platform can and cannot evolve into. Platform architecture—like DNA—imprints future evolvability of its ecosystem. But much like your and my DNA did not guarantee good outcomes in life without our own effort, a platform ecosystem's evolution must be guided, prodded, and nudged. Architecture therefore creates the potential trajectories for a platform's evolution, but much more is needed to realize its evolutionary potential.

Modularity in the platform's design (1) allows disaggregation of its production rather than having one organization produce it and (2) provides future flexibility to extend the platform's native capabilities in ways that cannot be anticipated at the outset by its original designers. These two advantages are much more powerful together than the sum of their parts: Many outsiders can extend the platform's capabilities far beyond what it started out with. This gives a platform emergent properties. Emergence is a property where new capabilities unforeseen by the platform's original designers are added to a platform by an app (Dougherty, 1992). By making apps more self-contained and autonomous, modularization gives them the freedom to evolve and grow. It therefore infuses self-organizing properties into a platform's ecosystem.

Modular architectures rely on stable, well-defined interfaces to ensure interoperability between a platform and apps, minimize unnecessary interdependencies, and ensure that the remaining interdependencies are well understood by the app developer. Platform interfaces are an important leverage point—places in a platform's ecosystem where a small change produces a disproportionately large evolutionary influence—and represent loci of power to nudge its evolution. Modularization entails minimizing dependence between the platform and apps, but maximizing it within each of them (Ethiraj and Levinthal, 2004a). Modularity, however, is not an absolute property of a platform ecosystem. A platform can intentionally be designed to be more or less modular. Platform modularization is a necessary but insufficient precondition for app modularization. If a platform is modular in its design, apps produced for it have the *potential* to be modular as well. Even if the platform is highly modular, it does not automatically follow that apps in its ecosystem will also be highly modular. Different apps for the same platform can have different levels of modularity, depending largely on the microarchitectural design choices made by the app developer. If an app is modular in its design, it can be designed and produced independently of the platform and other apps in the ecosystem. It is therefore important to distinguish between architectures at the platform level and at the app level; these two aggregate to describe the modularity of an ecosystem's overall architecture.

Modularity in platform ecosystems is achieved by (1) decoupling the platform from apps (i.e., minimizing their interdependencies) and (2) codifying the interface specifications for how an app interacts with the platform (Tiwana, 2008a,b; Tiwana et al., 2010). Modularization enables the two core functions of architecture in platform ecosystems: partitioning and systems integration. It facilitates partitioning by reducing design dependencies between the platform and apps, and in turn reduces dependencies in their development tasks. Changes in one app become independent of those in others. Modularization is therefore an antidote—and a vaccine—against growing complexity.

5.6.3 Design precedes production

A platform ecosystem's architecture determines how its production can be organized (Baldwin and Clark, 2000, p. 30). Recall the mirroring principle from Chapter 2. A modular architecture allows a multitude of app developers to participate whereas a monolithic architecture would have required a single integrated organization to do all the development work. The development of the platform and apps can then proceed independently and concurrently in different organizations without much need for day-to-day interactions among them. In economists' lingo, modularity thus reduces "transaction costs" between platform owners and app developers (Baldwin and Clark, 2000, p. 354; Williamson, 2010). Concurrent development of various apps not only means faster development but also potentially translates into market competition among multiple possible solutions to the same user needs by rival app developers. It also lowers the need for the platform owner to constantly monitor and watch app developers, whose alignment with the platform's goals can be guaranteed by self-interest through proper platform governance. The more profound benefits of such partitioning are in the evolvability of the platform, where modularization makes growing complexity tenable and embeds powerful "real options" in the design (Baldwin and Clark, 2000, p. 90; Gamba and Fusari, 2009). (These benefits are described in Part III of this book.)

Modularization also facilitates systems integration by reducing the need for explicit coordination and communication among the platform owner and the app developers to accomplish integration of apps with a platform (Baldwin and Clark, 2000, pp. 77, 216; Tiwana, 2008a,b). By reducing the dependencies between the platform and app to just their interfaces, compliance to interface specification is all that is needed to ensure that they will seamlessly interoperate. In economist's lingo, modularity thus reduces "coordination costs" among platform owners and app developers (Gulati and Singh, 1998). Systems integration costs are ongoing costs potentially faced by app developers every time they make changes to an app. By dramatically reducing them, modularization reduces their disincentives to rapidly innovate.

Keeping transaction costs and coordination costs in control is usually why organizations organize innovation work inhouse rather than outsourcing it. But modularity can wipe out these advantages of traditional organizations and make ecosystem-based models just as viable. It therefore enables partitioning and dispersion of innovation work across multiple organizations where it was not possible before (Baldwin and Clark, 2000, p. 354). This can accelerate the evolution of the entire ecosystem, generating fierce Red Queen competition for rival platforms. Faster evolution, however, leads to survival only under some conditions, which Part IV of this book explains. Modularization can therefore be a powerful organizing strategy that enables decentralized innovation to become viable while preserving ecosystem-wide coordination.

5.6.4 Design modularity enables production modularity

Modularization of platform architectures matters also because it determines whether development around a platform can feasibly be organized as an ecosystem or whether it must be done within the boundaries of a single organization. Different architectures impose different constraints on those who interact with it or are exposed to it (van Schewick, 2012, p. 4). The preceding discussion focuses primarily on modularity in design, overlooking another kind of modularity—modularity in production (Gamba and Fusari, 2009), which refers to modularity in the logic used to organize *production* of a design. A traditionally integrated organization represents a monolithic organizing logic whereas a distributed ecosystem composed on many independent app developers represents a modular organizing logic used for producing the design. Modularity of production is a platform governance decision (the focus of the next chapter), but one whose feasibility is determined by modularity of the platform's design. Lack of design modularity, in contrast, makes production modularity infeasible (Langlois, 2002; Sanchez and Mahoney, 1996). Architectural choices therefore preordain the realm of execution possibilities. This is the essence of the mirroring principle. Design modularity and production modularity are therefore fundamentally isomorphic (i.e., design modularity enables production modularity) (Baldwin and Clark, 2000, p. 12; Hoetker, 2006). A platform's architecture is therefore particularly decisive in the evolution of its ecosystem because it is closely intertwined with the organization of the ecosystem: who chooses to participate, how much they are willing and able to invest in creating complementary innovations around a platform, and their incentives to innovate.

5.7 GOLDILOCKS STRIKES AGAIN

On the surface, it might appear that modularity is then a desirable architectural property at every level of a platform's ecosystem. However, modularity introduces tradeoffs that might not be worth its cost in some circumstances. The key tradeoff between modular and monolithic architectures is that between immediate performance and future evolvability (Figure 5.18).

Monolithic architectures usually can outperform modular ones in the short run but lead to rigidity because they are hard to change in small increments. Modular architectures, in contrast, makes a platform ecosystem more evolvable even though short-term performance will usually be poorer than monolithic architectures. Therefore monolithic architectures optimize immediate performance but offer lower evolvability, and modular architectures compromise immediate performance but offer higher evolvability. An optimal, just-right level of modularity is somewhere between the two extremes that strikes a balance between this performance–evolvability tradeoff. Modular architectures should therefore be favored over monolithic architectures when rapid innovation is more important than overall performance (Ethiraj and Levinthal, 2004b). Let us put ourselves in the shoes of a platform owner and app developer to examine the upsides and downsides of modularization from their perspectives.

5.7.1 Upsides of modularization

Modular architectures have four advantages for platform owners and app developers, as summarized in Table 5.2.

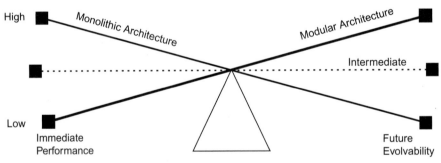

FIGURE 5.18

Tradeoffs between modular and monolithic platform architectures.

Table 5.2 Upsides of Modularizing a Platform for Platform Owners and App Developers

Platform Owner	App Developer
Massively distributed innovation	Less reinvention, more specialization
Increased variety of apps	Valuable ignorance
Greater volume of incremental innovation	Greater app evolvability
Control via architecture rather than ownership	Multihoming in rival platforms more feasible

The upsides of platform modularization for platforms owners are:

1. *Massively distributed innovation.* Modularization, like the de Prony trigonometric tables project, allows a platform owner to massively distribute innovation around a platform among thousands of independent app developers. A modular architecture wipes out the informational and coordination cost advantages of integrated organizations and makes mass collaboration across many organizations viable. Modularization enables a platform owner to leverage the distinctive capabilities of loosely coupled, independent, hungry app developers. Thus a modular architecture shifts the locus of innovation and risk-taking from the platform owner to more numerous app developers. This is particularly valuable when outsider app developers understand end-user needs and have diverse skills and capabilities that the platform owner does not possess inhouse (and cannot readily ramp up). Modularization also increases the future flexibility of the platform's trajectory ("option value" in Part III), which is most valuable when end-user preferences are diverse and unpredictable (Adner and Levinthal, 2001).

2. *Increased variety of apps.* By minimizing platform–app dependencies, app developers do not have to coordinate their own work with the platform owner yet are assured of subsequent systems integration. In other words, decreasing transaction costs between them reduces the costs of using the market to produce apps relative to developing them inhouse. With this come high-powered incentives that attract app developers, potentially increasing the variety of platform-specific apps. (Recall that outsiders usually have higher-powered incentives to perform well than inside employees.) This increases a platform's appeal to end-users and gives it a leg up in Red Queen competition with rival platforms.

3. *Greater volume of incremental and app-level innovation.* Innovation at the ecosystem can broadly be classified into four distinct modes—incremental, modular, architectural, or radical—as shown in Figure 5.19 (Henderson and Clark, 1990). It can involve refinement (incremental

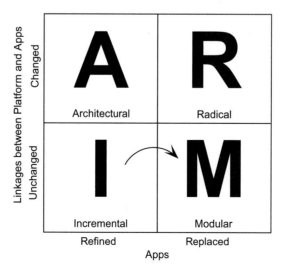

FIGURE 5.19

The four modes of innovation.

innovation) or replacement (modular innovation) of apps but leaving the linkages between the platform and apps unchanged. It can also involve changing the linkages between the platform and all its apps but leaving the apps largely stable (architectural innovation), or completely changing both the platform–app linkages and replacing the apps simultaneously (radical innovation). Modularization accelerates the quantity of innovation in the lower two cells. The reduced dependence of apps on the platform's innards allows the platform owner to make changes freely inside the core platform. Therefore, the threshold for modular innovation is much lower in modularized platforms. This potentially accelerates incremental innovation within the platform. (Modular innovation can be thought of as apps-driven innovation.) As a platform's architecture increases in its modularity, the innovation mode emerging around it shifts its evolutionary trajectory from being incremental tweaking (as in single-organization platforms) toward being modular innovation-oriented. Modularization of the platform architecture simplifies coordination with app developers, which is now achieved through design parameters and interface specifications rather than direct communication. Partitioning of apps also reduces the scope of troubleshooting and testing, reducing app development/revision timeframes (Parnas, 1972). Together, these changes speed up how fast app developers can introduce new apps and refine existing apps. New apps can rapidly extend the platform's own capabilities, and a rapid pace of introduction of new and revised apps continues to augment the usefulness of the platform. In contrast, the threshold for nonincremental innovation is much higher in monolithic platforms. Overall, this drives up the speed of app-level innovation around the platform. Therefore, modular platform architectures provide the advantage of variety today and evolvability tomorrow (Baldwin and Woodard, 2009).

4. *Control via architecture rather than ownership.* Finally, modularization of platform architecture potentially allows the platform owner to maintain some control and substantial influence over the ecosystem's evolutionary trajectory. Ordinarily, this level of control would require ownership of the entire ecosystem and the commensurate risk associated with developing apps to complement the platform. Maintaining sufficient control without compromising app developers' autonomy is a central aspect of governance of modularized platforms that we explore further in the next chapter.

The upsides of platform modularization for app developers are:

1. *Less reinvention, more specialization.* Platform modularization allows app developers to use the platform's services and reusable functionality as the *starting* point for their own work. The cognitive bandwidth freed from not having to reinvent the wheel allows them to invest more effort on functionality that differentiates their app in the marketplace. Put another way, it fosters specialization among app developers and reduces innovation costs.

2. *Valuable ignorance.* Apps in modularized platforms can be written with little knowledge of the code in the platform. This effectively reduces the conceptual design space that individual app developers must grasp.

3. *Greater app evolvability.* App developers can independently upgrade their apps without having to worry about interdependence or ripple effects elsewhere in the ecosystem. Each app is therefore free to evolve independent of the rest of the ecosystem, within the constraints imposed by the platform's interfaces (Gamba and Fusari, 2009). This increases evolvability of apps relative to monolithic platforms.

4. *Multihoming in rival platforms becomes more feasible.* Rival platforms are likely to share some common functionality, which app developers are less likely to reinvent if a platform is modularized. Therefore, more modular platform architectures increase app developers' incentives to join a platform and to remain engaged in developing around it (Baldwin and Clark, 2006). Furthermore, the cognitive bandwidth freed up by modularization and greater specialization in their app domain's functionality makes it more feasible for app developers to develop their app on multiple rival platforms, lowering their risk of being straddled with a losing platform.

5.7.2 Downsides of modularization

Modular architectures have four disadvantages, respectively, for platform owners and app developers, as summarized in Table 5.3.

The downsides of platform modularization for platform owners are:

1. *Modularity is not free.* Modularization is not free for platform owners. A platform owner must incur substantial upfront costs of modularizing a platform and establishing its interfaces. These upfront costs are usually much higher than those for more monolithic platform architectures.
2. *Technical performance takes a hit.* Modular architectures pay a modularization performance tax. The modular decomposition of a platform's ecosystem might split functionality that should have belonged in a single system instead of being split across many subsystems. The increased need for communication among these subsystems can decrease the overall technical performance of the ecosystem. It is usually not possible to fine-tune a modular system as precisely as a monolithic one (Langlois and Garzarelli, 2008). Therefore the technical performance of a modularized architecture is often worse than a comparable monolithic architecture for the same platform. Thus the assumption in modular systems thinking is that the benefits of decreased complexity and greater modification flexibility in apps and platforms offset the loss of overall system-wide performance.
3. *Modularization forecloses architectural innovation.* The choice of a platform's architecture puts it on a different trajectory in terms of the dominant mode of innovation (see Figure 5.20). More modular architectures are more conducive to incremental and modular innovation but often become hindrances to architectural and radical innovation (Figure 5.19). Recall that freezing a platform's interfaces is a precondition for modularization of its architecture. Platform interfaces, once widely adopted by app developers, lock in the platform for a substantial period of time even when a viable superior alternative subsequently becomes available (Langlois and Garzarelli, 2008).

Table 5.3 Downsides of Modularizing a Platform for Platform Owners and App Developers

Platform Owner	App Developer
Modularity is not free	Modularity imposes additional costs
Technical performance takes a hit	App performance takes a hit
Modularization forecloses architectural innovation	Modularity constrains experimentation
Increased risk of imitation by rivals	Leveraging the platform risks getting locked into it

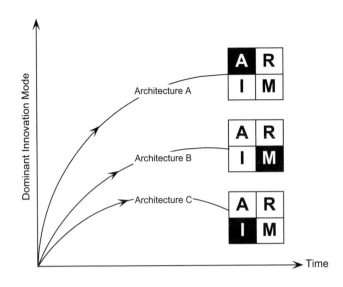

FIGURE 5.20

Platform architecture determines the dominant modes of ecosystem-wide innovation.

(Think of Apple's 30-pin i-device connector replaced by a 9-pin Lightning connector 10 years later in 2012, the QWERTY keyboard, USB, and the 30-year-old VGA connector. Although technologically superior alternatives became available—e.g., the Dvorak layout for keyboards and a plethora of potential successors for VGA interface standards—the legacy interfaces continue to widely persist.) The costs of poor architectural choices can therefore be high in the long run. Over time, modularization also reduces the platform owner's capacity for architectural innovation because balkanized expertise of the platform owner (from deepening its focus on the platform and away from apps) leads to a myopic understanding of the entire ecosystem. This focus serves it well, until the arrival of a different dominant design that offers sufficient improvements over the existing one surfaces. The platform owner's core competencies can then become its weaknesses. There are numerous examples of organizations that were unable to adapt to changes in their industry's dominant design. However, as Part IV describes, major innovations at the platform level are not impossible even with modular designs.

4. *Increased risk of imitation by rivals.* Monolithic designs usually take more time for rivals to understand and copy. Platform modularization therefore can increase the risk of imitation (Ethiraj et al., 2008; Pil and Cohen, 2006). A *nearly* modular design that retains some monolithic properties strikes an optimal balance between reducing ecosystem-wide coordination costs and risk of imitation by rivals (Figure 5.21). Therefore, intermediate levels of modularity are preferable.

Platform modularization has four downsides for app developers:

1. *Modularity imposes additional costs on app developers.* Developing for a modularized platform imposes costs of compliance with its design rules and interface specifications on app developers. These costs are often offset by the reduction in systems integration costs and gains in app evolvability.

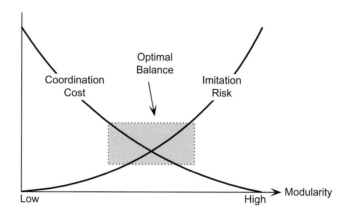

FIGURE 5.21

Modularization must balance the reduction in coordination costs against increased risk of imitation.

2. *App performance takes a hit.* Apps built around modular architectures often trade off technical performance (e.g., speed) by relying on a platform for some functionality. Such performance is likely to be higher in standalone, monolithic apps that are entirely developed by an app developer. Thoughtful app microarchitectures can compensate for this performance hit to some degree.

3. *Modularity constrains experimentation.* Complex modularized platform interfaces and their restrictions can constrain experimentation and flexibility of app developers as they attempt to develop new versions of their apps. Ingeniousness by app developers in app microarchitectures and their degree of tiering can sometimes help overcome such constraints, as we subsequently explain.

4. *Leveraging the platform increases app developers' vulnerability.* Modular platforms give platform owners an increased capacity to innovate *within* a platform. As a platform itself gains new or innovative platform-specific functionality and software services, app developers can leverage it in their own apps. (This is called increasing the *synergistic specificity* between a platform and an app (Schilling, 2000).) But this can be a double-edged sword if the leveraged functionality is unique to a platform because it makes an app more deeply dependent on and integrated with that platform. This increases the risk that an app developer will be locked-in with the platform and less able to multihome that app among rival platforms.

Overall, modularization is worth its downsides when a platform's markets are heterogeneous, riddled with uncertainty about technology trajectories and end-user preferences, and require deep pockets of specialized complementary knowledge that the platform owner does not have inhouse.

5.7.2.1 Why modular enough is good enough

Designing a perfectly modular platform architecture is almost impossible because it requires recognizing, anticipating, and resolving all app–platform dependencies in advance (Baldwin and Clark, 2000, p. 6). This is commonly problematic in practice because a platform's designers quickly run into the very human limits of bounded rationality. But the good news is that modular enough is good enough. Perfect modularity is still a useful ideal to aspire toward because even imperfect modularity reduces costs of software evolution and experimentation. Recent research has indeed shown that intermediate levels of modularity produce the most useful innovations (Ethiraj and Levinthal, 2004b). Architects aspiring to modularize platform architectures will likely end up somewhere short of perfect modularity and away from a monolithic design, which is a perfect place to be, as shown in Figure 5.18.

5.8 TWO MECHANISMS FOR MODULARIZATION

Modularization requires a mix of openness and secrecy. The logic behind modular architectures is to share information about the interfaces but keep the proprietary innards of individual apps and the platform secret. The secrecy in modular architectures comes from its first mechanism: decoupling. The openness in modular architectures comes from its second mechanism: standardization of interfaces. Decoupling facilitates decomposition of the ecosystem into relatively independent apps and the platform; interface standardization facilitates their reintegration after they are independently developed. This ability to separate and integrate subsystems is what software engineers call *composability* (Messerschmitt and Szyperski, 2003, p. 89).

5.8.1 Decoupling

Decoupling (or loose coupling) refers to the degree to which the components of an ecosystem are designed to be independent of each other such that changes *within* one component do not affect others in the ecosystem. At the heart of modular architectures is the idea of creating a "block-independent" structure, where the blocks represent the subsystems in an ecosystem (Baldwin and Clark, 2000, p. 61). The premise is that if details of a particular block of code are consciously hidden from other blocks, changes to one block can be made without having to change the other blocks (Parnas, 1972). Readers with programming expertise will immediately recognize this as the foundation of object-oriented programming languages, which are based on the idea proposed originally by David Parnas. In practice, this means that the platform and app should be designed to minimize interdependencies between them. Changes inside an app should not have an unpredictable ripple effect on the platform or on other apps. Conversely, changes inside the platform or in other apps should not adversely affect the functioning of that app.

Perfectly decoupled designs exist in theory but rarely in practice. Therefore, it is useful to think of decoupling as a slider scale with perfectly decoupled and tightly coupled on either ends of the scale. Decoupling lowers dependencies between the platform and an app, minimizing the need for coordination between the app developer and the platform owner when either the app or the platform is tweaked. Changes internal to one do not have a ripple effect on the other. A decoupled architecture can therefore potentially simplify interactions among app developers and the platform owner. This also means that coupling *within* an app and within the platform can be high such that subsystems within each can have strong dependencies. Therefore, decoupling means weak coupling between a platform and an app but strong coupling within a platform and within an app (Figure 5.22). Put another way, apps and platforms can be as monolithic internally as needed yet be a part of a highly modular ecosystem.

Decoupling is accomplished through a design process known as *encapsulation* (Baldwin and Clark, 2000, p. 63; Zweben et al., 1995). Any subsystem such as the platform involves two types of

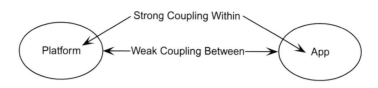

FIGURE 5.22

Weak coupling between a platform and an app and strong coupling within either.

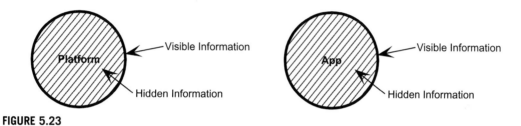

FIGURE 5.23

The distinction between visible versus hidden information in a subsystem.

information: visible information and hidden information (Figure 5.23). Information about what's inside a platform is its architecture's *hidden information*. It is information that is visible only to its developer. A well-decoupled platform should minimize the need for app developers in its ecosystem to have to know any hidden information. Internal details of its implementation should be invisible and untouchable by an outsider. The external view of the platform should display only its essential properties and hide unnecessary details of its internals. It must reveal as little as possible about its inner workings (Parnas, 1972). This property of information hiding is known as encapsulation of that subsystem. The external view is the platform's *visible information*, accessible to outsiders through its *interfaces*. The platform's interfaces are therefore the entirety of its visible information (Baldwin and Clark, 2000, p. 89). This means that only the interfaces of a platform are visible to app developers. The same logic can be applied to individual apps to encapsulate them by separating hidden information from visible information.

Interacting with the platform should require nothing more than access to its interfaces (i.e., the visible information) specified in its architecture. App developers can access the platform's functionality and services through its interfaces without having to know what goes on inside. The platform becomes a black box to app developers. It is much like driving a car: All you need to be able to drive is know how to use the car's controls; knowing how it works under the hood is not necessary. This allows app developers in a platform ecosystem to focus exclusively on their own app development work and have confidence that compliance with the platform's interface specifications will guarantee interoperability with the platform. Encapsulation of the platform therefore hides complexity (Ethiraj and Levinthal, 2004b). The same logic applies to encapsulation of individual apps. Encapsulating complexities and implementation details within subsystems not only preserves secrets about the functioning of the platform and individual apps, it also alters the competitive dynamics with rival platforms, as the next section of this book elaborates.

Decoupling requires creating and maintaining rigorous partitions of design information into hidden and visible subsets (Baldwin and Clark, 2000, p. 413). Decoupling can be accomplished in two ways: (1) splitting the ecosystem into high and low reusability subsystems and (2) specifying permissible assumptions.

5.8.1.1 Decomposition by reusability and variability – the five magic rules

The first way to decouple subsystems in a platform ecosystem is to partition it into stable and variable blocks, and high- and low-reusability blocks of functionality (Baldwin and Woodard, 2009). This requires evaluating each major element of functionality that is a candidate for consideration for inclusion in or exclusion from the platform core. Two premises of platform-based development can help guide this assessment:

- *Economies of scale across the ecosystem.* A platform achieves economies of scale in facilitating the development of complementary apps primarily by incorporating functionality that is reused by many apps.
- *Reduced costs of developing apps for the platform.* When including a function reduces app developers' costs of developing around the platform, it should be included in the platform.

Using these two guiding principles provides the following five heuristics—the magic rules—for deciding what functionality to include from a platform core.

1. *High-reusability functionality goes in the platform.* The subsystems with high reusability (i.e., shared by many apps) should go into the platform and those with low reusability (i.e., unique to a few apps) should be implemented as apps. Keeping the high-reusability functions within the platform allows that functionality to be improved much more rapidly because the subsystems used to implement them are colocated *within* the platform and can be tightly integrated. The platform itself can therefore be highly monolithic internally even though it is externally modular (i.e., when viewed by an app developer). Even the platform core of a modular platform can change over time; only the platform's interfaces need to remain stable. As long as the interfaces described in the next section remain untouched, internal functionality enhancement within the platform can be leveraged by all apps in the ecosystem without the need for much coordination between the platform owner and app developers.

2. *Generic functionality goes in the platform.* Functionality that is generic enough to be useful to many apps should go in the platform. These are the common components and functionality shared by many app implementations (Boudreau, 2010). This includes investments by a platform owner in foundational infrastructure, and shared assets and services that all app developers can potentially leverage. The exception to including only general functionality that can be used by all apps is functionality that a platform owner would want to completely control for strategic reasons (e.g., phone calls in iOS). However, nongeneric functionality that is idiosyncratic to a few apps should be implemented as apps but kept out of the platform.

3. *Any interfaces to the platform are an integral part of the platform.* Both the core codebase of the platform and its interfaces should be treated as inseparable parts of the platform because they have relatively long life spans and meet the criterion of high reusability.

4. *Stable functionality goes in the platform.* Stable functionality should go in the platform but immature, changing, evolving functionality should ideally be implemented as apps. Today's immature

functionality might become tomorrow's stable functionality; strategies for absorbing it into the platform without compromising architectural decoupling are discussed in Part IV of this book.

5. *Functionality with the highest uncertainty remains outside the platform.* The value of diverse experimentation is the highest for unproven functionality, where multiple solutions are viable and it is unclear upfront which solution or approach the market will prefer. Such functionality should be kept out of the platform and instead left to app developers. Including it in the platform risks premature commitment to what might turn out to be an inferior solution. Leaving it out of the platform can attract many diverse solutions from competing app developers aiming to meet the demand for it. The market will determine the winner out of the diverse experiments, provided appropriate incentives are in place. (It might be tempting for a platform owner to eventually subsume the winning solution into the platform, but this breach of trust with app developers can be a slippery slope, as we subsequently discuss.)

There are two exceptions to the fifth rule. First, a platform owner should integrate functionality that it deems critical to the attractiveness of the platform to end-users. If the platform owner also tweaks platform governance to match, it can foster strong healthy competition among app developers to improve the inhouse, native functionality. An example of this in mobile computing platforms is the inclusion of an email app and a Web browser in the iOS, Android, Microsoft Mobile, and Blackberry platforms, both of which were then also opened to app developers attempting fiercely to improve on them. Second, a platform owner should include functionality in the platform that it deems critical in terms of end-user expectations and norms set by rival platforms.

In summary, as shown in Figure 5.24, the platform should emphasize low-variety, high-reusability functions and relegate high-variety, low-reusability functions to apps.

5.8.1.2 Decoupling by specifying allowable assumptions

The second way to decouple subsystems is how a platform owner can explicitly specify assumptions that an app can make about the platform, and assumptions a platform can make about apps. Explicitly specifying allowable assumptions weakens dependencies among them. Neither apps nor the platform

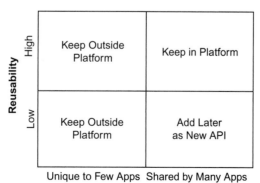

FIGURE 5.24

Strategically distributing platform functionality between a platform and apps.

are allowed to make any assumptions about each other beyond their visible information. Therefore access to a platform's functionality is restricted to its interface. This rule keeps the developers of the platform and the apps from relying on each other's hidden information as they do their own work and keeps them reliant on only the explicit, visible information provided by their architecture. Since the design of any app does not rely on the platform's hidden information, neither app developers nor the platform owner are affected by changes in the other's internals as long as the visible information remains frozen.

More decoupled apps are easier to comprehend, easier to change, and easier to test. If an app is weakly coupled to the platform, its interdependencies are completely contained in its interface to the platform. The app can therefore be implemented with limited knowledge of the platform's innards, relying largely on the interface specifications provided by the platform owner. In contrast, tightly coupled apps are designed to work closely with the platform and cannot be modified in isolation from the platform. This requires the app developer to understand the platform and the app as a whole, and possibly also the dependencies and interactions that the app might have with other apps in the platform ecosystem. Internal changes in the app can then cause errors in the platform's operations and changes in the platform can cause the app to malfunction. This creates a time-consuming coordination overhead that can slow down the app's evolution. Therefore decoupling decreases the likelihood of app malfunctions and speeds up its evolvability. The decreased need for an app developer to coordinate with the platform owner and to understand the inner workings of the platform allows the app to be changed more frequently and at a lower cost to the app developer. Similarly, changes within the platform are less likely to break the app as long as the platform owner remains faithfully compliant with the frozen interface specifications to the platform, as described in the next section.

5.8.2 Interface standardization

Interfaces are like a treaty between a platform and apps in a platform's ecosystem (Baldwin and Clark, 2000, p. 73). They are the platform's *visible* information. They specify the basic set of rules to ensure the technical interoperability of apps with the platform (Baldwin and Woodard, 2009; Boudreau, 2010).[5] A platform's interface standards are therefore sometimes referred to as the platform's design rules. *Interface standardization* refers to the degree to which an app communicates, interoperates, and exchanges data with the platform using predefined, well-specified interfaces, protocols, and rules that are not allowed to change. Interface standardization therefore means that all information about how any app must communicate and interact with the platform is explicitly documented in writing by the platform's owner and then frozen.

From an app developer's perspective, a platform's interfaces are the only visible embodiment of a platform seen and experienced by them. Apps are forbidden from communicating with the platform outside of its interfaces. The entirety of the interaction between a platform and apps occurs through the platform's interfaces. For all intents and purposes, from an app developer's perspective the interfaces *are* the platform. The platform's interfaces describe to all apps what they need to know to invoke and access the services and capabilities of the platform. The interface also specifies protocols, which

---

[5]Interfaces within the platform and within individual apps are their *intra*system interfaces. We concern ourselves with not intrasystem interfaces but rather solely with *inter*system interfaces—ones that connect an app to the platform, and both to external systems outside the ecosystem boundary—throughout this book.

describe how any back-and-forth sequence of interactions between an app and the platform should occur. A platform's interfaces therefore not only enable communication among the apps and platform, but also govern and discipline it (Langlois and Garzarelli, 2008).

Interface standardization does not require compliance with any public standards (such as CORBA) or joint development, just with the platform's own interface standards. In general, compatibility with rival platforms is undesirable for strategic reasons. Incompatibility among rival platforms' interface standards is a powerful strategic tool that subsequent chapters discuss in detail. Agreeing to common standards and interlinking rival platforms is likely to be profitable for all platforms only if no platform has a technological edge (Farrell and Saloner, 1985, 1992; Rohfls, 2003, p. 197).

Standardized platform interfaces are the key to opening up a platform's architecture. Openness of a platform architecture simply refers to whether outsiders need permission from the platform owner to build on it (Evans et al., 2006, p. 12).[6] If a platform is open, it means that outsiders can access its visible information using its interfaces to build complementary apps that augment the platform. A recent study of major platforms that thrived between 1990 and 2004 found that opening up platforms to outside developers increased the rate of innovation around that platform by 500% (Boudreau, 2010). Platforms can be open or closed to varying degrees, with most platforms neither completely open nor completely closed (Boudreau, 2010). For example, Apple's iOS platform is more closed than Google's Android platform because app developers need approval from Apple to distribute apps for the iOS platform. However, platform openness is as much a platform governance choice (Chapter 6) as it is a technical or architectural choice. But a platform's interfaces must be open to outsiders for an ecosystem to emerge. An interface is open standards-based when it is well documented, available publicly, nonproprietary, and not subject to intellectual property restrictions. Interfaces to a platform need not be open standards-based to foster vibrant ecosystems around them; they can be proprietary and open. Interface standardization therefore allows an app developer to treat the platform as a black box and focus her attention only on her own app. If the platform owner clearly and explicitly communicates how outsiders can build on the platform's capabilities in their own work, it can potentially become the basis for large-scale innovation around the platform (Meyer and Selinger, 1998). Such interface standardization must be ecosystem-wide but need not be applicable outside an ecosystem. Standards for the interface between a platform and app have three desirable properties to make them an effective coordination tool: precision, stability, and versatility.

5.8.2.1 Precisely documented

Interfaces of the platform are the glue that binds apps with a platform. Interface standards to a platform must be clearly specified, unambiguous, well documented, and stable to be useful to app developers. Ideally, the platform's visible information and interfaces are comprehensively and precisely documented, leaving no room for misinterpretation by app developers. They must also clearly lay out the design rules that describe how an app and the platform communicate, interact, exchange information, and interoperate. Information that is of relevance to more than one app must be nearly completely specified in the architecture design phase of the platform. As long as an app complies with the interface standards

---

[6]Openness of architecture should not be confused with open-source and closed-source architectures. Open source refers to platforms that make their *source* code freely available for others to use, augment, and build on. Google's Android platform is an example of an open-source platform.

prespecified by a platform owner, it should be able to interoperate with the platform independent of the app's internal implementation. A simple example of a standardized interface is a USB port. As long as a device (e.g., a printer, scanner, or camera) complies with the documented USB standards in how it communicates with a PC, it is able to communicate with it independent of the internal design of the device. Design rules provided by interface standards are particularly important after the initial platform architecture is chosen because they guide the implementation of the architectural decisions (such as decoupling). Their precision can substantially reduce the platform-wide inconsistencies between envisioned architecture and realized architecture, discussed earlier.

In platforms, such interface standards are often proprietary to individual platforms. But they must be documented in sufficient detail to provide app developers all the information they need to ensure interoperability with the platform. By isolating the interdependencies of the app from the rest of the ecosystem, platform interface standardization increases the flexibility of what an app developer can do and gives her more freedom to design and implement the functionality of the app. The utility of interface standards is that they allow app developers and a platform owner to leverage each other's strengths without sacrificing autonomy to innovate in their own work. Precisely documented interfaces between a platform and apps therefore help both app developers and platform owners innovate more effectively around the platform, guide interoperability at the app level, and provide an implicit coordination mechanism between the platform owner and app developers (Dougherty and Dunne, 2011; Sanchez and Mahoney, 1996). Thousands of app developers can then simultaneously work on their own apps in blissful ignorance of the technical details of the rest of the platform ecosystem.

A dominant way to provide such "hooks" for apps to interface with a platform are APIs. An API is simply a standardized interface designed to accept a broad class of apps (or add-ons/extensions/modules). APIs allow app developers to use the platform's capabilities without having to concern themselves with how those capabilities are implemented within the platform. App developers know how the platform behaves but do not need to know how it works. APIs play a central role in minimizing duplication of effort by app developers (Evans et al., 2006, p. viii). An API can include specifications for variables, routines, data structures, protocols, and object classes and behaviors. These APIs provide app developers well-defined means to access the platform's shared libraries, protocols, functions, and specific capabilities that they can use as a starting point for implementing their apps. An API specification can be compliant with a public open standard or protocol, or be platform-specific in the form of a platform software framework, libraries of a programming language (e.g., the Java API), or commands to invoke a Web service. Examples of widely used public API technologies include Pragmatic REST, JSON, and OAuth (for authentication without password propagation across the Internet). An open API allows an outside app developer to build on and extend the platform's native functionality by tapping into the platform's generic portfolio of services through a documented interface. An API or interface standards of a platform need not be completely open to all app developers. Openness of an API is a matter of degree; it can reside along a *continuum* ranging from completely open to completely closed. An API therefore enables a one-to-many relationship between the platform and apps. The advantage of APIs is that they allow extensions to the platform that could not even have been envisioned at the time the platform was created. They are also rich in embedded real options (see Chapter 8).

An API can become an industry standard in a platform's market, but can still be under the complete control of a single platform owner. (Maintaining such control, however, requires careful attention to platform governance.) An industry standard is a detailed specification that is agreed on by multiple players in the industry. Such standards can be formal *de jure* standards such as HMTL 5 or arise *de facto* through mass adoption (e.g., PDF format). While *de jure* standards are often created by industry consortia or regulatory bodies (such as IEEE or W3C), *de facto* standards often begin as a proprietary interface, protocol, or API that subsequently gains critical mass. Platform owners who maintain control over a *de facto* platform interface standard can enjoy considerable market power for long periods without getting under the skin of antitrust regulators.

Another way to implement interface standardization is through protocols. A protocol is a defined system of rules and semantics for exchanging messages between a platform and apps. These protocols may be platform-specific or based on public standards (such as HTML 5).

5.8.2.2 Frozen

Interfaces provided by the modularly architected platform must also be stable and unchanging (Baldwin and Clark, 2000, p. 76). Interface standardization provides an implicit coordinative function between the platform owner and app developers by documenting dependencies between a platform and apps. It specifies what assumptions app developers are allowed to make about the platform and what assumptions the platform owner can make about individual apps. These assumptions should not be allowed to change during the implementation of individual apps. Changes in the platform's interface standards can violate such assumptions, and in turn break apps. Even when they don't violate any previous assumptions that app developers were allowed to make, the added overhead for constantly verifying the safety of making an assumption about the platform can impose considerable unnecessary overhead on app developers while accomplishing little. Interface standards usually have long lifecycles and are loaded with legacy baggage. Think of standards that have persisted for decades: the VGA connector, 30-pin iPhone connector, QWERTY keyboard, and ASCII text. The widespread use of an interface standard by its adopters makes it difficult to dislodge even if a new replacement standard is technically superior.

An app must be able to assume that information about how it will interface with the platform will remain unchangeable. As long as a new version of an app (or new apps) complies with the interface specifications provided by the platform owner, any changes within the app cannot compromise its ability to interoperate with the platform. It is therefore important that any possible interdependencies between a platform and apps be captured in the interface specifications.

Paradoxically, this inflexibility in a platform's interface specifications dramatically increases flexibility in what app developers can do within their apps. New functionality that is added to a platform should therefore avoid touching existing interface specifications because stable APIs lead to predictability (Iansiti and Levien, 2004, p. 53). Instead, adding new functionality to a platform usually requires adding new APIs. This is why Apple's iOS had almost 15,000 APIs by 2013. Therefore, stability of interfaces used by the platform is critical to minimizing the interdependence between the platform and apps. They also must remain consistent across successive generations of a platform (Iansiti and Levien, 2004, p. 88).

5.8.2.3 Versatile

However, to support the ecosystem's evolution and the evolution of apps, such interfaces should also be versatile. Versatility means that the interfaces to the platform should be able to incorporate linkages in the future and permit future apps unforeseeable by the platform's original designers (Baldwin and

Woodard, 2009). Although stable interface specifications minimize the need for app developers to coordinate their app design decisions with the platform owner, they can severely constrain all subsequent designs to be bounded by those specifications. The more precise a platform's interface specifications, the more inflexible is this constraint. The more general a standard (HTML 5 vs. Flash), the greater its versatility.

To prevent the inflexibility of interface specifications from stymieing the evolution of the platform, good platform architecture should bundle together the functionalities that can most benefit from subsequent improvement in the platform itself. So functionalities that are likely to change together and are used by multiple apps should belong in the platform codebase itself. Monolithic-ness within the platform is therefore generally desirable. Put another way, the partitioning of the initial architecture of the ecosystem should be done in a way that places the functionality potentially shared by many apps into the platform core that is intended to be stable and the rest into a set of complementary apps that are encouraged to vary (Baldwin and Woodard, 2009). Versatility of a platform's interfaces is therefore inseparable from decoupling in its initial design.

5.8.2.4 Compliance with interface standards

Interface standards are like traffic lights; they simplify coordination only as long as everyone follows the same rules. Each driver must both know and follow the rules. To be effective coordination devices, interface standards must be binding on both the platform owner and app developers; app developers must obey them and also expect others to obey them (Baldwin and Clark, 2006; Ostrovsky and Schwarz, 2005). The degree to which an app actually complies with interface specifications encapsulates its behavior in practice. This in turn can generate variability in compliance among different app developers, with some app developers closely complying with the standards prescribed by the platform owner and others doing it half-heartedly. This variance in interface standards compliance among apps coupled with differences in app microarchitectures often creates variability in the architectural properties of different comparable apps even within the same platform. However, such compliance cannot readily be enforced, is rarely contractible, and is costly to verify (Ostrovsky and Schwarz, 2005).

Compliance with a platform's interface standards requires a carrot—demonstrable value and benefit to app developers—rather than a stick. What's in it for an app developer? Interface standards compliance decreases the complexity that an app developer must cope with, and the depth of knowledge about the platform that she needs to possess in doing her own work. This rationale, however, works better for established interfaces that have already been adopted by other app developers in a platform than it does for new interface standards. Early adoption of a new standard or API by an app developer can be particularly risky, especially one that develops the app on multiple rival platforms (i.e., produces a multihoming app). The platform owner must therefore credibly assure app developers against the risk of being stranded with high dependence on a platform interface standard that could be abandoned at will and also communicate precisely how it can enhance the app developer's own work. The platform owner must make it easier and less costly for app developers to adhere to the platform's interface standards and specifications. This requires investments by the platform owner in creating good app testing mechanisms that app developers can use themselves, and also in tools to help the platform owner determine whether an app complies with the critical interface specifications. Thoughtful platform governance—especially control mechanisms, described in the next chapter—can further alleviate this compliance problem. Enforcing a platform's design rules and interface specification is therefore an important role of governance (Baldwin and Clark, 2000, p. 13).

Table 5.4 Guiding Principles Influenced by Platform Architecture Decisions

Principle Affected	Platform Architecture	App Microarchitecture
Red Queen effect	●	●
Chicken-or-egg problem		
Penguin problem		
Emergence	●	●
Seesaw problem	●	
Humpty Dumpty problem	●	
Mirroring hypothesis	●	
Coevolution		●
Goldilocks rule	●	●

Different architectures can be used to implement the same functional requirements in a platform, and platform designers and app developers have relatively few constraints that keep them from freely picking one set of architectural choices over others at the outset. But these early choices can have strikingly different evolutionary consequences. Architectural decisions by platform owners and app developers therefore influence the evolution of platforms, apps, and entire ecosystems. Table 5.4 provides a preview of which of the key evolutionary principles are affected by their architectural choices. Parts III and IV of this book explain these ideas in depth.

CHAPTER SUMMARY

- *Complexity stymies innovation.* Platform ecosystems are complex to begin with and, as their complexity grows, interdependence among their many parts becomes paralyzing. Co-innovation is not additive but multiplicative, which stymies the prospects of even capable participants producing joint innovations. Architecture can reduce ecosystems' structural complexity but not their behavioral complexity.
- *Architecture is a platform's DNA that imprints evolvability.* Architectural choices irreversibly preordain the evolutionary trajectories open and closed to a platform's ecosystem. Platform ecosystems are intentionally designed complex systems composed of many interacting parts. Platform architecture specifies what these parts are, how they connect, and what they can and cannot do. These properties are inherited by apps in their own microarchitectures as well, but imperfectly so. Envisioning ecosystem architecture requires adopting a telescopic view of platform architecture; envisioning app microarchitectures requires adopting a microscopic view of platform architecture.
- *Architecture precedes organization.* Platform architecture determines whether transaction and coordination costs can be reduced sufficiently to make an ecosystem viable. It shapes the ability of outside app developers to join a platform and provides incentives to join.

- *Architecture partitions and reintegrates a complex system.* Architecture must serve two purposes: (1) it must partition a complex ecosystem so it can be decomposed into relatively autonomous apps and the platform and (2) it must facilitate ongoing systems integration among them so they can be put back together as a cohesive ecosystem.
- *Apps have internal and external microarchitectures.* Their internal microarchitecture is defined by how their four functional elements are split across the Internet. Their external microarchitecture is defined by how these functional elements are divvied up between the app and the platform.
- *Platform architectures have four desirable properties.* They should be simple, resilient, maintainable, and evolvable. The structure, governance, and evolution of modern cities offer useful lessons for designing vibrant platform ecosystems.
- *Modularization endows these desirable properties to architectures.* Modularization of architectures refers to how they can be designed so that changes within the platform or an app do not have a ripple effect on the rest of the ecosystem. Modularization is accomplished by decoupling the platform from apps and then freezing well-documented specifications for how they connect.
- *Decoupling in architecture uses two simple rules.* First, partition the ecosystem into low-variety, high-reusability functions that go into the platform core and high-variety, low-reusability functions that must remain outside it. Second, specify assumptions that apps can make about the platform and vice versa.
- *A platform's interfaces follow three criteria.* They must be precise, frozen, and versatile. Getting app developers to comply with them requires a carrot rather than a stick.
- *A platform's interface standards are like traffic lights.* They are useful as a coordination device only when everyone follows the same rules. Enforcing compliance is an important role of platform governance. A platform owner can invest in tools (such as developer toolkits, reference models, simulators, and module testers) that make it less costly for app developers to comply with them.
- *Goldilocks should not be forgotten.* Modularization has upsides and downsides both for app developers and platform owners. Modularization is usually worth it when a platform's markets are heterogeneous, riddled with technology and market unpredictability, and require eclectic knowledge that the platform owner does not have inhouse. The optimal level of modularity is *just enough* modularity. We discussed how to determine what is just the right level of modularity for a platform and for an app.

Even the most thoughtful platform architecture cannot nurture a vibrant ecosystem unless it is governed effectively. We turn our attention to platform governance in the next chapter. It provides a three-dimensional framework for platform governance that encompasses who decides what, mechanisms of control, and pricing. It also describes precisely how platform governance can be aligned with its architecture to help realize its strategic potential.

Platform Governance

Details create the big picture.
Sanford Weill

IN THIS CHAPTER

- Platform governance and its functions
- Three facets of platform governance: Decision rights, control, and pricing policies
- Who decides what (decision rights)
- The two functions of control
- The role of platform pricing policies
- Aligning governance with platform architecture, business models, and lifecycle stages
- Aligning decision rights, control portfolios, and pricing policies

6.1 PLATFORM GOVERNANCE AS THE BLUEPRINT FOR ECOSYSTEM ORCHESTRATION

If the metaphor for traditional organizations is an army, the metaphor for platform ecosystems is a symphony. The platform owner is like the conductor and the app developers are like the musicians. Each musician contributes a unique part of the overall musical score. The conductor helps the diverse musicians synchronize their own contributions to help ensure overall coherence in their collective performance. The conductor does not direct but rather orchestrates. The individual musicians *choose* to follow the lead of the conductor, who has limited direct authority or the depth of specialized musical talent of all of the musicians contributing to the performance. A good performance results from each musician being able to independently play her part but in synchrony with the others.

Like in a symphony, orchestration rather than control should be the focus of governance in platform ecosystems. Command-and-control structures work well in traditional organizations because legitimate hierarchical authority of managers over employees is accepted by both sides as a condition for employment. However, no such direct authority exists in a platform ecosystem. App developers are not employees of a platform owner; rather they often are free agents who typically specialize in niche domains outside those of the platform owner's. Performance-based rewards rather than punitive penalties are needed. The goal of good governance by a platform owner must therefore be to *shape and influence* its ecosystem, not to direct it (Williamson and De Meyer, 2012). And the goal of good

---

☆"To view the full reference list for the book, click here or see page 283."

117

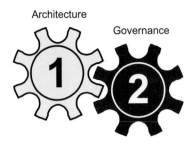

FIGURE 6.1

Governance is the second gear in a platform ecosystem's evolutionary motor.

governance is to respect the autonomy of app developers to do their thing while also being able to integrate their varied contributions into a harmonious whole. This is the essence of platform orchestration. Orchestration therefore entails influencing those whom the platform owner cannot control. The key function of governance is therefore to provide a context in which distributed innovation driven by app developers can emerge around a platform.

Platform governance is the second gear of platform orchestration (Figure 6.1). While architecture can reduce structural complexity, governance can reduce behavioral complexity. Platform governance matters because it determines whether innovation divisibility made possible by modular platform architectures is successfully leveraged (Boudreau, 2010; Rochet and Tirole, 2003; Tiwana et al., 2010). Governance of a platform ecosystem broadly refers to the mechanisms through which a platform owner exerts influence over app developers participating in a platform's ecosystem (Schilling, 2005, p. 159). Governance therefore flows from the platform owner who governs to app developers who are governed by the platform owner.

This chapter provides a foundation for understanding platform governance, beginning with its purpose and importance. It then explains the three dimensions of platform governance. The first is how the authority and responsibility for platform and app decisions are divvied up among app developers and a platform owner (decision rights). The second includes four mechanisms that a platform owner can mix-and-match to ensure goal convergence and coordination with app developers: gatekeeping, metrics, process control, and relational control. The third dimension is five platform pricing policies. It then explains why governance is inseparable from platform architecture and why realizing the potential of modular platform architectures requires aligning them. It finally explains how the three dimensions of governance—decision rights, control, and pricing—can be aligned with a platform's architecture, its business model, and its lifecycle stage. The mirroring principle provides a powerful mechanism for aligning decision rights in an ecosystem. But it also leaves some holes that must be plugged by platform control mechanisms. Aspiring for five simple rules can help design an effective but minimalist platform control system: simple, transparent, realistic, value-based, and fair.

6.2 THREE DIMENSIONS OF PLATFORM GOVERNANCE

Platform governance encompasses three dimensions (Table 6.1 and Figure 6.2): (1) the division of authority and responsibilities between the platform owner and app developers (decision rights partitioning), (2) the collection of mechanisms through which the platform owner exercises control over

Table 6.1 The Four Control Mechanisms and Their Prerequisites

Control Mechanism	Definition	Prerequisites
Gatekeeping	The degree to which the platform owner uses predefined criteria for what apps are allowed into the platform's ecosystem	• Platform owner must be competent to judge • Platform owner must be fair and speedy • App developers must be willing to accept such gatekeeping
Process	The degree to which a platform owner rewards or penalizes app developers based on the degree to which they follow prescribed development methods and procedures that it believes will lead to desirable outcomes	• Platform owner must have the knowledge to mandate methods to app developers • Platform owner should be able to monitor app developers' behaviors or verify compliance
Metrics	The degree to which the platform owner rewards or penalizes app developers based on the degree to which the outcomes of their work achieve performance targets predefined by the platform owner	• Metrics must be set by the platform owner, predefined, and objectively measurable
Relational	The degree to which the platform owner relies on norms and values that it shares with app developers to shape their behaviors	• Existence of shared norms and values between app developers and platform owner • Low app developer churn

app developers (the control portfolio, which includes the authority to accept or reject apps), and (3) decisions about how proceeds will be divvied up between a platform owner and app developers (pricing policies). Before we discuss each of these facets in detail, three important nuances must be emphasized. First, that these three dimensions of governance are interrelated; choices about one dimension can amplify or nullify the choices about the other two. Second, governance is costly. The optimal governance structure is the simplest one that achieves the goals of a platform at the least cost to both app developers and the platform owner. Third, governance structures are strategically inseparable from platform architecture. The same governance structure can be a disaster or a success depending on whether it is aligned well with the platform's architecture, the stage of its lifecycle, and its business model. Misalignment in any one of the three governance dimensions can lead to a collapse of the ecosystem. The role of each dimension of governance is shown in italics in Figure 6.2.

6.2.1 Decision rights partitioning

The first dimension of platform governance is decision-making authority or *decision rights*. A decision right broadly refers to who—the platform owner or app developer—has the primary authority and responsibility for making a specific type of decision—simply put, who makes what decisions

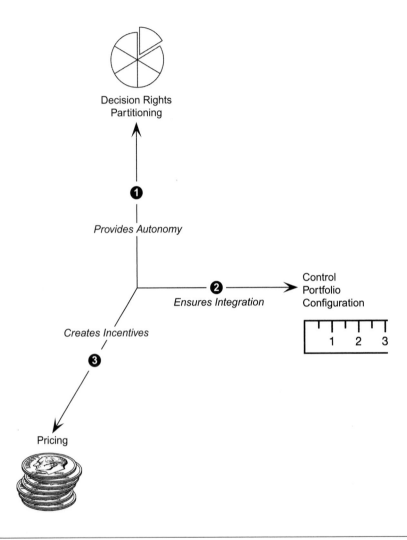

Decision Rights
Partitioning

1

Provides Autonomy

2 ———————➤ Control
Portfolio
Configuration

Ensures Integration

Creates Incentives

3

Pricing

1   2   3

FIGURE 6.2

The three dimensions of platform governance.

(Athey and Roberts, 2001; Vazquez, 2004). A decision right can reside primarily with the platform owner, which represents centralization of a decision right. Or it can reside primarily with an app developer, which represents decentralization of a decision right. Perfect centralization and decentralization exist mostly only in theory and are rarely ever observed in practice. In practice, a decision right can reside anywhere along the continuum of complete centralization and complete decentralization. This means that both the platform owner and app developers have some authority and responsibility for most decisions but it might lean more toward one party. It is therefore useful to think of any decision right as a slider that can be moved along the two extremes of centralization and decentralization (Figure 6.3).

6.2.1.1 *Platform versus app decision rights*

Thinking of each individual decision in a platform ecosystem can quickly devolve into an overwhelming and meaningless exercise. It is therefore necessary to reduce the broad notion of decision rights into a more comprehensible and tenable subset or classes of decisions. In a platform ecosystem, there are four broad sets of decision rights. The first distinction is whether decision rights pertain to the platform or the platform's apps. *Platform decision rights* refer to whether the platform owner or the app developers have the authority and responsibility for making decisions directly pertaining to the platform. Similarly, *app decision rights* refer to whether the platform owner or the app developers have the authority and responsibility for making decisions directly pertaining to apps. On first glance, you might conclude that platform decisions would be naturally made by the platform owner and app decisions by app developers. But this is a misleading oversimplification for four reasons.

First, decision rights can be placed anywhere along the continuum in Figure 6.3. It is a purposeful choice, not a given. This means that platform and app decision rights do not necessarily have a 1:1 mapping to platform owners and app developers, as the simple representation in Figure 6.4 would lead one to conclude. Instead, we must think of them in terms of their *degree* of decentralization. App decisions, for example, can be decentralized to a greater degree on one platform and less decentralized on another. This means that they are often *shared* to varying degrees between app developers and platform owners; the question is about the degree to which they are shared. We therefore refer to such sharing as partitioning of decision rights. Second, even slight differences in the degree of their centralization and

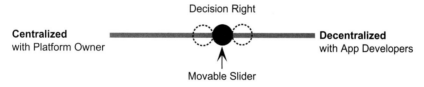

FIGURE 6.3

A decision right can be placed anywhere on the decentralization continuum.

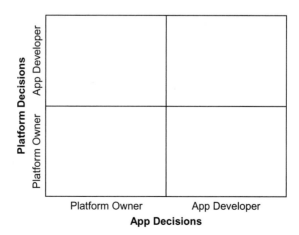

FIGURE 6.4

Platform and app decision rights can be assigned to platform owners or app developers.

decentralization can put two similar platforms on substantively different evolutionary trajectories. Such small differences in the degree of decentralization of platform and app decisions can amplify or mute the benefits of architectural choices made by platform owners and app developers. In other words, they have strong interactions and dependencies with architecture at the platform level and at the app level. A decision rights arrangement that enables efficient specialization among app developers under one architecture can become its Achilles heel under another. Therefore, the partitioning of decision rights must be aligned with the architecture of a platform and the microarchitecture of apps. Fourth, decision rights partitioning between two parties have an assigner and an assignee. The allocation of decision rights to an assignee might have little meaning if the assignee does not—or cannot—accept the responsibility for those types of decisions.

6.2.1.2 Two classes of decision rights: strategic and implementation

Decision rights for a platform or apps can be broadly split into two broad categories[1]: *strategic* and *implementation*. Strategic decision rights pertain to what a party (app developer or platform owner) should accomplish and implementation decisions are about how it should accomplish it. Strategic decision rights therefore are direction-setting, specification-oriented decisions. Implementation decisions are technical execution decisions that pertain to the choice of features, functionality, design, user interface, and implementation details of a software subsystem. Both classes of decision rights apply to platforms and apps. Therefore, *platform strategic* decision rights represent the authority and responsibility for specifying what the platform must accomplish and *platform implementation* decision rights represent how a platform actually accomplishes those objectives. Similarly, *app strategic* decision rights represent where the authority and responsibility for specifying what an app must accomplish reside and *app implementation* decision rights represent how an app actually accomplishes those objectives.

The division of app decision rights can vary by app, and the same platform can use different combinations of app decision rights partitioning for different apps. Similarly, an app developer with multiple apps on the same platform might see different decision rights structures used for various apps on the same platform. And a multihoming app developer with the same app on multiple platforms will likely encounter different decision rights structures for that app on different platforms. For example, the developer of the Skype Mobile app might see different decision rights structures on iOS, Android, and Windows Mobile platforms. The decision rights structure for an individual app on a given platform can succinctly be represented in the decision rights partitioning framework in Figure 6.5. The sliders are independently movable, must be aligned with platform architecture and app microarchitecture at the outset, and be moved over time to maintain alignment.

6.2.2 Control portfolio design

The second dimension of platform governance is control. Control refers to the means through which the platform owner ensures that the app developers' work is aligned with what is in the best interests of the platform. Control is implemented by the platform owner over app developers using a variety of control *mechanisms*. Therefore control mechanisms are the tools that platform owners use to implement and enforce rules that reward desirable behavior, punish bad behavior, and promulgate standards of behavior among app developers (Evans and Schmalensee, 2007). Control mechanisms can either be formal or

---

[1]For research on the distinction between these classes of decision rights, see Tiwana and Konsynski (2010) and Jensen and Meckling (1992).

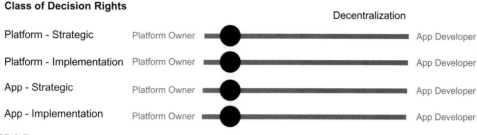

Class of Decision Rights

FIGURE 6.5

A decision rights partitioning framework.

informal. Several such mechanisms can be used together and this combination of control mechanisms represents the *control portfolio* used by a platform owner over an app developer. Different apps in the same platform can—but need not—have differently structured control portfolios.

Figure 6.6 summarizes the four control mechanisms that can be used by a platform owner.

A platform owner can use three formal control mechanisms and one informal control mechanism. All formal control mechanisms focus on imposing rules and standards that a platform owner expects app developers to aspire toward meeting (Evans and Schmalensee, 2007, p. 22). The formal control mechanisms include control through gatekeeping, process control, and control using metrics. An informal control mechanism that can be used in addition to these formal mechanisms is relational control. Table 6.1 summarizes these control mechanisms. Each control mechanism also has prerequisites for using it, also summarized in the table.

6.2.2.1 Gatekeeping

The first formal control is via *gatekeeping*. Gatekeeping represents the degree to which the platform owner uses predefined objective acceptance criteria for judging what apps and app developers are allowed into a platform's ecosystem. The platform owner sets this criteria, not just for *what* is allowed in but also *who* is allowed in. This formal control is also known as input control (Cardinal, 2001), much like how organizations select which candidates to hire as employees from a pool of applicants. In platforms, this entails an app developer submitting an app to the platform owner for evaluation for inclusion in the platform's ecosystem.

When gatekeeping is used by a platform owner, the platform owner reserves bouncer rights over apps that can be included as part of the ecosystem (Boudreau, 2010; Evans et al., 2006, p. 254). Apple,

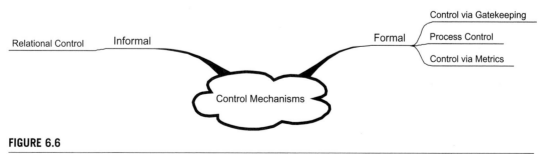

FIGURE 6.6

Control mechanism choices usable by platform owners.

for example, uses gatekeeping heavily as a control mechanism in its iOS platform. However, three important requirements must be met for control via gatekeeping to be viable. First, the platform owner must be sufficiently competent to judge app developers' submissions. Second, the platform owner must be able to do so fairly and speedily. Third, app developers must be willing to be subjected to such gatekeeping. If the platform owner is not perceived as being objective, fair, and speedy in judging inputs into the platform, it exposes app developers to considerable risk and uncertainty about platform-specific work they have already invested in completing. If deployed carelessly, it can discourage app developers from committing to developing for a platform.

6.2.2.2 Process control

The second form of control is *process control*, which refers to the degree to which a platform owner rewards or penalizes app developers based on the degree to which they follow prescribed development methods, rules, and procedures that it believes will lead to outcomes desirable from a platform owner's perspective. Such desirable outcomes in platforms refer to apps that will interoperate well with a platform, not whether they do well on the market. Such rules and procedures are prescribed by the platform owner, who then evaluates the extent to which individual app developers followed them. Compliance with prespecified processes is rewarded and noncompliance is penalized. These processes must be defined upfront and known to app developers for process control to be viable. In many software platforms, platform development and testing tools, simulation environments, and developer toolkits provided by the platform owner to app developers are mechanisms through which a platform owner attempts to implement process control. Process control, however, has two important requirements to be viable. First, the behaviors of app developers should be observable and monitorable by the platform owner. Such behavior observability need not be direct and can be through electronic audit trails and developer logs. Second, the assertion behind process control is that if app developers follow the processes prescribed by the platform owner rather than being left to their devices, the likelihood that they will produce technically better-performing apps is going to be higher. The platform owner must understand the work of the app developers sufficiently well—or better—in order to prescribe processes that will indeed improve the odds of their work being successful (particularly, app integration with the platform).

6.2.2.3 Metrics

A third formal control mechanism is through the use of *metrics*. This formal control refers to the degree to which the platform owner rewards or penalizes app developers based on the degree to which the outcomes of their work achieve predefined target performance metrics. Researchers call this output control because it evaluates the output of app developers' work (Ouchi, 1979). The requirement for metrics-driven control is that such metrics must be: (1) prespecified by the platform owner and (2) objectively measurable. The extent to which an app developer's completed work meets the targets determines the rewards or penalties that the platform owner imposes on the app developer. Metrics-based control comes from the legacy world of traditional software development where an internal manager or client could specify target criteria such as budget, project schedules, and acceptable defect levels to the internal IT department or an outside vendor. However, such metrics have little meaning if the platform owner does not—or cannot—prespecify target metrics such as development budgets or schedules that it expects app developers to meet.

In platforms, performance and survival of an app in the brutal marketplace serves as a powerful metric that eliminates the need for much metrics-based control (Armstrong, 2006; Bester and Krähmer, 2008). In many contemporary platforms, metrics-based control is therefore rarely used because the end-user market rewards high-quality output with strong sales and penalizes low-quality output with poor sales. In other words, the use of market competition can substitute for control using metrics. Examples of some *weak* app-level metrics in platforms can include performance, memory utilization, and speed at an operational level. They can also include *market-oriented* metrics such as unit sales, downloads, and end-user ratings. Use of market-oriented metrics such as these is also closely tied to the third dimension of governance: pricing structures used by the platform owner to divvy up proceeds with app developers. The sole purpose of market-oriented metrics is therefore simply measurement to implement revenue-splitting agreements.

6.2.2.4 Relational control

The fourth and only informal form of control is *relational control*. This control mechanism refers to the degree to which the platform owner relies on norms and values that it shares with app developers to influence their behavior. This control mechanism thus relies on the platform owner to provide an over-arching collective goal for the platform ecosystem; a sort of shared identity that defines the character of the platform ecosystem and rallies app developers around it by harmonizing their own goals with those of the platform. Such system-level goal-setting sets a trajectory to evolve the platform ecosystem and creates unity in effort without micromanaging app developers (Meadows, 2008, p. 165). Therefore, a shared culture, similar set of values, and shared norms provide a common ground that can align the objectives of the platform owner and the work of app developers. Researchers call this clan control because it relies on clannish behavior (Kirsch, 1997; Ouchi, 1980). Relational control is widely used in open-source platforms such as various Linux platform development communities. The upside to relational control is that it is often one of the least costly forms of control since it requires little enforce-ment and effort from the platform owner. However, the preexistence of shared norms and values in the app developer community is an important precondition for relational control to be viable. This require-ment is often not met if an app developer does not share a long history with the platform. It is also unlikely to be met in platforms that have an ongoing inflow of new app developers who join the plat-form but do not have the same shared history, professional values, and norms as existing developers. High app developer churn therefore reduces the viability of relational control. Therefore, relational control rarely suffices by itself, although it can nicely complement other formal control mechanisms.

The combination of these four control mechanisms at the platform level describes a control port-folio, as illustrated in Figure 6.7. Each control mechanism is an independent slider that can be omitted, used to some degree, or used extensively as part of a control portfolio. The control portfolio used by a platform owner can therefore be succinctly described using this template.

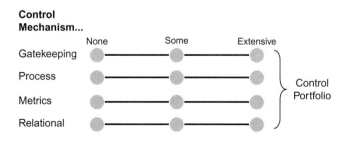

FIGURE 6.7

A control portfolio is a combination of the four control mechanisms used by a platform owner.

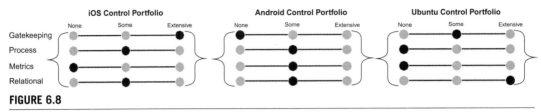

FIGURE 6.8

An illustration of the control portfolios used by three platforms.

Figure 6.8 illustrates the control portfolios used by three different platforms: iOS, Android, and Ubuntu. As this comparison illustrates, some platforms rely on a combination of some degree of diverse control mechanisms (e.g., Android) whereas others lean heavily toward the extensive use of one dominant control mechanism in designing their control portfolio.

6.2.2.5 Attempted versus realized control

Just because a platform owner decides to implement a particular control mechanism over all developers does not necessarily result in the expected behavior. In other words, there is a difference between control attempts by a platform owner and the degree to which the platform owner is actually able to realize it over individual app developers. A control mechanism is effective when the level of attempted control and realized control for that mechanism are not too far apart. This requires two things. First, the control mechanism should be accepted by app developers as being legitimate, fair, and reasonable. The power of a control mechanism requires the consent of the governed. Leadership is possible only when others choose to follow, so some consensus is always needed for any control mechanism to be realizable. Second, the prerequisites for it (Table 6.1) must be satisfied in the relationship between the platform owner and individual app developers. Both of these conditions are more likely to be met with some app developers and less with others. Therefore, there might be little variability in a platform owner's attempted control portfolio but considerable variability in the level of control realized by the platform owner over individual app developers. As illustrated in Figure 6.9, a uniform control portfolio that the platform owner attempts to use over three app developers might be realized differently with each of them.

The optimal control portfolio used in a platform should further multiple, often competing objectives of a platform and should also be aligned with the platform's architecture. We subsequently describe five guiding principles for how platform owners can design an optimal control portfolio in this chapter.

6.2.3 Pricing

The third dimension of platform governance is platform pricing policies. The goal of pricing policies is to create incentives that are compelling enough to encourage app developers to make personal investments to ensure the prosperity of their own app offerings, and in turn the vibrancy of the platform ecosystem as a whole. Pricing policies encompass five choices:

1. Whether pricing should be symmetric or asymmetric for the two sides of the platform
2. If asymmetric, who to subsidize and for how long?
3. Pricing for access versus usage?
4. Pie-splitting using a fixed scale or a sliding scale?
5. App pricing decisions

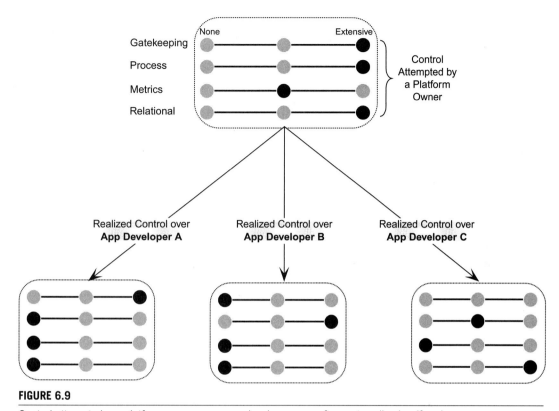

FIGURE 6.9

Control attempts by a platform owner over app developers are often not realized uniformly.

6.2.3.1 Decision 1: symmetric or asymmetric pricing?

Recall that there are at least two sides to a platform: app developers and end-users. The first pricing decision that a platform owner must make is whether you make money on one side and give a break to the other side (asymmetric pricing), or make money on both sides (symmetric pricing). The choices are illustrated in Figure 6.10. If a platform owner chooses to make money on only one side, it usually entails zero pricing or even negative pricing on the other side. For example, some platforms make money from end-users but subsidize app developers. Often, platform owners go even beyond subsidies by providing tools, hardware, and other costly incentives that cause them to lose money on one side. The subsidized side of the platform can often make up the losses in the form of increased profits from the other side. For example, Amazon Kindle and gaming console developers (e.g., Nintendo, Sony Playstation, and Microsoft Xbox) subsidize end-users. In contrast, mobile computing platform owners such as Apple, Google, and Blackberry subsidize app developers. In traditional businesses, this would be considered irrational and a recipe for the business model to collapse. However, in platform markets, strategically subsidizing one side can more than make up the lost money from the other side. It is important to make platform pricing decisions for long-term profitability, which might be at odds with short-term profitability. This is a tricky strategic decision and is tied directly to the stage of the platform's lifecycle, criticality of network effects, and competitive dynamics in the platform's immediate market, as we discuss later in this chapter.

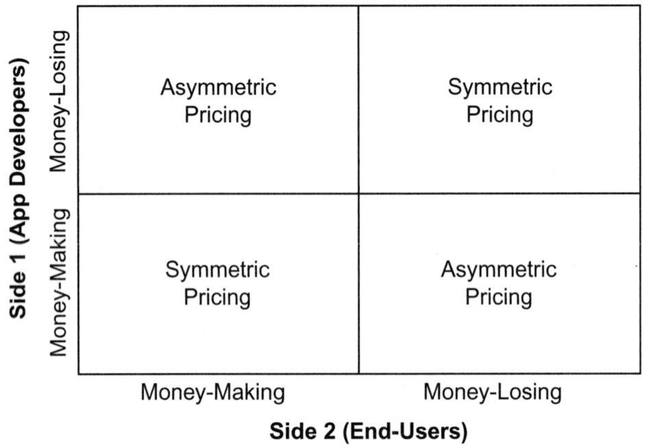

FIGURE 6.10

Asymmetric versus symmetric pricing across two sides of a platform.

6.2.3.2 Decision 2: which side to subsidize and for how long

The second pricing decision platform owners must make is which side to subsidize (if any) and for how long. For example, a platform owner might pay one side to join simply to attract the other side. The unsubsidized side should, however, always be the money-making side. If one side subsidizes the other, the platform owner must also decide how long this subsidy should last. Abruptly attempting to end the subsidy on the subsidized side can be challenging and must be planned in advance. For example, the newspaper publishing industry (e.g., the *New York Times*) subsidized readers by offering them free access to online content from the mid-1990s to the mid-2000s. This successfully attracted advertisers (the other side). But when they tried to end the subsidy to the readers by attempting to charge them access fees, it resulted in mass attrition of readership. If they had the foresight to plan to end the subsidy, a more feasible approach would have been to offer readers expiring monthly credit or points that they could have redeemed to gain free access during the intended subsidy period. We explain later how platform owners can make such subsidy decisions by considering various aspects of their platform and its competitive environment.

6.2.3.3 Decision 3: usage versus access pricing

The third pricing decision platform owners must make is about pricing for access and pricing for usage (Figure 6.11). It is important to set separate prices for access and usage. Access fees are the prices charged to app developers (but rarely to end-users) for gaining access to the platform. Usage fees are prices charged to app developers for actual usage of the platform. It often makes sense to set one of these prices to zero or even negative (e.g., where app developers are paid by the platform owner using side payments) depending on the platform's stage in its lifecycle, whether it is in the pre- or post-dominant design phase, and the accumulation of critical mass on the developer and the end-user sides. We subsequently explain how usage and access pricing policies can be aligned with these properties of a platform.

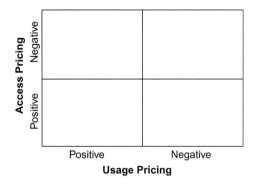

FIGURE 6.11

Access and usage pricing can be negative or positive.

6.2.3.4 Decision 4: pie-splitting using a fixed scale or a moving scale?

The fourth pricing decision that platform owners must make is about the pie-splitting structure. This means that for every dollar of revenue earned from an app, how the revenue will be shared between the app developer and platform owner. The choice is one of adopting a fixed scale or a moving scale. A fixed scale means that the platform owner keeps a predetermined percentage of each dollar of revenue (say, 30%, as in Apple's case). A moving scale means that the scale changes with an increase in the units of the app sold or in its usage. The percentage can either rise (a rising scale) or decrease (a sliding scale) with an increase in sales volume.

These three choices are illustrated in Figure 6.12. Mobile computing platforms most commonly use a fixed scale structure. The traditional book publishing industry, in contrast, frequently uses a rising scale where the first block of copies sold (say the first 5,000) pay the authors a small percentage (e.g., 5%), the next block pays a higher percentage (e.g., 7.5%), and all subsequent copies sold pay a higher ceiling percentage (e.g., 10%). As we subsequently explain, there is no one right model. The choice can have a strong impact on the incentives of app developers, and a model appropriate for one stage of the platform's lifecycle might not be appropriate for another stage.

6.2.3.5 Decision 5: app licensing decisions

The final pricing decision is app-specific pricing and licensing decisions. Unlike the preceding four pricing policies where the platform owner has the primary say, the app developer usually has considerable leeway in app pricing decisions. However, such decisions are likely to be constrained by the other four platform owner pricing choices. An app developer can use one of three pricing structures for an app:

1. *Single perpetual license*: This sort of license is perpetual in the sense that a one-time payment by an end-user grants nonexpiring rights to use the app. The license can either be an individual license (the buyer can use the app on a limited or unlimited number of her own instantiations of the platform), a machine license (which allows the end-user to use it on a particular machine that it was purchased for but not for any subsequent machine), or a floating license (which allows the user to use it on any one machine at a time and the host machine can change without constraints). This model is the most widespread in the traditional software industry. An app that is given away for

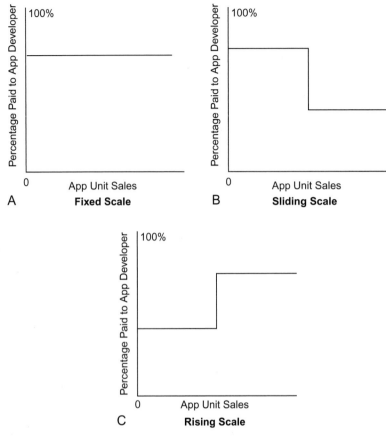

FIGURE 6.12

Pie-splitting between the platform owner and app developers can be on a fixed, sliding, or rising scale.

free is a single perpetual license priced at zero dollars, with revenue generated from a third side (e.g., advertising) or from the sales of a complementary product or service (e.g., department store sales, an airline flight, a banking relationship, or a credit card account).

2. *Subscription-based license*: This sort of license allows the user to use the app for the duration of an active subscription period (e.g., 1 year) and usually includes all future updates to an app during that period. This licensing model is a service-oriented model. The ubiquitous IP connectivity of contemporary software platforms allows this model to now be cost-effectively implemented because instant verification of an active subscription is possible each time the end-user attempts to use an app.

3. *Usage-based license*: This sort of model charges the user based on actual usage and requires some direct measure of usage (such as number of times used or number of hours used). This licensing model is a utility-oriented model, much like you pay for the actual amount of electricity or water consumed. The necessary condition for this licensing model is the ability to precisely and

cost-effectively meter usage. This is increasingly viable in software platforms due to their near-ubiquitous IP connectivity. The actual revenue need not directly be recouped from the end-user; it can be recouped from a third side (e.g., an advertiser) on a multisided platform. These three pricing strategies can directly be linked to free versus paid apps common in contemporary mobile app stores. The free model is a usage-based license subsidized by advertising. It generates an ongoing stream of revenue for the app developer, unlike the paid model that typically generates revenue from a one-time sale.

6.3 ALIGNING GOVERNANCE

Alignment is typically between two things. Table 6.2 summarizes what each of the three dimensions of platform governance must be aligned with. All the dimensions of platform governance must be aligned with its architecture. Innovation at the app level thrives on autonomy—granted by architecture—plus incentives of app developers for risk-taking—granted through governance. The decision rights dimension must additionally be aligned with the platform's business model. The pricing dimension of governance must additionally be aligned with the platform's lifecycle stage and its business model. Platform lifecycle refers to the three dimensions described in Figure 2.1 in Chapter 2: emergence of a dominant design, diffusion among end-users, and phase along the S-curve. We will stay clear of an academic treatise of what business models mean. In this book, it is sufficient to think of the business model simply as how a platform ecosystem's participants hope to pay their bills. It is how app developers and platform owners intend to generate revenue.

6.3.1 Aligning decision rights partitioning

Aligning the distribution of decision rights in a platform ecosystem requires analyzing primarily how they fit with the ecosystem architecture and secondarily with the platform's business model. As Table 6.2 shows, decision rights need to be aligned with ecosystem architecture and with the platform's business model. Two heuristics apply to aligning decision rights with architecture: the mirroring principle and specialized knowledge.

6.3.1.1 Aligning decision rights and architecture using the mirroring principle

The gist of the mirroring principle is that organization of the development teams in a platform ecosystem must mirror its technical architecture (Baldwin and Clark, 2000, p. 47). The division of authority over decisions (decision rights) is a defining property of organizational structure (Nault, 1998).

Table 6.2 Considerations in Aligning Governance Choices			
Governance Dimension	**Architecture**	**Lifecycle**	**Business Model**
Decision rights	●		●
Control	●		
Pricing	●	●	●

The architecture of a platform ecosystem determines the structure of dependencies between the task structure of the platform owner's work and the app developers' work. The boundaries of subsystems in an ecosystem determine feasible boundaries between groups that are responsible for each of them. Properties of a platform's architecture therefore determine whether the app development work can be done by outside app developers or is better done inhouse by the platform owner. Therefore, modularization of platform architecture provides a powerful mechanism for the separation of responsibility between the platform owner and app developers. Although a modular platform architecture provides a framework for making innovation effort divisible, the organization of the ecosystem must leverage this property to benefit from modularization.

The technical architecture of an ecosystem is therefore inseparably intertwined with the organizational structure of the ecosystem that is used. Architecture of an ecosystem imposes constraints on app developers who interact with it and build their work on it. It is of little consequence to attempt to resolve the debate about where architecture precedes organization or vice versa. Architecture and decision rights partitioning must be mirror images for them to reinforce each other's potential advantages. A misalignment between the two can create a severe coordination deficit (Sosa et al., 2004). Therefore, the relationships between the platform owner and app developers ought to be analogous to the relationship between the platform and apps. The boundaries of the development teams responsible for apps and the platform therefore usually follow the boundaries between apps and the platform within an ecosystem. Boundaries of individual organizations' responsibilities must align with boundaries of apps vis-à-vis the platform. If the platform's architecture is highly interdependent (monolithic), so should the linkages between app developers and the platform owner.

SHARED VERSUS PROPRIETARY ARCHITECTURE

If the ownership of a platform is shared among multiple owners or it is based on an open standard, it represents a shared rather than a proprietary platform (which belongs to one platform owner). These multiple owners of the platform must cooperate to make any changes to the platform architecture. Such distributed ownership mitigates the hold-up risk faced by app developers but also suffers from coordination challenges. It can result in a gridlock in making platform strategic decisions that can impede the evolution of the platform as well as its ecosystem. In contrast, a single platform owner has more power over the direction of a platform. It is therefore useful to view an increase in the number of platform owners as diffusion of power related to the platform's architecture.

Thus architecture precedes how an ecosystem is organized, and how much of the innovation work is done inhouse vis-à-vis outside developers. While the initial platform designers have knowledge of the entire platform, app developers do not need the same depth of knowledge of the platform if the architecture is sufficiently modularized. Their work can proceed independently, largely in ignorance of the inner workings of the platform. Compliance with the platform's interface specifications ensures that their apps will integrate and interoperate with the platform. This allows greater specialization by app developers in the domain of their apps. Thus technical division of the ecosystem through architecture enables division of cognitive labor.

How development tasks for a platform and its apps in an ecosystem are partitioned must match how authority for them is divvied up between the platform owner and app developers. In other words, the partitioning of decision rights should mirror the technical architecture of the platform ecosystem. Modular ecosystem architectures therefore require modular partitioning of responsibilities and authority across the ecosystem. A modular organizational structure is where each organization participating in the ecosystem is the owner-operator for their subsystem—autonomous, perhaps even in competition with others within the ecosystem. A modular organizational structure in an ecosystem is therefore one where the authority for platform decisions resides primarily with the platform owner and the authority for app decisions resides primarily with individual app developers. Architectural decoupling between a platform and apps must therefore be mirrored in the division of authority and responsibility across the ecosystem. The more modular the architecture of the platform ecosystem, the more modular should the partitioning of decision rights be for the platform and apps. Modularization of decision rights therefore economizes on the limited coordination capabilities of app developers and the platform owner (Ethiraj and Levinthal, 2004a,b; Simon, 1978). By extension, the more modular the microarchitecture of an app, the more modular should the partitioning of decision rights be for that app. In contrast, the more monolithic a platform's architecture, the more centralized and concentrated should the allocation of decision rights be. Such mirroring creates synergies such that governance amplifies the benefits of modular architectures. The implementation of the mirroring principle is illustrated in Figure 6.13.

6.3.1.2 Aligning decision rights with specialized knowledge

The second criterion for aligning decision rights is to locate the authority for each class of decisions where the specialized knowledge needed to make those decisions is located (Jensen and Meckling, 1992; Macher and Boerner, 2012; Tiwana, 2009). This criterion ensures that decision rights are aligned with the platform's business model. Recall that the four types of decision rights were the *strategic* and *implementation* decisions pertaining to the platform and individual apps. Using this logic, the optimal location for each of the four classes of decision rights can be determined. Decision rights are aligned with the platform business model when each class of decision rights is located with the core knowledge needed to make that class of decisions.

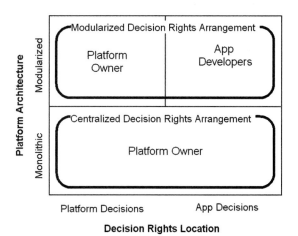

FIGURE 6.13

Using the mirroring principle to align decision rights with architecture.

Table 6.3 Aligning Platform and App Decision Rights with Ecosystem Architecture

Decision Right	Core Knowledge Needed	Complementary Knowledge Needed	Locus of Core (Complementary) Knowledge	Optimal Location
Platform: strategic	Platform's market	Some knowledge of user needs	Platform owner (app developer)	*Platform owner*, but with app developer input
Platform: implementation	Platform's technology	–	Platform owner	*Platform owner*
App: strategic	App domain user needs	–	App developer	*App developer*
App: implementation	App domain user needs	Some knowledge of platform technology	App developer (platform owner)	*App developer*, but with platform owner input

Table 6.3 summarizes the knowledge-authority co-location logic for aligning decision rights with the distribution of specialized expertise in a platform ecosystem. Consider each of the four classes of decision rights. Two classes of decisions—the platform's *implementation* decisions and an app's *strategic* decisions—are the most straightforward because they rely primarily on one specific type of core knowledge.

Platform implementation decision rights are operational decisions that pertain to the choice of features, functionality, design, and user interface of the platform (Tiwana, 2009). The core knowledge that they require is a deep understanding of the platform's technology, which is usually the platform owner's knowledge. Platform implementation decisions should therefore ideally be centralized (i.e., held by the platform owner). Centralization of platform implementation decisions also gives a platform owner architectural control over the ecosystem, which subsequently impacts the platform owner's ability to influence its evolutionary trajectory. Centralization of platform implementation decisions also potentially works well for app developers because it allows them to benefit from the scale economies generated by sharing the centrally managed commonalities in functionality that their apps might build on but that do not differentiate them in their own niche markets.

App strategic decision rights pertain to decisions about what an app should do. Recall that the value that end-users attach to a platform is often shaped by capabilities and functionality beyond those natively built into a platform. The source of such capability extension is apps. Apps require a deep understanding and in-depth knowledge of diverse user needs and application domains that might not be obvious to a platform owner but that app developers can bring to the table. These apps therefore target niche market segments of diverse sizes and structures subject to different levels of technical and business uncertainty (van Schewick, 2012, p. 134). These markets might also have different norms for compatibility across rival platforms (i.e., whether an app designed to work on one platform must also work on a rival platform) (Rysman, 2009). For example, social networking app users might expect cross-platform compatibility but instant messaging app users might not expect it. (These markets might also have widely varying norms for app microarchitectures, hence app-level modularity.)

Such sources of knowledge of users' needs in diverse, narrow application is increasingly dispersed (Dhanaraj and Parkhe, 2006). App developers are more likely than platform owners to have deep knowledge of such user needs in an app's domain. The locus of the core knowledge needed for decisions about what an app should do—app strategic decisions—is therefore app developers. Application strategic decision rights should therefore be decentralized (i.e., held by app developers). However, this is only appropriate when the platform architecture is sufficiently modularized. If the platform architecture were monolithic, app development would either have to be done by the platform owner or a combination of precise metrics and intense monitoring coupled with intense coordination between the platform owner and app developer would be needed.

As we subsequently describe in Part IV of this book, this has significant evolutionary consequences for apps. For example, decentralization of app strategic decisions gives app developers considerable control over cross-platform compatibility, business models used for revenue generation, and the power to adapt as fast as they need to. The diverse markets served by such apps can also vary significantly in how dynamic they are, often requiring different apps to adapt at different rates. Such decentralization therefore increases the prospects for individual app developers to maintain competitive differentiation, rebuff envelopment threats from the platform owner, and leverage network effects that create noncoercive lock-ins. Decentralization of app strategic decision rights also works well from the platform owner's perspective because it fosters "combinatorial" innovation around the ecosystem by mixing ideas from outside and inside its own organization.[2] Decentralization of app strategic decision rights also minimizes the burden on the platform owner for coping with the potentially large variability in evolution rates of the platform's app portfolio.

However, platform strategic decision rights and app implementation decision rights are not as straightforward to align with knowledge because they draw on a distinct core body of knowledge but also require a complementary body of knowledge that is usually not colocated with the same party in an ecosystem (Hoetker, 2005; Kapoor and Adner, 2011; Tiwana and Keil, 2007).

Consider *platform strategic decision rights*. These represent the authority for direction-setting decisions about what a platform should do. The core knowledge needed is an understanding of the platform's target markets, including an appreciation of rival platforms, industry needs, trends, and cost structures. The locus of such core knowledge is likely the platform owner. Therefore, on first glance, it makes sense to centralize platform strategic decision rights. Centralizing platform strategic decision rights also gives the platform owner the power to strategically maintain selective incompatibility that locks out rival platforms and (coercively) locks in app developers to the platform (Rysman, 2009). When the platform owner retains strategic decision rights for a platform, it also retains the power to alter the rights and privileges of app developers and set contractual obligations and rules of participation (Boudreau, 2010). This gives a platform owner the flexibility to tweak the degree of openness of the platform over time.

However, simply centralizing these decision rights with the platform owner runs the risk of overlooking a critical type of complementary knowledge that is likely to be a platform owner's weakness: deep knowledge of user needs. Recall that by definition a platform is at least two-sided. These two sides—app developers and end-users—are both users of the platforms.

---

[2]When a platform owner holds app strategic decision rights (i.e., they are centralized), the structure begins to resemble traditional software outsourcing. This is a viable decision rights structure only when the platform owner wants to dictate *what* an app developer should accomplish. It also alters the appropriate structure of control portfolios described in the next section, which must then emphasize output metrics set by the platform owner over any other control mechanism.

App developers must have some input in platform strategic decisions because they are likely to be able to contribute two distinct types of knowledge that are needed by the platform owner for making direction-setting decisions. First, app developers are likely to understand their own needs for their app development work around a platform better than the platform owner. External stakeholders such as app developers who were never in the picture in traditional organizations must therefore be given the opportunity to provide real input into platform decisions (de Weck et al., 2011, p. 19). Input from app developers allows a platform owner to appropriately evolve the interfaces to its platform to better meet app developers' evolving needs, while simultaneously protecting and selectively disclosing intellectual property that is core to the platform. By itself, control over the architecture of a platform gained by centralizing platform implementation decision rights does not guarantee that the platform will be able to sustain a win–win, pie-expanding proposition with app developers. A platform will survive only if it helps everyone in its ecosystem do better with it than without it. In order for a platform to thrive, platform owners must not only attract but also retain app developers. A platform owner must therefore continue to contribute unique capabilities valued by app developers that compare favorably with rival platforms, and capabilities that have no direct substitutes. Allowing app developers to have input in platform strategic decisions therefore enables a platform owner to remain sensitized to their emerging needs while also delivering the necessary economies of scale in the functionality shared by their apps.

Second, app developers are also likely to be closer to the pulse of emerging end-user needs from their specialized market segments of their own apps. End-user expectations of tomorrow's mass market end-users often stem from today's leading-edge user needs (Von Hippel, 1986). App developers are more likely to be better tuned to the emerging needs of such leading-edge users, who are typically found in niche segments of the broader end-user communities. In contrast, the platform owner's knowledge of end-user needs is likely to be more mass-market-oriented. Therefore platform strategic decision rights should lean toward centralization with platform owners but with app developers' inputs. In other words, they are optimally placed toward the centralization side of the scale but away from extreme centralization. This is illustrated in the range of possible placements for this class of decision rights in Figure 6.14. Where precisely within this range they are placed depends on the modularity of a platform's architecture. (When a platform owner holds app strategic decision rights, the platform model begins to resemble a traditional outsourcing arrangement.)

Finally, *app implementation decision rights* represent how app developers execute and realize app strategic decisions. The first core knowledge needed for app implementation decisions is likely to be with

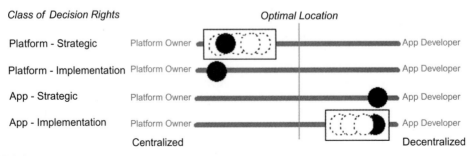

FIGURE 6.14

Optimal decision rights partitioning in modularized platform ecosystems.

app developers. The first advantage of greater decentralization of app implementation decision rights is that it places the authority over app implementation decisions where the core knowledge to make such decisions resides. Second, it frees an app's developer to upgrade and evolve an app unconstrained by the platform. Provided an app developer sufficiently modularizes an app's microarchitecture, this reinforces the potential advantage of the flexibility provided by architectural encapsulation (wherein the app displays no hidden internal details beyond its visible information to the rest of the ecosystem). A third advantage is that control over app implementation decisions provides an app developer the option to multi-home (i.e., to potentially make the app portable across multiple competing platforms). Portability means that an app can be readily executed on a different platform from the one for which it was initially designed. For example, an app such as Skype can readily be run on iOS, Android, or Blackberry OS. Portability is attractive to app developers and end-users, but not usually to platform owners.

However, simply decentralizing these decision rights with app developers runs the risk of overlooking a critical type of complementary knowledge that is likely to be app developers' weakness. Implementation of apps requires some knowledge of the platform technologies, especially to ensure that an app leverages the unique capabilities of a platform when appropriate, and to ensure interoperability with the platform. Therefore, such decisions should lean toward decentralization with app developers but with some input from platform owners. In other words, they are optimally placed toward the decentralization side of the scale but away from extreme decentralization. This is illustrated in the range of possible placements for this class of decision rights in Figure 6.14. Where precisely within this range they are placed depends on the modularity of an app's microarchitecture and how the four functional elements of the app are distributed across client- and server-side devices. The decision rights partition framework leaves unaddressed the question of who—platform owner or app developer—actually controls the relationship with an individual app's end-user. The answer depends on the microarchitecture for an individual app chosen by the app developer.

Figure 6.14 summarizes the resulting optimal pattern of decision rights partitioning in a modularized platform ecosystem. The more modular the platform's architecture, the more centralized should platform decisions be and the more decentralized should app decisions be. However, platform strategic decision rights can be anywhere in a range of levels leaning toward centralization but with some app developer say in them. However, app implementation decision rights can be anywhere in a range of levels leaning toward decentralization but with some platform owner say in them.

6.3.2 Aligning control portfolios
6.3.2.1 *The dual purpose of control in platforms*
The purpose of control mechanisms in an ecosystem is twofold: creating convergent goals and ensuring coordination between the platform owner and app developers.

Creating convergent goals. The first purpose of platform control is to ensure that the work of app developers furthers the interests and objectives of the platform. At the very least, it must not hinder them. App developers and platform owners are usually independent organizations that are likely to pursue their own self-interest, even if it is at the expense of the other party (Eisenhardt, 1989). Goal convergence can partially be accomplished by careful platform pricing choices that align the goals of app developers and platform owners. For example, pricing structures that split revenues create a shared fate that can bind together the interests of platform owners and app developers. But revenue-sharing models are not always viable in platforms (e.g., in open-source, nonprofit platforms). An alternative way to create convergent goals is through relational controls that rely on a shared sense of purpose, norms, and values that bind together the interests of a platform owner and app developers. Control mechanisms must also vet and weed out apps that are potentially damaging to the ecosystem. These can include outright malicious apps intended to harm the platform's end-users or apps that are designed to compromise or circumvent a platform's business model and rules.

Facilitating coordination. The second purpose of platform control is to facilitate coordination between the platform owner and app developers, primarily ensuring integration between the platform and apps. The potential power of platform ecosystems comes from leveraging the unique expertise of many, diverse independent app developers on a scale irreplicable within a single organization. However, this diversity can also be the root of utter chaos. Apps must seamlessly interoperate and integrate with the platform to ensure a cohesive platform ecosystem. This property—composability—is the degree to which an app can be readily integrated with the platform. After all, ecosystem-level innovation does not arise from the mere gathering—but from new *combinations*—of many app developers' capabilities (Dhanaraj and Parkhe, 2006).

We have already described two strategies in platforms that help facilitate such coordination: (1) an appropriate choice of architecture by the platform owner and app developers and (2) mirroring decision rights partitioning and architecture. However, even these two devices taken together leave one hole in ensuring coordination across the ecosystem, which a control portfolio must plug: variance in interface standards compliance. The implicit coordination capability of architecture works only if every developer is following agreed-upon standards for connecting their apps to the platform. Compliance by app developers to a modularized platform's interface specifications ensures integration of apps with the platform.

The challenge comes from variance in the extent to which different app developers comply with the interface standards. A roadblock in ensuring systems integration is the *repeated* need to ensure it. Different apps often evolve at different rates, and often evolve faster than the platform does. So, the need for ensuring seamless integration of apps with the platform is hardly a predictable, one-shot activity but rather an ongoing one. As an app evolves, it must maintain interoperability across each iterative release. Therefore, it is useful to think in terms of systems *re*integration rather than one-shot systems integration between a platform and apps. Mirroring modularized architecture with modularized decision rights does not eliminate the need for integration processes.

Paradoxically, this means that modular ecosystems organized around modular architectures require monolithic—not modular—*integration* processes (Brusoni and Prencipe, 2006). This is illustrated in Figure 6.15. By integration processes here we are referring to the processes used to integrate the outputs of app developers' work, not how they develop apps. (The latter are app implementation decision rights.) This ensures that app developers can be locally optimizing but globally aware. Freedom in app developers' work must therefore be coupled with strict specifications of contributions, expectations of performance, and appropriate rewards and penalties. This requires some degree of formal control by the platform owner over app developers. Control mechanisms can help address this challenge by ensuring better compliance to a platform's interface specifications and design rules.

This brings us back to the Goldilocks principle: Platform owners must get the control portfolio *just* right. The challenge for platform owners is to manage the delicate tension between developer autonomy and ecosystem-wide integration. Control portfolios must simultaneously support the entrepreneurially oriented independence of app developers and seamless integration of their output into the platform's ecosystem. Too much control can stifle innovation by app developers. Too little control can compromise ecosystem-wide coherence (Boudreau, 2010). Granting access by opening a platform

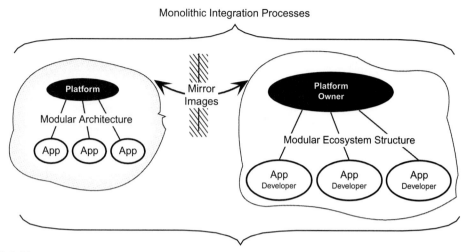

Monolithic Integration Processes

FIGURE 6.15

Modular ecosystems organized around modular architectures still require monolithic integration processes.

therefore does not entail giving up control. In going overboard with giving up control, a platform owner can position itself out of the ecosystem altogether. (Think of IBM and the PC business that it literally created.) A 16-year study of platforms found evidence that giving up control did not increase innovation in platforms beyond an incrementally trivial level; instead it put them on a devolving path to failure (Boudreau, 2010). Therefore, a platform ecosystem that thrives will neither be like a democracy nor a centrally planned regime. Instead, it must be like a benevolent dictatorship (Tiwana et al., 2010).

6.3.2.2 Rules of thumb for designing a platform control portfolio

Platform-based businesses represent a shift from closed innovation models to open innovation models. The closed innovation model—the mainstay of traditional organizations—was based on the philosophy that *innovation requires control*: Companies generated their own ideas, developed and implemented them, and then took them to market. Self-reliance was the prized virtue, and the key task of managers was to screen out bad ideas. This model dominated most of the past century. This internally focused approach to innovation is increasingly becoming obsolete as traditional organizational structures are being supplanted or altogether replaced by distributed innovation networks such as platform ecosystems. The platform model is based on the philosophy that *innovation requires giving up some control*. Five rules of thumb should guide the design of a platform's control portfolio to accomplish these goals.

1. *Simple.* The first rule of thumb is that a control portfolio should be as simple as possible in its structure. Simply put, less is more. Controls impose costs on the platform owner who must design, implement, and most importantly enforce control mechanisms (Anderson and Dekker, 2005). These costs must be commensurate with their realized benefits. A control mechanism that cannot be reliably enforced is likely to deliver little benefit but will nevertheless impose costs. Controls

also impose compliance costs on app developers. These costs are not only direct financial costs but also indirect costs such as discouraging frequent releases of apps. This can slow down—even cripple—the evolution of individual apps, create a destructive pattern of missed windows of opportunity, and increase time lag between updates. Such costs are borne immediately by app developers, but their damage to the vibrancy of a platform can easily exceed the damage they can do to individual app developers. Rapid iterative refinement is usually critical in highly competitive app market segments. If controls stymie the speed of such refinements in apps, they can amplify the destructive power of the Red Queen effect that we discussed in Chapter 2. A useful heuristic is therefore to structure a control portfolio that is least costly for both app developers and for the platform owner. Remember that architecture itself is a form of control. By defining the architectural rules for app developers, a platform owner invokes a source of real power in a platform ecosystem (Meadows, 2008, p. 158). Control though architecture can substitute for many of the costlier, overt control mechanisms. But overt control is effective only in extreme moderation. Therefore, the minimal subset that gets the job done (i.e., ensures that the app developers are working in the best interests of the platform and ensures easy integration of their work into the ecosystem) is optimal. Instead of asking themselves how much of each control mechanism to use, it is more fruitful to ask the question of whether a specific control mechanism is even necessary. If it is, can it be realized in practice? Can it be enforced? If a control mechanism is absolutely necessary, it is the platform owner's responsibility of minimizing the cost imposed by it on app developers.

2. *Transparent.* The second rule of thumb is that a control portfolio should be transparent to app developers. Compliance with a set of controls imposed by the platform owner is more likely to happen if app developers clearly understand precisely how their work will be evaluated. Ambiguity about this (as was the case with Apple's iOS) can make compliance so cryptic that it can discourage existing app developers from sticking with a platform and dissuade new app developers from joining the platform. To have high transparency, a platform owner can take two steps. First, be explicit about expectations and how performance on specific criteria related to how those expectations will be measured. Second, make the process of evaluation on such criteria visible to app developers.

3. *Realistic.* The third rule of thumb is that a control portfolio should be based on a good understanding of how the app developers' work is done. The platform owner must therefore consider whether each control mechanism chosen for the control portfolio is a realistic reflection of app developers' day-to-day routines and practices. To the extent possible, a platform owner must seek to establish guidelines—not rulebooks—for app developers and also make a few nonnegotiable principles explicit.

4. *Shared values.* The fourth rule of thumb is that a control portfolio must conform to the platform owner's philosophy about the platform. This philosophy is effective only if it is also shared by other members of the ecosystem, particularly app developers. A well-designed control portfolio should reinforce this philosophy and at the very minimum not contradict it. (An important control mechanism that can promulgate shared values, norms, and a shared culture among app developers and the platform owner is relational control.)

5. *Fair.* The final rule of thumb is that a control portfolio should be fair. This means that it should be consistently applied to all app developers, it should have no contradicting rules, and must be fairly applied and interpreted by the platform owner. Fairness also includes fairness to the

platform's other sides such as the end-users. An important role that controls must therefore also serve effectively is to prevent members of either side to take unfair advantage of the other (Evans and Schmalensee, 2007, p. 35).

6.3.2.3 *Aligning individual control mechanism choices*

Platform owners must ask three questions to pick which of the four control mechanisms to deploy and to what degree:

1. Is it needed? If not, skip it.
2. Whether something else can substitute for it? If yes, use the substitute instead.
3. Is it viable? Viability requires that the preconditions in Table 6.1 for using it are met. If not, skip it.

The forthcoming logic is summarized in Table 6.4.

Table 6.4 Evaluating Individual Control Mechanisms for Inclusion and Exclusion

Control Mechanism	Needed?	Substitute?	Viable if...
Gatekeeping	When creating performance metrics or monitoring processes is not possible	None; but prescreening app developers helps	• App developers accept a platform owner's authority to play gatekeeper • Compliance criteria are known and considered fair by app developers • Platform owner can cost-effectively verify compliance
Process	Not needed if performance metrics are used	• Gatekeeping • Use of metrics-based control • Allocation of app implementation decision rights to app developers	• Platform owner has credible expertise to dictate methods • Platform owner can verify process compliance by app developers
Metrics	Not needed if app developers retain app strategic decision rights	• Use of process control • If market determines winners and losers among app developers	Metrics are objectively measurable
Relational	• Fills gaps left by formal controls • Lower cost than formal controls	None, but prescreening app developers helps	• App developer churn is low • App developers and platform owners are bound by clan-like shared values

6.3.2.4 Aligning gatekeeping with platform architecture

Gatekeeping is required when a platform owner can neither reliably use predefined performance metrics nor cost-effectively impose or monitor process compliance by app developers. Both of these challenges often exist in platforms, leaving platform owners with no good substitutes for gatekeeping. But gatekeeping requires that criteria for their app being allowed into the platform ecosystem is explicitly known and considered fair by app developers and that the platform owner can cost-effectively verify compliance. The more visible—but less important—role of gatekeeping is to keep ill-intentioned apps out. The more important role of gatekeeping is to ensure the integrity of apps and their compliance with the design rules, constraints, and interface standards to proactively ensure interoperability with the platform. Recall that modularization of platform architecture facilitates app integration with the platform only if individual apps comply with the platform's interface specifications and design rules. Therefore, the primary purpose of gatekeeping is ensuring app developer compliance.

However, testing costs are the Achilles heel of modular architectures (Baldwin and Clark, 2000, p. 272). Gatekeeping can become very costly and time-consuming for a platform owner as the frequency of updates to individual apps increases and the size of the app developer pool grows. Over time, this can become enough of a bottleneck that a platform can fall behind in the competitive race against rival platforms. Therefore, a platform owner has a strong incentive to invest in tools and mechanisms that lower app developers' costs and its own costs of verifying compliance of apps with the platform's design rules and conformity with its critical interface specifications. Developer toolkits, reference models, integrated development environments, and app testing tools are examples of such tools (Evans et al., 2006, p. 413; Parker and Van Alstyne, 2005). Two additional ways to reduce gatekeeping costs upfront include (1) prescreening who is allowed to join the platform (a form of relational control) and (2) being clear about constraints on what apps are *not* allowed to do. An example of the latter is Apple's prohibition on apps duplicating the native functionality of the iOS platform. In summary, gatekeeping has almost no direct substitutes and is essential for fully extracting value out of modular designs.

6.3.2.5 Aligning process control with platform architecture

Process control is required when the platform owner either (a) cannot prespecify objective metrics to evaluate app developers' outputs or (2) has a better understanding than app developers of how to successfully develop apps. The first condition is often met in platform settings but the second one holds true only occasionally. The platform owner can rarely dictate to the developers how to do their day-to-day app development work because it lacks the legitimate authority to issue commands and independent app developers are not obligated to obey (Dhanaraj and Parkhe, 2006). Nor can it inexpensively monitor or micromanage how app developers do their own development work. Decentralization of app implementation decision rights to app developers also contradicts the use of process control because it translates into granting autonomy to app developers for how to implement their apps.

However, a platform owner often *can* credibly prescribe development and testing procedures that will ensure app interoperability with its platform. Modular platform interfaces themselves provide some app integration mechanisms that reduce the need for ongoing coordination between a platform owner and app developers. Furthermore, use of gatekeeping by the platform owner also reduces the need for extensive process control. This leaves only one potential use for process control: to help app developers pass gatekeeping checks. Therefore, *some* process control can increase the value of extensive gatekeeping in ensuring apps' compliance with a platform's interface specifications and design rules.

A platform owner can invest in four things to facilitate such compliance using noncoercive, facilitative process control:

- *Programming resources.* Examples of such resources include documentation such as technical specification, manuals, programmers' guides, and programming tools used to write apps. Apple's investments in such resources for its iOS developers have paid back handsomely (Burrows, 2011).
- *Integrated development environments* (IDEs), software development toolkits (SDKs), and reference models are other common ways for platform owners to assist app developers with compliance to a platform's interfaces (Evans et al., 2006, p. 79; Parker and Van Alstyne, 2005). They automate rote tasks such as tracking changes, managing source code versions, and testing of apps using simulators. Providing such tools can help improve app developer productivity and better manage complexity associated with developing for a platform. The platform owner should rarely charge for such app developer tools. The focus should be on enabling everyday development processes and helping improve app developer productivity. The objective is to reduce the cost and effort incurred by app developers in developing around the platform.
- *Mock-up and prototyping tools.* These are tools that allow app developers to inexpensively create prototypes of what a finished app would look like before having to implement it in code. The purpose of such tools is what Michael Schrage (2000, p. 126) calls demand articulation: End-users cannot readily tell app developers what app features that they need but recognize them when they see them. This allows app developers to quickly refine app design concepts before they make irreversible investments in implementing apps that eventually turn out to be duds. A platform owner providing such tools also reinforces the decentralization of app strategic decision rights to app developers in modularized platform ecosystems. This subsequently has much larger payoffs in a platform's evolution and survival in Red Queen competition against rival platforms.
- *Integration protocols and testing standards.* These are procedures that allow the app developers to proactively assess how well an app conforms to a platform's rules and interface specifications (Baldwin and Clark, 2000, p. 77). The earlier in the app development process an app developer can test standalone apps for compliance, the cheaper it will be to fix potential problems (Hibbs et al., 2009).

6.3.2.6 Aligning metrics-based control with platform architecture

Control via metrics is rarely required in platform ecosystems for two reasons. First, when app strategic decision rights are decentralized, app developers—rather than platform owners—set most criteria and metrics for judging the performance of their apps. However, metrics-based control requires platform owners to set predetermined metrics for evaluating the app developers' performance. Objective measurement of app developers' performance using metrics, even if possible, is meaningless when the platform owner does not set them. (Recall from Section 6.3.2.3 that this information-intensive, costly control mechanism is a legacy from the traditional software development model.) Second, competitive markets determine winners and losers among apps in platform ecosystems. End-user markets therefore provide high-powered incentives for app developers to create apps that do well in the marketplace. These incentives, coupled with their own investments in their apps, suffice to motivate app developers to use their distinctive capabilities and to leverage their unique expertise to ensure that their apps compete well in meeting the needs of their end-users. Third, process control and metrics-based control do not mix well (Tiwana and Keil, 2007). If process control is used by a platform owner—as is often done in platform ecosystems—it provides a direct substitute for metrics-driven control. Therefore, control via metrics is rarely needed[3] or viable, and often has less costly substitutes in modular[4] platform markets. Only a small set of objective performance metrics such as sales or usage is sufficient to implement the revenue-sharing agreement between the platform owner and individual app developers.

6.3.2.7 Aligning relational control with platform architecture

Relational control fills gaps left by formal controls, especially in dealing with outside-the-contract situations not covered by the formal agreements between the platform owner and an app developer (Bernheim and Whinston, 1998; Tadelis, 2002). Relational control is among the least costly control mechanisms. However, it is difficult to implement right off the bat because shared values, norms of behavior, peer pressure, and the shared mindset among the app developer community—especially a globally distributed one with markedly different values and norms—that it relies on take time to emerge. The app developer community must also be stable enough over time for it to be viable. Platforms often have developer churn, with new developers lacking the shared history of existing developers. The potential diversity of app developers, the churn in membership, and the youth of the platform can therefore decrease the viability of relational control.

Relational control will therefore rarely suffice by itself but can be a useful complement to the other formal control mechanisms. The platform owner can help foster a clan-like culture by promulgating a sense of shared values, norms, sense of purpose, and mindset among its developer community by (1) setting examples through its own actions (e.g., fairness, impartiality, design ethos), (2) reinforcing a common identity among members of the ecosystem (Dhanaraj and Parkhe, 2006), and (3) organizing socialization opportunities among its app developers (e.g., developer conferences). Prescreening who is allowed to join the app developer community is another way to accelerate the development of shared norms. Prescreening might use criteria such as prior history of the developer on other platforms to ensure that members of the app developer community meaningfully complement the platform owner's own capabilities.

The litmus test for an ideal control portfolio is one that is simple, transparent, fair, and realistic. The ideal mix of controls is to use one formal control mechanism as a dominant form of control and supplement it with relational control if possible. When relational control is not viable, use gatekeeping with either process control or metrics-based control.

6.3.3 Aligning platform pricing policies

Pricing decisions by platform owners are key to creating incentives that can encourage a critical mass of app developers to create platform complements that can keep a platform ahead of rival platforms in Red Queen competition. The five pricing decisions in platforms must be aligned with the architecture, platform lifecycle stage, and the platform's business model, as summarized in Table 6.5.

---

[3]The only rare exception is when app strategic decision rights are centralized (i.e., the platform owner rather than app developer makes direction-setting decisions for an app). In this case, the platform model begins to resemble a traditional outsourcing arrangement where metrics-based control should largely replace process control and gatekeeping.

[4]In contrast, if the platform architecture were monolithic and output metrics were unavailable, development of the app would have to be done by the platform owner.

Table 6.5 Considerations in Aligning Pricing Policies

Pricing Decision	Business Model	Lifecycle	Architecture
Symmetry	●	●	
Subsidy-side	●	●	
Access/usage fees		●	●
Sliding scale?	●	●	●
App pricing model			●

6.3.3.1 Aligning the pricing symmetry decision

The first criterion in deciding whether to price the two sides asymmetrically is the platform's business model. If a platform is two-sided *from the beginning*, getting both sides on board is critical to getting it off the ground. Recall that most successful multisided platforms started out as one-sided services that added a second side only after a critical mass of adopters was on board on the first side. For example, Dropbox, the popular file-sharing service, added app developers (the second side) only after it had a large end-user base (the first side; initially the only side).

In two-sided platforms, one side is often the loss leader and the other side is the profit center. Money lost on the money-losing side is usually made up on the money-making side. Only in rare cases do platforms make money on both sides; this is often when it starts off as a dominant early mover that started out as a successful product (e.g., iPhone) or service (e.g., Dropbox and YouTube) with a lot of adopters. Platform pricing therefore often must be asymmetric such that either the app developers *or* the end-users are the side that pays a lot less than the other side.

A second consideration is whether the platform's business model depends on cross-side network effects for its success. If so, asymmetric pricing can accelerate the creation of cross-side network effects in the early stages of its lifecycle; if enough subsidy-side users are attracted to a platform, the money-side users will pay a premium to reach them (Eisenmann et al., 2006). An example of this is Amazon's Kindle platform. Amazon subsidized end-users (by selling devices based on the platform at a loss) to create a large potential reader base. This attracted major book publishers to the Kindle platform, jumpstarting cross-side network effects. The initial subsidies can then be reduced, possibly even eliminated. This approach, however, can fall flat if there are no early-mover advantages in the platform's market.

Being a first mover to sell in a product or service category does not necessarily guarantee success. A first mover can be riddled by an underdeveloped or immature pipeline of adopters on the subsidized side and unclear market requirements, which can make being an *early follower* a more attractive proposition for entering a potential platform market. The ability to create switching costs[5] among the subsidized-side adopters, exploiting scale and increasing returns advantages and possibly network effects is necessary for first-mover advantage to be plausible. Dropbox is an example of a platform

---

[5]Switching costs arise when the initial investment in complementary products such as purchased apps, going up the learning curve for a platform, and the whole hassle of replicating her setup on a rival platform can discourage the subsidized-side user from leaving the platform for another one. Learning costs and familiarity with the QWERTY keyboard, for example, kept users from switching to a technically superior Dvorak keyboard. The same logic often applies in platforms.

that inspired many copycats attempting to replicate its offering. Such copycats who enter the market after the product or service has begun to penetrate the mass market are known as late entrants. They were able to replicate Dropbox's offering but were unable to overcome the strong same-side network effects that Dropbox had used to create a first-mover advantage.

6.3.3.2 Aligning the choice and duration of the subsidized side

If a platform owner decides to subsidize one side, which one should it be and for how long? The first criterion in deciding which side to subsidize is the platform's business model, particularly if it depends on cross-side network effects. The trick is to subsidize the more price-sensitive side and charge the side whose demand increases more strongly with growth on the subsidized side. A platform owner should charge the lowest prices to the side it needs most to get cross-side network effects started. Put another way, charge more to the side that derives more value from the presence of the other side. Even if a platform owner makes a loss on one side, it can recoup the losses from the other side provided the demand on the other side is sufficiently strong.

Consider two examples. Adobe's portable document format (PDF) did not catch on until Adobe priced the PDF reader at zero. Subsidizing end-users substantially increased sales of PDF writers, from which Adobe earned all of its revenues. Now, think of a trade press magazine as another example. If readers of a magazine value the number of ads less than advertisers value the number of readers, then magazine publishers should do better to subsidize readers relative to the advertisers (Armstrong and Wright, 2007). This approach works well for many trade magazines that are free to readers but that charge hefty fees to advertisers. Therefore, as a general rule, use prices that lead to zero (or negative profits) from the side that is more valuable to the other and has greater ambiguity about the value they will derive from adopting the platform (Evans and Schmalensee, 2007, p. 84). However, such subsidies are needed only until critical mass is achieved by a platform on both sides. Achieving critical mass triggers a self-reinforcing bandwagon effect because the value of a platform to either side increases approximately proportional to the square of the number of users (Rohfls, 2003, p. 55). Subsidies can be reduced after critical mass is reached, although it is unadvisable to completely eliminate them.

The question for platform owners to ask themselves is whether app developers value access to end-users more, or end-users value apps more. Will subsidizing app developers increase end-user demand for the platform by increasing the number of apps they can use, particularly in comparison to rival platforms? If so, subsidize the app-developer side. This is the case with many smartphone platforms. In such markets, availability and variety of apps is decisive in end-user platform choice. Superstar apps and so-called killer apps that end-users value highly can have a disproportionately large effect on end-user platform adoption; their developers are often prime candidates for subsidies. Conversely, will subsidizing end-users increase the demand from app developers by increasing the prospective pool of willing buyers of their apps for that platform? If so, subsidize the end-user side. This is the case with many gaming console platforms. The same logic can be used by app developers when an app attempts to grow into a nested, mini platform (see Chapter 11).

The second criterion is the platform's stage in its lifecycle. Two considerations enter this decision: (1) whether a platform is in its pre- or post-dominant design stage and (2) its diffusion among end-users. In the pre-dominant design phase, app developers are usually stronger candidates for subsidizing because a winning industry-wide design is yet to emerge. At this stage, the platform's market can be a winner-takes-all kind of competition. Therefore, rapid adoption of a platform by app developers can boost the rate of innovation, increase end-users' perceptions of its usefulness, and accelerate its mass adoption. Together, this can increase the likelihood of a platform becoming *the* dominant design that rivals will eventually be forced to follow. Negative pricing can therefore become optimal when a platform owner's viability (and profits) are contingent on promoting network effects (Parker and Van Alstyne, 2005). Second, same-side network effects are difficult to initiate in the early stages of diffusion among end-users but are self-reinforcing once they take off. Having app developers on board shapes end-users' expectations about the platform's future; such expectations heavily influence their present adoption decisions (Rysman, 2009). A useful metric for tracking progress in diffusion among end-users is a platform's installed base (Rochet and Tirole, 2003). Real-time information about this metric can readily be collected in ubiquitously networked software-based platforms. Subsidies might be reducible for the subsidized side once a platform reaches the early-majority stage in its diffusion among end-users.

6.3.3.3 *Aligning usage and access pricing*

The first criterion in deciding whether to charge access and usage fees is the platform's stage in its lifecycle. A platform owner can theoretically charge all sides (e.g., app developers, end-users, advertisers) platform access fees (typically fixed upfront fees) and usage fees (typically variable fees), or both (Hagui, 2006). Or platform owners can choose to charge neither to two of their sides (e.g., app developers and end-users) and instead make up for the loss from a third side (e.g., advertisers). The correct choice of access and usage policies and fees depends on the platform's business model, its industry, and the norms among direct and indirect rivals. Indirect rivals can be particularly tricky to recognize for platforms and apps that are attempting to create new "blue ocean" markets. For example, iOS's competitors were dumb phones and Blackberries but Android OS's competitor was iOS. Similarly, Dropbox's competition was the inexpensive USB thumb drive, not other file-sharing services. Therefore, the choice of the primary fee model is one that does not have easy answers. However, two general rules usually should be followed. As a first general rule, platform owners must keep access fees low to encourage prospective adopters on all sides to try the platform. But access fees for the subsidized side should *not* be zero for an established platform but can be zero or negative in fledgling platforms. Willingness to pay a token access fee can be just enough to signal credible commitment and seriousness from app developers. Apple, for example, charges its iOS app developers a token $99 annual fee for access to the platform. For fledgling platforms yet to attract a critical mass of app developers, access fees can even be negative. Blackberry, for example, guaranteed to underwrite a minimum revenue for $10,000 for new apps on its BBOS 10 platform, effectively *paying* app developers to join. Poor pricing decisions about access fees for upstart platforms can keep them from building the right mix or critical mass of participants from one or both sides, leading to failure even before they've had a chance to take off. As a second general rule, a platform should charge either access fees or usage fees to individual sides, but not both. However, access and usage fees can be mixed within a platform but not on the same side of the platform.[6]

---

[6]For example, it is possible for a platform to charge access fees to app developers, nothing to end-users, and usage fees to advertisers.

The second alignment criterion is app microarchitecture. A platform owner should charge usage fees to at least one side—either end-users or app developers—if (1) an app's microarchitecture *heavily* uses native services of the platform and (2) such services lack scalability. This permits recouping expenses from the usage of apps that hog platform resources and scale-limited services. But this imposes a considerable overhead of metering usage by individual apps on the platform owner.[7] However, having to resort to such pricing policies is often symptomatic of two larger problems. First, it might be a red flag that the platform's architecture itself lacks sufficient scalability, often a sign of larger looming problems as the platform grows. Second, app microarchitecture is a decision largely made by app developers but it is heavily influenced by platform architecture. Having to charge fees for platform services could *potentially* signify weaknesses in modularization of the platform's architecture.

6.3.3.4 Aligning the pie-splitting scale choice?

The first criterion in deciding how to split the revenue pie with app developers is the platform's business model. To remain attractive, a platform must allow app developers to profit sufficiently from their work (Gawer and Cusumano, 2008). Pie-splitting choices by a platform signal are also an important credible signal to app developers that a platform owner will not abuse its power and that they share a common destiny. Although fixed scales are most common in contemporary platforms (e.g., Apple splits revenues using a 30–70% fixed scale), moving scales can serve a useful role in various stages of a platform's lifecycle. A rising scale model is fairly common for author royalties in the traditional book publishing industry. If used in a platform ecosystem, rising scales create stronger rewards for apps that perform better in the marketplace. This can create strong incentives for app developers to study their own niche markets more intensively, invest in understanding user needs more closely, and evolve their apps. When app developers maintain presence on more than one rival platform and when platform owners cannot dissuade or restrict such multihoming, rising scales can also encourage them to invest more heavily in developing their app for that platform. This subtle strategy to deter multihoming is known as *steering* (Rochet and Tirole, 2003).

The platform's lifecycle stage provides a second criterion for aligning pie-splitting choices. The earlier a platform is in its lifecycle, the more intense is the competition for app developers. Incentives matter even more in such early stages because app developers are potentially more mobile and can move to a competing platform. The vibrancy of a platform ecosystem then critically hinges on attracting new app developers and retaining existing ones. By using a rising scale in a platform's early lifecycle stages, a platform owner can offer stronger incentives than rivals to app developers. In the long run, app developers are more likely to opt for a smaller piece of a bigger pie than a smaller pie.

Architecture provides a third criterion for aligning pie-splitting choices. If an app intensively uses the platform's native services in its microarchitecture and the platform has scalability limitations (or scaling is costly for the platform owner), a sliding scale is a viable option. Platform owners should generally refrain from using sliding scales.

---

[7]An alternative is to insist that app developers use multi-tiered app microarchitecture as an alternative capacity scaling strategy.

6.3.3.5 Decision 5: app licensing decisions

The choice of perpetual, subscription-based, or usage-based licensing by an app developer for an app largely depends on the *app developer's* business model. A platform's architecture and portfolio of software services, however, can constrain viable business models that app developers can implement. For example, integration of advertising services into iOS and Android platforms makes it more viable for an app developer to create advertising-supported apps rather than being limited to revenue-generating apps. Furthermore, app microarchitectures play a direct role in how easy it is to create variants of a single app. These variants are often priced differently. This strategy (called app *versioning*) means different customers pay different prices for more or less capable variants of an app. However, the possible choices of app microarchitecture available to app developers are also constrained by platform architecture. Therefore, the connection between app licensing and platform architectures is at best indirect. The app licensing decision has consequences for versioning of apps by app developers. We describe in detail several strategies for versioning in our discussion of app evolution in Part IV.

Table 6.6 summarizes the foregoing discussion of how each of the five pricing choices can be better aligned with a platform's business model, its lifecycle, and its architecture.

Platform governance decisions by platform owners impact several of the ecosystem evolution principles over the life of a platform. Table 6.7 provides a preview of these. The next section explains these ideas in depth.

Table 6.6 Summary of Considerations in Aligning Platform Pricing

Pricing Decision	Business Model	Lifecycle	Architecture
Pricing symmetry?	Asymmetric if two-sided from outset and dependent on cross-side network effects	Asymmetric if first mover advantage can be secured through network effects or switching costs	–
Subsidized-side?	• If one side values the other more • "Superstar" apps	• Dominant design emerged? • Diffusion among end-users?	–
Access fees?	• Generally avoid • Token access fee from app developers to signal credible commitment	Negative or zero access in early but nonzero in later lifecycle stages	Usage fees for native services-intensive app microarchitectures
Moving pie-splitting scale?	Rising scale if app developers multihome rival platforms	Rising scale if intense cross-platform rivalry	Sliding scale if low platform scalability
App pricing model?	–	–	Viable app licensing models are constrained by platform architecture

Table 6.7 Consequences of Governance Choices in Platform Ecosystems

Principle Affected	Governance Dimension		
	Decision Rights	**Control**	**Pricing**
Red Queen effect	●	◗	◗
Chicken-or-egg problem			●
Penguin problem			●
Emergence	●	●	
Seesaw problem		●	
Humpty Dumpty problem		●	
Mirroring principle	●		
Coevolution	●	●	
Goldilocks rule			●

CHAPTER SUMMARY

- *Governance is how a platform owner influences its ecosystem.* App developers are not soldiers in an army but rather like musicians in a symphony. The role of governance is to coherently orchestrate the integration of their unique contributions into a platform's ecosystem. Good platform governance must respect app developers' autonomy while ensuring ecosystem-wide integration.
- *Governance complements architecture.* Platform governance determines whether thoughtful architecture pays off. The two must be aligned.
- *Governance has three dimensions.* These are (1) who decides what (decision rights), (2) how a platform owner controls app developers (control mechanisms), and (3) pricing policies.
- *Governance must aspire to be simple and cheap.* The optimal governance structure is the simplest one that achieves the goals of a platform at the least cost.
- *Decision rights are division of authority among a platform owner and app developers.* The authority and responsibility for four classes of decisions can be split any way between a platform owner and app developers: strategic and implementation decisions about the platform, and strategic and implementation decisions about individual apps. Strategic decisions are decisions about what it should do and implementation decisions are about how it should do it. Centralization and decentralization of decision rights refer to whether they lean toward the platform owner or app developers.
- *Control is how a platform owner creates goal convergence and facilitates coordination with app developers.* A portfolio of control mechanisms used by a platform owner can mix-and-match different levels of formal (gatekeeping, metrics, and process control) and informal (relational) control mechanisms.
- *Pricing policies involve five decisions.* These involve decisions about whether app developers or end-users are subsidized by the other side, for how long, whether a platform owner charges access or usage fees, the pie-splitting structure, and app licensing choices.

- *Aligning decision rights follows the mirroring principle.* The partitioning of decision rights among a platform owner and app developers must mirror the platform's architecture. Decentralization of design in platform architecture must therefore be mirrored in the decentralization of authority. It must also be aligned with who has the knowledge to make each class of decisions. The optimal structure requires some sharing of decision rights between a platform owner and app developers.
- *Control complements decision rights.* Modular ecosystems organized around modular architectures require monolithic integration processes, which a platform's control mechanisms provide.
- *Aligning a control portfolio uses five simple rules.* It should be simple, transparent, realistic, reflect shared values, and fair.
- *Platform pricing policies.* Pricing policies must be aligned with the platform's business model, its stage in its lifecycle, and its architecture.

Chapters in the next section delve into the evolution of ecosystems, platforms, and apps.

Dynamics and Metrics of Ecosystem Evolution

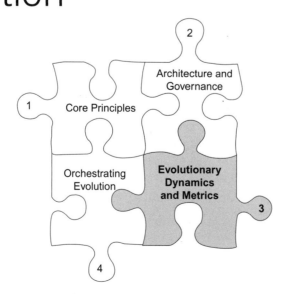

III

Architecture and Governance

2

1 Core Principles

Orchestrating Evolution

Evolutionary Dynamics and Metrics

3

4

Metrics of Evolution

If you don't know where you are going, any road will get you there.
Lewis Carroll

IN THIS CHAPTER

- The roles of evolutionary metrics: steering evolution, separating signal from noise, and managing tradeoffs
- Overarching principles for metrics selection
- Differences between metrics of evolution and traditional software engineering metrics
- Short-term metrics: resilience, scalability, and composability
- Medium-term metrics: stickiness, platform synergy, and plasticity
- Long-term metrics: envelopment, durability, and mutation

The evolution of platform ecosystems is a journey, not a destination. In a journey, you need markers—pins on the map—to keep track of your bearings in order to decide whether you are indeed headed in the intended direction. Metrics of evolution are such markers.

Dictums in the popular press such as "platforms must innovate or die" are not very helpful in practice because it is often difficult to measure innovation. This chapter brings the lofty notion of platform innovation down to earth, with tangible metrics to measure different aspects of the amorphous notion of innovativeness over time. This chapter first describes the three roles of metrics of evolution: steering evolution, separating signals from noise, and managing tradeoffs. It then describes three overarching principles that guide the selection of metrics used to help guide evolution: an outside-in vantage point, focusing on the short term without losing sight of the long term, and the consideration of costs versus value of tracking any particular metric. We then explore nine strategic and operational metrics of evolution spanning three time horizons: the short, medium, and long term. These metrics encompass resilience, scalability, and composability in the short term; stickiness, platform synergy, and plasticity in the medium term; and envelopment, durability, and mutation in the long term. We also explore how these metrics directly influence others in the longer term, and ones where improvements simultaneously bolster another metric. These metrics apply to both platforms and apps; we therefore generically refer to these as "subsystems" in a platform's ecosystem. For both platform owners and app developers, we also offer a few ways to tangibly measure each metric.

☆"To view the full reference list for the book, click here or see page 283."

7.1 THREE ROLES OF EVOLUTIONARY METRICS

Metrics of evolution serve three roles in assessing the evolution of a platform or app: (1) they help steer evolution in ways that enhance its fitness in its evolving competitive environment; (2) they separate signals from noise to avoid pursuing dead ends and not miss out on promising opportunities; and (3) they help manage tradeoffs among design choices in forks along its evolutionary trajectory.

7.1.1 Metrics steer evolution

Passive adaptation to an unfavorable environment is the road to mortality. Evolutionary metrics focus attention on what's important, not just on what is quantifiable. An obsession with translating a metric into a quantifiable measure can often result in measuring the wrong things. This can lead a platform owner and app developers to diligently pursue goals to produce the result measured by that metric—which is not what anyone in the ecosystem actually wants. MindSpring is an example of how wrong metrics can lead well-intentioned individuals to do the opposite of what is intended. In the late 1990s, MindSpring wanted to improve its customer service. So it started tracking the amount of time that its service representatives took to address a customer problem when they called its technical support hotline. It soon found that the duration of the calls significantly decreased, but, unexpectedly, customers became even more dissatisfied with its technical support. To its surprise, its technical support staff was rushing customers through support calls, sending them on wild goose chases to get them off the line, or outright hanging up on them. Mindspring's support staff maximized precisely what was being measured, but producing exactly the opposite of the intended goal. Platform owners and app developers are therefore much better off with an approximate measure of a relevant evolution metric than with the precise measurement of a wrong metric. Just because a metric cannot readily be measured does not mean that it does not matter. Pretending that a property does not exist if it is hard to quantify can lead to faulty mental models and dysfunctional dynamics (Meadows, 2008, p. 176). Just remember that the singly critical long-term goal of a platform ecosystem is survival.

7.1.2 Metrics separate signal from noise

A second function of evolutionary metrics is to amplify meaningful signals and filter out noise. Tracking what's important in a platform ecosystem is like looking for a needle in a haystack because of a low signal-to-noise ratio. Signal refers to things that really matter, or indicators of the evolutionary health of a platform. Noise is information other than the meaningful signal such as readily available data, factoids, assertions, and beliefs. Confounding signal for noise and noise for signal can result in strategic blunders by a platform owner and app developers that can lead them down blind alleys, push them to pursue dead ends, and even put them on a death spiral.

Software platforms and the rise of big data mean that platform ecosystems are inundated with previously unimaginable streams of real-time data. This overabundance of information creates a poverty of attention. Software developers have historically dealt with data points, not data streams. The existing professional toolkits of software metrics focus largely on short-term, operational metrics that are appropriate for projects with a clear end point and rely primarily on data points (see "Evolution Versus Metrics of Implementation Performance").

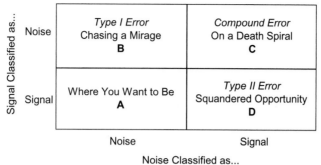

FIGURE 7.1

The evolutionary consequences of confounding signal and noise.

Errors in judgment that result from misclassification of signals and noise are illustrated in Figure 7.1. Confusing signal for noise can result in a failure to make timely investments in an emerging technology and markets that subsequently turn out to be disruptive to the platform or an app (cell D in Figure 7.1). Confusing noise for signal can result in investing in emerging technologies and markets that turn out to be dead ends (cell B in Figure 7.1). Statisticians call these errors in judgment Type I errors (aggressively pursuing an opportunity that eventually turns out to be a mirage) and Type II errors (failing to pursue an opportunity that would eventually turn out to be big). The greater the technological and market uncertainty in a platform market, the greater is the likelihood of such errors in judgment. The Red Queen effect can make it challenging to recover from either one of these errors. The worst position to be in is the right half of Figure 7.1, where simultaneously committing both errors in judgment is guaranteed to put a platform on an accelerated death spiral. The metrics of platform evolution developed in this chapter alleviate the signal-to-noise ratio problem by reducing noise and amplifying weak signals. Good evolutionary metrics of platform evolution should ideally move you as close as possible to cell A in Figure 7.1. Real options thinking, described in Chapter 8, provides the framework for designing architectures that include strategic flexibility for coping with both technical and market unpredictability.

7.1.3 Metrics help manage tradeoffs

There's an old saying in the software business that you can have a project on time, within budget, and of high quality—just pick any two. Evolving platform ecosystems involves similar tradeoffs, except their consequences are not immediately visible because they can span long timeframes. By focusing attention on multiple time spans, metrics help ecosystem participants recognize the long-term consequences of their immediate choices. In other words, they help deliberately and consciously manage tradeoffs that are otherwise invisible until much later.

7.2 THREE GUIDING PRINCIPLES

Tracking multiple metrics can be costly and time-consuming, and not all metrics are worth tracking. Three overarching principles should guide a platform owner's and app developers' choice of metrics of evolution to track: (1) they should provide an outside-in vantage point, (2) they should focus on the short term but without losing sight of the long term, and (3) they should be worth more than their measurement cost.

7.2.1 Look from outside in

The first guiding principle for choosing metrics of evolution is to start from the outside, looking in. Responsiveness to existing and prospective customers' latent needs should overshadow everything else. The primary customers of a platform are app developers and the primary customers of apps are end-users. Starting on the outside focuses attention on what matters most in an evolving marketplace, potentially riddled with rival platforms and rival apps. An outside-in approach is a constant reminder that you, as an ecosystem participant, live and die with the ecosystem. The fate of a platform owner is inseparably intertwined with the fate of its app developers. It is particularly important for the platform owner to remember that competition exists among platform ecosystems, not among individual platforms. Nokia once dominated the mobile telephony business, but it was beaten not by Apple or Google but rather by their ecosystems. Nokia was not challenged by a firm, but by an ecosystem. One company, no matter how dominant or successful, is hardly a match for an army of companies rallying together as an ecosystem. It is chaotic, like a properly attired regiment of soldiers pitted against a much larger rag-tag band of revolutionaries. Eventually, the rag-tag band, in spite of its chaos, will likely prevail by its sheer overwhelmingness and diversity of self-organized tactics. Ecosystems—with a systems advantage and high collective evolvability—will usually overwhelm and leapfrog even the most leading firm. And in Red Queen competition, the platform that looks the most attractive to its app developers and end-users will win in the survival of the fittest.

7.2.2 Focus attention on the short term without losing sight of the long term

The second guiding principle for choosing metrics of evolution is to focus on the short term without losing sight of the long term. Measuring the evolution of a platform and its apps requires tracking the key properties that indicate whether it is evolving along a favorable or unfavorable trajectory. Evolution in complex systems occurs over long timeframes (de Weck et al., 2011, p. 65). Therefore, the tracked metrics of evolution must span shorter and longer time scales.

Let us momentarily go back to the idea of evolution as a journey. Trying to orchestrate a platform without good short-term metrics is like trying to drive a car without a speedometer. Trying to orchestrate it without medium-term metrics is like driving in an unfamiliar city without a map. Missing long-term metrics is like driving without a compass, particularly with your author's sense of direction. As we subsequently explain in this chapter, what is short and long term is subjective and varies from one category of platforms to another. It should always be defined using the lifespan of comparable platforms as a reference point (Tiwana et al., 2010).

Another way to think about metrics along the three time horizons are as three lenses of a telescope; each provides a different view of what's ahead. This is illustrated in Figure 7.2. Together they provide a much better view of reality along a platform ecosystem's evolutionary trajectory.

Simultaneously using metrics for evolution over the short, medium, and long term provides three evolutionary advantages for platform owners and app developers:

* *Imagination-driven innovation.* Using multiple lenses to track evolution provides a future-looking perspective, allowing ecosystem participants to see the platform's technology not as it is today, but what it can become. Some of the most profound innovations of our era resulted from someone imagining a technology that was impossible then and then working diligently to make it

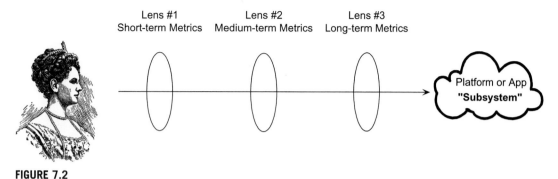

FIGURE 7.2

Three lenses for measuring evolution in platform ecosystems.

a reality. Take the iPad, for example; the entire concept was envisioned in a 1988 inhouse video called the Knowledge Navigator that took over two decades to realize. (Google it.)

- *Recognizing the long-term consequences of today's choices.* Today's design choices by platform owners and app developers can also have irreversible evolutionary consequences; seeing the connections requires a prepared mind using the linkages among short-, medium-, and long-term metrics of evolution. The lens that we fixate on influences not only what we do see but also what we do not see.
- *Avoiding force-fitting.* Using just one type of lens will also subconsciously bias us to force-fit the unfamiliar with what we recognize. (Remember the story of the elephant and eight blind men in Chapter 5?) Tracking evolution metrics spanning multiple timeframes also mitigates the human tendency to overvalue short-term and undervalue long-term consequences of design decisions, which is pervasively observed in technology development decisions (Gamba and Fusari, 2009).

Using these three timeframes to track evolution in platform ecosystems provides us a telescopic view that prevents us from isolating the context from our decisions. However, this telescopic view also needs to be complemented by a "magnifying-glass view" that prevents us from missing the little operational details. This magnifying glass is real options thinking, described in Chapter 8.

7.2.3 The cost of tracking a metric should never exceed the value of tracking it

The third guiding principle for choosing metrics of evolution is that the cost of measurement should not be more than the value that you—the platform owner or app developer—get out of a metric. In practice, this means that app developers should focus more on app-specific metrics and less on platform-level metrics. However, app developers must also be cognizant that they will sink or swim with the platform unless they multihome. For platform owners, it is important to distinguish between public and private metrics. While private metrics are for the platform owner's eyes, public metrics are the ones that app developers can use in their own work. These are typically app-specific metrics and ecosystem-wide metrics. To make sure that the right public metrics are used, stick with the overriding principle that a metric first should do no harm (i.e., not push the ecosystem in an undesirable evolutionary direction). The platform owner should also seek to automate data-gathering for assembling metrics where possible. This will lower app developers' measurement costs and help them better self-organize around your platform in a more evidence-driven manner.

EVOLUTION VERSUS METRICS OF IMPLEMENTATION PERFORMANCE

This chapter focuses on metrics of evolution but not implementation-oriented, technical performance metrics. Most software developers are familiar with software implementation performance metrics and there exist excellent reference books on that topic. Implementation performance metrics are necessary but insufficient preconditions to survive and prosper in platform markets. They focus heavily on projects with discrete end points or individual coders ("coder metrics") as the unit of analyses but little on evolution, which is the focus of this book. In other words, they focus on how well a project was done rather than how well a system evolved to improve its fitness that predicates its survival and mortality. Put another way, they are more like a rearview mirror rather than a GPS screen.

Evolution should not be confused with maintenance (Kamel, 1987); the former is functionality-expanding and the latter is corrective in nature. The focus on software implementation metrics made perfect sense in the pre-platform paradigm, where efficiency and reliability—not evolvability—was the emphasis in developing software. These include defects density (number of defects per thousand lines of code), development productivity (development person-hours required per thousand lines of code), coder productivity (improvements in coder productivity over time) (Banker et al., 1992, 1994; Fenton and Neil, 1999). We therefore do not focus on software implementation metrics, which are backward-looking rather than forward-looking (Dekleva and Drehmer, 1997; Tiwana et al., 2010). We directly build on a few key concepts from the traditional software engineering metrics literature in developing our metrics of platform evolution. These concepts apply to the code used to implement both platforms and apps.

- *Release*. A software release is a collection of compiled software code prepared for distribution and installation on end-user devices. It consists of replacement code implementing new features and functionality and modifying the undesirable characteristics of earlier releases. Quality of a release of a platform or app can be approximated by the number of patches released after its initial introduction to repair a defect in a small portion of the previously deployed code. These patches are often known as bug fixes and should not be confused with updates that add new capabilities to the system.
- *Version*. Although releases are sometimes referred to as *versions* in colloquial use, we reserve the term *version* in this book to refer to a distinctly different concept: a variant or an edition that is a modification of a platform or app that adds or deducts features as the basis for price discrimination. A single release of a platform or app can have multiple versions at the same time (e.g., free vs. paid; or light vs. standard vs. professional).
- *Fidelity*. Fidelity is the accuracy with which an app or a platform achieves the desired functionality (Messerschmitt and Szyperski, 2003, p. 56). A simplistic metric for fidelity is the inverse of defect density (defects reported per thousand lines of code), which can be compared across apps in the same platform (since they likely use the same programming language) but not across platforms. This simple metric captures real defects, which might be different from perceived defects, which are more noticeable and therefore matter more to end-users even when few real defects are present in an app or platform.

7.3 AN OVERVIEW OF METRICS OF EVOLUTION IN PLATFORM ECOSYSTEMS

Metrics of evolution measure emergent properties of platform ecosystems. They tap into unfolding ecosystem behavior over time. Metrics of evolution described in this chapter therefore capture *changes*—increases or decreases—in some evolutionary property of platforms and apps over time rather than a snapshot at one point in time. Emergent properties—unlike lines of code, defect counts, system speed, and person-hours of development work—cannot be measured directly but only by their manifested effects and consequences. To reliably measure emergent properties, one must measure more than one manifestation of that property. We therefore use a bundle of three metrics for each of the short, medium, and long timeframes. Each of these metrics applies to both platforms and apps—any subsystem in a platform ecosystem. We therefore refer to these metrics as properties of a "subsystem," where the subsystem can either be the platform or an app.

Each of these nine metrics can therefore apply to the platform or an individual app. These metrics can broadly be categorized as operational or strategic evolution metrics, and span the short, medium, or long term. *Strategic metrics* relate to the strength of the competitive positioning of a subsystem in its environment. *Operational metrics* are tactical measures that feed into strategic goals by breaking them down into workable actions.

The definition of short term and long term is inherently subjective and relative to the lifecycle of a population of comparable platforms. *Each* release of a PC operating system, for example, has a 5- to 10-year lifespan, mainframes about 40 years, and mobile phone operating systems about 2 years. It would be erroneous to define long term as the lifetime of one release of a platform. Instead, each release of the same platform should be added up to guesstimate what constitutes short term and long term. For example, the iOS platform in 2014 originated as iOS 1.0 in 2007, implying that the same platform has survived for 7 years. This realistically makes 7 years no more than the medium term in its lifespan. Similarly, Windows 8 in 2014 is simply a continuation of Windows 1.0 introduced in 1985, giving the Windows platform a lifespan of about 30 years *so far*. So a conservative definition of long term will span 7 and 30 years, respectively, for these software platforms. One could argue that iOS can be traced back to MacOS, which can be traced back to Unix; so iOS did not truly begin in 2007. This is where the concept of platform mutation, described in this chapter, makes the definition of the beginning of a platform more clearly delineable. A derivative platform's age begins when it mutates— or splits off—into a different environment, free of any ongoing linkages to a parent platform.

The common underlying theme in the metrics of evolution is evolution speed, which is grounded in the evolvability of subsystems in a platform ecosystem. Evolvability is the capacity of a subsystem to efficiently change as new requirements, needs, and possibilities emerge (de Weck et al., 2011, p. 187). User needs and market dynamics evolve over time. As soon as a fertile new market niche is identified and a platform or an app emerges to successfully meet that need, it is likely to encourage copycats. It must evolve to remain differentiated. Architectural choices—a platform's DNA—have an enduring influence on evolvability of a platform, the type of innovations that do and do not emerge around it, and the vibrancy of its ecosystem. However, whether its evolutionary potential is realized in ways that enhance its fitness in its competitive environment depends on how well its governance reinforces its architectural properties. This match between architectural properties and governance of platform ecosystems is what we call *architecture–governance alignment*, discussed in Chapters 10 and 11.

Here we focus only on metrics of evolution (Table 7.1), specifically sidestepping commonly used software implementation metrics. If they substitute for tracking evolutionary performance, fixation on software implementation metrics, used widely in software engineering practice, can be fatal in platform markets. We also do not cover metrics that can be used for implementing process control; existing metrics in the software industry—such as capability maturity metrics, integration test metrics, standards compliance, and build test metrics—can be used as a complement to the metrics of evolution.

Two types of relationships exist among the nine metrics of evolution: causal linkages (●) and correlations (○). These are summarized in Table 7.2. Causal linkages, also indicated by the arrows in Figure 7.3, exist when one metric influences another in the longer term. Improving a causal metric is necessary to improve the other. Two metrics are correlated when actions that improve one metric also help improve the other, but one does not directly cause the other (Table 7.3).

Table 7.2 summarizes ideas to measure each of the metrics, as described in detail previously.

Table 7.1 Definitions and the Strategic Versus Operational Nature of the Nine Metrics of Evolution in Platform Ecosystems

Metric	Operational	Strategic	Definition (Subsystem Can Be a Platform or an App)
Short Term			
Resilience	●		Capacity of a subsystem to function acceptably in the event of a failure elsewhere within or outside the ecosystem
Scalability	●		The degree to which the functional performance and financial viability of a subsystem is size-agnostic
Composability		●	Ease with which changes can be made within a subsystem without compromising its reintegration with the ecosystem
Medium Term			
Stickiness	●		"Eyeball time" between a subsystem and its primary users
Platform synergy		●	Degree to which an app is designed specifically for a particular platform
Plasticity		●	The degree to which a subsystem can deliver functionality that it was not originally designed to deliver to its primary existing and prospective users
Long Term			
Envelopment	●		Swallowing by a subsystem of the functionality of a solution in an adjacent market with overlapping users
Durability		●	A subsystem's endurance in a competitive marketplace
Mutation		●	Unanticipated, serendipitous creation of a spinoff subsystem that inherits some of the properties of the parent system but with a different purpose

7.4 SHORT-TERM METRICS OF EVOLUTION

7.4.1 Resilience

Resilience refers to the degree to which a subsystem is able to maintain an acceptable level of service when it encounters an unexpected fault in another subsystem in the ecosystem or disruption in an external service with which it interoperates. Variants of the resilience property are fault tolerance, reparability, and robustness. This property describes the degree to which the subsystem is internally immune to uncontrollable *external* factors that are difficult for the subsystem's developer to directly control (de Weck et al., 2011, p. 71). The property of resilience is an important short-term operational metric of evolution that complements common short-term metrics of performance such as reliability, stability, responsiveness, and performance.

Two key features of resilience are germane to subsystems in platform ecosystems vis-à-vis software systems from the pre-ecosystem paradigm. First, the subsystem's *internal* immunity is to failure *external* to it, such as in another subsystem with which it interoperates or due to changes in its environment

Table 7.2 Relationships Among Metrics of Evolution

	Resilience	Scalability	Composability	Stickiness	Platform Synergy	Plasticity	Envelopment	Durability	Mutation
Resilience									
Scalability									
Composability				O		●			
Stickiness							O	●	
Platform synergy				O			O	O	
Plasticity									●
Envelopment								●	
Durability									
Mutation									

●, one leads to the other; O, the two are correlated, but not causally.

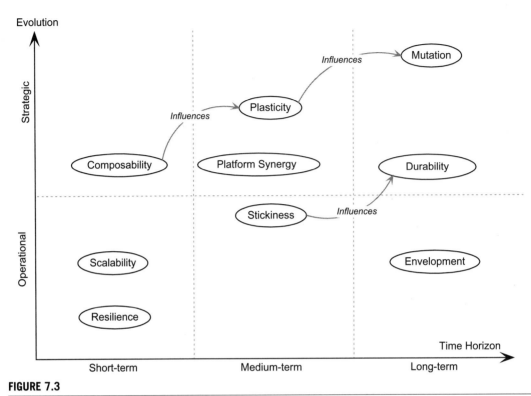

FIGURE 7.3

The nine metrics of evolution.

(de Weck et al., 2011, p. 90). Second, the important attribute is not failure avoidance but rather fast recovery to restore normal functioning—a capacity to bounce back—from a failure outside the subsystem. This means that it is robust to malfunctions in other subsystems in the ecosystem. This requires a design that can quickly isolate perturbations affecting the subsystem. At the platform level, this means that the platform is capable of bouncing back or recovering to resume functioning normally when an app malfunctions. At the app level, this means that an app is capable of functioning normally when either the platform or another app that it interacts with malfunctions or fails. Even in the best-designed platforms, apps can be resilient to perturbations from malfunctioning apps but are rarely resilient to failures at the platform level. Figure 7.4 compares subsystems with two levels of resilience.

7.4.2 Scalability

Scalability refers to the degree to which the functional and financial performance of a subsystem is size agnostic. This translates to the capacity of a subsystem to support a larger or smaller number of something—end-users, app developers, apps, or external software services. Scalability is a short-term operational metric of evolution that is applicable both to platforms and to apps. In practice, scalability then is the degree to which a subsystem can maintain its performance and function, and retain all its

Table 7.3 Some Proxy Measures of Evolution in Platform Ecosystems

Metric	Measurable Proxy
Short Term	
Resilience	• Recovery time of a platform or app after a failure *outside* it
Scalability	• Increase in the subsystem's latency, responsiveness, or error rates per additional 1,000 users • Direction of the shift in the subsystem's financial breakeven point per 1,000 fewer users
Composability	• Integration effort (person-hours) per internal change
Medium Term	
Stickiness	• Change in hours per end-user session over time • Change in averaged end-user sessions per week over time • Change in API calls made by an app on average as the platform ages (platform-level only)
Platform synergy	• Change in the number of functions called by app to APIs unique to platform
Plasticity	• Average count of major features added to a subsystem per release over its lifetime
Long Term	
Envelopment	• Count of successful envelopment moves • Count of envelopment attacks rebuffed • Percent of *new* subsystem adopters using enveloped functionality
Durability	• Change in the percentage of a subsystem's initial adopters who remain active users • Change in a platform's percentage of apps released that are subsequently updated at least once a year
Mutation	• Number of *unrelated* derivative platforms relative to rival platforms • Percentage of carryover users at outset of derivative subsystem • Growth of an app into a platform

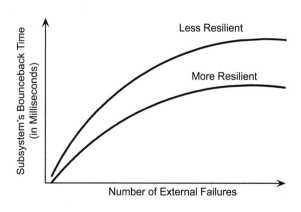

FIGURE 7.4

Resilience.

desired properties without a corresponding increase in its internal complexity (de Weck et al., 2011, p. 187). There are two important differences between scalability in platform ecosystems vis-à-vis traditional software systems. First, we normally think of scalability as the capacity of a software system to scale upward. However, in platform settings, the capacity to scale downward is just as important. Therefore scalability must capture the subsystem's capacity to expand or contract, upward or downward (Parnas, 1979). Second, performance can mean technical performance in the commonly accepted view of scalability, but it can also mean financial performance.

If a subsystem lacks downward scalability, it might not be financially sustainable below a minimal threshold of end-users or apps. This often-overlooked problem has caused many a technically promising offering to crash and burn in platform environments. For example, Blackberry's BBOS 10 platform lacked downward scalability because it was not sustainable below a minimal threshold count of apps on its new platform. That prevented the platform from successfully taking off. Similarly, apps that rely on network effects among end-users have been unsustainable because they did not reach a minimal critical mass of adopters for network effects to get started. An example of this is Apple's Ping social network built into iTunes, which was subsequently shut down due to lack of downward scalability. As we subsequently describe, upward scalability is impacted most by the architecture of a subsystem and downward scalability by governance and business model decisions.

Scalability in terms of technical performance can be measured as the change in latency, responsiveness, error rates for each additional or fewer end-user or app at the platform level, and changes in counts of end-users or external services invoked at the app level. Figure 7.5 illustrates this for upward scalability of two subsystems. Scalability in terms of financial performance can be thought of in terms of where the breakeven occurs (i.e., where revenues exceed costs), illustrated in Figure 7.6. A less downward scalable subsystem will shift to the negative net revenue region faster as the scale of the relevant "something" (end-users or apps) shrinks. This means that the subsystem on curve B will be less financially sustainable than the subsystem on curve A as the *something* count decreases. The point at which the breakeven point occurs can be shifted through thoughtful governance and business model design, giving a subsystem greater downward scalability.

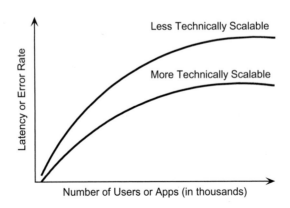

FIGURE 7.5

Technical scalability.

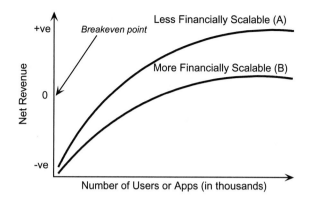

FIGURE 7.6

Financial scalability.

7.4.3 Composability

Composability refers to the ease with which internal changes can be made to a subsystem without compromising its integration with other interdependent subsystems, including those inside and outside the ecosystem. Composability can be measured in terms of effort, in person-hours, needed for reintegrating a subsystem with others in its ecosystem after one internal change is made to it. A subsystem that requires more person-hours of effort to integrate with the ecosystem is less composable than one that requires fewer person-hours of effort (see Figure 7.7). Other ways to think about this property is to think of the maintainability of a subsystem or its capacity to maintain interoperability after changes are made within the subsystem. The opposite of composability is brittleness, wherein a change inside a subsystem breaks its ability to interoperate with other subsystems within the platform's ecosystem with which it interacts. Although composability is a property of a subsystem, the same subsystem may be less composable in one ecosystem and more composable in a different one. Therefore, composability is

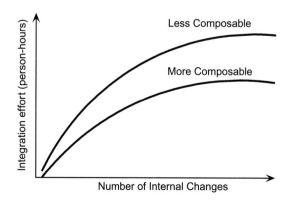

FIGURE 7.7

Two levels of composability.

a relative property definable only in the context of the ecosystem in which a subsystem functions. It is also a less immediately observable system property than responsiveness or speed.

Composability is an important evolutionary property for three reasons:

1. *Every dollar invested needs seven more for maintenance.* Lifetime maintenance costs of software far exceed its initial development costs, by a margin of about 700%. We often tend to think of changes as corrective changes that fix flaws in the initial implementation. However, typically only about 25% of post-release maintenance expenses come from bug fixes and about 75% of maintenance expenses over the lifetimes of typical systems come from functionality-enhancing changes (Eick et al., 2001). Therefore, the costs of changing a subsystem can be more important over its lifespan than its initial development costs. However, consideration of maintenance costs is often an afterthought in most software projects (de Weck et al., 2011, p. 79).

2. *Outside innovations are more absorbable.* Composability influences the ease with which a subsystem within the platform ecosystem can evolve to exploit technological advances from outside the ecosystem to enhance its functional capabilities. An inability to change the software code within a subsystem quickly and reliably means that fleeting business opportunities are likely to be missed, putting it further and further behind in Red Queen competition. Well-designed subsystems should be able to rapidly absorb newness and incorporate innovations from the outside or else face obsolescence and competitive irrelevance.

3. *Different parts of an ecosystem do not evolve in synchrony.* Different subsystems within an ecosystem often evolve at different rates. These differential rates at which individual subsystems face the pressures and encounter the opportunities to change means that it is more useful to think of composability as ease of systems reintegration rather than systems integration. In traditional software systems, systems integration of modules or subsystems is often a one-shot activity. However, in platform ecosystems, it is an ongoing, dynamic activity where changes in any app or in the platform can introduce integration problems. It is therefore important to recognize the ongoing, dynamic nature of systems integration in platform environments. A single change in a single subsystem in a platform ecosystem can potentially require bringing all subsystems together again to realize overall ecosystem functionality. This means that the lower the composability of a subsystem, the less readily it can evolve independent of other subsystems in its ecosystem. This requires changes to be implemented in large blocks spanning multiple subsystems in an ecosystem rather than on a piecemeal basis as needed. On the other hand, changes can be made to composable subsystems at differential rates, allowing them to evolve independently at the pace that is individually appropriate for them. Composability is therefore a strategic metric of evolution.

Composability is a property of a platform as well as an app that interoperates with a platform. For a platform, this property means that a change does not require much effort to reintegrate it with apps within the platform's ecosystem. It can also continue to work together with apps and with other platforms and external services that are not owned by the platform owner (de Weck et al., 2011, p. 93). At the app level, composability therefore means how readily a tweaked app can be reintegrated with the platform, and also possibly with other apps with which it might interoperate. Composability of a subsystem in the short term influences a strategic medium-term metric, its plasticity. Therefore, emergence of ecosystem-wide new capabilities is heavily influenced by the composability of subsystems within it. Interactions among them determine the ecosystem's evolution speed. We subsequently describe how speed is one of the few reliable sources of competitive advantage that ecosystem participants can count on.

7.5 MEDIUM-TERM METRICS OF EVOLUTION

7.5.1 Stickiness

Stickiness is a measure of "eyeball time" between a subsystem and its primary users. It taps into the subsystem's ability to sustain their attention; attention is a scarce resource and the currency in platform markets. Stickiness addresses questions such as *changes* in how much a subsystem is used by its primary users after its adoption and how much sustained use it sees. Use of the subsystem can be active use (where the primary user directly interacts with a subsystem) or passive use (where the primary user uses the services of the subsystem in the background). The emphasis on active use is more meaningful in assessing stickiness.

Stickiness applies to both apps and platforms. The primary users of apps are end-users and the primary users of the platform are apps (rather than app developers). For apps, a good way to measure stickiness is the change over time in hours per session or the number of sessions per week by their end-users. Remember that we are interested in averaged changes—increases or decreases—in this metric to understand the evolutionary trajectory of the app. Figure 7.8 illustrates both increasing and decreasing stickiness of an app over time (e.g., over 3 months). Stickiness avoids the risk of overrelying on measuring its installed base—number of end-users who have purchased or acquired the app—to gauge its health (a common practice in the software industry). This might create an illusion that the app is doing well when in reality it might be seeing little use after its novelty has worn off for end-users. As apps are often subsidized by advertising revenues, ensuring stickiness is critically linked to the app's business model as well.

For a platform, its stickiness for its secondary users can be measured in the same way as it is for apps. However, for the primary users of a platform—app developers—its stickiness can be approximated as the change—positive or negative—in the API calls made by each app on average as the platform ages. A platform with an increase in API calls per app would indicate increasing platform

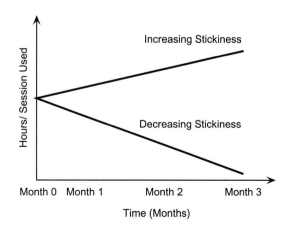

FIGURE 7.8

App stickiness.

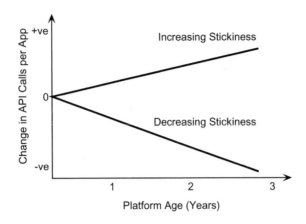

FIGURE 7.9

Platform stickiness.

stickiness for its app developers. Figure 7.9 illustrates both increasing and decreasing stickiness of a platform with an app as it ages.

7.5.2 Platform synergy

The concept of platform synergy is derived from the broader concept of "synergistic specificity," which is the degree to which a subsystem and another subsystem are made for each other (Schilling, 2000). This is a property of a subsystem that is always relative to something else, which is the referent. It is an attribute of a subsystem that is a combination of two concepts: synergy with another subsystem and specificity to that subsystem. It is useful to think of increases and decreases in synergistic specificity over time rather than its level at a snapshot in time. Our focus on platform ecosystems here means that we focus on synergistic specificity of an app relative to other apps for that platform rather than external services (e.g., an app designed specifically for an external service like Gmail or Dropbox). It is therefore most useful to think of synergistic specificity as a property of an app relative to a specific platform. Platform synergy in this narrower sense then refers to the degree to which an app increases—over subsequent releases—and the degree to which it uniquely exploits the evolving native capabilities of the platform in its own implementation. Put another way, it is the degree to which an app achieves greater functionality by being specifically designed for a particular platform. An increase in platform synergy means that an app is able to integrate and exploit the power of a specific platform to a greater degree over time. It also means, however, that the app becomes increasingly more dependent on that platform to deliver that functionality. An increase in platform synergy is therefore a double-edged sword, potentially increasing an app's performance and integration with a platform on one hand and potentially increasing its lock-in with the platform on the other. This tradeoff is illustrated in Figure 7.10.

From a platform owner's perspective, an increase in an app's synergy with a platform can increase an app developer's lock-in to the platform while also potentially enhancing its platform-specific performance. Lock-ins can either be coercive or value-driven, and platform synergy is a value-driven form of lock-in. Coercive lock-ins are those created by setup, learning costs, or complementary investments

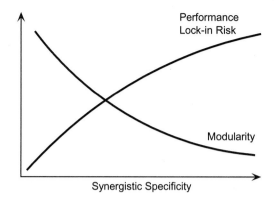

FIGURE 7.10

Tradeoffs in increasing platform synergy.

that app developers must make to develop apps for a platform, or through the use of proprietary standards. Such investments have limited salvage value in a rival platform. But such lock-ins are not sustainable in the long run and are technologically breakable using translators, middleware, emulators, and adapters. We describe these strategies in later chapters.

Value-driven lock-ins are primarily created by offering apps unique functional capabilities in the platform that differentiate an app created specifically for a platform vis-à-vis the same app created for rival platforms. Although this type of value-driven lock-in over app developers is technological capabilities-based, other forms of value-driven lock-ins include access to a larger pool of app adopters (market access-based), a stronger prospect for network effects from a larger platform user base, or knowledge-based (wherein greater access to end-user usage metrics data provides better actionable insights to app developers for developing their apps). Therefore, an increase in platform synergy non-coercively increases app developers' costs for defecting to a rival platform. Given the potential for sustaining app developers' commitment to the platform as well as increasing app performance, it is usually in the platform owner's best interest to increase the platform synergy of apps developed for that platform.

From an app developer's perspective, increasing platform synergy needs to be approached with more caution for two reasons. First, app developers must often make investments specific to a platform to increase platform synergy of their apps. These investments include acquiring technical skills of the programming language, APIs, and architecture of a particular platform that are more valuable in relation to that platform but of lesser value in a rival platform. This increases app developers' exposure to the risk of opportunistic behavior by the platform owner (e.g., unilaterally changing the rules of the game at a later time). This risk is usually more pronounced for platforms that use proprietary interface standards than it is for ones that use open standards. Second, increasing platform synergy limits the degree of modularization of an app; increasing an app's tie-in to a platform by definition gives it more monolithic properties in relation to the platform. The more platform-specific the functionality of an app is, the harder it is to change it without constraints. This can make it progressively more difficult to evolve the app independent of the platform. App developers can limit these risks in two ways. First, intentionally limit increasing platform synergy to avoid excessive lock-in with a platform, particularly in its early lifecycle stages. Second, multihoming—or simultaneously developing the app for multiple rival platforms—hedges against stranding risk (i.e., being stuck with a platform that eventually turns out to be the losing bet among rival platforms).

7.5.3 Plasticity

Plasticity is a pragmatic antidote to the alarming overuse of adjectives such as *innovative* and *dynamic* to describe subsystems in platform markets. Plasticity refers to the degree to which new releases of a subsystem delivers new functionality to its primary users that it was not originally designed to deliver. Plasticity is directly correlated with the rate of innovation that is accomplished in a subsystem. Malleability, extensibility, and the capacity to morph are other ways to envision plasticity of a subsystem. Plasticity is a direct measure of the emergent properties of software-based systems because it reflects a subsystem's capacity to morph to meet new needs and possibilities that did not exist at the time of its original creation (de Weck et al., 2011, p. 85). Two nuances are important in assessing plasticity. First, the extension of capabilities should not have been preplanned. Preplanned capabilities reflect incremental refinements rather than plasticity. Second, the changes that result in plastic behavior should be internal to the subsystem. Plasticity therefore reflects a subsystem's capacity to internally change to better fit changes in its environment (de Weck et al., 2011, p. 187), reflecting the ease and rapidity with which it can be evolved to meet the changing needs of its existing and prospective users or to exploit technological advances.

Primary users for the platform are app developers, and for an app are its end-users. It is important to remember that end-users are secondary—not primary—users of a platform. Plasticity of a platform is therefore the degree to which it can deliver new capabilities for the platform's app developers. It can include gaining the ability to work with other platforms and external services that are neither owned by the platform owner nor originally designed to work with (de Weck et al., 2011, p. 93). For example, iOS does things today that were simply not possible at its inception. Plasticity of an app is the degree to which an app developer can rapidly, over subsequent releases, add new functionality, capabilities, incorporate user feedback, and address evolving user needs. A subsystem with high plasticity provides such new—related or unrelated—capabilities in addition to its originally intended functionality (de Weck et al., 2011, p. 86). Plasticity is comparable to properties akin to a Swiss army knife that can perform many different functions, including some that were not preplanned. The simplest metric for plasticity is a count of major features added to a subsystem averaged per major release over its lifetime.

7.6 LONG-TERM METRICS OF EVOLUTION
7.6.1 Envelopment

Dominant platforms are often hard to displace because once they successfully create network effects, those network effects create large incentives to existing users to stick with them even if a technically superior alternative subsequently appears. Therefore, the functionality of the new solution has to be revolutionary enough to warrant switching to it plus foregoing all benefits of the existing network effects that are already in place. Envelopment is an alternative strategy to overcome this barrier for new entrants in platform markets.

We described envelopment in Chapter 2 as an evolutionary dynamic where one subsystem expands into the turf of another solution with which it has an overlapping user base by offering its functionality as part of an expanded multiproduct bundle of functionality (see Figure 7.11). Successful envelopment

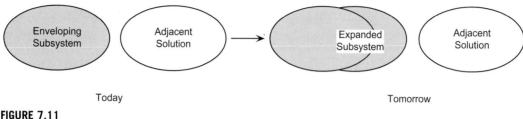

Today   Tomorrow

FIGURE 7.11

An illustration of envelopment.

attacks have three requirements: (1) there must exist shared economies of scale across the original and the target solution markets, (2) the key leveraged asset should be relevant and readily transferable to the targeted enveloped market, and (3) the enveloped functionality must be adjacent to the enveloping subsystem's domain. Envelopment depends on leveraging overlapping user bases and common components to offer a bundle that includes both the original subsystem's functionality and the target solution's functionality. The enveloping subsystem can either progressively tip-toe into the enveloped solutions' space or outright swallow it. Adjacencies between enveloped solutions and enveloping subsystems can be of two key types:

1. *Customer adjacency.* The enveloping subsystem and the enveloped solution have substantially overlapping customer bases (Eisenmann et al., 2011; Evans and Schmalensee, 2007, p. 154). An example would be the existing pool of users of email applications that overlap extensively with the existing pool of digital camera users. Envelopment occurs here when the enveloping subsystem expands to offer the functionality of a different solution that is also used by a large percentage of its own users.
2. *Value chain adjacency.* The enveloping subsystem and the enveloped solution occupy different but proximate links in a value chain. Envelopment occurs here when the enveloping subsystem expands to span a different link in the value chain that was previously served by a different solution. An example would be digital photography software users versus digital printing services users or electronic scanner users. Similarly, the incorporation of inexpensive GPS chips in smartphones allowed them to progressively swallow the functionality of standalone GPS devices and mapping services.

We call envelopment based on customer adjacency *horizontal envelopment* and that based on value chain adjacency *vertical envelopment*. As Figure 7.12 illustrates, vertical envelopment can be downstream or upstream.

Opportunities for envelopment arise primarily due to convergence of unrelated industries or applications either due to the convergence of previously disparate technology solutions or due to regulatory changes. Such envelopment opportunities arise from the application of existing or new technologies to deliver the functionality of the enveloped solution in a completely new way. For example, voiceover IP allowed software to envelop residential telephony; an increase in wireless data speeds and a simultaneous decline in costs allowed streaming services such as Pandora to offer the functionality of satellite radio in automobiles; Internet video-streaming services such as Netflix enveloped rent-on-demand entertainment services offered by cable television companies.

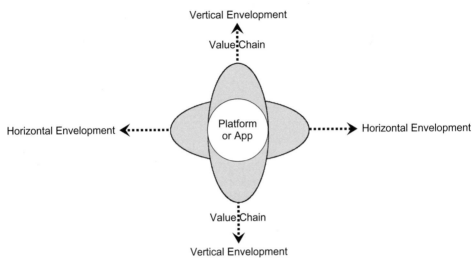

FIGURE 7.12

Two types of envelopment in platform ecosystems.

Envelopment becomes increasingly pronounced as product and service markets evolve into platform markets. This potentially poses a threat to nonplatform businesses that might find their bread-and-butter business under attack from a platform from an unrelated industry attempting to envelop their core market. Envelopment attacks often come from platforms in unrelated industries and from nontraditional, unexpected competitors, which makes incumbent solution providers especially vulnerable and unable to respond by matching the attacking platform or app's functionality. For example, Craigslist versus local newspaper classifieds or Google Catalog versus print catalogs were not obvious substitutes, traditional competitors for the latter nor were they from the same industry. Successful envelopment attacks usually offer users of the enveloped solution a better value proposition based on different value-added functionality or a lower cost. For example, electronic catalogs such as Google Catalogs not only reduced mailing costs but also offered interactivity to clients such as L.L. Bean (which mails about 200 million printed catalogs each year). Google has progressively enveloped using its search platform electronic payment services (Google Checkout), software (Google Docs), email (Gmail), browsers (Chrome), advertising, and mobile OSes (Android) (Eisenmann et al., 2011). Similarly, iOS has progressively enveloped diverse solutions such as PDAs, hand-held gaming consoles, ebook readers, video recorders, cameras, and personal computers (Eisenmann et al., 2011).

Envelopment is a powerful way for new entrants in a platform market to overcome the competitive blocking caused by rivals' existing network effects (Eisenmann et al., 2011). By using an envelopment strategy, a late entrant can become a dominant player in an adjacent market if it holds a dominant position in a related market. Recall the network effects shield platforms and apps from new competitors, who must offer functionality that is not merely better but so revolutionary that it is sufficient to convince end-users to abandon the network effects that they might already enjoy. This rarely happens in practice and the bar for defining revolutionary is often higher than new entrants presume. For example,

Apple introduced FaceTime, which competed directly with Skype. However, the simpler interface, better integration with iOS devices, and lower bandwidth requirements were insufficient for it to displace Skype due to Skype's strong network effects. In short, its technological merits were insufficient to entice Skype users to abandon their existing networks of peer users. Envelopment does not require revolutionary new functionality to displace a dominant solution (Eisenmann et al., 2011). Envelopment attacks instead harness network effects that previously sheltered the incumbent platform to their own advantage.

The key to breaking network effects barriers through envelopment is the notion of carryover (Adner, 2012). Carryover means that the enveloping subsystem simply replicates its existing network of users in the space of the enveloped solution. For example, iOS users of the iPhone provided an existing base of several million registered users to Apple when it introduced the iPad; the clever tactic was to use the same iOS account credentials across the two families of devices. Google has repeatedly used this tactic by adding enveloped services to its existing set of users, in essence instantly replicating their existing network of peer users in the space of the enveloped solution. Since the user bases of the Google platform and the target solution were substantially overlapping, the network effects that previously sheltered envelopment targets (such as Facebook) were no longer as protective. Such requirements for leveraging of a shared user base is the primary reason that envelopment attacks require a substantial overlap in user bases.

Envelopment is a significant evolution metric for both platform owners and app developers, who can both exploit envelopment opportunities and must also successfully rebuff envelopment threats in order to survive. The simplest way to measure envelopment is a raw count of successful envelopment moves by a subsystem and successful envelopment threats rebuffed. Another way of measuring successful envelopment moves is the percentage of *new* adopters of a subsystem that actively use the enveloped functionality after an envelopment move is completed.

For platform owners, envelopment therefore provides a way to grow the market occupied by a platform. It also offers a useful heuristic to anticipate envelopment attacks from adjacent platforms. For app developers, the envelopment threat not only comes from rival app developers but also from the platform itself. App developers must hedge against the risk that the platform owner might itself vertically integrate the functionality of an app into the platform, essentially wiping out instantaneously demand for the app. Although a platform owner might have its reasons for doing so (e.g., generating more competition in a critical piece of functionality or attempting to set a gold standard for app developers), this can damage the platform's ability to attract app developers if this strategy is attempted too often. App developers can protect themselves from such attacks from platform owners by multihoming and embedding "real options" in the design of their app, as described in further detail in Chapter 11.

7.6.2 Durability

Durability refers to the competitive persistence of a subsystem's advantages and distinctiveness over time (Barnett and Hansen, 1996; Pil and Cohen, 2006; Tiwana et al., 2010). Unlike performance durability that reflects a short-term property of resilience, competitive durability reflects a subsystem's competitive endurance in a marketplace. An app that initially had 1 million adopters but only 50,000 actively using it 2 years later is therefore less durable than one that had half a million. Durability is therefore a more granular way of thinking of a subsystem's survival and mortality over time.

Durability is an important long-term metric for how well a platform or an app adapted to improve its fitness in a changing competitive environment, rivals, and rebuffed envelopment threats. This can be measured objectively in two possible ways: (1) for an app or a platform, the change in the percentage of

initial adopters who remain active users over an increasing time span (see Figure 7.13) and (2) for platforms, the change in the percentage of apps released that are subsequently updated at least once a year
(see Figure 7.14). A coarser approach to measuring this at the ecosystem level is the change in the
survival rate over time of a platform's app developers. This metric can be compared across two platforms to compare the durability of rival platforms relative to each other.

7.6.3 Mutation

Mutation refers to the unanticipated, serendipitous creation of a spinoff platform or app that inherits some
properties of the parent subsystem but with a completely different function than its parent (Tiwana et al.,
2010). Unlike envelopment, which expands the subsystem's functionality, mutation creates a distinct

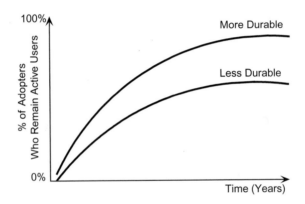

FIGURE 7.13

App durability.

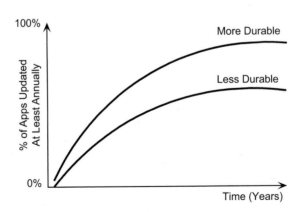

FIGURE 7.14

Platform durability.

derivative system. Evolutionary biologists describe this process as speciation: taking an organism in one domain and transplanting it to another. When separated from its parent species and placed in a different application domain, the derivative system can develop very different characteristics from its parent species and grow quite distinct. In other words, derivative mutants diverge. Mutants can become distinctive enough to be the founders of the next generation of species of software systems; for example, the Mac OS platform mutated into the iOS platform in 2007. Mutation often results from the application of an existing solution to a new application domain. For example, face recognition technology combined with Amazon's app resulted in Amazon's Price Check app, which allows real-time price comparisons by its end-users in rivals' stores. The radical discontinuity was not the technology itself but its application domain. The advantage of mutation is twofold: diversification and carryover. First, by creating a product or service that does not directly compete with existing ones, it offers a solution to being trapped in a Red Queen race by diversifying a subsystem's core market (Meadows, 2008, p. 129). Second, the derivative system conserves some advantageous features of the parent subsystem. Evolutionary biologists refer to such genetic features that are highly conserved to mean that the same core features are redeployed in a very different species. *Carryover* that such inherited features facilitate refers to the process of leveraging the original subsystem's ecosystem of users to jump-start the creation of a derivative, second ecosystem (Adner, 2012, p. 194). In software-based platforms, carrying over existing users of the parent subsystem to the mutated spinoff can give them a leg up in evolutionary competition. It exploits the original app or platform's success in one setting to create an advantage in constructing a new ecosystem (Adner, 2012, p. 205). Carryover can therefore be used by platform owners to induce end-users as well as app developers to adopt the derivative platform. It can similarly be used by app developers to induce the original app's end-users to adopt a derivative app. An example of such carryover is Google's Google + social network: While Facebook and Twitter took about 2 years to reach a user base of 10 million users, Google + was able to do it in 2 weeks. Similarly, Apple used this strategy to introduce the iPad, putting it ahead of rivals even before it launched. Steve Jobs famously said when introducing the iPad to iPhone users that they already knew how to use the iPad.

Mutation applies to both platforms and apps in platform ecosystems, and can also apply to entire ecosystems. However, it is most often observed at the platform level. Measures of mutation in the evolution of a platform or app include the number of unrelated derivative platforms that grew out of a platform relative to rival platforms or the percentage of users at the outset of a derivative platform that were carried over from the parent platform. Apps can also mutate and grow into nested platforms—platforms within platforms.

7.7 LESSONS LEARNED

- *Evolution is a journey, and evolutionary metrics are the pin markers on the map.* They help keep tabs on whether a platform or an app is headed in the intended direction.
- *Metrics of evolution apply equally to platforms and apps.* Both are generically referred to as subsystems in this chapter.
- *Metrics of evolution play three roles.* They help steer evolution to enhance a platform or app's fitness in its evolving competitive environment; separate signals from noise to avoid pursuing dead ends and not miss out on promising opportunities; and help manage tradeoffs.

- *Three guiding principles guide the choice of a few metrics of evolution.* Tracking multiple metrics can be costly. The chosen set of metrics must provide an outside-in vantage point, should focus on the short term but without losing sight of the long term, and they should deliver more value than what it costs to measure them.
- *Metrics of evolution measure changes—increases and decreases—in an evolutionary property over time.* This makes them distinctively different from implementation performance metrics commonly used in software development, which are inherently backward-looking rather than forward-looking.
- *Metrics of evolution can be operational or strategic, and span the short, medium, and long term.* The metrics of evolution encompass resilience, scalability, and composability in the short term; stickiness, platform synergy, and plasticity in the medium term; and envelopment, durability, and mutation in the long term.
- *Some metrics are causally linked and others are correlated.* A metric in the shorter term can directly influence another metric in the longer term. Some others do not have such cause-and-effect linkages. Instead, improving one requires doing the same things that can improve another.

Real Options Thinking in Ecosystem Evolution

8

The menu is huge, sophisticated, and very creative but I keep to simple choices.
Jean Reno

IN THIS CHAPTER

- An introduction to real options as a way of thinking
- Coping with technology and market volatility in platform projects
- Six types of real options
- Applying real options thinking in practice
- Exercising real options

The architecture of platforms and the microarchitecture of an app can create different types of flexibility to adapt to volatility in technology and in end-user needs. When the design of a project creates such future flexibility without the obligation to use it, it is said to have a *real option* embedded in it. The value of such flexibility is greater when a project involves more volatility in either the technology or the market needs addressed by the project. This chapter describes real options thinking as a tool for designing and exploiting the six different types of real options, primarily by platform owners and to a lesser extent by app developers.

8.1 AN INTRODUCTION TO REAL OPTIONS THINKING

Real options are a *way of thinking* that disciplines how projects—both platforms and apps—can be structured to protect against potential losses while preserving potential gains. It is an approach to position for the upside by hedging against possible futures. A real "option" is simply the right to do something without the obligation to do it (Trigeorgis, 1993). It refers to the flexibility to do something along a project's evolutionary trajectory—grow, scale, switch ingredients, stage expansion, or kill a project—in the future without having to do it. When the flexibility specific to any type of real option is present in a project, that real option is said to be embedded in it (Bollen, 1999; Hilhorst et al., 2008; Huchzermeier and Loch, 2001). Although traditional approaches to strategy are often seen as an answer to uncertainty and dynamic markets, they are based on an assumption of predictability in the environment. Real options thinking, in contrast, is based on the assumption of uncertainty and unpredictability, which is precisely the kind of environment where the flexibility provided by real options is valuable. The

---

☆"To view the full reference list for the book, click here or see page 283."

value of embedding real options in a platform project lies in the future flexibility to defer, expand/contract, repurpose, or terminate projects, without the obligation to do so. Often, this flexibility relates to when and how to implement specific features and functionality. Thinking in terms of creating real options allows firms to prepare today for an unpredictable future.

8.2 VOLATILITY IN TECHNOLOGIES AND MARKETS

Generally, the greater the variance—or volatility—involved in a project, the *more* valuable is any real option. Real options therefore tend to be most valuable as well as more plentiful in fast-moving, unpredictable markets and in large, complex projects with greater disparity between the upside and downside outcomes (Fichman et al., 2005). The flexibility provided by embedded real options is valuable under two conditions: (1) greater technical and market (e.g., how end-users will respond) volatility and (2) how long an option can be held before the flexibility provided by it disappears (known as an option's expiration period). By corollary, options are of lesser value in predictable markets and when platform projects use stable technologies and have short development timelines. Figure 8.1 summarizes the key sources of technical and market volatility. Technical volatility is largely an uncertainty on the supply side of a platform and market volatility is largely on the demand side of a platform.

8.2.1 Technical volatility

Technical volatility arises from the immaturity of technology, unpredictability of how it will evolve, the need for integrating a system with other existing systems within and outside a platform ecosystem, and a platform project's sheer complexity. Such technical volatility is reduced only through small-scale, tip-toeing investments (McGrath, 1997); by cautiously "doing something," unlike market volatility, which is reduced simply by waiting (if the risk of being preemptively locked out of a market by potential rival platforms is low). The greater the technical volatility involved in a platform project, the greater is the value of flexibility created through options thinking.

8.2.2 Market volatility

Market volatility arises from not knowing how potential end-users will respond to a project, how fast they will adopt it, and whether rival platforms will quickly replicate to match the features and capabilities introduced by the project. Market volatility also arises from attempting to target a market where

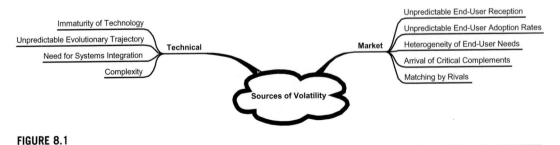

FIGURE 8.1

Two types of volatility and their sources.

the needs of users are diverse (both end-users and app developers are a platform's users). The value of a real option is low when consumer preferences are homogeneous and predictable and high when they are heterogeneous and unpredictable (Adner and Levinthal, 2001). The latter is likely to be the case in the early lifecycles stages of a platform where users are diverse and it is unclear what functionality they will value more. This means that any project targeting a group with heterogeneous needs will have to make compromises in what it can and cannot offer to its average user. Real options simply provide a way to reverse those choices if they turn out to be wrong. Although the volatility of new markets is greater than established markets, real options have much greater value in such markets (McGrath, 1997). Therefore, real options are more useful in new platform markets than in well-established ones. A final source of market volatility is from uncertainty about whether and when critical complements such as apps will arrive. If a platform project introduces functionality that is of limited appeal without the arrival of complementary apps that make it useful in practice, it can be a death knell for the platform. This is precisely why Blackberry drummed up new apps for its Blackberry 10 platform long before its public release in 2013. (It guaranteed minimum payouts of $10,000 to each app developer for its new platform.)

Expiration period of a real option refers to the time remaining during which the option can be exercised after it is created. This means that the longer the development schedule of a project, the more valuable it is to embed real options in it. Such projects should also have the shorter gaps between periodic project reviews and smaller stages. The expiration period of a real option also depends on the length of the product lifecycle in the platform's market, its stage along the S-curve, and the intensity of competition in its core market (e.g., number of rivals and prevalence of race-to-the-bottom pricing).

Besides technical and market uncertainty, three additional sources of uncertainty influence the value of real options in platform projects because they alter the volatility surrounding them (McGrath, 1997).

- *Feature matching by rival platforms.* A greater likelihood of feature matching retaliation by rival platforms *reduces* the value of real options. In contrast, uncertainty about whether a rival platform will move to match a new feature added to a platform increases its volatility, in turn increasing the value of real options.
- *Blocking-related uncertainty.* If rival platforms or complementary services (such as external APIs) block access to the project, it reduces the variance in returns, therefore reducing the value of real options.
- *Slow adoption.* Slow adoption by app developers or end-users reduces the variance in cumulative returns, therefore reducing the value of a real option embedded in a platform project.

Risks can be managed proactively using options thinking only if the platform owner plans for such uncertainties in advance. The emphasis should be on recognizing upfront the key technical and market uncertainties inherent in a new project. Each of these key uncertainties can then be approximately classified into four levels, illustrated in Figure 8.2 (Courtney, 2001, p. 22); real options thinking is most useful at levels 2 and 3.

- *Level 1.* A clear trajectory and predictable view of the future exists for the focal volatility. At this level, traditional strategic planning techniques work well and investments to create flexibility and diversification solely to manage risk are wasteful (Courtney, 2001, p. 103). Real options thinking has little value at this level.

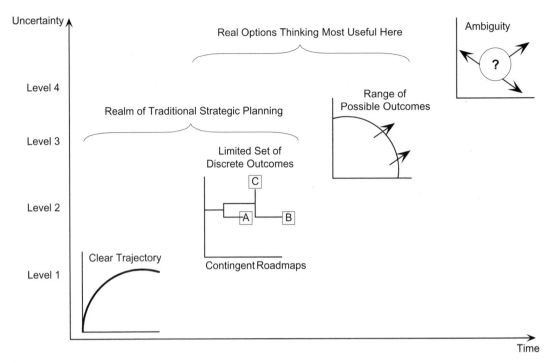

FIGURE 8.2

Four levels of technical and market volatility.

- *Level 2.* A limited set of possible outcomes can be readily identified on a contingent roadmap, one of which will occur. For example, two different dominant designs for a platform or two competing standards (e.g., Flash vs. HTML 5) might exist, one of which will prevail. Real options selectively embedded in a project begin to become valuable. In the preceding example, a switch use option would be key. Scenario planning techniques that actively track the relative probabilities of each evolutionary path are useful complements to real options thinking at this level.
- *Level 3.* A range of possible outcomes can be identified, but there is considerable ambiguity within that range. At this level, real options thinking becomes most useful. It is also necessary to actively track the changes in the key technical and market uncertainties to update the value of embedded options and to determine the timing of exercising the flexibility associated with them.
- *Level 4.* True ambiguity where not even a range of possible outcomes can be predicted. Real options thinking has limited usefulness at this highest level of uncertainty. Reversibility of decisions in the form of embedded abandonment and switching options, and some ability to insure against worst-case scenarios, is valuable at this level (Courtney, 2001, p. 103).

The simplified options exercise framework described in Figure 8.5 is immediately applicable for creating, holding, and exercising possible real options in a project. Such tracking not only requires actively monitoring the sources of key uncertainties but also small-scale experiments that can generate new information to reduce ambiguity. Other tools such as latent demand discovery of user needs using methods such as conjoint experiments (discussed in Chapter 11) can therefore also be useful. Such experiments with app developers and end-users can allow an app developer or a platform owner to develop preliminary hypotheses about functionality that they would likely value and then confirm or disconfirm such hypotheses. This approach allows iterative refinement and narrowing down of the range of possible outcomes, effectively reducing uncertainty to Level 2 in Figure 8.2.

8.3 TYPES OF REAL OPTIONS

Real options can either be strategic or operational, as shown in Figure 8.3. Table 8.1 summarizes the six types of real options that can be embedded in a platform project and how each can create value. A *strategic* option (also known as a growth option) refers to future flexibility to use the project as a foundation or stepping-stone for yet-unimagined follow-on projects through further investment. Strategic options are obvious in hindsight but usually challenging to foresee. *Operational* options relate to the operational implementation of a project and consist of five types:

1. *Defer.* This option is embedded in a project if it can be delayed without missing a market opportunity. The key requirement is that the upside opportunity must not be imperiled by delaying the project and the risk of preemption or lockout must be minimal. The presence of a defer option allows market volatility to be resolved by allowing the developer to delay implementing functionality whose value to a platform's or app's primary users is not yet clear. The presence of a deferral option is the key mechanism for reducing market volatility. A deferral option embedded in a platform project therefore provides a way to cope with volatility by providing an opportunity to delay an investment decision with uncertain future value until the uncertainty has been resolved or reduced. The pitfall associated with defer options is the risk of a false illusion that a project can be deferred without imperiling its potential. In reality, the creation of network effects by a rival and the initiation of the Red Queen effect can cause a project to fall irrecoverably

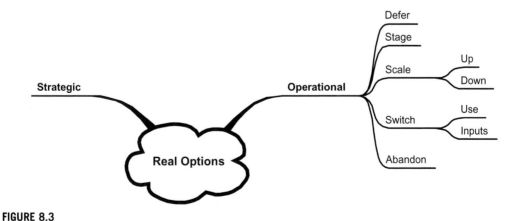

FIGURE 8.3

Six types of real options.

Table 8.1 Spotting Embedded Real Options and Their Sources of Value

Option	Present if...	How It Creates Value
Strategic growth	The initial baseline project opens the door to pursue a variety of follow-on projects, including ones that could not be initially envisioned	Over time, the value of follow-on projects becomes clearer and new technological innovations open up unanticipated opportunities for using the original project as a foundation for follow-on projects
Defer	A decision of whether to implement a stage can be delayed without wiping out market opportunity or facing lockout	Reduces risk of being first to market when market volatility is too high and the risk of being locked out is limited
Stage	A project can be divided into distinct stages, where pursuit of each stage is based on a reassessment of costs and benefits after the preceding stage is completed	Completion of each stage reduces ambiguity about the payoff from the subsequent stage, which is pursued only if a positive payoff is clear
Scale	The project can be scaled up or down	New information about favorable/unfavorable market prospects allows the investments to be expanded or contracted
Switch	A project can be redeployed for a different application (switch use) or a key foundational technology can be swapped out for another (switch inputs)	A project can be more valuable in a different application domain or a chosen technology building block that proves less robust can be replaced with an alternative one
Abandon	A project can be terminated midstream and the unused resources can be redeployed elsewhere	As a project progresses, actual costs and benefits become clearer; losses can be cut by terminating a failing endeavor

behind. Recall that network effects can protect early movers because end-users' willingness to adopt a network effects-dependent system is a function of the number of existing users.

2. *Stage*. This option exists if the project can be implemented in sequential stages, where the functionality in each stage can be implemented independent of subsequent stages. The new information generated in each stage allows a better assessment of the value of proceeding to the next stage. Embedding a staging option is one of the most powerful ways to apply options thinking in platform markets, beginning with a minimalist project footprint and progressively expanding it.

3. *Scale*. A scale option is embedded in a project if it can be scaled up without increasing a system's complexity or scaled down without compromising its viability. The scaling option therefore captures both the flexibility to expand and contract the scale of a project. As described subsequently, the option to scale up is embedded in architectural choices and the option to scale down is closely related to choice of business models and governance. The scale-down option is a milder form of the abandonment option.

4. *Switch*. The switch option is embedded in a project if it has the flexibility to either be switched to a different use than the one it is designed for or if a key foundational technology used in it can be swapped out for another one. In software systems, switching use rarely requires discontinuing the original application due to low reproduction costs for software. This is valuable when a project is better used in a different application domain than the one for which it was intended, or if a

selected building block technology proves less robust than an alternative that subsequently emerged. This option provides a springboard to envelopment and mutation of apps and platforms.

5. *Abandon.* A project carries an abandonment option if it can be terminated midstream and the freed-up resources can be salvaged and redeployed for a different project. In theory, any project can be abandoned. But in practice, sunk costs, morale damage, and the desire to save face can make it impossible to terminate projects that are on a failing course. The abandonment option can most readily be embedded in a project by (1) setting upfront explicit and clear exit criteria and (2) separating the authority to pull the plug from those directly involved in a project.

Multiple real options can simultaneously be embedded into a project, some naturally but more through deliberate design. The level of flexibility in implementing a platform is not preordained but deliberately *designed* into its initial design and architecture. For example, staging options can be embedded by carefully structuring a larger platform project into smaller, staged subprojects that cumulatively build on each other. Switch use options can be embedded by internally modularizing a core technology component in a platform or app that could later be swapped out with a rival one. It is through this process of deliberate design and restructuring at the outset of a project that real options are embedded.

8.4 APPLYING REAL OPTIONS THINKING IN PRACTICE

The tactic for applying real options thinking in practice is to decompose a project in a series of sequential subprojects. This requires first decomposing a larger project into smaller, shorter subprojects and then sequencing them using options thinking. Consider an example of a system for collaborative file synchronization (such as Dropbox), as illustrated in Figure 8.4. For simplicity, assume that the project has three intended pieces of functionality: (1) file synchronization, (2) text message notifications of file changes, and (3) social networking capabilities. For simplicity, let's assume that the project would take three months of development effort and the expected payoff of the project is $3 million, equally attributable to the three pieces of functionality. The traditional big-bang approach to software development would treat it in a monolithic fashion, as illustrated on the left-hand side of Figure 8.4. If all goes well, the project would be completed on schedule and would realize its payoff at the end of the third month, when the project goes live. However, this assumes that its users' needs would remain stable over that time and that no glitch or technical challenge will appear. Such monolithic implementations also tend to incorporate rigid assumptions about users and user needs. If the development team runs into an insurmountable technical problem or if user needs turn out to be different from what the project team had assumed, say in the second month, the project can stall and realized payoff would be zero. Put another way, there is not much to show for the $2 million already spent.

Embedding real options in the same project requires decomposing the project into smaller subprojects and then appropriately sequencing their implementation. Consider the same example, but broken down into three subprojects: A (file synching), B (text notifications), and C (social networking capabilities). This provides two advantages. First, if something goes awry after stage A is completed but stage B is in progress, there will be some return to show, as shown in the shaded area on the right-hand side of Figure 8.4, even if stage B is never completed. This payoff would have been forfeited if the project were not decomposed. Second, new information might be generated at the end of stage A that might reduce the uncertainty about whether proceeding to stage B is likely to be worthwhile. The staged nature of investments lowers downside risk, which is capped at the money already invested in the

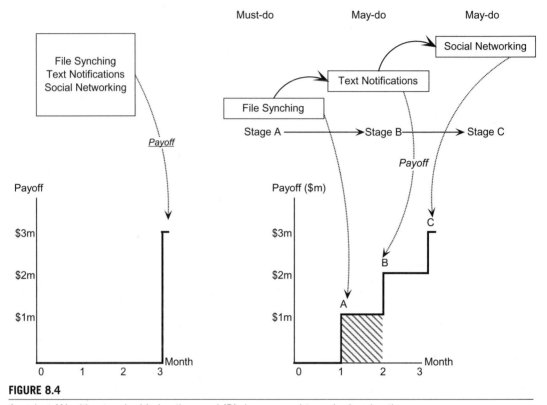

FIGURE 8.4

A project (A) without embedded options and (B) decomposed to embed real options.

ongoing stage. However, the upside remains open because the decision to invest in further stages can be made after the completion of one stage generates new information about the prospects of the subsequent stages. Such information generated at the end of each subproject would not be available if the project had not been decomposed.

The decomposed version of the project therefore separates calculated risks from foolish risks, disciplines investment decisions, and safeguards against misreading the writing on the wall. It contrasts starkly with the big bets approach, which are riskier in the presence of volatility.

Therefore, in the presence of volatility, a project with embedded real options is more valuable than one without them.

8.4.1 Decomposing a project into smaller subprojects

There are two possible ways to decompose a project into standalone stages (Fichman and Moses, 1999): (1) successive stages involve the same systems but with additional detail and features added to them (akin to adding layers of paint on a canvas, called *canvas painting incrementalism*) or (2) successive stages involve functionality that was intentionally excluded from preceding stages (akin to adding slices to a pie, called *pie slice incrementalism*). We recommend the second approach, which is more conducive to applying real options thinking to platform evolution. However, for the advantages of project decomposition to be realized, both decomposition and the sequencing of stages require forethought. The decomposition must follow three simple rules of thumb:

1. *Separate must-do and may-do elements.* The first step to begin applying options thinking is to distinguish what a project must do and what it may do. The must-do element is a project's "minimum viable footprint," or minimal baseline functionality that it must deliver (Adner, 2012, p. 194). For things that a project must do, there is no flexibility by definition, thus no option value. Think of the leanest configuration of functionality that can be implemented to create a distinct, functioning platform (or app), focusing on its distinctive feature set and nothing more. This allows you to begin by tackling the subset of problems that you are currently in the best position to solve, and enables cheaper and faster iterations. The must-do and may-do elements of the larger project must first be clearly separated. All options are embedded in the may-do elements of a project, where value can be created by structuring these may-do elements as options. To identify the may-do elements, think of which additional elements can be added on top of the must-do elements so that each new may-do element cumulatively benefits from the preceding stages.

    Increasing the may-do to must-do ratio expands opportunities for embedding real options in a project by increasing the number of stages. The must-do subproject creates the flexibility without the obligation to proceed to the next stage. Its outcomes generate new information about the true value of proceeding to the first may-do subproject, which is appropriate given the milestone-driven, iterative management processes that underlie real options thinking. This approach also curbs scope creep and overengineering of solutions by keeping the implementation focused on a few key attributes that the completed project must deliver at each stage (Fichman and Moses, 1999). Overengineering otherwise produces a proliferation of complexity (Fichman and Moses, 1999).

2. *Segregate by volatility.* Segregate functions with the least technical and market volatility into a different stage from those with the greatest volatility.

3. *Each stage must be discrete with a measurable value proposition.* Each stage must deliver clear measurable benefits even if no further stages (the may-dos) are ever completed (Fichman and Moses, 1999). Each increment must implement *everything* required to produce the desired results for that subproject, and must be doable in a relatively short timeframe.

8.4.2 **Sequencing subprojects**

The may-do stages must be cleverly sequenced to maximize the potential for extracting value from embedded real options. Sequencing stages follow three additional rules of thumb:

1. *The planned functionality implemented in any stage should not be dependent on later stages.* Each stage must produce a distinct outcome that is not dependent on the subsequent stages. In other words, each stage must provide a standalone value proposition. Later stages can, however, cumulatively build on the outcomes of preceding stages. This ensures that each stage is cumulative

such that accomplishments from each stage feed into and provide foundations for the subsequent stages.

2. *Sequence the lowest uncertainty stages first and highest uncertainty stages last*. Schedule stages with the greatest uncertainty as late as possible in the overall project roadmap. The must-do elements must focus on opportunities with the least technical uncertainty and the highest immediate payoff, ensuring that the stream of benefits will begin accruing earlier rather than later. However, defer functionality to a later stage only if there is no clear first-mover advantage (i.e., the upside opportunity is not imperiled by delaying it and there is no realistic danger of preemption or lockout from the market due to rivals). This approach can reduce challenges in subsequent stages by generating new information during the implementation of the preceding stages. Even if some later stages are never implemented, some payoff is generated from what is feasible instead of pursuing an all-or-nothing proposition.

3. *Sequence stages with the most cumulative learning first*. Start with a set of features where conditions are most favorable to success and where learning is most cumulative (i.e., lays the foundation for the subsequent stages). Resolving uncertainty should be dependent on the direct experience that can be gained through learning-by-doing in the earlier stages. The upside is that uncertainty about later stages can potentially be decreased by new information generated during each stage, allowing a more informed decision about whether to proceed to the next stage.

This decomposed sequencing approach sounds logical in theory, but is challenging in practice because of a penchant for an all-at-once mindset prevalent in software projects (Fichman and Moses, 1999). Furthermore, the project must also be technologically divisible into stages, which has a lot to do with the choice of its architecture.

8.5 EXERCISING REAL OPTIONS: THE DEVIL IS IN THE DETAILS

Recognizing and embedding flexibility in a project in the form of real options is only half the story. Such flexibility is not of much value unless it is exercised appropriately, which is where its value is extracted. This requires recognizing when to exercise the flexibility, when to keep it in the back pocket, and when to ditch each embedded option.

The simplified options exercise framework in Figure 8.5 provides a simple way to make such decisions (Courtney, 2001, p. 143). On the *y*-axis is the volatility involved in a project, which can be technical or market volatility. Embedding a real option in a project often has a direct cost and some value. On the *x*-axis is the ratio of value to cost for a specific real option. This ratio is 1 when value and costs are equal; greater than 1 when value exceeds cost; and less than 1 when cost exceeds value.

8.5.1 Cost of an option

There is no free lunch because creating options in a project incurs both direct costs and opportunity costs. Embedding real options can therefore add to the initial development cost. Direct costs are the costs of additional development work that is needed to embed various flexibilities in the design of the project. Opportunity costs are the costs of not being able to do something else (e.g., implementing a feature) because of the time and effort expended on creating that flexibility. Creating such flexibility

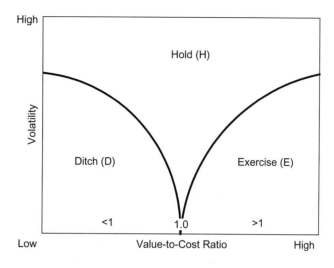

FIGURE 8.5

A simplified real options exercise framework.

often requires upfront investments such as restructuring or decomposing a project into stages or designing it to allow for swapping out one ingredient technology with another. You must weigh the potential loss of fleeting opportunities because embedding a real option can also add to the development time. This is the cost of embedding that option, the loss if that option is not subsequently exercised. The cost of embedding an option is usually the same, no matter what the level of volatility surrounding the project.

8.5.2 **Value of an option**

The value of a real option, unlike cost, is a lot harder to estimate. Various methods, including partial differential equations, dynamic programming, and simulations, have been developed to estimate the value of options. However, research is ongoing and these techniques are typically beyond the grasp of most other than a few specialists who can read research papers written mostly in Greek symbols! In fact, Professors Black and Sholes won the 1997 Nobel Prize for their attempt to solve the options valuation problem. However, applying real options thinking in practice does not require acquiring arcane academic skills to value real options.

8.5.3 **Exercising an embedded option: when to hold and when to fold**

The simple question to ask is whether—given the known cost of embedding a *specific* real option in the design of a project—its value is likely to exceed its cost. If not, the option falls in the left half of Figure 8.4. Here, if volatility is low, it falls in the *ditch* region (D) of the framework. Such options are not worth investing in creating and if they are already present in a project, they are safe to ditch. A flexible design is valuable only in the presence of volatility but is suboptimal when volatility is absent. An inflexible design optimized to a particular set of stable circumstances can often outperform a flexible one when volatility is absent. Because embedding a real option such as switching use or inputs in the initial design of a project costs real money, when volatility is low or expiration time short, the cost of creating the option can exceed its potential value. However, if the volatility associated with the option is very high, it falls in the *hold* region (H) of the framework. Such options are worth holding on to if they are already present in a project, and worth investing in creating if the project is new. As volatility declines, it shifts to the *exercise* region (E) in the framework. Such options should immediately be exercised to extract their value. Poorly timing the exercise of an option can wipe out its potential value.

This simple options exercise framework emphasizes that the *changes* in volatility associated with an option are the key factor that can shift it from the hold (H) to ditch (D) or exercise (E) regions in the framework. Volatility is a simplified representation of reality and is based on assumptions help by the system's designers. Like any subjective representation based on assumptions, it should evolve over time. Therefore, volatility is a dynamic rather than a static attribute. Active tracking and constant monitoring of the key volatility and proactively monitoring unfolding trends associated with each embedded real option is therefore key to realizing their value. This also requires frequently testing and updating assumptions about the core technologies and adopters of a platform. In software-based platforms, such data can often be gleaned inexpensively from usage patterns and metrics. What cannot be predicted can also often be gleaned through small-scale experiments with feature tweaks (e.g., users find one interface option easier to use than another). But such information is of value only if the new information they generate is acted on and used to update volatility estimates used in real options thinking.

The common traps in failing to recognize when to exercise the flexibility provided by an embedded real option include the lack of diverse inputs from multiple project stakeholders, looking only at existing end-user and app-developer pools while neglecting prospective new ones, and basing decisions on a static project roadmap rather than one that is a living document.

8.6 LESSONS LEARNED

- *Real options discipline imagination.* Real options thinking disciplines projects to safeguard against potential losses while preserving their upside potential.
- *Real options are more valuable under uncertainty.* Uncertainty can be in either the technology or the market needs addressed by a platform or app project.
- *Real options are of six types.* Real options embedded in a project provide the flexibility to use a project as a foundation for strategic growth, defer, stage investments, change scale, switch its components or purpose, or abandon it.
- *Staging is the most common real option.* This requires decomposing a project into must-do and may-do elements, and then implementing them in an options-driven sequence. Real options thinking guides both the decomposition and sequencing of such subprojects.
- *Timed exercise extracts real option value.* Embedded real options must be exercised using a simple options exercise framework, described in this chapter.

The next chapter delves into five discrete operations called *modular operators* that can be performed on a platform or an app, and within the ecosystem to evolve it using real options thinking. These modular operators provide the language to precisely describe evolution in platform ecosystems.

Modular Operators: Platform Ecosystems' Evolutionary Baby Steps

9

IN THIS CHAPTER

- An overview of modular operators
- The role of modular operators
- The SPLIT operator
- The SUBTRACT operator
- The SUBSTITUTE operator
- The AUGMENT operator and its INVERT and ENVELOP special cases
- The MUTATE operator and its PORT special case
- A stylized representation of evolution using modular operator sequences

Modularization of platform interfaces embeds flexibility in the form of real options in their ecosystem. This flexibility is manifested in five discrete operations that can be performed on a platform or an app, and within the ecosystem to evolve it. These discrete steps are called *modular operators*. Evolution of an app, platform, or the entire ecosystem can be mapped on a timeline with nothing but this small set of modular operators. Think of modular operators as the alphabet—or baby steps—to precisely describe evolutionary paths taken in platform ecosystems. In this brief chapter we describe each of the five operators along with some of their special cases. We subsequently use these operators in Chapter 10 (on platform evolution) and Chapter 11 (on app evolution) to explain how platform owners and app developers can use them to evolve platforms, apps, and entire ecosystems using these five discrete operators.

9.1 AN OVERVIEW OF MODULAR OPERATORS

Modular operators are a repertoire of discrete actions that can be performed in modularized platform ecosystems. These operators are actions that change the existing structures of platform ecosystems into new ones in well-defined ways (Baldwin and Clark, 2000, p. 129). Complex evolutionary changes in a platform can be understood and envisioned using sequences of modular operators applied successively over time. Modular operators can therefore be iteratively applied to a

---

☆"To view the full reference list for the book, click here or see page 283."

modularized design to incrementally refine the ecosystem. Modular operators are therefore baby steps representing the trajectories and pathways through which a platform's ecosystem evolves.

There are five modular operators. Table 9.1 briefly defines each operator, what levels in an ecosystem it applies within and to, and provides a notation for each operator. Figure 9.1 illustrates the operated-upon system before and after each modular operation.

Most operators, with the exception of *SPLIT*, work only on modular systems, entire "modules" or subsystems (i.e., the platform or an app) at a time *as a whole* (Baldwin and Clark, 2000, p. 131; Gamba and Fusari, 2009). Therefore, all of the operators can be applied *within* platform ecosystems, and to the entire platform or entire apps *as a whole*. Except for SPLIT, they cannot be used within an app or platform unless it is internally modularized, a move that should be avoided for the many reasons, described in Chapter 5 on architectures in Part II of this book. They can, however, be used within a platform or an app once the SPLIT operator has been used on it.

9.1.1 Split

The SPLIT operator involves subdividing a monolithic system into two smaller, possibly modularized subsystems. Applying the SPLIT operator is the only way a monolithic system can be modularized (Gamba and Fusari, 2009). This operator is involved in refactoring of software systems, which is how a monolithic system can be given modular properties. This is the only operator that can be applied to nonmodular/monolithic systems. Splitting a monolithic pre-platform system is often the first step to evolve an existing system into a platform; competition among rival apps arises only after splitting makes app-level substitution possible within the ecosystem of the modularized platform. SPLIT can therefore be applied *within* a platform or an app, unlike all other operators that can only be applied *to* a platform or an app as a whole.

9.1.2 Subtract

The SUBTRACT operator applies only to modular systems and involves removing an app or the platform from the ecosystem. Therefore, removing an app from a platform's ecosystem is an example of a SUBTRACT operation on an app. Similarly, removing the platform from an ecosystem while retaining the apps is the application of the SPLIT operation on the platform. An example of this is the removal of the Android platform from the Android ecosystem and subsequently replacing (the SUBSTITUTE operator) it with the Blackberry Tablet operating system (using emulation). In this example, the subtraction allowed the Blackberry Tablet operating system to exploit the existing pool of Android apps for use with its own platform. However, since apps and platforms are often internally modular though externally modularized, this operator cannot be applied within individual apps or a platform, only *to* them taken as a whole. Exclusion—by leaving out a selected subsystem—creates a minimal design now with the opportunity to subsequently increase its scope and functionality using the AUGMENT operator (Gamba and Fusari, 2009).

9.1.3 Substitute

The SUBSTITUTE operator involves substitution of a subsystem (i.e., an app of a platform) within an ecosystem with another one. It is usable within an ecosystem but usable only on individual

Table 9.1 Scope of Application of Each Modular Operator in a Platform Ecosystem

Evolutionary Operator	Notation	Usable *Within*			Usable *On*			Definition
		Ecosystem	Platform	App	Ecosystem	Platform	App	
Split[a]	$\neq$	●	●	●		●	●	Subdivision of a monolithic system into two smaller subsystems; modularizes monolithic systems
Subtract	$-$	●				●	●	Removal of a subsystem from the ecosystem
Substitute	$\rightleftarrows$	●				●	●	Substitution of one subsystem in the ecosystem with another
Augment	$+$	●				●	●	Addition of a new subsystem to the ecosystem, adding new functionality
Special case: Invert	$+^i$	●				●	●	Addition of the functionality widely used by other interacting systems to the original ecosystem. Invert potentially *demodularizes* by converting a modular pair of systems into a monolithic system
Special case: Envelop	$+^e$	●				●	●	Addition of the functionality of an adjacent solution with a shared user base to the original ecosystem, swallowing the target's functionality
Mutate	$\approx$	●			●	●	●	Replication of a system to create a distinct derivative system intended for use in a different application domain
Special case: Port	$\approx^p$	●				●	●	Replicating the functionality of an app to allow it to function on a platform different from which it was originally implemented

[a]*Can be used in monolithic systems as well; all others can be used only within modular ecosystems.*

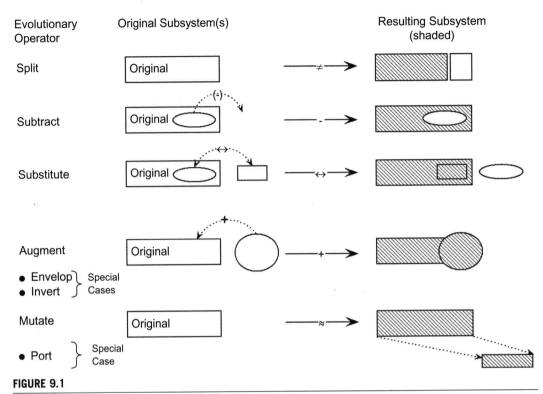

FIGURE 9.1

Before and after the use of each modular operator.

subsystems taken as a whole. It is therefore not usable on systems that are internally monolithic, unless they are first internally modularized using the SPLIT operator. The SUBSTITUTE operator is the key to accelerating evolution in modularized platform ecosystems because it allows one version of an app to be replaced with an improved version, without causing a ripple effect in the ecosystem. It is also key to creating competition among rival apps in platform ecosystems because it allows one app to be swapped out for a different one by end-users. For example, a Web browser in a mobile computing platform can be substituted for an existing one. The substitute operator allows platform ecosystems to evolve through modular recombination (Garud and Kumaraswamy, 1993; Simon, 2002), giving an ecosystem a plug-and-play property with respect to individual apps (its subsystems).

9.1.4 Augment

The AUGMENT operator involves adding a new subsystem—usually an app—that adds new functionality to a platform's ecosystem without requiring any other change elsewhere in the ecosystem (Gamba and Fusari, 2009). This operator therefore is usable on an app and within an ecosystem. The AUGMENT operator is the primary mechanism for adding new capabilities and giving emergent properties to an ecosystem.

9.1.4.1 Special case 1: Invert

Inversion is the first special case of the augment operator. Inversion is used to subsume into a platform functionality that is widely shared by many apps in the platform's ecosystem. Such recurring functionality might have emerged after the original system was implemented but is widely used by many apps. Therefore, it meets the criteria for high reusability and low variability, making it a prime candidate for integration into the core platform. Evolutionary theorist Brian Arthur (2009) describes this as the congealing of a heavily used subsystem into a platform. This operator often requires the addition of new interfaces (usually in the form of new APIs) that apps can use to invoke the now-integrated functionality (Baldwin and Clark, 2000, p. 138). Inversion is the opposite of the split operator because it reduces modularity by potentially combining two modularly interacting subsystems into a larger monolithic system. Inversion is the key mechanism through which redundant implementations of common functions recurring and spread across many apps can be consolidated into the platform (Gamba and Fusari, 2009; Kamel, 1987). This reduction in duplication of effort across apps in turn improves the scale economies obtained by a platform's app developers, increasing the value of the platform to future apps. However, inversion can also wipe out the business of app developers who might have previously specialized in providing the inverted functionality. An example of inversion is iOS subsuming cut-and-paste functionality and system notifications that were required by many apps but absent in the earlier versions of the iOS platform. Paradoxically, inversion speeds up the evolvability of the ecosystem as a whole because it allows any apps that use that common functionality to benefit from improvements in it when that functionality is implemented in the platform itself.

9.1.4.2 Special case 2: Envelop

Envelopment is the second special case of the AUGMENT operator because it involves adding a new module to an ecosystem that replicates the functionality of an adjacent solution or product whose user base overlaps with that of the original ecosystem. This operator is the primary mechanism through which an ecosystem can expand to swallow solutions offered in adjacent markets (Eisenmann et al., 2011).

9.1.5 Mutate

The MUTATE operator involves making a copy of the original system to create a derivative system intended for use in a different application domain. Mutation creates a distinct derivative system, leaving the original intact (Tiwana et al., 2010). The spin-off inherits some properties of the parent system but with a function distinctive from its parent. The mutate operator can be used on both modular and monolithic systems at all levels. Therefore the mutate operator can be used on—but not within—an ecosystem, a platform, or an app.

9.1.5.1 Special case: Port

A special case of the MUTATE operation is the PORT operation, which applies primarily to apps. It can sometimes also be used on a platform. Porting involves replicating the functionality of an app to allow it to function on a different platform from the one for which it was originally implemented. The core functionality of the app remains unchanged but its implementation is unique to the new platform. An example of porting would be implementing the Skype Mobile app originally developed for iOS on the Android platform. The advantage of porting is that the app does not have to be redesigned from scratch for the target platform. However, the implementation often must be done from scratch because of cross-platform differences. There have been attempts to create universally portable "write-once-run-everywhere" software, but they have had limited success. Portability often conflicts with an app's platform specificity (i.e., the degree to which it can leverage capabilities unique to a specific platform in its own operations). Therefore, universal portability is rarely an attainable goal and is often not desirable given the performance tradeoffs that it often introduces. However, the use of virtual machines (e.g., Java virtual machine and Microsoft's .NET framework) allows a limited degree of cross-platform portability.

A growth in platform-specific APIs can discourage multihoming and reduce portability. App developers can and often do spread their development costs across multiple platforms, hedge bets on multiple rival platforms than being tied down to one that might end up failing, and also access a larger pool of potential customers. An indistinguishably similar pool of apps on rival platforms reduces platform differentiation. Therefore, it is generally in the interest of app developers to increase portability but in the interests of a platform owner to reduce it. Platform owners can reduce portability by rapidly adding new APIs and platform functionality that differentiates the app on their platform, increasing incentives for app developers to reduce modularization of their app in order to take advantage of the platform's unique capabilities. App developers in contrast can increase portability by increasing modularity vis-à-vis a platform, relying on virtual machines, and relying less on platform-specific capabilities (instead investing in building their own).

Each of the modular operators can be applied in any sequence, one at a time to a platform, app, and an entire ecosystem. The stylized representation in Figure 9.2 illustrates how the evolutionary trajectory of platform subsystems using the exhaustive set of modular operators described in this chapter can be compactly tracked. We return to these operators in guiding the evolution of platforms and apps, respectively, in Chapters 10 and 11.

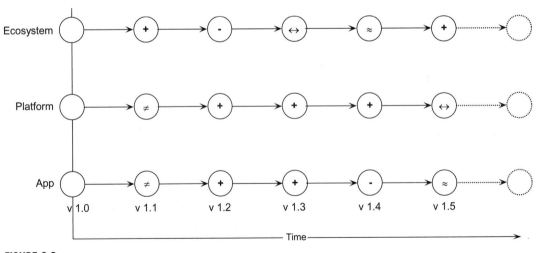

FIGURE 9.2

A stylized representation of evolution using modular operators.

9.2 **LESSONS LEARNED**

- *Modular operators are five discrete evolutionary actions.* Modular operators are a repertory of discrete actions that change the existing structures of subsystems in a platform ecosystem into new ones in precisely defined ways.
- *Modular operators can only be applied one at a time.* Complex evolutionary changes in a platform can be envisioned using sequences of modular operators applied successively over time, one at a time.
- *Modular operators can be used on all types of systems but only within some.* All operators can be used on an ecosystem, app, or platform taken as a whole. SPLIT can be applied *within* a platform or an app.
- *The SPLIT operator* breaks a monolithic system into two smaller subsystems and can be used to modularize a monolithic system.
- *The SUBTRACT operator* removes a subsystem from the ecosystem.
- *The SUBSTITUTE operator* swaps out one subsystem in the ecosystem with another.
- *The AUGMENT operator* adds a new subsystem to the ecosystem. Its two special cases are the INVERT and ENVELOP operators.
- *The MUTATE operator* replicates a system to create a distinct derivative system for use in a different application domain. Its special case PORT operator reimplements its functionality in a different platform ecosystem.
- *Modular operators on a timeline convey evolution.* A stylized representation of evolution using modular operators conveys its evolution trajectory.

The next chapter delves into how platform owners can orchestrate the evolution of a platform.

Orchestrating Evolution

IV

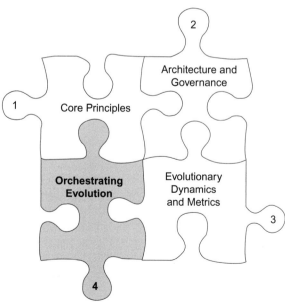

2 — Architecture and Governance

1 — Core Principles

Orchestrating Evolution

Evolutionary Dynamics and Metrics

3

4

Evolving a Platform

It is not the strongest or the most intelligent who will survive but those who can best manage change.
Charles Darwin

IN THIS CHAPTER

- Parallels between platforms and evolutionary biology
- The "bathtub model" of innovation stocks and flows
- Creating and sustaining a competitive advantage: The litmus test
- Lessons on evolution speed from American military doctrine
- Aligning architecture and governance
- Ensuring platform resilience, scalability, and composability
- Growing platform stickiness with app developers and end-users
- Evolving the platform core and its boundary
- Growing platform synergy
- Orchestrating platform plasticity
- Orchestrating vertical and horizontal platform envelopment
- Orchestrating platform durability
- Orchestrating platform mutation

The central idea in evolutionary biology is that multiple species compete over scarce resources in a changing environment. Charles Darwin (Figure 10.1), the originator of this idea, suggested that the ones that survive are not the strongest or the cleverest but the ones that are most adaptive to their environment. Evolution is then simply the process of adaptation, rewarded by the survival of the fittest. This biological analogy is a powerful metaphor for understanding the evolution of platforms. Rival platforms are akin to competing species, competing for the same pool of adopters in a complex, turbulent environment.

Like living organisms, platforms have the potential to adapt and evolve to sustain themselves over long periods. Thinking of a platform as a living entity then implies that its primary goal becomes survival. It will survive only if there is a symbiotic relationship—an implicit contract—between the platform owner and its app developers to help the latter reach higher in return for their support of the

---

☆"To view the full reference list for the book, click here or see page 283."

FIGURE 10.1

Charles Darwin (1809–1882) originated contemporary ideas of evolutionary survival.

Source: Hutton Webster, Modern European History, *D.C. Heath & Co., Boston, 1920.*

platform's goals. It requires a mindset that is tolerant of new ideas, being fair, and focused primarily on longevity rather than profitability.

However, grasping the evolution of software platforms is challenging for most of us who were trained to think of software projects in terms of operational and implementation metrics such as efficiency, effectiveness, and quality. Thinking of platform evolution as software development is a counterproductive analogy for orchestrating ecosystems. A more productive analogy is the production of a daily newspaper, which must deliver a fresh edition every morning. Its structure, such as its major sections, does not change from day to day, but the content evolves. Stock tickers and economic indicators in the financials page change little, but their content is updated each morning. A platform's ecosystem must similarly constantly balance change and stability as it evolves.

This chapter delves into how a platform owner can orchestrate the evolution of a platform. We begin by describing a "bathtub model" of innovation stocks and flows and then describe a litmus test for identifying which resources in a platform's ecosystem can give it a competitive advantage. We emphasize how the only source of sustainable advantage that a platform owner can count on is evolutionary speed. We then describe how dynamic alignment of a platform's architecture and its governance accelerate its evolution. We trace the influence of these two levers for orchestration on the short-, medium-, and long-term metrics of platform evolution, described in Chapter 7. We first tackle how a platform owner can bolster a platform's resilience, scalability, and composability in the short term, followed by stickiness, synergy, and plasticity in the medium term. We conclude with a discussion of how a platform owner can orchestrate envelopment by a platform while rebuffing envelopment attacks on the platform, ensure its durability, and orchestrate platform mutation in the long run.

10.1 THE BATHTUB MODEL: ECOSYSTEM INNOVATION AS STOCKS AND FLOWS

Complex systems such as platform ecosystems are partially designed and partially evolved (de Weck et al., 2011, p. 168). Evolution of a platform ecosystem can be envisioned as inflows and outflows of innovations, as illustrated in Figure 10.2. Think of this as the "bathtub theory" of platform evolution. Inflows are innovations that enter an ecosystem, contributed primarily by app developers and the platform owner, and to a lesser extent by end-users, upstream suppliers in the platform's value chain, and

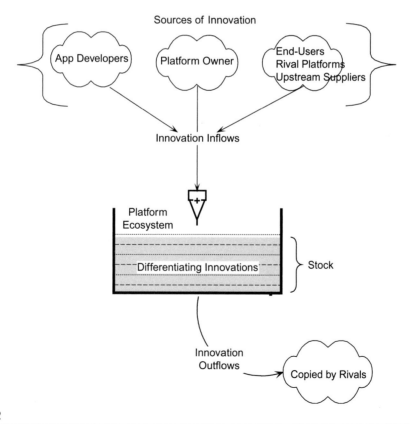

FIGURE 10.2

Innovation stocks and flows in the bathtub model of platform evolution.

ideas copied from rival platforms. Outflows are innovations that are copied by rival platforms. The net difference between inflows and outflows—what is left in the reservoir—are a platform ecosystem's stocks of innovation that can *potentially* differentiate it from rival ecosystems. (The stock is the shaded portion in Figure 10.2.) These are features, functions, and assets that are unique to a platform's ecosystem. Differentiation using the shaded part of Figure 10.2 is the essence of platform strategy and the key source of competitive advantage. In the long run, it is the shaded stock unique to a platform's ecosystem that determines its long-term prosperity.

The goal of effective ecosystem orchestration by a platform owner then is twofold: (1) growing the stock of innovations and (2) using these to competitively differentiate a platform from its rivals.

10.1.1 Growing the stock

Growing the stock of innovations unique to a platform ecosystem requires reducing the outflow and increasing the inflow. The outflow is a function of the intensity of rivalry among competitive platforms and the occasional protections using patents. In competitive platform markets, reducing the outflows is usually challenging. This is especially true when a platform establishes a dominant design, and its core features are so readily replicated that they become merely the cost of entry into its market but no longer serve as differentiators. For example, Android had a late start and lagged in its capabilities compared to iOS, which subsequently became the smartphone industry's dominant design. However, it replicated almost all core features of iOS's dominant design in about half a decade (from 2007 to 2013) and gained a billion end-users in the process by 2014. Once replicated, new innovations do not differentiate a platform from its rivals. They simply become a baseline expectation among potential adopters of a platform. This pattern repeats itself like clockwork in almost every era of technology innovation, beginning with Citibank's introduction of ATM machines that differentiated it only during the 6 months it took its rivals to introduce theirs. If the speed of outflows through copying is high, inflows must be increased to keep the stock stable and substantially increased to grow it relative to rival platforms. Platform owners usually have a limited ability to reduce outflows, so must focus primarily on increasing inflows. A platform ecosystem's capacity to nurture a *stream* of valuable new functionality can allow it to innovate faster than rivals can replicate it (Boudreau, 2010).

10.1.1.1 Architecture–governance alignment

Increasing innovation inflows into a platform's ecosystem requires two things from a platform owner with respect to app developers.

1. *Motivation.* Creating the motivation to innovate around a platform is primarily done through governance that creates strong incentives for app developers. It also enriches the diversity of the pool of ideas for augmenting the native capabilities of a platform.
2. *Ability.* Creating the ability to innovate around a platform is primarily the role of platform architecture that makes it easier, cheaper, and faster for app developers to use a platform as a springboard for their own development work. A recent study of platforms from 1990 to 2004 found that opening up platforms to outside developers increased the rate of innovation by 500% (Boudreau, 2010). However, a rich pool of diverse ideas dispersed across the ecosystem will not add up to much without a capacity—platform owners' and app developers'—to act on them. For this, a platform's ecosystem must be evolvable. Evolvability is a platform ecosystem's capacity to

rapidly adapt to unanticipated changes in its competitive environment (Baldwin and Woodard, 2009; de Weck et al., 2011). Evolvability is determined in large part by the choice of a platform's architecture (de Weck et al., 2011, p. 141; Iansiti and Levien, 2004, p. 152). This is because the viability of various modular operators, described in Chapter 9, are directly enabled and constrained by its architecture. A platform's architecture serves as its DNA—largely irreversible and enduring—that provides a blueprint for the evolutionary trajectories that a platform can and cannot pursue, the types of innovations that do and do not emerge around it, and the vibrancy of its ecosystem.

Motivation without ability is as worthless as ability without motivation. Therefore, platform governance must be aligned with platform architecture (Tiwana, 2008b; Tiwana and Konsynski, 2010). One must mutually reinforce the other so their joint effect exceeds their sum of parts. Architecture and governance are deeply interwoven and inseparably intertwined in shaping the evolutionary trajectory of platforms. Alignment allows their evolution to be propelled by the invisible hand of the market and orchestrated by architecture. This is why we described platform architecture and governance as the two gears of a platform's evolutionary motor (see Figure 10.3). Such architecture–governance alignment is the predictor of a platform's evolution, and the majority of this chapter describes how such alignment can be achieved. The two must interlock for the evolutionary motor to move forward; their mis-locking exacts evolutionary penalties. It is therefore platform evolution where platform architecture meets platform governance.

Governance and architecture can act as a system, mutually reinforcing each other. Neither alone is as effective as the two together. They have a two-way effect; both are affected by each other and affect each other. It is not only platform architecture that determines feasible governance strategies but also governance choices by platform owners that lead to architectures evolving along different trajectories over time. We therefore must think in terms of the codesign and coevolution of architectures and governance (Tiwana et al., 2010). The same architectures will lead to different types and levels of innovation under different governance structures. However, the consequences of different architectures on

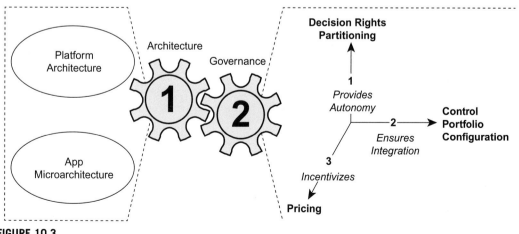

FIGURE 10.3

Architecture and governance—gears of a platform's evolutionary motor—must interlock.

innovation within a platform's ecosystem cannot be predicted without considering the motivations and incentives of app developers and the broader competitive environment within which a platform exists. Platform governance can therefore reinforce or weaken the benefits of platform architecture depending on whether they are aligned or misaligned. Their alignment encourages and also allows the ecosystem to absorb variety and experimentation in apps that augment the platform. (Architecture–governance alignment also shapes the evolution of apps, which is discussed in the next chapter.)

10.1.2 Creating and sustaining a competitive advantage

Merely growing the stock of innovation—what's left in the bathtub in Figure 10.2—does not create a competitive advantage for a platform. A platform owner's responsibility is for developing and sustaining a competitive advantage that differentiates a platform from rivals. Even if a platform begins with a clear competitive edge or technical superiority, it is only a matter of time that rivals will erode any such advantage if the payoffs are large enough. Put another way, beginning with a competitive advantage does not mean that it will be sustainable. Therefore, one must think in terms of *sustainability* of a temporary advantage rather than search for the Holy Grail of durable competitive advantage.

Platform owners must begin by abandoning the fantasy that there even exists such a thing as a durable competitive advantage. The idea belongs with the likes of the Tooth Fairy and the Abominable Snowman. (I will refrain from putting Santa Claus on this list.) Instead, any competitive advantage is temporary and fleeting. A platform must become adept at finding new sources of temporary advantage. Therefore, success in platform markets depends on maintaining a steady stream of innovation inflows into the ecosystem that is faster than the speed at which rivals can copy it. Evolution speed then becomes a source of competitive advantage.

10.1.2.1 The resource litmus test

To understand how competitive advantage is created and sustained, focus on an ecosystem's stock of "resources" (i.e., what is left in the bathtub in Figure 10.2) at any point in time. A resource refers to tangible assets such as a platform's capabilities, functionality, user base, complementing apps, and patents as well as its intangible resources such as brand recognition and reputation.[1] Intangibles such as brands are messier to count on because once they define the dominant design for a platform's market category, there are no guarantees that their value can be captured exclusively by the platform owner. Xerox copiers, Scotch tape, the IBM PC, and iPhone define their entire product categories to such a large extent that they have become generic labels used to describe their many clones. This is particularly true of software-based platforms.

Identify the *key* resources of a platform, focusing specifically on what the platform owner directly contributes to the platform's ecosystem. To keep this list focused on the key resources, put it on one side of an index card. For each resource, use the *resource litmus test* below to identify whether it can competitively differentiate a platform from its rivals. The resource litmus test is based on an assessment of four properties of a resource (Table 10.1).

---

[1]This perspective, called the resource-based theory of competitive advantage (Coff, 1999; Mezias and Mezias, 2000; Wernerfelt, 1984), is based on Edith Penrose's (1959) work in the 1950s that rose to prominence 40 years later.

Table 10.1 The Resource Litmus Test

Resource Property	Competitive Advantage	
	Creates	Sustains
Valuable?	●	
Rare?	●	
Inimitable?		●
Nonsubstitutable?		●

1. *Valuable*: Is it of value in the platform's market and industry?
2. *Rare*: Do very few rival platforms have it?
3. *Inimitable*: Is it difficult (prohibitively costly or time-consuming) for a rival platform to imitate?
4. *Nonsubstitutable*: Can something else substitute for it?

The more of these properties a resource possesses, the more likely it can help competitively differentiate a platform from its rivals. A resource can help create a competitive advantage if it is valuable and rare. A resource can help sustain a competitive advantage if it is inimitable and nonsubstitutable. The mere possession of a resource does not give a platform a competitive edge; a platform owner must have the capability to widely exploit it as well. Alignment of a platform's architecture with governance facilitates this.

As an illustration, Table 10.2 uses this resource litmus framework for a back-of-the-napkin comparison of one platform (iOS) with three rival platforms (Android, Blackberry, and Windows Mobile). The table succinctly helps recognize the competitive edge of individual rival platforms and therefore helps envision an actionable roadmap for evolving a platform. The list of resources in this example is merely illustrative and by no means comprehensive. A valuable resource must also be rare to create a temporary advantage for a platform (i.e., very few rival platforms should possess it). It must be inimitable and nonsubstitutable for it to sustain that edge. Therefore all four resource properties should have checkmarks in them for a resource to be an enduring source of differentiation. None of the resources in the quick-and-dirty analyses meet those criteria, suggesting that there is no durable source of competitive advantage in the market of these platforms. This is the norm for platform markets with Red Queen competition and the only source of advantage for any platform is evolving faster than rivals.

10.1.3 Evolution speed: lessons from the American military doctrine

If no temporary advantage is sustainable in the evolutionary Red Queen race, a platform must become adept at finding new sources—streams rather than events—of temporary advantage. Think of baby steps to create a steady flurry of temporary advantages. Evolution speed matters (Baldwin and Clark, 2000, p. 404); faster evolution increases the odds of gaining an unchallenged edge for at least as long as the time it takes rival platforms to replicate new innovations. In Red Queen-dominated platform markets, it is better to act quickly and iteratively than perfectly. In contrast, slower evolution leads to missed windows of opportunity.

Although business strategists often compare competition among rivals to a game of chess, viewing platform orchestration as playing a chess master is a counterproductive exercise. Multiple chess pieces

Table 10.2 An Illustration of the Application of the Resource Litmus Test

| Resource | Rival Platforms | | | | Resource Litmus Test Properties | | | |
| | | | | | Create Edge | | Sustain Edge | |
	iOS	Android	Blackberry	Windows Mobile	Valuable?	Rare?	Inimitable?	Nonsubstitutable?
Perceived ease of use	●	●			✓	✗		✓
Native cloud services	●	●			✓	✗	✗	✗
Integration with Gmail		●			✓	✓	✗	✗
Platform-wide messaging services	●	●	●		✓	✗		
Multiple form factors (phone, tablet)	●	●	●	●	✓	✗	✗	✗
Existing proprietary network effects	●	●	●		✓	✗	✓	✓
Large app developer community	●	●			✓	✗	✗	✓
Large end-user base	●	●	●		✓	✗	✗	✓
Stickiness with end-users	●		●		✓	✓	✗	✓
Brand recognition	●		●		✓	✗	✓	✓

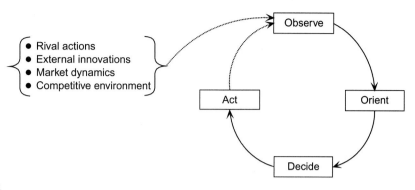

FIGURE 10.4

The military doctrine of OODA loops applied to platform ecosystems.

don't move simultaneously and they don't have vested interests and their own mind. Insights into speeding evolution instead come from an unexpected source: the American military doctrine in the 1950s Korean War. John Boyd, an American Air Force colonel, is credited with introducing the idea of the *OODA loop*. The OODA acronym refers to the cycle of Observe → Orient → Decide → Act, as illustrated in Figure 10.4. The key idea in this military doctrine was the emphasis on executing faster OODA loops than an enemy plane, which is widely believed to be instrumental in many aerial combat dogfight victories. If this notion reminds you of the Red Queen phenomenon, it would be useful to translate John Boyd's ideas into a platform setting to see its direct applicability.

1. *Observation*: collection of data from across the ecosystem
2. *Orientation*: analysis and synthesis of data to develop an evolving mental model of the platform or app in the context of its current competitive environment
3. *Decision*: deciding on a course of action based on the above
4. *Action*: the execution of that decision. The actions in modular platforms are typically one of five modular operators described in Chapter 9. Sometimes, when the environment changes in the midst of an OODA loop, it is necessary to cancel the action at the end of an OODA loop. In real options terms, this is exercising the abandonment option.

Boyd's premise was that faster OODA loops provide a momentary edge over rivals. Agility is more important than raw power in this perspective. The key to creating an edge over rivals is to shorten the lag between the four steps of the loop. This is identical to the premise of Red Queen competition where the goal is to adapt faster than rival platforms.

Rivalry within and among platform ecosystems is more akin to encounters between fighter planes. Arial dogfights have much more in common with platform markets than does chess: Brief air combats parallel shorter technology lifecycles in platform markets, unfamiliar terrains parallel emerging markets, unpredictable weather parallels a volatile environment, and actions with immediate consequences that might kill you before the next move parallels the surprisingly fast mortality of dominant platforms. Each OODA loop in platform markets can use as its input (observation) not only information about the consequences from the previous loop but also from rival actions, changes in the competitive environment, new technology advances outside the ecosystem, and insights into the dynamics of the platform's market. Feedback delays in absorbing such new information can lead two similar systems to evolve very differently (Meadows, 2008, p. 2). The same signals are often available from the environment to all competing platforms; the difference in their evolution then results from variance in their ability to decode them and rapidly act on them, or the speed and numbers of *concurrent* OODA loops. All else being equal, the lesson from this military doctrine is that the platform that wins out in Red Queen competition is one that evolves faster than its rivals.

However, the Goldilocks rule applies to the speed with which feedback is incorporated in evolving a platform as well. While reducing lag in feedback loops mitigates decay in evolution speed, feedback that is absorbed too fast can create instability because of overreacting to inputs in subsequent OODA loops. There must therefore be a balance between inertia and momentum (Shy, 2001, p. 83). Too much of either can derail platform evolution.

The key to increasing innovation inflows into a platform's ecosystem is then to (1) shorten the lag in one or more of the arrows in Figure 10.4 and (2) have many more of these OODA loops autonomously running in parallel. Aligning platform governance with architecture accomplishes the first task by placing app decisions with app developers and platform decisions with platform owners, while relying on platform architecture to decouple and reintegrate their work. Modularized platform architectures also reduce *unnecessary* coupling among feedback loops within an ecosystem by reducing the interdependencies between apps and the platform. Decentralizing the ecosystem's governance accomplishes the second task by increasing the platform's sensory points from few to many app developers, and giving each of them the power to act autonomously and without unnecessary lag. The alignment of platform architecture and ecosystem governance therefore addresses the Humpty Dumpty problem described in Chapter 2.

Three other ideas in Boyd's theory are noteworthy in a platform market. We return to each of these later in the chapter.

1. *Emphasis on what, not how.* The emphasis in the OODA doctrine is on decentralized command that uses objective-based control rather than method-driven orders. This is identical to our earlier idea of platform governance where the minimal expectations for outputs from app developers are specified by a platform owner but they are given complete autonomy in how they develop their apps.

2. *Continuous immersion in the platform market.* Maintaining an accurate grasp of reality requires a continuous cycle of interaction with the environment. This idea is identical to our notion of the need to use emerging information from app developers', rivals', and platform owners' own observations on the competitive environment, rivals, and outside innovations. This idea applies to both the platform in this chapter and to apps in the next chapter.

3. *Fast and frequent—not perfect—actions.* A lag in adapting to new information and updated forecasts can lead to instability in evolution, just as delay is a killer in dogfights. The key to survival in dogfights is the ability to adapt to change, not perfect adaptation. Speed trumps perfection. While one platform goes through one carefully thought-out loop, if a rival platform can go through a hundred much littler OODA loops, it will be much more likely to win out in evolutionary competition. This mirrors our subsequent emphasis on the need to simply adapt faster than rival platforms, even if it is imperfect and involves occasional missteps in between.

10.2 ORCHESTRATING PLATFORM EVOLUTION: A PREVIEW

Table 10.3 previews and Figure 10.5 summarizes how the design of platform architecture, platform governance, and their alignment can be used by a platform owner as levers to orchestrate the evolution of a platform in the short, medium, and long term.

HOW DISTRIBUTED OWNERSHIP CAN GRIDLOCK INNOVATION

In 1955, millions of American kids participated in a Klondike land rush. Quaker Oats Company, a cereal manufacturer, bought land in the Yukon Territory of Canada for $1000 and divided it into 21 million parcels of land, each a square inch in size. It then enclosed a mail-in form in boxes of its cereal products—Quaker Puffed Wheat, Quaker Puffed Rice, and Muffets Shredded Wheat—that buyers were asked to mail back to the company. The company in return sent back a deed to one square inch of land in the Klondike. This went on to become one of the most successful marketing campaigns in history. What do you do with a 1-inch piece of land? The land was technically unusable by any one because ownership was spread too thin (Heller, 2008). One kid tried to donate his 3-inch parcel to create the world's smallest park. The land office of the Yukon currently has an 18-inch-thick file folder of correspondence regarding the promotion. Too much fragmented ownership can wreck markets and firms and dampen rather than boost innovation. The architecture of an ecosystem defines ownership of assets in a platform ecosystem but extracting the potential benefits of fragmented ownership requires aligning with ecosystem governance.

Table 10.3 A Summary of How Platform Design Drives its Evolution

Platform Evolution Metric	Influenced by			Pertinent Governance Dimension		
	Architecture	Governance	Architecture–Governance Alignment	Decision Rights	Control	Pricing
Short term						
Resilience	●		●	●	●	
Scalability	●		●			●
Composability	●		●	●		
Medium term						
Stickiness	●	●		●		
Platform synergy		●				●
Plasticity	●		●	●		●
Long term						
Envelopment		●		●		
Platform durability			●	●	●	
Mutation			●	●		

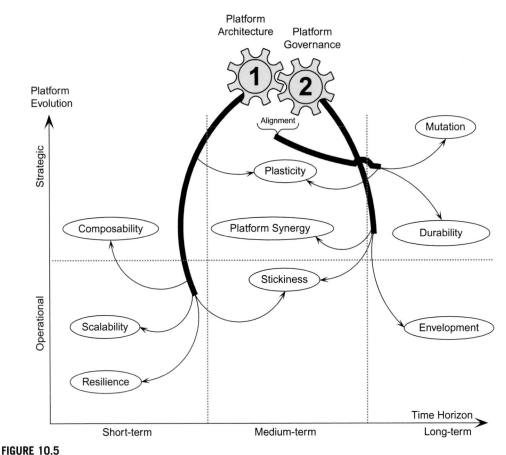

FIGURE 10.5

A summary of the primary drivers of the nine metrics of platform evolution.

10.3 ORCHESTRATING SHORT-TERM PLATFORM EVOLUTION

10.3.1 Orchestrating platform resilience

The resilience of a platform is its capacity to function acceptably in the event of a failure elsewhere within or outside the ecosystem. In contrast, a platform that breaks many apps due to internal changes in it is brittle (Meadows, 2008, p. 76). A platform's architecture and how well it is aligned with the control dimension of platform governance are the key drivers of its resilience. What makes a platform's ecosystem work is not its parts in isolation but the platform's interactions with apps. The key source of failure arises from the awry interactions of the platform with apps and external services that a platform uses. In complex systems, evolutionary changes in one subsystem can affect other subsystems. Complexity is a function of three things: the number of unique apps in the platform's ecosystem, the density of connections between these apps and the platform, and the rate of change in the ecosystem as a whole. Such complexity begets more complexity over time. When a platform is connected to other systems such as apps and external services, they can jointly exhibit highly complex behavior due to their interdependence. Dependence of a platform on other systems leads to inflexibility as a small change in one place can have an unpredictable ripple effect cascade through the ecosystem. The larger the ecosystem, the greater such interdependencies (Evans et al., 2006, p. 49). Increasing a platform's resilience requires (1) modularizing a platform's interfaces, (2) deliberately introducing some redundancy in its internal design, and (3) increasing the degree to which the platform is internally monolithic.

Modularization of platform interfaces. The greatest complexities arise at the interfaces of the platform within its ecosystem. It is important to remember that platform-to-app boundaries are artificial conceptual simplifications. They are mental castles that serve merely as a conceptual crutch to assist with sense-making (Meadows, 2008, p. 95). Modularization of a platform's interfaces creates a design optimized for flexibility and resilience rather than efficiency. It also reduces the amount of information about the internal functioning of the platform that any app has to keep track of—or even be aware of—because a platform's interfaces govern the outputs of app developers. While modularization does not eliminate the connections between the platform and an app, the standardization of interfaces entailed by modularization creates an explicit shared understanding between an app developer and a platform owner of how the two must interact. Therefore, they shape expectations of both the platform owner and app developers (Evans and Schmalensee, 2007, p. 36). App developers can be assured that as long as they conform to the platform's interface specifications, their apps will readily interoperate with the platform. Similarly, the platform owner has a well-documented implicit contract that as long as the interfaces of the platform remain untouched, changes within the platform will not undermine the functioning of existing apps. Furthermore, modularization decouples the implementation of the platform and individual apps in its ecosystem. This ensures that a maintenance change in the internal design of the platform does not require compensating changes in the apps that interoperate with it. Modularization of a platform's interfaces therefore improves maintainability without compromising the platform's capacity to evolve (de Weck et al., 2011, p. 80). This approach creates autonomy within apps and within the platform yet disciplines the interconnections among them. Modularization of a platform's interfaces therefore improves the reliability and ease with which new functionality can be implemented within a platform, in turn making the entire ecosystem more resilient. This design approach allows the platform owner to incrementally tweak and refine the platform's internal implementation as frequently as needed without inadvertently undercutting the apps in its ecosystem. In contrast, changes in a platform with undermodularized interfaces can lead to a propagation of errors from the platform to apps and vice versa (MacCormack et al., 2006), reducing a platform's resilience. Similarly, poorly documented interfaces to the platform can make apps in the ecosystem fragile, with errors propagating from the platform to the rest of the ecosystem in unpredictable ways.

The second architectural technique to improve platform resilience, feasible only occasionally, is to create some degree of redundancy in external services that the platform's own functioning might depend on. The simplest way to accomplish this is to use public, industry-standard interfaces to external services where possible; they permit swappability of such services (e.g., allowing 3G and WIFI to be used interchangeably for data transport). If the platform is unavoidably dependent on an app in the ecosystem to derive some of its critical functionality, it is useful to preserve some redundancy and swappability of such apps. This ensures that the loss of one critical app will not cripple the ecosystem.

This runs counter to the idea of minimizing redundancy to maximize efficiency that is espoused in the design of traditional organizations and of traditional large-scale software systems. A third architectural technique also usable occasionally is to reduce the platform's *internal* modularity. As long as internal implementation of the platform is under the platform owner's control, this internal demodularization reduces the likelihood of internal failures for the same complexity vis-à-vis a more modularized internal architecture. The last two techniques can be combined over time, with the platform owner taking over the inhouse provisioning of external services on which the platform critically depends. Apple did precisely this by integrating cloud storage services into the iOS platform (as iCloud) that it once accessed externally (as iCloud).

Alignment with governance. Modularization of a platform's interfaces relies on standardizing—explicitly documenting and adhering to simple rules for—the interfaces from the platform to the apps in a platform's ecosystem. However, standards are like traffic lights on busy streets—they are only useful as a coordinating mechanism if everyone follows them. This is where the role of platform governance comes into the picture. However, governance is not an end in itself in improving platform resilience; rather, it is the alignment of governance with architecture that enhances platform resilience. Power over rules—or setting the rules of the game—is real power in complex systems (Meadows, 2008, p. 158). Such power should be wielded by a platform owner in extreme moderation (remember the Goldilocks principle). It is a delicate balancing act: Imposing too much control can stymie app developers' freedom to be creative and imposing too little control can hurt the platform ecosystem's resilience. The platform owner and app developers in self-organizing platform ecosystems must retain the freedom and autonomy to experiment in their own work.

The enforcement of interface specifications requires aligning the governance mechanisms discussed in Chapter 6—specifically the platform decision rights and control dimensions of governance—with its architecture. Modularization of the code used to implement the subsystems in the ecosystems must match the partitioning of responsibility for those subsystems (MacCormack et al., 2006). In this instance, modularization decouples the platform from apps. Such decoupling must also be mirrored in the ecosystem's governance by partitioning of decisions between the platform owner and app developers.

The greater the modularization of the platform's interfaces, the more valuable it is for the platform owner to centralize platform implementation decision rights but decentralize most app decision rights to app developers. This partitioning of decision rights creates a system of distributed control and autonomy between the platform owner and app developers. Furthermore, this partitioning of decision rights between a platform owner and app developers must also be complemented by a minimal set of simple, nonnegotiable rules. Greater use of gatekeeping and compliance-oriented metrics by a platform owner can help enforce platform interface standards among app developers. Aligning platform architecture modularization with governance provides cooperative advantage within the ecosystem, which can give it a competitive advantage against rival ecosystems where such alignment is poorer.

However, it is preferable that platform owners rely on peer-to-peer reinforcement—what we called *relational control* in Chapter 6—where possible. Relational control fosters self-organization by getting everyone in the platform's ecosystem on the same page, and in turn improves its resilience. If the platform ecosystem is amenable to the use of relational control, it can be used as a less-expensive alternative to metrics-based control. Peer reinforcement provided by relational control can be far more effective than formal metrics, provided the app developers share the platform owner's values and norms. Greater reliance on relational control, however, requires that app developers be able to self-monitor their own compliance with the platform's interface standards. This can be accomplished by sharing freely compliance data for individual apps with app developers (e.g., data from testing and integration tools). This allows app developers to self-adjust their own development work, particularly when they appreciate that their own fate is intertwined with that of the platform.

Platform owners need not use other control mechanisms such as process control with the assumption that they need overt control over the implementation of apps. Therefore, modularization of the platform's interfaces and alignment of governance with the platform's architecture improves the platform's resilience in the short term.

In summary, increasing platform resilience requires:

- A modularized platform architecture
- Alignment of governance with the platform's architecture such that
    - Platform implementation decision rights reside with the platform owner but apps decision rights reside with app developers
    - Just enough control to ensure compliance with a platform's interface standards by app developers

10.3.2 Orchestrating platform scalability

Platform scalability is the degree to which a platform's functional performance and financial viability is size-agnostic. Platform scalability encompasses size agnosticism with respect to two facets: (1) upward and downward changes and (2) apps and end-users (the two sides of the platform). This means that the platform must be able to maintain its desired properties with an increase or decrease in the number of apps and end-users without a corresponding increase in its internal complexity. This is illustrated in Figure 10.6, where all four cells being covered represent a *perfectly* scalable platform.

Platform scalability is influenced by platform architecture and its alignment with the pricing dimension of governance. While attention to platform architecture improves its *capacity* to scale, aligning governance with its architecture reduces its *need* to scale.

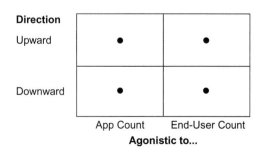

FIGURE 10.6

Platform scalability.

10.3.2.1 Platform architecture and platform scalability

A platform can improve its scalability by (1) minimizing the need for unstructured communication between the platform and apps by standardizing platform interfaces and decoupling apps; (2) starting with a minimum viable footprint for the platform, rich in embedded real options; and (3) using tiered pricing and service-level agreements (SLAs) with apps.

Minimizing unstructured communication between the platform and apps is accomplished through the standardization and explicit documentation of the platform's interfaces. This ensures that all interactions between a platform and apps in its ecosystem use an agreed-upon set of interface standards specified by the platform's APIs. The emphasis is not on reducing the need for communication but rather the need for communication that is unstructured (i.e., not covered by the platform's interface standards). A crude indicator of this is the chattiness of the platform's core APIs. The chattier a platform's APIs, the less likely it is that apps interoperating with a platform rely on communicating in ways that are not formalized in the APIs. This results in a more flexible platform design that is scalable both upward and downward. As a platform gains more apps, the stability of its latency and responsiveness for every thousand new apps is a simple way to evaluate its scalability. However, no matter how modular a platform's architecture, architecture always imposes limits to growth. These limits can be relaxed by using a tiered architecture that is neither completely monolithic nor excessively modular, allowing only parts of the platform that need to grow in their capacity to be upgraded without having to grow the entire platform. This allows functions that exhibit high growth in usage by apps and end-users to independently be scaled up. For example, using a tiered architecture for a platform-wide notification system would allow a platform owner to increase the capacity of just the notification function without having to grow the other functions across the platform. Similarly, a platform owner should also encourage tiering of app microarchitectures by app developers. This approach also helps increase a platform's scalability with respect to both apps and end-users.

The second approach to bolstering a platform's scalability is to design the platform for a dream audience but provision for the expected load. Recall that the platform's audience includes its two sides: apps and end-users. Ensuring downward scalability requires that the platform be financially viable even if the number of apps or end-users that adopt it turns out to be fewer than expected. A less downward scalable platform will shift to the negative net revenue region faster as the scale of the end-users or apps shrinks. The point at which the breakeven point occurs can be shifted through thoughtful design, giving a platform greater downward scalability. Platform designers must first grasp the implications of fixed costs and variable costs to build financial scalability into the design of a platform. Fixed costs should be decreased for a platform to have downward financial scalability. This requires starting a platform with a minimum viable footprint (which is often also rich in embedded real options), or what we described as the "must-do" elements of the platform in the discussion on real options thinking in Chapter 8. This ensures downward scalability by reducing fixed costs vis-à-vis variable costs per additional user (on either side). Fixed costs are the costs that a platform owner bears to keep the platform operating independent of the number of users. These are the baseline costs that would be incurred (e.g., initial development costs, services provisioning costs, operating expenses) even if the platform had zero users on either side. These fixed costs are spread over the number of users, which means that the fixed costs per user decline as the number of users grows. Variable costs are the additional costs that increase with an increase in the number of users (e.g., bandwidth costs, end-user support costs, or storage costs). The total costs incurred by the platform owner are fixed costs plus variable costs. The revenue generated by the platform owner depends on the number of platform users. These costs are

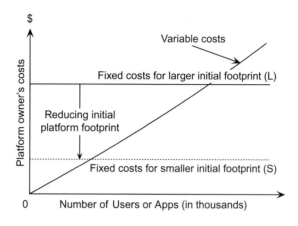

FIGURE 10.7

Fixed costs plus variable costs are a platform owner's total costs.

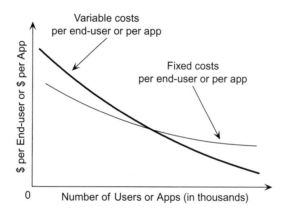

FIGURE 10.8

Both a platform's fixed costs and variable costs per user (or app) usually decline as their numbers increase.

illustrated in Figures 10.7 and 10.8. Reducing the initial footprint of the platform reduces the fixed costs by shifting the fixed cost line from line L to line S in Figure 10.7. By reducing the fixed costs, the platform owner lowers the minimum number of users or apps needed for the net revenue (difference between revenues and costs) to be positive. An alternative to growth through scaling that can also sometimes be viable is replication of a platform (making a copy of the system) for use in a different application domain (i.e., using the mutation operator).

10.3.2.2 Aligning architecture with governance to enhance platform scalability

A complementary way to improve a platform's upward scalability is to align its governance—specifically the pricing dimension—with its architecture. This tackles the scalability challenge by reducing the *need* to scale, in contrast with the earlier approach that improves its *ability* to scale. Aligning governance requires promising service levels to apps in exchange for agreements on tiered quotas on how an app uses a platform. SLAs include error rates, latencies, and other operational performance metrics such as maximum downtime that a platform owner guarantees to app developers along with explicit documentation of remedies for outages, service interruptions, security breaches, and response latencies. These metrics are relatively easy to track due to the ubiquitously connected nature of contemporary software platforms. In exchange, a platform owner can impose quotas to limit API calls from individual apps to the platform or use a tiered pricing structure, particularly if a platform cannot absorb a level of traffic beyond a designed threshold. This naturally segments apps and app developers into segments or tiers with different quota levels. Twitter, for example, permits app developers to check their timelines between 150 and 350 times an hour, depending on the current state of the Twitter platform. The platform owner can often readily track the actual usage data to track the most popular and the least popular API calls to a platform. This creates a natural incentive for app developers to limit the demands that their apps place on the platform, reducing its need to scale. This allows a platform to grow, but in a controlled manner. It also helps maintain the delicate balance between the interests of app developers and the platform owner.

In summary, improving platform scalability requires:

- A modularized platform architecture that begins with a small initial footprint rich in embedded real options
- Using tiered pricing and quotas for the pricing dimension of platform governance

10.3.3 Orchestrating platform composability

Platform composability encompasses the ease with which changes can be made within a platform without breaking its interoperability with apps in its ecosystem. To be high in composability, changes within a platform should not impose integration costs on app developers.

It is important to recognize the ongoing, dynamic nature of systems integration in platform markets. Unlike traditional software systems, different subsystems in a platform ecosystem can evolve at different rates. A single change in the platform can require tweaks to apps to ensure their continued interoperability. Therefore a platform owner can encounter two types of platform-to-apps reintegration costs: (1) from changes that elaborate and extend the platform itself and (2) from new apps and changes to existing apps. Such reintegration costs can be unpredictable in their timing and cumulatively debilitating to a platform's ecosystem. The imposition of such coordination costs can stunt a platform's evolutionary potential and wipe out any benefits of intellectual division of labor across a platform ecosystem (Langlois and Garzarelli, 2008).

Platform composability is embedded in its architecture, particularly the modularization of its linkages to the rest of the ecosystem. Modularization decomposes an ecosystem into distinct apps and a platform that are subsequently composed. The decoupled apps rely on explicitly documented interfaces (such as APIs) to interoperate with the platform. A platform's interfaces are therefore a contract between a platform and apps. Apps are built on top of that contract, which requires that an API and similar interfaces be stable, documented, and predictable. Compatibility with apps is achieved through interface standardization, defined as an explicit agreement to do certain things in a certain way (Farrell and Saloner, 1992). Following the platform's interface specifications means that the platform owner describes exactly what functionality the platform will offer, how apps should access it, and the technical constraints on the apps' interactions with the platform (e.g., how often an app is allowed to access an API or specific platform services per minute). This disciplines interactions of apps with a platform exclusively to its interfaces, which tell apps all they need to know to interact with and use the platform's services. It also hides all internal implementation details about the platform from apps, which rely only on the documented protocols and APIs to communicate and interoperate with a platform. Platform modularization is therefore an important means for coordination of distributed work across a platform's ecosystem, allowing apps to be developed independently by app developers but interoperate harmoniously with the platform (Arthur, 2009, p. 43; Messerschmitt and Szyperski, 2003, p. 173). Therefore, apps can be assured of composability with a modularized platform simply by complying with its interface specifications. This allows a platform to be changed internally as often as necessary provided its interfaces are left untouched.

Changing existing interfaces violates the premise of modularity. It is important to rigorously maintain separation between internal implementation and interfaces of a platform as it evolves (Kamel, 1987). In contrast, poor modularization messes up composability precisely when it is much more challenging to fix reintegration problems. Flaws in decomposition of functionality between the platform and apps, unrecognized dependencies, and ambiguity in interface specifications show up later only when the independently developed apps are brought together for integration with the platform.

Modularization, however, requires compliance with architectural rules by app developers and by the platform owner (Langlois and Garzarelli, 2008). Governance enforces compliance with architectural rules. As diverse expertise and resources accumulate among app developers in a platform's ecosystem, it is standardization of a platform's interfaces that allow this distributed constellation of capabilities to cost-effectively coalesce. Modularization of platform architecture must therefore be aligned with its governance, particularly its decision rights dimension. The more modularized the platform ecosystem, the more decentralized must decision rights be. Paradoxically, the more modularized and decentralized the architecture, the harder it becomes for a platform owner to control, provide direction, and maintain oversight over app developers. Therefore, decision rights decentralization must be granular and deliberate for each of the four types of decision rights in a platform ecosystem, described in Chapter 6.

Each ecosystem participant must be crystal clear about which decisions they are responsible for and how they affect the ecosystem. Both app developers and the platform owner must be clear on what implementation decisions they should and should not be making. Simple rules—not micromanagement—should guide app developers' work. Clear accountability among app developers and the refrain from micromanagement by a platform owner therefore go hand in hand. This ensures that the technical boundaries of apps vis-à-vis the platform mirror the ecosystem-wide distribution of responsibility for them. Such mirroring-based alignment requires that the more a platform is modularized vis-à-vis its ecosystem, the more platform decision rights reside predominantly with the platform owner.

In platform markets, the platform owner must encourage diversity among apps and let the market determine winners and losers. But some control is still needed to ensure integrity and quality of app developers' work. The control portfolio used by a platform owner should emphasize principles over rules and policies. The former liberate while the latter constrain app developers. App strategic and implementation decision rights should also reside largely with app developers, provided the platform's interfaces are sufficiently modularized. This grants them freedom to work as they see fit, knowing in advance how they will be judged.

This match between architecture and governance allows changes to be made within a platform without requiring extensive coordination with app developers in its ecosystem. Such architecture–governance alignment mitigates the Goldilocks problem by giving a platform owner just enough centralized control to achieve integration across the ecosystem and enough autonomy to app developers to pursue their own ideas unfettered by a burdensome set of rules. Any need for extraneous coordination between them is a symptom of insufficient modularization of the platform's interfaces. Linux and Mozilla's Firefox are examples of platforms with strong architecture–governance alignment (MacCormack et al., 2006; Tiwana et al., 2010). These are also platforms where informal processes, a shared system of norms and values, and peer monitoring—all relational forms of control—are the predominant control mechanisms.

In summary, improving platform composability requires modularizing the platform's interfaces and mirroring the allocation of decision rights for the platform and apps across the ecosystem.

10.4 ORCHESTRATING MEDIUM-TERM PLATFORM EVOLUTION
10.4.1 Growing platform stickiness
Platform stickiness refers to the pattern of active use of a platform by end-users and app developers (its two sides). We care more about changes (increases or decreases) in active use over time. The prevalence of the Red Queen effect means that a platform has to deliver more value to keep its stickiness from declining and much more to increase stickiness over time. For a platform to grow stickier over time, both sides—the end-users and app developers—must progressively be better off as a platform ages. The fiercer the rivalry among platforms, the higher is this bar.

10.4.1.1 Growing platform stickiness with end-users
There are three approaches to increasing platform stickiness with end-users: (1) focusing on increasing app developer stickiness knowing that it is highly correlated with end-user stickiness, (2) creating value-driven, noncoercive switching costs to rival platforms, and (3) strategic incompatibility with rival platforms.

1. *App developer stickiness correlates with end-user stickiness.* The single most effective way to increase end-user platform stickiness is to remember that the same things that increase stickiness with app developers often increase stickiness with end-users. End-users value improvements in functionality and usefulness of a platform, which comes largely from app developer-driven innovations. Create strong incentives and make it easier for app developers to innovate in their own work and you create a virtuous cycle: More users attract more app developers to the platform, increasing the variety of apps available to end-users. This in turn attracts more end-users to a platform, creating a feedback loop that feeds on itself. This is illustrated in Figure 10.9.

   However, platforms that grow solely reliant on external innovation stagnate and die. A platform owner must therefore not abdicate responsibility for bolstering a platform's native functionality for app developers. Instead, app developers' effort should be complemented by the platform owner's own efforts at proactively retiring platform features that have run their course and steadily

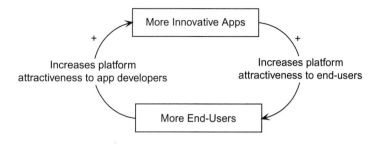

FIGURE 10.9

The virtuous loop between end-user stickiness and app-developer stickiness.

increasing the native capabilities of the platform in ways that end-users value. (Techniques used by app developers to recognize end-users' latent needs, described in Chapter 11, can also be used by platform owners.)

2. *Create end-user lock-in based on value rather than coercion.* Lock-in means that an end-user incurs a switching cost associated not just with having to abandon her investment in a platform but from also having to abandon benefits that accumulate from having used a platform. Such costs can be coercive or noncoercive. Coercive lock-in (such as refusal to port data to a rival platform) is rarely sustainable and rival platforms can often devise ways around it. Noncoercive lock-in does not occur by force or binding contracts but by adding compelling value that cannot be replicated outside the ecosystem. The more effective and less breakable lock-ins are noncoercive ones created in three ways: nonportable network effects, personalization, and lowering end-users' search costs.

    (a) *Nonportable network effects* are specific to a platform and have little value in a rival platform. For example, Blackberry and iOS platforms provide functionality that is available only between users of the same platform. As a user accumulates a peer group of users on the same platform, the value of a platform comes to a large degree from the collaborative activities that an individual end-user can do with her peer network on that platform. For example, a messaging function (such as iMessage in iOS) that allows rich interactions between users of a platform but cannot function in the same way across rival platforms creates a value-adding lock-in. This has often shielded platforms facing intense rivalry and prolonged the useful life of withering platforms. For example, a Skype user with a hundred Skype contacts would find it difficult to convince her entire network to abandon the Skype platform and migrate to a competing platform that offers the same—or even superior—functionality. Similarly, Blackberry's messenger service created strong network effects among Blackberry OS users, which kept them loyal to the platform even as it was fading from the marketplace. However, sustaining such network effects requires that they remain nonportable to rival platforms. Therefore, the design of a platform that emphasizes strong same-side network effects in its functionality is more likely to increase platform stickiness for end-users.

    (b) *Personalization* is a second technique to increase a platform's stickiness with end-users. This involves implementing ways to make the platform more useful the more an end-user uses it. Mobile OS platforms, for example, learn and adapt to user behaviors, preferences, and idiosyncrasies (such as learning typing patterns and commonly used words). Similarly, eBay, Amazon, and Netflix learn user interests and preferences and use correlation data to generate product recommendations that a user will increasingly find helpful. You cannot transfer Amazon's product recommendations to a competing site, nor readily transfer Skype contacts to Google Voice to FaceTime; or Netflix's deep and fine-grained knowledge of likely user interests to rival services like iTunes, Hulu, or Amazon Video. As a platform owner gains more knowledge of end-users' preferences and behavior, it must creatively use it to make the platform even more useful and valuable to them. Such personalization creates a powerful incentive to stick with a platform because abandoning it in favor of a rival platform also requires abandoning the value that the platform is able to deliver to that end-user through learning effects. This does not eliminate the threat of platform abandonment, but simply raises the bar for how revolutionary a rival platform must be and how far it must leapfrog the incumbent platform to convince an end-user to jump ship. However, personalization is effective in increasing stickiness only if it is idiosyncratic to a platform (i.e., not portable to a rival platform) and if the end-user truly finds it valuable.

(c) *Lowering end-users' search costs* is the third noncoercive technique for increasing platform stickiness. A platform owner must make it easier and lesser expensive for an end-user to find apps that would increase a platform's functionality that she would perceive as being valuable in her own use of the platform. Increasing the variety and number of apps potentially increases the odds that an end-user can find apps that meet even the most eclectic and idiosyncratic needs at the tail end of long-tail markets. Paradoxically, this also makes it increasingly difficult to find an app in a larger pool. As a platform evolves, the platform owner must work to reduce search costs incurred by end-users in acquiring them. The goal should be to help end-users find apps more efficiently (Evans and Schmalensee, 2007, p. 33). This can be done by designing and then refining tools, methods, and capabilities for filtering, selecting, and aggregating information about apps (e.g., reviews) and app developers in ways that the end-users could not accomplish without the platform.

3. *Strategic incompatibility with rival platforms* is the third technique to increase platform stickiness for end-users. Platforms owners can choose to make a platform incompatible with a rival platform, one-way compatible (where the focal platform can interact with a rival platform but not the other way around), or compatible both ways (where a rival platform can interact with the focal platform as well) (Farrell and Saloner, 1985). How much should a platform allow its end-users to interact with users of rival platforms? Interoperability with rival platforms is a strategic choice, sometimes desirable and sometimes undesirable from the platform owner's perspective. This choice should not remain static and can change as a platform progresses through different stages of its lifecycle. Incompatibility is more profitable when end-user needs and preferences are more heterogeneous and the threshold to trigger network effects is relatively low. Incompatibility makes it more difficult for rival platforms to dislodge a platform because a rival platform would not only have to deliver a better price/performance ratio but would also have to rally a critical mass of app developers and end-users around it. Platform owners must tread with caution in even pondering any move away from incompatibility. IBM, which literally created the PC business yet managed to let later copycats drive it out of the very business that it created, should serve as a poignant reminder of the risks of too much compatibility.

Breaking incompatibility barriers imposed by a rival platform is possible through the use of adaptors or middleware that translate or emulate data from one standard to another (Armstrong and Wright, 2007; Rysman, 2009). Although this permits interfacing with rival platforms, it is possible for a platform owner to block such adaptors from accessing the platform's APIs. They are also usually not very scalable, costly to develop, and the overhead of the translation process often degrades performance and quality (Farrell and Saloner, 1992).

One-way compatibility is more profitable only when a platform owner faces a higher threshold for initiating network effects (i.e., needs a larger critical mass of end-users at the outset). This choice exploits network effects for a platform while denying them to rival platforms (Farrell and Saloner, 1985). Modularization of a platform's interfaces—by preserving secrecy of a platforms' internal implementation details—can make it more challenging for rivals to make their own platforms interoperable with it. The only condition under which two-way compatibility is likely to be profitable for all rival platforms is if and only if no platform has a clear technological edge (Rohfls, 2003, p. 197). This usually happens after the emergence of a dominant design, where competition is no longer among platform designs but *within* designs. Two-way interoperability is therefore likely to emerge when rival platforms are indistinguishably close in their features and when none of them perceives an opportunity to drive rivals out of the market by amassing a proprietary user base.
This usually happens in the more mature phases of a platform market and signals a march toward commoditization and a race toward the bottom in terms of profit margins. Agreement on common standards and interlinking of rival platforms is widely seen in this phase.
This should serve as a loud signal that the platform market is devolving into a zero-profit industry, as has happened repeatedly in consumer electronics industries including televisions, refrigerators, digital cameras, and personal computers. Surviving this lifecycle phase of a platform market's evolution requires the platform owner to pay close attention to the three longer-term evolutionary metrics: platform envelopment, durability, and mutation.
Although platform stickiness with end-users is challenging to develop, it is easier to recognize and measure. End-user stickiness of a platform can readily be tracked as the increase or decrease in average hours per session or number of sessions per day per user over time.

10.4.1.2 Growing platform stickiness with app developers

A platform owner cannot just play orchestrator and expect to last very long. It must itself contribute something distinctive with sustaining value to the ecosystem. Stickiness of a platform vis-à-vis its apps is indicated by the direction of the change—increase or decrease—in the API calls made by an app on average as the platform ages. A platform with an increase in API calls per app generally indicates increasing platform stickiness. Recall the two key value propositions that platform must deliver to app developers: (1) the technical foundations to use as the starting point for their own work and (2) market access. Growing platform stickiness with app developers requires that a platform continue to deliver on these promises better than rival platforms. Therefore, a platform owner must focus on making it cheaper, easier, and faster for app developers to develop apps for the platform and grow the prospective pool of end-user app adopters that they can reach through the platform.

10.4.1.2.1 Cheaper, easier, and faster app development

The first mantra to increase app developers' platform stickiness is to make app developers' work around the platform cheaper, easier, and more productive. Recall that app developers value a platform for the technical foundations on which they can build their work. The premise was that this would save them the effort of duplicating functionality that does not differentiate their apps and spend the effort saved on developing functionality that better leverages their unique expertise and skills. A platform's value to app developers therefore lies primarily in the scaffolding that it provides for apps to reach higher than they could without the platform. The closest parallel is the folks who made the most money during America's Gold Rush: the ones who sold pots, pans, and digging implements to the gold prospectors. The app developers are the prospectors, and the platform owner must provide them tools that they value. App developers therefore value a platform for the reuse of designs and common functionality, sharing of resources, and productivity-enhancing tools. Therefore, expanding the platform's native capabilities that apps can leverage requires growing the platform's capabilities and making it easier for apps to leverage its existing capabilities. The platform must evolve gradually on the exterior, but it can evolve rapidly internally. This is only possible if its interfaces are modularized.

All else being equal, consumers are more likely to prefer—and even be willing to pay a premium for—a platform with a greater variety of apps over one with fewer. The higher the cost of development faced by app developers on a platform, the lower the variety of apps that will be produced for that platform. The primary customer of a platform is therefore app developers; delight them and the rest will naturally follow. Therefore, a platform owner must ensure that a variety of apps emerge and sustain on a platform. Without sufficient variety vis-à-vis competing platforms, fewer users will eventually adopt the platform, owing to the lower value they ascribe to it, and trigger a death spiral for the platform. Lowering developers' costs is rarely a one-shot initiative because app developers also repeatedly incur such costs in updating and evolving their apps. This has a close connection to platform architecture: Platform architectures that enhance platform composability also enhance platform stickiness with app developers.

All else being equal, a platform that more consistently creates new opportunities for its app developers will outpace rival platforms in the value that it delivers to its end-users. A platform owner should therefore keep reducing developers' app innovation costs and app-to-platform integration costs by enhancing the platform's development environment. This encompasses the platform's portfolio of app development tools, debugging tools, test automation and integration tools, best practice guidelines, reference app designs for new app developers to build on, and development processes (Boudreau, 2010; Williamson and De Meyer, 2012). The development environment provided by Apple to iOS app developers—the collection of technical specifications, manuals, and programming tools—is largely credited with the development of its highly successful ecosystem (Burrows, 2011). A platform owner can assess how well it is reducing app developers' costs by tracking changes in app developer productivity over time. Is it faster and cheaper to develop an app for the platform than it was in the previous year? Has the platform made it easier for the app developers to exploit new technology developments and business opportunities in their own work?

Platform owners can identify opportunities to reduce app developers' costs by keeping three things in mind: remembering the parallels to the evolution of cities, recognizing opportunities to move elements in and out of the platform core, and recognizing when to maintain and when to sacrifice backward compatibility.

10.4.1.2.2 Evolving the platform core

Recall the parallels between the evolution of cities and the evolution of platform ecosystems in Chapter 5. A platform provides the infrastructure on which apps operate, much like buildings in a city connect to shared city infrastructure (e.g., water, sewers, and electric grids). Much like a city's infrastructure, a platform serves as a backbone for apps, providing consistency and order. As the residents of a city evolve, so do their needs. This requires a platform owner to retire legacy functionality, expansion with new interfaces and APIs, and recognizing once-unique services and functionality whose use is now widespread among many apps. Like a city with changing resident needs, a platform must also evolve to meet the changing needs of app developers and end-users.

As a platform ages and new generations of technologies emerge outside it, there can be a natural progression of what is feasible. A platform owner cannot sit still and hope that the external innovations will not be disruptive to the platform. A fledgling innovator will put those pieces together, just as Blackberry did after Palm grew too comfortable, and Apple did as Blackberry grew too comfortable. This requires the platform owner to proactively build on external innovations that can be added to the platform that would potentially be of shared value to many of the app developers. This role of evolving the platform itself cannot be left to outsiders, nor does it require consensus from the ecosystem.

Adding new APIs while retiring functionality that has run its course has the effect of shrinking the platform core and expanding the periphery (Figure 10.10).

10.4.1.2.3 Evolving the platform's boundary

The platform owner's choice of the platform boundary discussed in the earlier chapters—where the platform ends and its ecosystem begins—is important to remain mindful of as the ecosystem evolves. Boundaries in complex systems cannot remain static (de Weck et al., 2011, p. 99). The platform boundary itself must evolve over time using the simple heuristic described in Chapter 5: Highly reusable functionality used by a lot of apps goes into the platform itself; all else remains outside it (see Figure 10.11). Where change and variability are low, you want to create a stable, reliable, and robust foundation for apps to build on. As long as a platform continues to free app developers from the responsibility of provisioning the supporting infrastructure and building undifferentiating, redundant functionality, a platform is likely to remain valuable to them (Messerschmitt and Szyperski, 2003, p. 204). Therefore, the evolving platform must emphasize genericness with respect to the functionality that it provides to apps in its ecosystem. It is important that the platform continue to provide capabilities

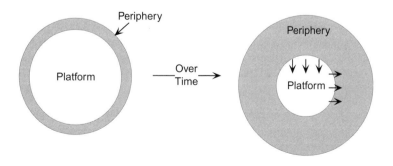

FIGURE 10.10

Adding APIs and retiring functionality shrinks the platform core and expands its periphery over time.

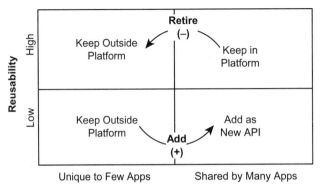

FIGURE 10.11

Two pathways for evolving the core of a platform over time.

that are generic enough to be of value to a large pool of app developers, and that they evolve to support a wide variety of current and future applications. As a platform's ecosystem evolves, widely shared services must be moved into it and those that are no longer used must be moved out of it.[2]

Platform interfaces have long lifetimes and the burden of their legacy is often inescapable in systems evolution (de Weck et al., 2011, p. 140). This does not mean that an API can never change, just that the changes are in the internal implementation but not to the interfaces. However, the rigid constraint of interface stability can become a challenge as a platform ages. Changes inside a platform are often intended to add new functionality and capabilities made possible by new technologies that might have appeared long after the initial design of a platform. As a platform evolves, elaborating elements added to it often increase its internal complexity and often need different interfaces (Arthur, 2009). The existing platform interfaces might not be able to accommodate such newly added functionality, which a platform owner might want to make accessible to app developers to leverage in their own work. Remember that innovation in platform markets is often combinatorial; a new capability added to a platform delivers more mileage in evolutionary competition when many app developers can build on it.

A platform owner can never tweak *existing* platform interfaces. In reality, platforms often lag in evolving the infrastructure they offer apps; this imbalance can be a major source of risk to a platform's long-term prospects. Instead, a platform can introduce new functionality to its ecosystem by adding new interfaces and APIs without touching existing ones. Other alternatives include supporting multiple versions of an API (which is inefficient), adding a mediation layer that can translate between different versions of an API (which is unscalable), or holding off altogether (which stunts evolution). If versioning is used to change an API, it must maintain backward compatibility to preserve the contract with app developers. Adding new platform interfaces in the form of APIs does not require any changes to existing apps, preserving composability. The appeal of extending the functionality that a platform provides

---

[2]This includes adding new functionality to the platform via new APIs that is now widely used by apps but was not previously. Such stability in the platform enables the rapid evolution of the apps in the platform's ecosystem, where the rate of change is higher and code reusability is lower. Stability of the platform translates a greater capacity to absorb high variety and experimentation in the apps that augment it.

apps by adding new APIs therefore explains the proliferation of APIs in platforms over time. (On last count, the iOS platform had about 15,000 APIs.)

10.4.1.2.4 Spotting such opportunities

A platform owner can recognize candidate generic functionality to move into a platform by looking for upstream complements now used by app developers that can be bundled into the platform and made available to all apps. (This has a direct connection to upstream envelopment in the longer term.) Other strategies that a platform owner can use to recognize such opportunities include learning from leading-edge app developers, discovering app developers' latent needs manifested as frustrations with rival platforms, and anticipating inflections where a niche technology trend takes off and becomes main-stream (using S-curves and chasm models described in Chapter 2).

10.4.1.3 Expanding app developers' market access

The second approach to increasing a platform's stickiness with app developers is by improving the findability of apps by end-users. This requires reducing end-users' app search and discovery costs, dis-cussed earlier, which simultaneously increases platform stickiness with app developers and end-users. Fail to do this well, and one of two outcomes are likely. Either the platform will lose the loyalty of both app developers and end-users. Or, the market will create alternative ways such as Amazon's creation of its own version of an app discovery marketplace that attempts to fix the gap left by Google in its Android platform. Growing the app developers' addressable market and improving findability, how-ever, requires that a platform owner largely control platform strategic and implementation decisions. A democratic arrangement involving app developers has its place, but not in such decisions.

10.4.2 Growing platform synergy across the ecosystem

Platform synergy is the degree to which app developers of a platform develop an app specifically for the platform, meaning that the apps integrate with the platform and build on its native capabilities to a greater extent vis-à-vis rival platforms. Platform owners would want apps to grow more platform-specific over time for two reasons. First, greater platform specificity translates into a better end-user experience and greater opportunities for differentiating a platform from rivals. Exploiting the function-ality unique to a platform means that small improvements in a platform's capabilities can have a wide-spread impact on the level of innovation across its ecosystem. Second, as apps become more dependent on a platform, they become less generic and in turn make a platform less readily interchangeable with a rival platform. This lowers the likelihood of either app developers or end-users defecting to a rival platform. In other words, it can increase stickiness on both sides of a platform.

However, increasing platform synergy is a catch-22 from an app developer's perspective: While it allows them to better exploit a platform's capabilities in their work, it can lock them into a platform and make them vulnerable to opportunistic behavior by a platform owner. Managing expectations is key to improving apps' platform synergy. App developers will invest in a platform based on their *expectations* of how a platform owner will behave (Evans et al., 2006, p. 254). Platform owners will occasionally engage in downstream vertical envelopment (i.e., integrate the functionality of an app into the plat-form) either to extend the platform's native functionality or as a hedge against the failure of app devel-opers to supply that functionality. A platform owner should rarely ever engage in such envelopment because it can signal that the platform owner will change the rules of the game, and in turn discourage an increase in platform synergy. A platform owner must offer compelling reasons to app developers for them to expose themselves to such vulnerability. Three things, all under the platform owner's control, can give app developers such reasons:

1. *A large installed base of end-users.* Growing the installed base of end-users provides app developers a larger prospective pool of users for their app. A larger installed base offers greater opportunities for exploiting the platform's network effects to an app's advantage. When a platform symbiotically serves as a gateway to access a larger market, app developers are more likely to increase the platform synergy of their apps.
2. *Economizing the code developed by app developers.* The primary economic value of a platform from the app developers' perspective is economizing on the amount of code that app developers must write themselves to deliver a working app to the app's end-users (Evans et al., 2006, p. 58). Therefore, the same things that increase a platform's stickiness with app developers—easier integration, more productive development, and better app development tools—also encourage an increase in the platform synergy of apps.
3. *Differentiated platform capabilities vis-à-vis rival platforms.* If a platform offers technical capabilities made available to apps via APIs that rival platforms do not offer, app developers are more likely to increase their apps' platform synergy. However, such capabilities must pass the resource litmus test: These capabilities must not only be rare, they must also be valuable to app developers.

In summary, improving platform synergy requires attention primarily to platform governance.

10.4.3 Orchestrating platform plasticity

A platform exhibits plasticity when it learns to do new things and gains new capabilities over time. In other words, it can morph to deliver new functionality and meet needs that did not exist at the time of its original creation for its existing and prospective users on both sides. Plasticity is a way to measure the level of innovation that is successfully realized around a platform. To grow in plasticity, a platform needs to be more a sponge than an inventor. This requires speeding the inflow of innovations into the platform, which can be done in three ways: (1) strengthen the ecosystem's capacity to innovate (via platform modularization) and make them want to out of pure self-interest (via governance, especially pricing), (2) expand the diversity of the pool supplying new ideas to the ecosystem, and (3) recognize what innovations will not occur naturally and take responsibility for them.

10.4.3.1 Catalyzing ecosystem innovation capacity with developers' self interest

A flexible architecture and dispersion of decision rights across the ecosystem are the two powerful levers for improving platform plasticity. The distribution of subsystems across a platform's ecosystem means that their ownership is widely dispersed. Too much ownership can create a gridlock by imposing daunting coordination requirements in which everybody loses. A gridlock is a human creation; an artifact of ownership gone awry (Heller, 2008). A preventive measure against gridlock is platform architecture modularization, which allows app developers to work unfettered on their own projects without waiting on changes elsewhere in the ecosystem.

A modularized architecture gives a platform ecosystem an evolutionary advantage. While monolithic designs can only be improved as a whole, modular designs can be improved one subsystem at a time. A monolithic platform simply cannot replicate the innovation potential of a larger, diverse pool of outsiders rallied around a modularized platform with a fire in their belly. Modularizing a platform's interfaces strengthens a platform's plasticity by bolstering its ecosystem's capacity to innovate around a platform in four ways:

- *Decouples app evolution from platform evolution.* Modularization of a platform decouples the internal implementation of the platform and those of apps by hiding within-subsystem implementation decisions (Pil and Cohen, 2006). This creates technical autonomy within all major subsystems of a platform's ecosystem; changes inside one do not have a ripple effect nor require changes in the others. In contrast, innovation in a monolithic architecture is system-wide rather than in little subsystem-level chunks. Greater within-platform freedom and a lower need for overt coordination with apps increases its freedom to evolve (Baldwin and Clark, 2000, p. 221). This is why modular systems tend to evolve faster (de Weck et al., 2011, p. 85; Ethiraj and Levinthal, 2004a,b; Simon, 2002). Such technical autonomy enables independence in how the owners of the platform and individual apps implement them and how often they can tweak them. The platform and apps can be internally monolithic yet interoperate solely by complying with the interfaces and APIs. This allows the platform and apps to evolve independent of each other, at a rate that is appropriate to their own specialized domains, market dynamics, and varied end-user needs. This reduction of the need for coordination with anyone else in the ecosystem allows fast, autonomous—almost continuous—market experimentation by app developers (Kamel, 1987; Sanchez and Mahoney, 1996). Similarly, the platform can be tweaked more rapidly and assimilate technology advances outside the ecosystem, unconstrained by app dependencies, and therefore is likely to come out ahead in Red Queen competition. Therefore partitioning the platform through modularization does not just lower complexity but exponentially reduces it. In contrast, a platform with a more monolithic architecture will simply be unable to absorb new capabilities at the same rate. In real options terms, platform modularization therefore creates real options as each app gains independence within the constraints of the platform's design rules (Gamba and Fusari, 2009).
- *Deepens specialization across the ecosystem.* The use of decentralized solutions search processes by many diverse designers is a fundamental premise of the theory of modular evolution (Baldwin and Clark, 2000, p. 14). Modularization reduces the need for a platform owner to understand the domains of its app developers, and the need for app developers to know internal details of the platform. The key, as Linus Torvalds puts it, is to keep people from stepping on each others' toes. This requires minimizing the need for communication, even forbidding it (Langlois and Garzarelli, 2008). Each app developer needs to be concerned with only *what* the platform does, not *how* it does its job. This simplification of their respective solution spaces creates a valuable form of mutual ignorance that allows the platform owner and app developers to specialize more deeply in their own domain (Tiwana, 2008a). The platform owner can then treat apps as black boxes, unconcerned with their implementation.
- *Reallocates platform owner resources toward platform innovation.* Recall that the greatest complexities in platform ecosystems arise at the interface of the platform and apps. Standardization of platform interfaces through modularization eases integration of apps with the platform, lowering platform owners' recurring and unpredictable app integration costs (Argyres and Bigelow, 2010; Moneverde, 1995). These interfaces provide the glue that holds the platform and its apps together. This in turn frees up resources that a platform owner would need for integrating apps, which can now be reallocated to innovating within the platform. Modularization

therefore speeds platform capability enhancement by freeing up more resources for enhancement of native platform functionality and by requiring less time for integrating apps (Kamel, 1987).

- *Protects platform secrets.* Platform modularization limits how much of the innards of a platform are visible to app developers and rivals without discouraging the emergence of complementary apps. This selective disclosure of proprietary technology safeguards platform innovations by maintaining a layer of secrecy around their implementation, reducing the outflow of innovations from a platform. It also increases a platform owner's control over the interfaces, which is a subtle but potent form of control through architecture instead of overt power.

Opening up a platform using an architectural modularization strategy often amplifies innovation around the platform by an order of magnitude, provided its governance structure encourages it as well. Amazon Web Services (AWS), Twitter, Netflix, NPR, Facebook, and SalesForce have successfully used this approach through APIs to stimulate external innovation around their platforms. Cloud-based Salesforce.com, for example, opened up its core services to outsiders to augment; external apps based on its API now account for about 75% of the company's business.

But the plasticity-enhancing potential created by platform modularization requires that platform governance be aligned with its architecture. In particular, the pricing dimension of platform governance should provide strong incentives for app developers to actively engage in innovating around a platform purely out of self-interest. Failing such alignment, app developers' goals can dominate at the expense of ecosystem interests; this behavior is known as suboptimization in complex systems thinking. Furthermore, allocating app decision rights primarily to app developers in modularized platforms ensures that app-level strategic and operational decisions are rapidly translated into action.

10.4.3.2 Increasing ecosystem diversity increases platform plasticity

An old adage says that the best way to good ideas is to generate a lot of ideas. The best way to generate a lot of ideas around a platform is to have a lot of different people generate them in parallel. A second way to bolster platform plasticity is therefore to increase the diversity and size of the pool of app developers in the platform's ecosystem (i.e., increasing the inflows of innovations by tapping into ideas from all corners of the ecosystem). The diversity and size of the app developer pool matters more when there is greater heterogeneity in the platform end-users' needs and greater technology and market volatility (van Schewick, 2012, p. 9). Decentralized innovation by a large and diverse pool of app developers means that a variety of experiments and ideas will be tried, resulting in more innovation inflow into the platform's ecosystem. The more independent approaches that are experimented with, the greater is the likelihood that one solution will solve a focal open problem particularly well. Decentralized ecosystem governance will therefore generally produce more diverse apps, increasing its odds of producing diverse solutions that meet diverse end-users' needs, and in turn a more sustainably attractive platform. This requires a platform owner to be tolerant of app developers' activities at the margins, unusual experiments, and outliers. Such activities can stretch the platform owner's own understanding of the possibilities for the platform. Platform architecture—by altering the degree to which the platform owner and app developers are independent and overlapping in their responsibilities—influences the composition of app developers that choose to join the ecosystem, their incentives and disincentives, and their ability and constraints to innovate freely.

The key is to ensure that platform modularization is aligned with governance. All three dimensions of governance are important. Decision rights for apps should be sufficiently decentralized for app developers to be able to act on opportunities that they spot; revenue-sharing incentives should be

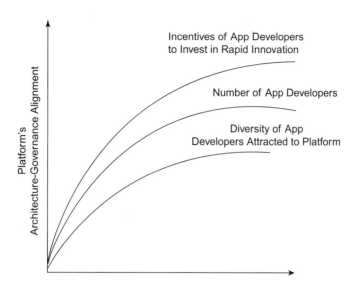

FIGURE 10.12

Architecture–governance alignment influences who participates in a platform's ecosystem from the app developer side.

sufficiently motivating vis-à-vis rival platforms for them to bear the risk; and the control portfolio should be lean enough to not get in their way yet ensure that the quality of what goes into the platform's ecosystem is not degraded. As Figure 10.12 illustrates, the better such alignment, the greater the growth in the diversity and numbers of app developers that are likely to be attracted to a platform.

Input control is particularly critical in the early stages of a platform ecosystem's lifecycle to ensure that the apps that enter the ecosystem increase the perceived value of a platform in end-users' perceptions. Google used minimal input control in its Android ecosystem, which encouraged a lot of junky apps. Junky, half-baked apps and minimal ports from rival platforms of dubious value and quality can drown out the fewer strong apps by their sheer volume. This substantially increases end-users' search costs, reducing the long-term prospects of the platform.

10.4.3.3 Recognize the platform innovations that will not naturally occur

Finally, a platform owner must recognize that modularized platforms are good at generating rapid incremental improvements within individual apps in an ecosystem but terrible at producing ecosystem-wide ones. Different architectures will impose different idea implementation costs on app developers. Therefore, different ecosystem architectures will lead to different types of innovation activity emerging as dominant in a platform's ecosystem over the long term. Recall from Part II of the book that modularized platform ecosystems amplify innovation vis-à-vis monolithic systems by shifting the innovation mode from incremental to modular. In modularized platforms, the dominant mode of innovation will therefore be modular, within-app innovation. This is shown in Figure 10.13. Incremental innovations come from both platform owners and app developers, while radical innovations will almost never occur in the absence of scrapped-and-rebuilt platforms. A platform owner must take responsibility for architectural or ecosystem-wide innovations will not occur naturally in the platform's ecosystem. This has consequences for a platform's durability; we subsequently discuss ways in which a platform owner can address this challenge.

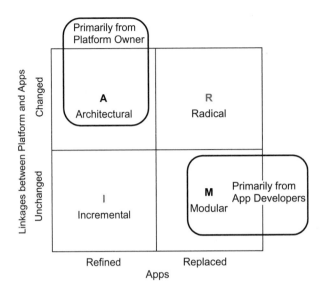

FIGURE 10.13

The origins of two classes of innovations in modularized platform ecosystems.

10.5 ORCHESTRATING LONG-TERM PLATFORM EVOLUTION

10.5.1 Orchestrating platform envelopment

Envelopment by a platform can span expansion of a platform into the turf of adjacent markets (horizontal envelopment) or adjacent parts of the ecosystem's value chain (vertical envelopment) (see Figure 10.14).

10.5.1.1 Horizontal envelopment

Horizontal envelopment is the most widespread envelopment move through which a platform can swallow the functionality of a product or service—or even a platform—in an adjacent market. A horizontal envelopment move primarily attempts to offer new services to existing customers (Zook and Allen, 2003), as illustrated in Figure 10.15. Horizontal envelopment has two prerequisites. First, there must be a considerable overlap between the platform's users and the users of the adjacent solution. This allows the enveloping platform to carry over—simply replicate—its existing network of users in the space of the enveloped solution. For new entrants in a platform market, envelopment is therefore a powerful way to circumvent the blocking caused by rivals' existing network effects. Second, the enveloping platform's assets should be leverageable in the enveloped solution's domain. Whether the enveloped solution offers a stronger value proposition by offering better functionality or lower costs, it must be strong enough to convince the target solution's installed base of users to adopt it. Horizontal envelopment can preemptively prepare a platform for saturation and decline in its core market by providing a segue into a future core business. Your next core business, however, will not introduce itself with fanfare (Zook and Allen, 2003).

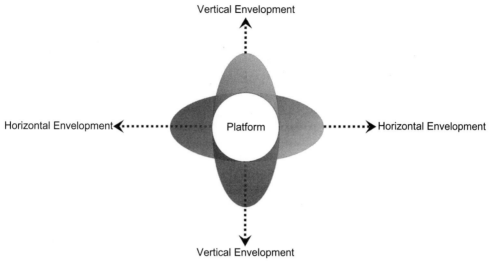

FIGURE 10.14

Two types of envelopment moves by a platform.

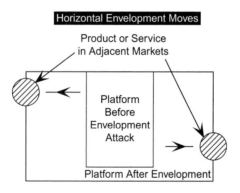

FIGURE 10.15

Horizontal envelopment by a platform.

A platform owner can spot opportunities for horizontal envelopment in five ways.

1. *Identify adjacent bundling opportunities*. Identify standalone products and services that existing end-users of your platform value that could possibly be bundled profitably into the platform.
2. *Watch S-curves in adjacent markets*. Flat or declining adoption rates usually indicate mature markets with stable products or services. There is little product innovation going on in such markets and the focus has usually shifted to process innovations. These are often targets for envelopment attacks if (a) a platform can offer the same functionality cheaper or offer improved functionality and (b) the user base of the platform and the target market overlaps. The assets of a platform must be leveraged to either reduce costs of delivery or significantly enhance the value

proposition of the target solution. For example, the digital camera industry was successfully enveloped by smartphones, which offered somewhat weaker photography capabilities but with better integration with email and social networks that a large proportion of digital camera users also used.

3. *Watch for convergence of previous independent streams of technology.* Opportunities for horizontal envelopment also arise due to the convergence of previously disparate technology solutions, which allows one platform to expand its functionality to include an adjacent product or service and offer it to end-users as a multiproduct bundle. Technological convergence can therefore help anticipate envelopment attacks from adjacent platforms. Convergence is driven particularly by packetization, discussed in Chapter 1, associated today with the ongoing technological leaps around the Internet of Things and additive manufacturing (3D printing). Every horizontal envelopment opportunity is also potentially an envelopment threat. Watch out for competition from innovators in adjacent markets, who could offer a directly competing product created and distributed with a very different business model. The entrée of open-source Linux projects into the smartphone OS market in 2014 is an example of such a threat to companies such as Apple since the former use open-source and GPL-licensed code for their platforms.

4. *Track regulatory changes.* Watch for external, regulatory changes in mature industries outside your own industry that alter the rules of competition in those industries. For example, the regulatory change allowing the use of enhanced emergency calling services (E911) in the United States allowed voice-over-IP service providers to directly envelop the residential telephony market.

5. *Watch envelopment attacks by rival platforms.* Envelopment attacks, no matter how feeble, by rival platforms that your own platform directly competes with can also help identify envelopment targets.

10.5.2 Rebuffing envelopment attacks on a platform

Launching envelopment attacks requires an aligned platform governance structure, particularly decision rights. The foregoing strategies for horizontal envelopment require that a platform's strategic decision rights reside primarily with the platform owner. The evolutionary metrics described in the preceding sections also require such partitioning of platform decision rights. A platform owner's alertness to envelopment opportunities is also potentially valuable to app developers because it expands the pool of potential end-users to which they have access. In this sense, envelopment goes horizontal envelopment attacks launched by a platform hand in hand with platform stickiness with app developers. Eighty percent of successful adjacency moves are built on deep insights into end-users' needs, behaviors, and frustrations (Zook and Allen, 2003). App developers are usually far more tuned into these than a platform owner. Involving app developers in seeking envelopment opportunities can help identify underdeveloped adjacencies, exploit untapped insights into customers, and identify unrecognized market segments. Therefore, platform strategic decision rights should include input from app developers. In other words, they should reside primarily—but not exclusively—with platform owners.

A platform owner is also likely to encounter horizontal envelopment attacks by indirect competitors, who can exploit the same convergence dynamics to foreclose existing markets and overlapping end-users. A platform owner must first decide whether an envelopment attack is a real threat. If the side on which a platform makes its money—either app developers or end-users—perceives that the enveloping platform delivers a better value proposition than your own, then the envelopment threat is real.

How can a platform owner rebuff horizontal envelopment attacks that it encounters? There are three defense mechanisms that a platform owner can use. First, tight control over a platform's interfaces only protects against existing rivals but does little to deter horizontal envelopment attacks (Farrell and Saloner, 1992). One logical response is to reciprocate with a reverse horizontal envelopment attack if the threat of envelopment is credible. Second, altering the business model used by a platform owner can sometimes rebuff an envelopment attack. For example, a platform owner might shift to an ad-supported business model that it can viably use profitably but the envelopment attacker would not be able to financially capitalize. Third, cross-licensing partnerships and mergers of two vulnerable platforms can give the merged platform greater ability to survive an attack. An example of this is the fusion of Nokia's Symbian platform and Microsoft's Windows Mobile platform, which plausibly made them better able jointly to compete with rivals such as Android and iOS.

10.5.2.1 Vertical envelopment

A second type of envelopment move is one where a platform owner expands the scope of a platform to occupy a different link in the platform's value chain (Zook and Allen, 2003), as illustrated in Figure 10.16. This involves swallowing the functionality provided by a participant in either the upstream or downstream part of the platform value chain. An upstream envelopment move can involve integrating an upstream ingredient provider, either consensually or by brute force. These can be providers of external services that a platform uses, licensed intellectual property that goes into a platform, and suppliers of software components (such as Flash and VPN technology). An example of such a move is Apple integrating cloud storage services into iOS in 2011; these were previously provided by external service providers such as Dropbox. Such envelopment moves typically threaten the bread-and-butter business of the upstream partner and should be attempted only when vertically integrating an upstream ingredient can increase the value and stickiness of a platform both for end-users and app developers significantly beyond the level possible without integrating. In this instance, introduction

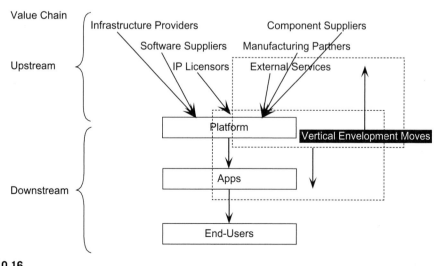

FIGURE 10.16

Vertical envelopment by a platform.

of iCloud into the platform significantly increased app developers' stickiness by allowing them to integrate and build on cloud storage capabilities into thousands of apps, thereby reducing app developers' innovation costs. The service had 300 million users by the end of its first year. Upstream envelopment moves however are often high risk and costly, and opportunities are relatively infrequent.

Downstream envelopment involves assimilation into the platform of a downstream complement—specifically the functionality of an existing app. Opportunities for downstream vertical envelopment are relatively abundant compared to any other envelopment opportunities. However, downstream envelopment is often a challenging dilemma because it puts the platform owner in direct conflict with the interests of its app developers. Such envelopment moves can destroy an existing app developer's business model overnight (Evans et al., 2006, pp. 53, 254). A platform owner must approach downstream envelopment with kid gloves. As a general principle, a platform owner should credibly signal that it will keep out of its app developers' niches. Steamrolling app developers is not an effective way to attract and retain them. Intel, for example, assists outside developers of promising applications of its core products and promotes them, but does not dabble directly in their markets. As apps become more specialized and begin addressing smaller niches, it is no longer possible for the platform owner alone to address them. When the *long-tail effect* kicks with a platform at the center, everyone in a platform's ecosystem wins. The penalties for paralyzing the long-tail effect usually exceed the short-term financial gains from downstream vertical envelopment by a platform owner. Put another way, because horizontal envelopment can destroy a platform owner's credibility with app developers and alienate them, the long-term damage to a platform's ecosystem can often exceed the immediate improvement in a platform's native functionality. Commitments by a platform owner to prospective app developers must remain credible to be effective (Rysman, 2009). Although platform owners should avoid app developers' markets, they invade their turf often enough to make many app developers wary.

10.5.2.2 When is downstream envelopment by a platform acceptable?

So, when it is acceptable for a platform owner to initiate a downstream vertical envelopment attack? A platform owner should make its own apps—or envelop vertically downstream—only under three conditions:

1. *Strategic functionality.* First, when the functionality of the app can strategically differentiate a platform from its rivals and a platform owner wants to foster dramatic improvements by app developers in its functionality. By setting a benchmark for app developers to beat, this can foster intense competition to improve app functionality. This has an effect on ratcheting up performance of app developers (Bradach and Eccles, 1989; Kim et al., 2011). It can engender intense competition from app developers, who can survive only by providing more value to end-users than the platform owner's own app does. While it is important to provide direction and foster competition among app developers, a platform owner must be careful not to take it so far that there's no money left on the table. A platform will then fail to attract new app developers and fail to retain existing ones. However, when new functionality previously absent from the platform is introduced as an app, it does not put app developers' interests in conflict with the platform owners' interests.

2. *Gap-filling functionality.* Second, when the app market is unlikely to provide functionality that a platform owner believes is needed by a platform. In this scenario, the platform owner-provided app simply fills a void that might otherwise be left unfilled. An example of this is the development of presentation software (Keynote) by Apple for the iOS platform. When such

apps are created by the platform owner from the outset of a platform, it does not have the credibility-damaging effect typical of downstream vertical envelopment. The only other instance in which a platform owner will vertically envelop a downstream app is in retaliation to an app developer attempting to vertically envelop a platform. A recent example of this was the introduction of a mapping app by Apple, intended to replace Google Maps as Google attempted to envelop the iOS platform with its own Android platform. Platform owners must remain cognizant of today's app evolving into tomorrow's rival platform.

3. *The common good outstrips the few that are penalized.* Third, downstream envelopment is more acceptable when the number of app developers that benefit from the move vastly outnumbers those hurt by it. Finally, when a platform's existing *end-users* significantly benefit from it or it attracts new users to the platform on either side, the upsides of downstream envelopment can outweigh its downsides. This final criterion can be a slippery slope.

10.5.3 Orchestrating platform durability

A platform's durability refers to its endurance in the marketplace in the face of competition. Recall that we are more interested in changes—increases and decreases—in a platform's durability rather than its survival or mortality. A platform's durability is a function of its direct contribution to the platform's ecosystem, always relative to rival platforms. The platform must contribute resources that pass the lit-mus test—they must be valuable, rare, inimitable, and nonsubstitutable from the perspective of both sides of the platform, end-users and app developers (Figure 10.17). A platform will endure only if it *continues to* offer a compelling value proposition to its current and prospective app developers and end-users. Platforms that fail to create a win–win for their app developers wither and die. For a platform to be durable, both sides of the platform must remain better off being part of its ecosystem than outside it (Evans et al., 2006, p. 56). (Recall that indicators of a platform's durability include changes in the sur-vival rate of apps, the proportion of apps that are updated at least once a year, and the changes in the percentage of platform adopters on both sides who remain active users.) Given that a platform's primary users are its app developers, we focus primarily on them. Tending to this side of the platform usually accomplishes the same things that a platform owner must do to increase its durability with its end-users.

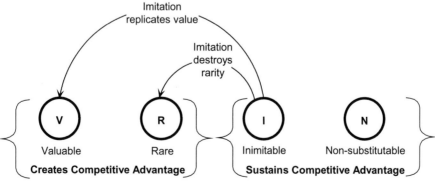

FIGURE 10.17

Imitation by rival platforms destroys the rarity of valuable platform resources.

A test for the competitive advantage of a platform is the resource litmus test. A platform initially gains traction by contributing capabilities and resources that are *valuable* to its app developers but *rare* in rival ecosystems. To sustain its initial advantage, these resources must also be *inimitable* and *nonsubstitutable*. But the intrinsic properties of software often make it imitable through replication and reverse engineering, notwithstanding the mild protections of patents and copyrights that are often challenging to enforce in global markets. In a sufficiently competitive market, imitation by rival platforms often replicates valuable functionality and destroys its rarity. Today's rare capability becomes tomorrow's norm, as illustrated in Figure 10.17.

That leaves only two viable solutions to enhance a platform's durability: (1) adding valuable new capabilities faster than rivals can replicate them, giving them temporary rarity, and (2) developing nonsubstitutable assets. As we subsequently explain, accumulating nonsubstitutable resources is not a bulletproof strategy because convergence-enabled envelopment attacks can altogether bypass the need for them.

10.5.4 Consistently contributing valuable resources to the ecosystem

The first step for a platform owner is accepting that any competitive advantage is temporary. No positional advantage is durable, but the ability to evolve is. The hallmark of a durable platform is not solely focusing on doing some things well but rather being good at learning how to do new things that app developers and end-users value. A platform owner must pay attention to six things in evolving a platform's value proposition in ways that enhance its durability vis-à-vis rival platforms.

10.5.4.1 Many eyes are better than few

A platform's biggest asset in recognizing new ways of adding valuable resources to its ecosystem is to use app developers as its many eyes. Since app developers are likely to be far better tuned to diverse end-user needs, granting them sufficient autonomy by decentralizing governance across the ecosystem can increase the volume and variety of new ideas for a platform to generate new value. Recall that the best way to generate good ideas is to generate lots of them. This autonomy, however, must be coupled with strong win–win propositions for app developers, as dictated by the pricing dimension of governance. A platform owner that remains receptive—not necessarily agreeable—to inputs from app developers is likely to find new ways to keep the platform valuable to its app developers and remain at the center of its ecosystem. Platforms that fail to contribute nonsubstitutable capabilities that app developers' value and at a pace that at least matches rival platforms will soon be at a competitive disadvantage.

As we enter the era of "big data," think of signals, not data. The amount of data confronting organizations has increased nearly tenfold in the past decade and is expected to increase a thousandfold in another decade. Managers used to thinking in terms of data points must therefore shift their thinking to data streams. Episodic information processing must be replaced with dynamic information processing. These data streams must be quickly mined for insights, extracting the right signals, and acting on them.

Leveraging app developers as its many eyes increases a platform owner's capacity to decode weak market signals embedded in such data streams and act on them before rivals can. In contrast, platform companies that withered and died—Palm, Blackberry, Nokia—all failed to notice ground shifts in the market, usually caused by fledgling entrants that were too little to even notice. The ability for a platform owner to detect weak signals from the ecosystem's eyes and ears coupled with the flexibility maintained by investing in real options can endow a platform unrivaled ambidexterity to serve today's markets but be prepared for tomorrow's. All of this, however, requires a mindset that is humble, mutually respectful, and open to diversity of divergent opinions and unorthodox viewpoints of app developers. It also requires a culture that encourages members of the ecosystem to experiment rapidly, frequently, and economically with technologies and business models.

10.5.4.2 Coevolving platform governance with aging platform architecture

The second way in which a platform owner can maintain the inflow of new value into a platform is by adapting and coevolving platform governance to mirror an aging platform's architecture. Even if a platform is codesigned with perfect architecture–governance alignment at the outset, unintentional architectural drifts that accompany aging can cause them to fall out of alignment. Put another way, a platform's age is a liability to its plasticity. A platform becomes less and less malleable as it ages. This phenomenon, known as *code decay*, occurs due to the violations of the prescribed design principles and deviations from the intended architecture that accumulate over time, both within the platform and across the ecosystem (Eick et al., 2001). It gets worse over time: As a platform ages, its complexity grows due to undocumented dependencies and workarounds to its interface standards, in turn worsening its plasticity over time. This makes it increasingly challenging to make internal changes to a platform without fracturing the ecosystem. Implementation shortcuts and modular principle violations by the platform owner and app developers can be considered a technical debt that must be paid at some point in the future as a platform evolves. Symptoms of code decay are bloated and excessively complex code, the need for widely dispersed changes (i.e., the span of a code change is not as localized as it used to be for a platform of that level of modularization), and an excessive proliferation of many interfaces that often results from adding new APIs (Baldwin and Clark, 2000, p. 416; Eick et al., 2001). Taken to an extreme, code decay eventually transforms the platform's ecosystem into a monolithic block. Changes in architecture are then needed to "refactor" the platform to fix these problems. This is often an impossible task in mature platforms with many apps, which will likely break and have to be reimplemented. Changes in platform architecture—even small ones—can then wreck a platform because they often are inseparable from changes in its interfaces. It is a hit or miss bet for a platform owner: Firefox rebuilt Firefox with version 2 with much success and Microsoft rebuilt Windows XP as Windows Vista with little success. In either case, the existing apps on the original platform ceased to function with the rebuilt platform. While effective governance can discourage behaviors that intensify the liability of age, they cannot eliminate the problem.

Instead, this requires the platform owner to coevolve the governance of a platform to mirror the current as-it-really-is architecture rather than keeping it aligned with architecture as it *used to be* earlier in the platform's lifecycle. This age-driven architecture–governance "remirroring" is illustrated in Figure 10.18. Since the effect of age is increasing monolithicity of the platform's architecture, realigning governance primarily requires reducing the degree to which app implementation decision rights are decentralized and increasing the use of formal control in the portfolio used by the platform owner to regulate app developers' work. A failure to coevolve governance to mirror devolving architectural modularity will otherwise increase the platform owners' integration costs by unbalancing the integration–autonomy seesaw, described in Chapter 2.

Such coevolution of architecture and governance driven by age must also be complemented by consideration of forces exogenous to the platform ecosystem (Figure 10.19).

10.5.4.3 Expanding the scope of a platform through vertical envelopment

The third way to expand the value of the resources contributed by a platform to ensure its durability is through vertical upstream envelopment, described earlier in our discussion on increasing stickiness. Doing this more aggressively than rival platforms allows the Red Queen effect to be multiplied in favor

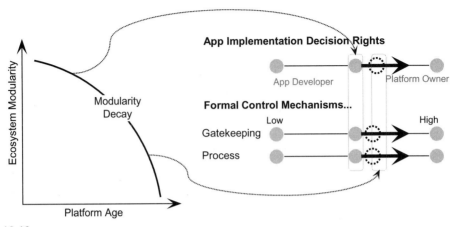

FIGURE 10.18

How ecosystem governance must evolve with platform age to maintain architecture–governance alignment.

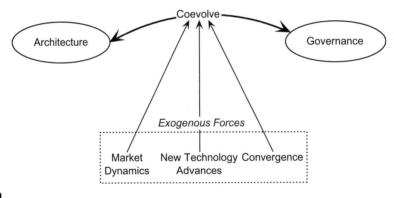

FIGURE 10.19

Exogenous drivers of architecture–governance coevolution.

of the platform because upstream capabilities that are adopted by many app developers raise the bar for what a rival platform must replicate to keep up. iOS adding cloud storage service that apps could build on is an example of such a durability-enhancing envelopment move.

10.5.4.4 *Maintain modularity by adding new APIs*
Fourth, adding native new functionality that builds on external technology advances using new APIs, as described earlier in this chapter, maintains the benefits of platform modularity without accelerating architectural decay. However, there is a limit to the proliferation of APIs after which the sheer complexity of the platform makes it challenging to attract new app developers.

10.5.4.5 *Plug the gap in system-wide innovations that will not naturally occur*
The fifth way to expand the value of the resources contributed by a platform is for the platform owner to recognize that ecosystems of modularized platforms will not produce system-wide, non-app-level innovations. A platform owner must take responsibility for pursuing such innovations to ensure its

durability, illustrated in Figure 10.13 in our discussion of platform innovation. Examples include new system-wide services that apps can leverage. Paradoxically, the rigidity of frozen platform interfaces that enable rapid innovation at the ecosystem level stymies radical innovation at the platform level. Recall from our discussion on platform plasticity that platform modularization increases the inflow of app-level innovations but forecloses systemic innovation by incapacitating changes to the platform's interfaces. Platform modularization is therefore good for making lots of little hops but terrible for making large technological leaps. In the long term, this reduces the durability of a platform, particularly when new rivals—unencumbered by legacy interfaces and APIs—are able to exploit systemic advances in new generations of underlying technologies in their own platforms (Brusoni and Prencipe, 2006; Pil and Cohen, 2006). Radical changes in platform architecture are even more unlikely because specialized knowledge is eventually fragmented across members of the ecosystem, making it impossible for the platform owner to possess detailed knowledge of the emergent dependencies across the ecosystem (Baldwin, 2008). An ecosystem's core competencies then become its core rigidities, as app developers and the platform owner become more deeply focused on the niches where they excel. Managing this tradeoff requires applying the Goldilocks principle in the initial design of the platform so it has an intermediate level of modularization—neither too much nor too little. A related tactic is to ensure that the interface standards are designed to be versatile so their restrictiveness does not retard innovation (Farrell and Saloner, 1992). Unfortunately, determining what is a just-right level for modularity is a tricky question with no straightforward answers.

10.5.4.6 Mutate into markets when a platform's existing assets are still rare
The final tactic to counter the durability-diminishing effects of replication by rivals is to mutate the platform into horizontally adjacent markets where the platform's existing assets are still rare and potentially valuable. This was described in depth in the discussion on platform envelopment earlier in this chapter.

10.5.5 Accumulating nonsubstitutable assets
The second approach to improving a platform's durability is to accumulate nonsubstitutable assets in the platform's ecosystem. The single hardest to substitute asset is cross-side and same-side network effects created by a platform. As we described earlier, network effects create a value-driven, noncoercive lock-in on both sides and protects a platform. However, we described how new rivals using mutation, envelopment, and carryover can break past network effects that previously protected a platform. The other two nonsubstitutable assets are more of a nuanced mindset that guides platform evolution.

10.5.5.1 The Icarus paradox: the other thing besides taxes that is an absolute certainty
Platforms encounter the "Icarus paradox" as they age: The very reasons that led to its market success hinder its ability to respond to new generations of technology, eventually causing its downfall. As Chuck Palahniuk says in *The Fight Club*, on a long enough timeline, the survival rate for everyone drops to zero. The core capabilities that are honed over successive generations of a platform can become its core rigidities, largely because architectural change becomes almost impossible once a modular design has taken off and has enlisted a large ecosystem of app developers around it. While there is no recipe for avoiding the Icarus paradox, platform owners can delay it by changing what they focus on as a platform progresses through different stages in its lifecycle. As a platform ages and a dominant design is well established in its core market, the rate of fundamentally new innovations sharply decreases. At this point, the focus must shift toward process innovations. This leaves all

platforms following the industry's dominant design vulnerable to new entrants who enter the market with a fundamentally new dominant design that incumbent platforms cannot readily switch to. Therefore, a platform owner must focus on technological and business model innovations in the predominant design era of the platform's industry, and focus on innovating in content and substance more than the mechanisms and routines used to orchestrate the ecosystem. However, the focus reverses in the post-dominant design phase to innovating in the platform's processes as fundamental product innovations become harder. However, process innovations simply delay the inevitable; incumbent platforms almost always fail to make the leap across technological discontinuities.

Another nonsubstitutable asset therefore is the capacity to recognize the role of lifecycle effects and change a platform's focus to align with its stage in the evolutionary lifecycle. Two key lifecycle attributes discussed in Part I are relevant: emergence of a dominant design and progression along the S-curve. Platform owners must shift expectations for what they focus on accomplishing to be in line with a platform's current stage in its lifecycle. First, the emergence of an industry-wide dominant design shifts competition from among designs to within variants of the design. When a platform establishes or follows a dominant design, its core technological features are so effectively replicable that they merely become the cost of entry and are no longer a differentiator. At this point, modular innovation is the dominant mode for differentiation. This means that differentiation among platforms is driven primarily by improvements at the app rather than platform level. Second, as a platform moves from the upward trajectory to its peak on the S-curve, radical improvements become progressively harder to make and the rapidity of new innovations levels off. It does not matter how hard a platform owner tries, less improvement occurs per investment dollar. The rate of finding improvements slows exponentially over time as a platform ages; each major advance increases the difficulty of finding the next one. The emphasis should then shift away from fundamental product innovations and more toward process innovations (i.e., doing existing things better). The platform owner's mindset should enable such process innovations across the ecosystem, or at least not constrain them. To paraphrase an old saying, platform owners must have the serenity to accept the things they cannot change, changes the ones they can, and the wisdom to know the difference. The Icarus paradox is in the category of unchangeable things.

THE ORIGINS OF THE ICARUS PARADOX

The *Icarus paradox* is a term coined by Canadian economist Danny Miller for the phenomenon that businesses fail abruptly after enjoying considerable success in the marketplace. Their initial success brings about their own downfall due to subsequent overconfidence and complacency. The term comes from Icarus—the son of the master craftsman Daedalus—in Greek mythology who flew too close to the Sun and melted his own wings, which were made of feathers and wax (Figure 10.20). This, according to the legend, caused him to drown to his death in the sea, which is known in the present day as the Icarian Sea near Samos in Greece.

The Icarus paradox eventually brings every successful platform to a fork in the road where either path leads to mortality. The choice is to stick with an obsolete core or to reconstruct the platform from scratch. Sticking with a stagnating platform core can be disastrous but fixing the problem requires a complete overhaul or reconstruction. Core reconstruction is necessary when the platform owner is faced with a generation of technologies or business models that straddles the platform with inherently inferior economics that it cannot shake off or sustain relative to new kids on the block (Zook and Allen,

FIGURE 10.20

The Icarus paradox is named after the legend of Icarus in ancient Greek mythology.

Source: Thomas Bulfinch, The Age of Fable, *Henry Altemus Company, Philadelphia, 1897, p. 202.*

2003). Successful platforms repeatedly stumble in their attempts to catch up by using a binge-and-purge strategy. Such bet-the-company moves are almost always a loser's game (Zook and Allen, 2003). Replacing the platform core outright almost always fails because it often requires breaking backward compatibility from the existing generation of the platform, which in turn requires rebuilding apps. Maintaining compatibility between successive generations of a platform—of what economists call *vertical compatibility* (Rysman, 2009)—is necessary to avoid alienating existing app developers. Examples of such abrupt overhauls that failed include Microsoft's attempt to radically reinvent its Windows platform using Windows Vista and Zune's tile-based interface, Palm's attempt to rebuild PalmOS as WebOS, Nokia's attempt to reinvent its Symbian platform, Psion's attempt to do it with its Psion OS, and Blackberry's attempt with Blackberry 10 OS.

10.5.5.2 Recognize whether a platform is in a winner-takes-all or pie-splitting market

A platform owner must also recognize whether its market is a winner-takes-all market. In other words, whether it is possible for one platform to dominate or whether multiple platforms will coexist in the same market. One platform will dominate only when three conditions are simultaneously met (Eisenmann et al., 2006, 2011):

1. *Multihoming costs must be high for both end-users and app developers.* When multihoming costs are high only for end-users but low for app developers, multiple rival platforms can coexist. This by itself is a sufficient condition for the coexistence of multiple rival platforms.
2. *Cross-side network effects must be positive and strong.* When cross-side network effects are positive and strong, a single platform will dominate. End-consumers prefer a platform with many complements, and app developers prefer a platform with many users. This is the case in the mobile computing/smartphone markets, where end-users value the presence of a large number of app developers and vice versa. (Recall that same-side network effects in the absence of cross-side network effects are in one-sided systems (Skype, FaceTime), which are not platforms by our definition—they fail to meet the two-sided requirement.) Recognizing this property of your platform's market also guides how pricing subsidies should evolve. If you followed penetration pricing to catalyze the creation of network effects (by accelerating critical mass generation, scale economies, or switching costs), should the subsidy be ended or made permanent for one side? Subsidies for early adopters are driven primarily to prime the pump to overcome a cold-start problem typical of network effects. A platform owner might profit more from permanently subsidizing one side if Red Queen competition persists.
3. *End-users have low demand for hard-to-copy differentiated features from platforms (i.e., end-users' needs are relatively homogenous).* If the demand for differentiated features is high (i.e., end-user needs are diverse), multiple platforms can coexist.

If even one of these conditions is not met, multiple platforms will coexist and the platform is not in a winner-takes-all market. Rival platforms will remain substitutable in the minds of end-users, which guarantees that fierce competition will persist in the platform's market. In the absence of a winner-takes-all market, a platform owner is better off specializing in tackling one segment of the broader market where its resources give it an edge over rivals. (Use the resource litmus test to assess this.)

10.5.6 Orchestrating platform mutation

Unlike envelopment, which expands a platform's functionality, platform mutation creates a distinct derivative platform in a *different* application domain. Unlike envelopment, mutation does not require an overlap in users across the existing and mutation target market. Figure 10.21 illustrates the key differences between platform mutation and envelopment. The result of platform mutation is a serendipitous spinoff platform that inherits some of the properties of the parent platform but with a different purpose. Mutation is akin to exercising a growth option in real options lingo. Just as species can break out of competitive exclusion by diversifying, platforms can break out of the race to the bottom by diversifying into different markets where their existing assets give them some advantage over the incumbent

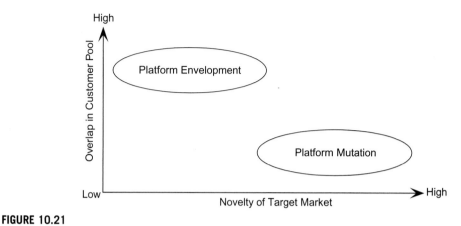

FIGURE 10.21

Differences between platform mutation and platform envelopment.

rivals. A platform owner must first clearly articulate exactly how—using the resource litmus test—its assets can be a distinctive advantage in the target market.

Unlike envelopment, mutation often requires a break from the platform's existing business model. Apple is a good example of mutation of a platform into the music industry. Perhaps bigger than the technology innovations that Apple brought to the mobile computing market were the business innovations that it introduced into the music business. Within a few years it transformed a company with zero market share into the world's largest music retailer. Similarly, Amazon mutated its existing electronic retailing infrastructure into the software business by introducing AWS. In either case, the company leveraged a set of assets that were rare in the targeted industry and coupled it with a disruptive business model. Mutation in Apple's case involved carryover of its existing end-users into the target market, but Amazon did not use a carryover strategy due to the lack of a distinctive overlap in the customer pools in its existing and mutation target markets.

The need for mutation is often created by fading markets in which a platform currently competes. These are signaled by a decrease in the growth rate of the platform's core existing market, attrition of customers to rival platforms, and the emergence of commoditization of platforms in the post-dominant design phase of the platform market's lifecycle. This often creates race-to-the-bottom price wars that make a platform's industry a zero-profit business. To identify opportunities for mutation, a platform owner must look outside its existing core markets. Historically, in industries ranging from photography, lighting, glass making, and refrigeration, major disruptive competency-destroying innovations have come from industry outsiders, unlike competence-enhancing innovations that are as likely to come from insiders as they are from outsiders. Recall that nascent markets are plagued by a low signal-to-noise ratio and a platform owner can use all the help that it can get from its ecosystem to discern the signal behind a prospective mutation opportunity.

The key enabler for platform mutation is appropriate platform governance, particularly the partitioning of decision rights. The platform owner must centralize platform strategic decision rights to be able to act on mutation opportunities but also decentralize apps decision rights so that its app developers can act as its many outside eyes and ears to sense latent opportunities for the platform to mutate. Fortunately, the governance structures that enhance platform composability and durability are also conducive to platform mutation.

10.6 LESSONS LEARNED

- *Adaptation drives survival of platforms.* Platforms that survive in evolutionary competition are not the strongest, largest, or the cleverest but are the ones that are most adaptive to their environment. Rapid adaptation improves fitness with their changing environment.
- *The bathtub theory of innovation.* The net difference between innovation inflows that enter a platform's ecosystem and outflows that are copied by rivals is its stock of innovation that can potentially differentiate it. Growing the stock requires increasing the volume of inflows and curbing the outflows.
- *The resource litmus test tells us what resources in the stock can competitively differentiate a platform from its rivals.* A resource is any tangible asset such as a platform's capabilities, functionality, user base, apps, and patents as well as its intangible resources. A resource must be valuable and rare to create a competitive advantage and inimitable and nonsubstitutable to sustain it. Few resources will simultaneously meet all these conditions. Therefore most resources create only a temporary advantage. Speed with which new resources are added then becomes the only reliable source of competitive advantage.
- *OODA loops in the American military doctrine help accelerate platform evolution.* Shortening the lag in each link in the Observe → Orient → Decide → Act loop accelerates evolution. This can be done by modularizing platform architecture to reduce lags in each loop and by using decentralized governance to create many concurrently executed loops.
- *Three other ideas from Boyd's theory of dogfights apply to platform owners.* These are a platform owner's need to emphasize *what* over *how* for app developers, maintaining an accurate grasp of reality through continuous interaction with the platform's competitive environment, and the emphasis on fast and frequent rather than perfect actions.
- *Architecture–governance alignment drives evolution.* Platform governance must be aligned with platform architecture. They are deeply interwoven and inseparably intertwined because they respectively supply ecosystem-wide motivation and ability to innovate around a platform.
- *Orchestrating for resilience, scalability, and composability.* In the short term, platform architecture–governance alignment shapes its resilience, scalability, and composability. Each of these properties require attention to different dimensions of platform governance.
- *Orchestrating for stickiness, synergy, and plasticity.* In the medium term, platform stickiness with both app developers and end-users is influenced by architecture and governance; its synergy with apps primarily by platform governance; and platform plasticity by platform architecture as well as architecture–governance alignment.
- *Orchestrating platform envelopment, durability, and mutation.* In the long term, envelopment by a platform as well as its capacity to rebuff envelopment attacks is influenced by platform governance, and platform durability as well as mutation by architecture–governance alignment.

In the next chapter, we turn our attention to the evolution of apps. Many of the ideas used in orchestrating platform evolution also apply to apps. We therefore focus primarily on ideas that are distinctive to evolving apps from an app developer's perspective but apply less to platforms.

Evolving an App

People don't know what they want until you show it to them.
Steve Jobs

IN THIS CHAPTER

- Dynamics of apps in platform markets
- The Eureka moment and the origin of apps
- How an app's microarchitecture influences its evolvability
- Ensuring app resilience, scalability, and composability
- Growing app stickiness
- Managing tradeoffs in platform synergy
- Enhancing app plasticity
- Orchestrating vertical and horizontal app envelopment
- Bold retreats and envelopment survival tactics
- Enhancing app durability
- Orchestrating app mutation

In the late 1990s, a major US chemicals manufacturer stumbled upon a promising market opportunity: There was not one single brand of bug spray that customers were unequivocally happy with. The company invested millions of dollars in research and development to create the most effective bug spray ever created. It refined the packaging to eliminate everything about existing brands of canned bug sprays that irritated consumers. It priced it competitively and launched with a glamorous advertising blitz on television and in print. It was an investment in the future, the company thought, to make the product a household name. Sales immediately took off nationwide and it looked like it had a winner on its hands. Until a week later, when, to its utter surprise, sales stalled. Instead, the company's warehouses were flooded with returns. It immediately sent the returned cans of bug spray back to the lab. It found nothing wrong. Every can consistently killed bugs more effectively than any product on the market. Puzzled, it interviewed a sample of consumers to figure out what went wrong. To its surprise it found that when the consumers used the bug spray, the sprayed bugs scurried away, only to die a few minutes later. This created the perception that the formula was not effective. Instead, what the consumers were expecting was that the bugs would die on the spot. The company tweaked the

---

☆"To view the full reference list for the book, click here or see page 283."

formula to add a paralyzing agent to it, which immediately paralyzed the bugs and then slowly killed them in the same amount of time. The revised formula went on to become one of the leading brands of bug spray since then. The company's mistake: Failing to recognize that the customers' latent need was not just to kill the bugs but to *see* the bugs squirm and die.

Perception is as important as substance. Any product must meet its customers' *latent* needs. In platform markets, perceived value often trumps technological superiority, otherwise Linux would have a 90% market share and Windows 10%. The lesson for app developers is that the key to thriving in competitive markets is discovering and meeting their end-users' *latent* needs—needs that they often might not be able to even articulate. Evolving apps is then the process of discovering and satisfying end-users' latent needs, and doing it better than rivals.

This chapter focuses on how app developers can evolve apps in platform markets. It begins with an overview of the dynamics of platform markets from an app developer's perspective, and describes how an app can be designed and then evolved through a careful combination of app microarchitecture within the constraints of a platform's governance. We first describe how apps can be evolved in the short term to be resilient, scalable, and composable. We then describe how app developers can improve their stickiness, manage the tradeoffs in choices about platform synergy, and improve their app's plasticity in the medium term. We then describe how, in the long term, app developers can exploit envelopment opportunities and rebuff envelopment attacks from other apps as well as from the platform owner. We also describe two strategies that app developers can use to grow an app into a platform in its own right. We conclude with a description of how app durability and survival in a competitive market and mutation into different markets can be orchestrated.

11.1 DYNAMICS OF PLATFORM MARKETS

Like the book publishing and movie business, app development—particularly in consumer-oriented platform markets—is a hits-oriented business. Apple alone paid on average over a billion dollars a year in royalties to app developers in the first 5 years of its iOS platform's existence, a number that rose to $4 billion a year by 2013 (Strietfeld, 2012). However, the payoff was very unevenly distributed: 25% of its app developers made less than $200 and about 4% made over a million dollars. App development is therefore an ecology weighed heavily toward a few winners (Strietfeld, 2012)—a classic winner-takes-most market. It is the prospect of a huge payoff and the modest upfront investment that attracts new app developers into platform markets.

The numbers tell this story. The "app economy" surrounding mobile computing platforms created 500,000 new jobs in the United States alone (Strietfeld, 2012). For an app developer, one big hit can make up for the losses on many duds. The top 250 apps in iOS and Android platforms had an average daily audience of about 52 million users, which roughly equals the circulation of the top 200 US weekend newspapers or the three top-rated primetime TV shows in the United States in early 2013.[1] This market grew from almost zero to $25 billion in revenues in five years by 2013. On average, users of iOS and Android platforms actively used eight different apps on an average day.

App development can be costly and multihoming even costlier from an app developer's perspective. For example, apps for iOS average about $10,000 in upfront development costs (Economist, 2012a,b). When competition is fierce—as it often is in growing markets—introducing a decent app alone does

---

[1]http://blog.flurry.com.

not guarantee success in a crowded marketplace (Strietfeld, 2012). Neither does aggressive pricing. An app must solve a fundamental but widespread enough problem in a novel way, as described in the next section. If an app meets this criterion, it will not be long before it has many clones. Evolving the app to introduce new features faster than rivals can copy them is the only shot at surviving. In other words, an evolvable app is a more competitively adaptable app. Such evolvability is determined by the app's microarchitecture. While these patterns illustrate dynamics specific to consumer-oriented mobile computing platforms, they are just as applicable to any other platform market.

11.1.1 A rising tide floats all boats

When entering or creating a new market segment, an app developer is likely to see an initial period of slow growth followed by a sharp takeoff (Agarwal and Bayus, 2002). For example, the auto industry was created in 1899 but the mass market did not take off until 1909 (Agarwal and Bayus, 2002). The popular belief is that new entrants put downward pressure on price, and that price decreases attract new adopters. This is only part of the story. How much downward price could possibly exist when apps are priced at zero, as was typical in mobile computing platforms in the mid-2010s? The other part of the story is that new entrants often also raise all boats because they also grow the market. As economists would describe it, the new entrants shift the "demand curve" (Agarwal and Bayus, 2002). In particular, the entry of big firms legitimizes the new app category. Initial sales are often slow due to the primitiveness of new apps in new categories, where new entrants subsequently foster more features-driven competition. As new rivals enter the category created by such an app, the actual and perceived product quality improves (Agarwal and Bayus, 2002). Therefore sales growth does not have to come at the expense of profitability compression associated with declining prices. In other words, the initial innovator *can* be better off because there is now a much bigger pie to be split. A study of 30 major product innovations over a 150-year period showed precisely this: Price decrease accounted for only 5% of the takeoff growth but new entrants accounted for about 50% of the takeoff of a new market (Agarwal and Bayus, 2002).

11.2 THE EUREKA MOMENT AND THE ORIGIN OF APPS

To understand how apps evolve, we must begin with the question of where the ideas for the most successful apps come from. Innovation theorists and marketers often think of end-user needs as hidden, waiting to be discovered by a clever entrepreneur. However, in platform markets, this is a tricky assumption and only half the story. Sometimes new needs are created by the introduction of technologies themselves, which create a need that did not exist until recently (Arthur, 2009, p. 175). As complexity scientist Brian Arthur (2009, p. 175) once said, possession of rocketry technologies created the need for space exploration. Similarly, the introduction of new technologies can generate new needs that are unobvious to the naked eye.

The commonality in blockbuster apps? They surface and address needs that end-users don't even realize they have. There is no substitute for deep immersion in an ecosystem as an end-user to recognize such emergent needs spot an app opportunity. Would-be app developers often discover a fresh opportunity when they realize that some difficulty that they are experiencing might be faced by other end-users as well. Deep immersion as an end-user in an app's application domain can be a rich source of deep, firsthand insights into real problems, frustrations, and irritations that spark an idea that becomes an app's Eureka moment. The most successful apps begin with one insight about an unrecognized

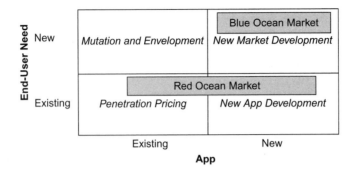

FIGURE 11.1

Blue ocean apps often originate with a Eureka moment.

problem and a potential solution to it. Such insights, grounded in knowledge of the app's application domain, can play a primary role in defining opportunities for new apps. The Eureka moment that led to Dropbox was when Drew Houston (Dropbox's founder) left his USB thumb drive at home when he showed up at work. The Eureka moment for the Polaroid instant camera was when founder Edwin Land's daughter asked him why she could not see the photograph that he had just taken. App developers that enter a platform market in this way are often new entrants who see opportunities that existing app developers might have failed to see.

If the problem is real and widespread, an app that addresses it can *create* an entirely new market within a platform's marketspace. Such markets are what we describe as *blue ocean markets* that expand the entire ecosystem, as opposed to *red ocean markets* where rival apps compete over existing end-users in existing markets (see Figure 11.1). The former create new segments of the market and address unmet end-user needs, as opposed to the latter that engage in a bloody fight over an existing pool of end-users.

Such "blue ocean apps" have little precedent or historical demand data because their market has not yet emerged. Traditional market research methods are of limited value in such markets. Evaluating the idea then requires answering a few elementary questions.

1. How widespread is the problem that the app addresses?
2. Who will be the primary adopters, how will they use the app, and why?
3. What will they be prepared to pay? What will stop their adoption dead in its tracks?

11.2.1 Who is the incumbent? Think again

A trickier question is identifying what the app must compete against. The obvious answers are usually the wrong ones. Dropbox, for example, succeeded where many other file synchronization services failed because Houston recognized that his competition was not other file-sharing services but inexpensive USB thumb drives. Palm succeeded in creating a PDA market where Apple, Texas Instruments, Sony, Microsoft, and Sharp failed because it recognized that its competition was the plain old paper organizer, not users' desktop PCs or laptops. Their offerings were designed from the outset to outdo the value proposition of incumbent technologies very different from what their failed predecessors had envisioned. This led to a different prioritization of functionality that they focused on and also led to consequential decisions about what their solutions were *not* going to attempt to accomplish. From the get go, Dropbox and Palm focused solely on outdoing the value proposition of a thumb drive and a paper organizer.

End-users' perceptions matter tremendously in the success and failure of new market offerings. It is therefore critical to recognize what they'll actually compare your app against rather than what you think they will compare it against. In entering such nascent markets, it is important to not attempt to go for the big market at once. Understanding this origin of blockbuster apps can guide app developers to evolve just about any app by recognizing sources of fresh insights and ideas that compensate for the lack of the rare Eureka moment. Successful category-creating apps will soon attract new rivals out of thin air, initiating a Red Queen race within that category. This brings us to app evolution.

11.3 HOW APP MICROARCHITECTURE SHAPES APP EVOLVABILITY

Platform architecture constrains but does not determine the microarchitecture of apps in its ecosystem. Apps within the same platform can have considerable variance in their internal microarchitecture because of two choices made primarily by app developers. First, identical apps with identical internal microarchitectures can vary in their compliance with a platform's interface standards. This gives them different architectural properties that impact their evolvability. Second, different app microarchitectures partition the app's functionality differently between the code implemented in an app and the functionality leveraged from the platform. This choice changes the parts of an app that are built from the ground up by an app developer and those that are reused from the platform through application programming interfaces (APIs) and platform interfaces. Recall that the four pieces of functionality in an app are:

- Presentation logic, where the interaction with an end-user is handled
- Application logic, where the core function of the app is implemented
- Data access logic, where access and retrieval of data are handled
- Data storage logic, where data are stored

The division of these four functions across a client device and a server results in cloud, client-based, client–server, and peer-to-peer app microarchitectures. (If all four functions are implemented on the client side, it results in a standalone app.) In a platform environment, an app developer can choose how much of each of these four functions is implemented from the ground up in an app and how much is implemented by calling on the services of a platform. This is illustrated in Figure 11.2.

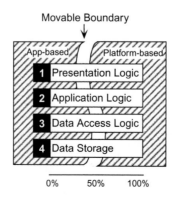

FIGURE 11.2

The four functions in an app's microarchitecture can flexibly be split between an app and the platform.

Table 11.1 A Comparison of the Key Properties of Various App Microarchitectures

	Standalone	Cloud	Client-Based	Client-Server	Peer-to-Peer
Resilience	●	◖	●	◖	●
Scalability	●	○	○	◖	●
Processing power of client device	~	○	●	◖	○
Need for network robustness	○	●	●	◖	●

○, Low; ◖ medium; ●, high; ~, varies.

The choice of app microarchitecture influences the evolutionary trajectories that are open and closed to an app. Put another way, an app's microarchitecture embeds real options and allows an app developer to subsequently repartition the division of the functions that are platform-based versus app-based. This has consequences for what an app builds and leverages. It also has implications for an app's potential for resilience, scalability, requirements of processing power on client devices, and dependence on a robust data network, as summarized in Table 11.1.

A few noteworthy properties of each of these app microarchitectures have implications for app evolution:

- Cloud-based microarchitectures are the modern reincarnation of dumb terminals in host-based systems. Their advantages are that they are the most conducive of all app architectures to running on "weak" client devices with low processing power, updates can be centrally pushed out to app users instantaneously, and the app developer usually has almost complete control over the app. However, this microarchitecture's weaknesses are a single point of vulnerability shared by all end-users, costliness to scale, and the potential to be sluggish as its usage grows.
- Client-based microarchitectures keep only the data storage logic on the server side. It is most appropriate when app data storage needs are high but the devices that it is deployed on are modest in their own storage capacity (e.g., devices connected to the Internet of Things). It is also network-intensive because of the large volume of data that must flow between a client and the server.
- Client–server microarchitectures follow a balanced partitioning of the four functions. They are average in every property but excel at nothing. They are also the most conducive of all app microarchitectures to placing the most server-side functionality on the platform.
- Peer-to-peer microarchitectures are the most scalable of all app microarchitectures and have the strongest potential for positive same-side network effects. However, they leave an app developer with the least control over the app. They are also harder to implement in their pure form in platform environments because some app developer control and centralized coordination is often needed for most apps.
- The implementation of any of these app microarchitectures can also involve tiering, which is splitting the implementation of at least one of the app's core functions across multiple server-side devices. (Tiering, as we subsequently explain, increases an app's scalability.)

Standalone app microarchitectures are the most resilient simply because they do not do much. Standalone architectures are like using a computer without an Internet connection. It will never fail, but you will not be able to do much with it to begin with. Leveraging a platform in building an app inevitably means exposing the operation of an app to some vulnerability. Once an app developer accepts this risk, the choice of app microarchitecture has irreversible strategic consequences. Therefore, the choice of microarchitecture should not be made lightly. An app's microarchitectural choice is made in the initial implementation of an app and therefore largely irreversible.

11.4 EVOLVING AN APP: A PREVIEW

Table 11.2 summarizes the influence of app microarchitecture and app governance on app evolution in the short, medium, and long term. Their influence on the nine individual metrics of app evolution is described next. These are summarized in Figure 11.3.

11.5 EVOLVING AN APP IN THE SHORT TERM
11.5.1 Managing app resilience

The resilience of an app is primarily a function of its microarchitecture. Overall, an app should err on the side of being internally monolithic but externally modular to follow the mirroring principle. Four high-level principles can help improve resilience of the app:

1. *The KISS principle.* Keep the four functions simple by not splitting too many of them across the app and a platform. When faced with two alternative design choices in the implementation of your app, the correct choice is always the simpler solution.
2. *Follow the rules.* Stick with standardized platform interface guidelines and API conventions. This ensures that the relationship between the platform and the app remains sufficiently modularized. Avoid workarounds, which often result in architectural debt that must be paid back with often too much interest along the evolutionary trajectory of an app. A simple proxy to estimate the modularity of an app is to count the number of function calls by an app to the platform (MacCormack et al., 2006). By reducing the span of changes needed to implement a change in the app, modularization facilitates efficient testing and verification of the integrity of app-level changes (Baldwin and Clark, 2000, p. 88). Compliance with the platform's interface standards also ensures that the app can readily integrate with the platform every time an internal change is made in either the app or the platform.
3. *Understand your decision rights.* Clearly understand what decision rights belong to you and which ones to the platform owner. Decision rights that are assigned to you as an app developer encompass both the authority and the accountability for those decisions.
4. *Internal design redundancy provides future flexibility.* Designing some internal design redundancy within your app embeds real options that can provide valuable future flexibility. For example, redundancy in the design of the data storage logic would allow relocating to local storage from cloud-based storage services provided by the platform (e.g., iCloud) or to external storage services (such as Amazon Elastic Cloud). Also minimize cross-app dependencies and stick with standardized, open interfaces where possible.

Table 11.2 A Summary of How App Design Influences Its Evolution

App Evolution Metric	Influenced by		Pertinent Governance Dimension			
	Microarchitecture	Governance	Microarchitecture–Governance Alignment	Decision Rights	Control	Pricing
Short term						
Resilience	●					
Scalability	●		●			●
Composability	●		●	●	●	●
Medium term						
Stickiness	●		●			●
Platform synergy	●		●			●
Plasticity	●		●		●	
Long term						
Envelopment		●		●		
Durability		●	●	●		
Mutation	●	●		●		

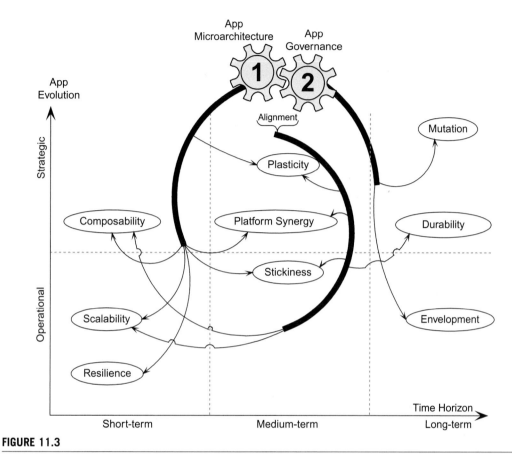

FIGURE 11.3

A summary of the primary drivers of the nine metrics of app evolution.

11.5.2 **Improving app scalability**

The scalability of an app refers to its ability to maintain its functional performance and financial viability with increases or decreases in the number of app end-users. Scalability is heavily influenced by an app's microarchitecture, as summarized in Table 11.1. From a technical scalability perspective, the peer-to-peer architecture is the most upward and downward scalable. However, this microarchitecture is limited in its viability to a few apps where centralized coordination requirements on the part of the app developer are modest. The next best choice in terms of scalability is client–server architecture, which provides a middle-of-the-road value on all evolutionary metrics. The cloud-based microarchitecture will provide high scalability under one of two conditions: (1) if the most data-intensive functionality such as the data storage and data access logic resides on the platform or (2) if some core aspects of an app's application logic builds heavily on the platform's native capabilities or ecosystemwide services and APIs that cannot viably be implemented within the app. Platforms such as iOS and Android provide such services, for example, in the form of voice recognition capability. App developers must, however, be wary that their app's performance is then critically dependent on the resilience and scalability of the platform, which a platform owner ought to be able to guarantee in the form of service-level agreements and uptime promises. A second technical consideration for app developers is the preference to use tiering. This embeds real options in the app in the form of the *SWITCH INPUTS* option.

To cope with a growth in demand and the associated need for upward financial scalability, app developers can create a menu of different versions or editions of an app, each priced differently to cover the costs of features that are scale-intensive. See also the subsequent discussion on app versioning strategies.

In terms of an app's financial scalability, building in downward scalability also has implications for the design of the initial implementation of the app: Its fixed costs should be low for it to have a scale-down option. Cloud microarchitectures have the most downward scalability when the four app functions are implemented primarily on the platform rather than app side. This minimizes the app developer's upfront investment on the app side, reducing the app's fixed costs. In turn, this reduces the number of end-users needed to reach the positive financial breakeven point using the same logic as platform scalability that was described in Chapter 10. In developing the initial release of the app, an app developer must first deliver baseline standalone value to end-users to be viable before a critical mass of users is reached. A valuable standalone application is very powerful in overcoming the critical mass problem at the outset (Rohfls, 2003, p. 197). Recall that most successful platforms started out as products or services that were useful in isolation. Similarly, an app that it useful even in the absence of network effects faces a less uphill battle in getting off the ground. Think in terms of the must-do elements of the app in a real options sense, starting with the minimum viable footprint. Focus on the anchor features and unique functionality in the initial version that you get out of door. This is the smallest subset of features needed to validate the key assumptions in your app's business model. It should be accompanied by an app roadmap—the "may-do" list in real options lingo—that articulates the plan for adding new features and functionality over time. Tweaks, refinements, and nice-to-have features can come later as cognitive bandwidth and app development resources permit. Networks effects-based features are a good add-on, but often as a subsequent may-do stage of the app development project. Alternatively, if the app's concept depends on the need for network effects, an app can sometimes ride on the platform's end-users network from the get-go. Many platform owners, however, explicitly prohibit apps from doing this. If they do allow it, it introduces the risk of making the app too dependent on the platform and making it more vulnerable to downstream vertical envelopment by the platform owner.

11.5.3 Enhancing app composability

Evolvability of apps is even more important than the evolvability of the platform because different apps will often face differential market pressures, to which they must adapt at different rates (de Weck et al., 2011, p. 125). We described in the previous chapter how modularization of a platform's interfaces and their alignment with how a platform owner governs the platform ecosystem allow the ecosystem to absorb differential rates of change in apps. The same alignment that facilitates platform composability facilitates app composability. (The linkages between a platform and a particular app are identical from the app developers' vantage point and the platform owner's perspective.)

Recall from Part I of the book that app developers face two types of costs in developing for a platform: app innovation costs incurred in developing capabilities unique to their app and systems integration costs

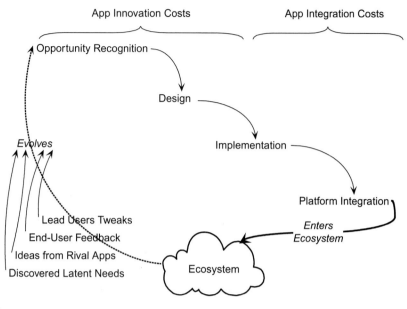

FIGURE 11.4

Reducing app integration costs frees up more resources for app innovation.

incurred in getting the initial app and every subsequent revision working with the platform. Figure 11.4 illustrates the approximate breakdown of these costs across different stages of the app lifecycle. The stages in the development cycle of an app can be summarized as follows. In reality, they are rarely as linear or sequential as suggested by their oversimplified representation in Figure 11.4.

1. *Opportunity recognition.* A latent need is recognized and a market for a future app is identified.
2. *Design.* A vision for what an app will accomplish is first developed. This is the app's high-level design that also spells out a detailed description of the app's features and capabilities in the sense of the classic waterfall model. This is followed by the detailed design, where app features are prioritized, mockups are field-tested with representative prospective end-users, and microarchitectural choices are made. The microarchitectural choices are usually one-time choices that are subsequently not reversible in subsequent revisions of the app. Most of the app innovation costs are incurred in these two stages and the work in the subsequent stages is largely grunt implementation and integration work.
3. *Implementation.* The actual implementation of the detailed design in code is done in this stage.
4. *Platform integration.* The completed app is integrated with the platform at this stage. Most testing tools and simulators provided by a platform owner are used to reduce costs at this stage.

The app developer's total app development costs are the sum of app innovation costs and app integration costs. Modularizing the connections between the app and the platform reduces app integration costs. Modularization grants within-app freedom while also lowering the need for coordination, thus making an app more free to evolve (Baldwin and Clark, 2000, p. 221). This in turn frees up cognitive resources that an app's developer can now reallocate toward innovation in the functionality of an app, increasing the potential for increasing the inflow of new innovations into the app.

Modular linkages with the platform allow app developers the autonomy to decide how the app is implemented and to freely make changes *inside* an app. An app developer can treat the rest of the ecosystem largely as a blackbox, paying attention to only how the app will interact with it. This is akin to driving a car: You don't need to know how its parts work; just knowing how to interact with them is sufficient. This allows an app to evolve faster, reduces cycle times for new releases, and allows the app to evolve at a rate that is appropriate for the dynamics of its own market rather than be constrained by the platform's tempo. Put another way, modularization speeds app evolution and minimizes the cost of change (Ethiraj and Levinthal, 2004a,b; Sanchez, 1995; Simon, 2002). This increases the likelihood that an individual app can—but not necessarily will—adapt faster to its environment, hence be more likely to survive in evolutionary Red Queen competition (Simon, 2002).

However, platform modularization without an alignment with decision rights does not grant sufficient autonomy to app developers to pursue app evolution. Similarly, decentralized governance without modularization of the linkages between an app and the platform will spiral app developers' integration costs out of control. The integrating mechanisms provided by modularized architectures must therefore be complemented by decentralized app governance for the two to reinforce each other. Therefore, for an app developer to realize the advantages of modularized linkages with the platform, the app decision rights granted to app developers must be accepted by an app developer to make this mirroring arrangement work. This requires compliance by an app developer with the platform's interface standards and platform API guidelines described in Chapter 5. This is a function of the decision rights and control dimensions of governance. As long as an app developer complies with the interface standards of a well-modularized platform, successful integration is virtually assured. Therefore, an externally modularized app architecture coupled with an internally monolithic app microarchitecture enhances an app's plasticity, and subsequently its competitive durability in the long run.

11.6 EVOLVING AN APP IN THE MEDIUM TERM
11.6.1 Growing app stickiness

Stickiness of an app is with the app's end-users. Stickiness is a challenging objective for app developers. Recent surveys show that while end-users, on mobile platforms for example, are using apps more intensively, only half of the apps that they were using heavily in the preceding year were still in use a year later (Economist, 2012a,b). This app abandonment rate of about 50% is a troubling number, especially because it is for apps that broke through the crowd of rivals to become heavily used apps. Increasing app stickiness begins with the prerequisite that an app's end-users perceive it as valuable and easy to use. After this, app developers can use six distinct strategies to enhance the stickiness of an app over time:

1. *Discovering and meeting the latent needs of existing and prospective end-users.* While a platform owner can have a large number of app developers feeding ideas and innovations into a platform's ecosystem, who can an app developer turn to for generating a stream of new ideas that expand an app's stickiness? Three sources: (a) discovering latent end-user needs, (b) learning from lead users and early adopters, and (c) insights from the analysis of embedded in-app analytics.

- *Discovery of latent needs.* Steve Jobs once said that customers do not know what they want. As Apple's success in the past decade demonstrates, consumers' self-stated opinions of what they want in a product can be a poor predictor of market success. Asking consumers what they want will give you a list of needs that they *can articulate*, not needs that they don't even realize they have. These are their latent needs. Discovering latent needs requires the same kind of deep immersion in the end-user context as the one that leads to bigger Eureka moments, described earlier. What you need are insights into what your end-users want to accomplish, not what they say they want or need. Figure out the "job to be done" in a better or more affordable way. But identifying, say, three latent needs still does not tell you which one matters more in the mind of an end-user. How much would they be willing to pay if an app met that need?[2]

- *Watch to your lead users.* Your app's lead users and early adopters are a second rich source of new ideas. These are your app's users who tweak, hack, and modify an app to make it do things they would want it to do. Lead users have specific needs that arise before the mass market and often have very high expectations. Their pressing needs today might eventually be widespread in your app's core market because they face them ahead of the mass market. By incorporating and monitoring ideas from the lead users, app developers can enhance their offerings, reduce the risk of market failure, and reduce their own design costs (Baldwin and von Hippel, 2011; von Hippel, 1986, 1988). However, be wary of the widespread blindspot created by having app evolution decisions inordinately influenced by the needs of its existing end-users while neglecting prospective ones.

- *Embedded in-app analytics.* A third source of new ideas for extending an app is by embedding deep analytics into an app that show how an app is actually used. Analyzing such usage data can provide unexpected insights into functionality that is not being used, tasks that require more steps than they should, and features that end-users most use. Subtract what gets in the way of the functionality that an app's users really value. Retire features that have run their course and no longer match users' real needs. In-app analytics can also be used to run mini-experiments with iterative tweaks to an app and seeing how users' respond in their behavior. The data-rich nature of software platforms and their near-ubiquitous connectivity allows probing markets, testing hypotheses, and making evidence-driven app evolution decisions.

2. *Create multiple versions or editions of an app to target multiple end-user segments.* Book publishers often release new books in hardcover editions first followed by lower-priced paperback versions a year or two later. The idea is that readers who value the book more will pay for the higher-priced hardcover edition and those who value it less will wait for the lower-priced paperback edition. Similarly, movie studios sequentially release movies in theaters, followed by DVDs, and then into the rental market. This strategy, which segments prospective consumers by their willingness to pay, can also be used to create variants of an app that target different segments of end-users with different levels of willingness to pay.

   Having lower-priced, crippled apps with in-app upgrade options similarly lowers the barriers for end-users to try and app before they commit to buying a full-priced version of an app.

---

[2]Questions like this are best addressed by conjoint studies (which stands for CONsidered JOINTly). These are short survey-like studies that can be used to reverse-engineer a prospective consumer's mental model, which they otherwise would not be able to articulate even if they wanted to. The output of the conjoint technique is a rank-ordered list of priorities that influence an end-user's app adoption decision.

Two related tactics are the use of vanity pricing and Goldilocks pricing. Vanity pricing uses a high-priced version of an app to anchor end-users' perceptions of the value of all other versions; it is priced so high that it makes other versions appear like a bargain in comparison. The expectation is that few end-users, if any, will actually spring for the vanity-priced version. Restaurants and car companies routinely use this strategy effectively. A restaurant that has a $1200 steak on its menu makes an $80 steak look like a steal. Similarly, Lexus sells a $400,000 car, which makes its $60,000 model look like a bargain. The same tactic can be used for pricing apps, with a free version, a $2 version (the one that the app developer hopes to sell the most), and a $10 anchoring version. This strategy only works well if end-users' ability to comparison-shop across rival apps is limited.

Goldilocks pricing is based on the idea that if a customer is offered three different models of a product, they will usually go for the middle choice. If you price the middle one to make the most profit, this strategy can maximize profits. Fast-food chains and coffee shops frequently use this technique, offering three sizes of a drink with the expectation that customers will almost always gravitate to the middle size. It is perceived as neither too small nor too big but just right. App developers can use this approach to create a light, standard, and professional version of an app as long as they are careful to price their business models on the premise that the middle version will sell most. This strategy does not work if the low-end version is free and is advertising supported. In that case, the middle version should be priced to at least equal the expected lifetime advertising revenue of the low-end version. App stickiness, described subsequently, also then becomes crucial to sustaining the app developer's business.

3. *Develop app-specific rather than platform-specific network effects.* Just as a platform's network effects protect platform owners from rival platforms, an app's network effects can protect an app developer from its rival apps as well as from downstream envelopment by a platform owner. However, to be effective, such network effects should be unique to the app and based on that app's users rather than a broader base of a platform's users. They should also be nonportable to rival apps. For example, Dropbox's users value their ability to share files with other Dropbox collaborators. For an end-user to abandon the service for a rival offering not only requires the rival to have to deliver better functionality but also be high enough to justify losing Dropbox-specific network effects that an end-user might have developed and values.

4. *Develop end-user lock-in through nonportable, app-specific personalization.* This noncoercive lock-in involves implementing ways to make an app more useful the more an end-user uses it. Such personalization can create a powerful incentive for an end-user to stick with an app because abandoning it in favor of a rival app also requires abandoning the value that the app is able to deliver to that end-user through learning effects. However, app personalization is effective in increasing stickiness only if such personalization is (a) nonportable to rival apps and (b) perceived as value-enhancing by an app's end-user. App developers must be careful to keep such personalization under their complete control and in a proprietary rather than standardized format to prevent rival apps from being able to import it with the end-users' consent.

5. *Multihoming across nonrival platforms.* If a platform's users multihome across nonrival platforms, having an app on those nonrival platforms can increase app stickiness. For example, an app that allows an end-user to access its functionality on a mobile device and a personal computer can be stickier than one that exists on just one platform.

6. *Multihoming across rival platforms.* When should an app developer multihome across rival platforms? In deciding whether to multihome across rival platforms, an app developer must also recognize the risk of getting stranded with a platform that eventually turns out to be the loser. The choice of platform has significant consequences for the audience that an app reaches: In 2014, less than 100 devices were responsible for 80% of the 50+ million daily app sessions on the two leading mobile computing platforms, iOS and Android (Strietfeld, 2012). Hedging bets requires multihoming, which is easier said than done because multihoming can be costly. The safe way to avoid backing the wrong horse requires the app developer recognizing whether a platform's core market has properties that make it as winner-take-all market or whether multiple rival platforms will persist for the foreseeable future. An app developer is better off single-homing if the platform's market is a winner-takes-all market and a clearly dominant platform has emerged. However, a developer should multihome across rival platforms if a clearly dominant platform has not yet emerged. A single dominant platform will emerge only if three conditions are simultaneously satisfied in the platform's market: (a) multihoming costs are high for both end-users and app developers, (b) cross-side network effects are positive and strong, and (c) end-user needs for a platform are relatively homogenous (Eisenmann et al., 2011). If even one of these conditions is not true, an app developer is better off multihoming (i.e., developing the app for multiple rival platforms). This also protects app developers from the threat of downstream envelopment by a platform owner. Furthermore, the existence of multiple rival platforms is an opportunity for an app to gradually evolve into a small platform in its own right.

11.6.2 Tradeoffs in managing an app's platform synergy

Increasing an app's platform synergy means that more of an app's application logic and presentation is moved out of the app's own code and into the platform over time. Figure 11.5 illustrates a growth in platform synergy.

Increasing an app's platform synergy is a catch-22 from an app developer's perspective for reasons. First, it can reduce the app developer's app innovation costs but make the app developer more dependent on the platform owner. Second, it can increase an app developer's costs of multihoming if the platform services leveraged by the app are unique to the platform and not widespread across rival platforms. Increasing app synergy can therefore make an app developer more vulnerable to downstream

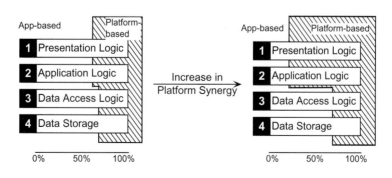

FIGURE 11.5

Increasing platform synergy involves reallocating more of the presentation or application logic to the platform.

vertical envelopment by the platform owner. (Apple is notorious for doing this with iOS developers.) Until a dominant platform has emerged, an app developer is better off multihoming, emphasizing genericness, and deemphasizing platform synergy in the app's implementation.

App developers should increase their app's platform synergy only under two conditions, in this order. First, when increasing platform synergy allows an app to deliver unique functionality that the app's end-users value. Second, when it dramatically increases the size of the app's prospective adopter pool. Whether it economizes the amount of code that an app developer must write to implement an app often matters less unless: (1) the app developer single-homes only on that platform or (2) the app's partitioning of the four functions in its microarchitecture is heavily skewed toward being implemented in the platform rather than in the app.

11.6.3 Enhancing app plasticity

App plasticity measures how extensively an app morphs over time to allow its end-users to do new things that it was not originally designed to do. It is an emergent property rather than a preplanned one, indicating how rapidly new innovations and capability extensions flow into the app. Plasticity is primarily a function of (1) the modularization of an app's platform-facing interfaces into the ecosystem and (2) use of open standards within the app's microarchitecture where possible. The first attribute embeds flexibility in the form of real options within the app's microarchitecture, allowing it to evolve independently of the platform. An app developer can make changes *within* an app to extend its functionality without needing to coordinate with the platform owner. All it requires is compliance with the platform's interface standards and APIs to ensure interoperability. It also allows the app developer to rapidly exploit and integrate new innovations within the platform into the functionality offered by the app. The second attribute allows the app developer more flexibility to repartition the division of the four core functions in an app across the app and the platform. It also allows some of these functions to be moved entirely outside the ecosystem, for example, to exploit innovative external software-based services that did not exist at the time of the app's original creation. Therefore, app plasticity is driven primarily by app microarchitecture and secondarily by an alignment in the app developer's work with the platform's control dimension of governance.

11.7 EVOLVING AN APP IN THE LONG TERM

11.7.1 App envelopment: how apps evolve into platforms

Envelopment moves by apps provide a pathway for an app to evolve into a platform in its own right. Like platform envelopment, app envelopment can either span the turf of apps in adjacent markets (horizontal envelopment) or adjacent portions of the app's place in the platform value chain. These are illustrated in Figure 11.6.

11.7.1.1 Horizontal envelopment by apps

Horizontal envelopment involves incorporating the functions of another app or a standalone product or service experiencing technological convergence that is also widely used by an app's current end-users. (Tapping into a nonoverlapping pool of end-users is mutation.) This is a promising move only when the expanded app can deliver a stronger value proposition (lower cost, better capabilities) to the users of the enveloped target app by leveraging its existing capabilities or economies of scale. As in platform

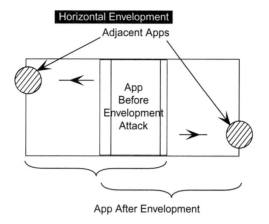

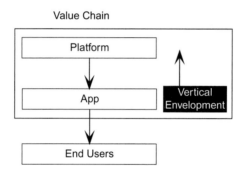

FIGURE 11.6

Horizontal and vertical envelopment by an app.

envelopment, there must be some overlap in the user base of the app and the envelopment target app. However, the enveloping app's existing users that overlap with the target app matter less than the non-overlapping users in assessing the value proposition of the expanded app. Nevertheless, an app developer can expect a reciprocal envelopment attack. Therefore, horizontal envelopment attacks should only be attempted if the app's own assets leveraged in the target app's domain cannot readily be matched by the target app's developer. Examples of such assets include unique functional capabilities, large user base, or brand recognition.

The same strategies that platform owners use to spot horizontal envelopment opportunities, discussed in the previous chapter, can also be used by app developers. The more insights an app developer has into the mini-sized segments of the broader platform userbase, the more likely it is to recognize a horizontal envelopment opportunity. Recall that it is precisely this sort of contextual immersion that also helps bolster app stickiness and durability. Unlike platforms, an additional way in which apps can make such horizontal envelopment moves is by recognizing geographic or segment adjacencies (Zook and Allen, 2003). This involves creating an adaptation of the same app to new prospective end-users in different geographical areas or a previously unaddressed segment of the market (e.g., creating a French translation of an English app). This approach simply repeats the execution of an app's core business idea—which already has a solid foundation elsewhere—in adjacent markets.

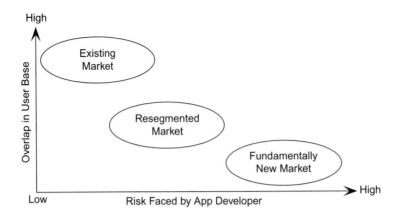

FIGURE 11.7

Overlaps in user bases open up three types of markets to apps through horizontal envelopment.

Horizontal envelopment offers the first pathway for an app to begin growing into a platform. As the native functionality of an app expands and provided it is of value to other apps as well, app developers can begin providing access to it by introducing its own APIs. By following this strategy, an app can potentially evolve into an infrastructural component for other apps to build on (Messerschmitt and Szyperski, 2003, p. 200). Today's app can therefore become tomorrow's platform by executing a series of envelopment moves. Dropbox and Twitter did precisely this over time, growing into a nested "platform within a platform." Similarly, Google has—with mixed success—slowly grown its Chrome browser into an ecosystem with its own apps, and then into a standalone operating system (Chrome OS). Skype also attempted to grow its service into a platform by adding a second side but had almost no success, largely because the two sides (end-users) did not have a compelling need for each other and the business model lacked compelling incentives to attract enough developers (i.e., the pricing dimension of governance was weak).

The key requirement for facilitating horizontal envelopment is governance, specifically that the app developer possess app strategic decision rights to a much greater degree than the platform owner. Horizontal app envelopment allows an app to either resegment its existing end-user base or to reach a pool of prospective end-users that is relatively new to the app (Figure 11.7). Horizontal envelopment therefore offers app developers an opportunity to grow an app's end-user base. The risk faced by an app developer in attempting horizontal envelopment moves increases as the overlap in the user base of the app and the target app shrinks.

11.7.1.2 Vertical envelopment by apps and on apps

Vertical envelopment involves selectively incorporating functionality originally provided by the platform into the app. Vertical envelopment primarily expands an app's functionality upstream in the platform's value chain. This will often put an app developer in direct competition with a platform owner. An app developer can expect a retaliatory downstream envelopment attack from the platform owner, especially if the app's functionality is of sufficient usefulness to other app developers in the platform's ecosystem. Vertical envelopment is therefore a second pathway for an app to evolve into a nested platform (a platform within a platform), especially when it either spans multiple nonrival platforms used by the same end-users (e.g., mobile and tethered operating systems) or multiple rival platforms (e.g., iOS, Android, and Blackberry).

11.7.1.3 Thwarting envelopment attacks by a platform owner

How does an app developer thwart an envelopment attack by a platform owner? We described several reasons that can compel a platform owner to justify such moves, but none of those reasons change the likelihood that it jeopardizes an app developer's survival. Although platform owners should ideally avoid invading their app developers' turf, it has historically happened often enough that app developers should take any promises with a grain of salt. An app developer facing a downstream envelopment attack by a platform owner often has little choice but to either sell out or quit the business. However, this no-win scenario can be avoided if an app developer plans ahead for it. How can an app developer safeguard against vertical envelopment of its app by a platform owner, which can otherwise instantly destroy an app developer's business? There are three ways to protect against downstream vertical envelopment by a platform owner. First, such an attack is less likely to happen if a platform owner cannot innovate in ways that an app developer can. Second, network effects that are unique to an app but that it does not share with the platform offer an additional protection against such threats. This protected Twitter from an envelopment attack from Apple, which instead chose to partner with it by creating deep hooks into iOS (thus exploiting Twitter's network effects to its own advantage). Third, an app developer can hedge against this risk by multihoming across multiple rival platforms. These three things were precisely what saved Dropbox when iOS enveloped its functionality with iCloud. It continually innovated in cloud storage technologies faster than Apple, had a network of end-users who valued strong network effects with their collaborators spanning a wide array of mobile and tethered platforms, and it multihomed extensively.

11.7.1.4 A bold retreat as an alternative to quitting

When it is not possible to thwart an envelopment attack by a platform owner—often the case—the next best bet is to pursue what Adner and Snow, (2010) calls a *bold retreat*. An app developer can engage in a bold retreat by retrenching to a niche of the existing market where it has an advantage over the platform owner in addressing end-user needs (Adner and Snow, 2010). This can sometimes be more effective than fighting a losing battle or quitting the market altogether. This allows an app developer to pursue a less vulnerable, sustainable niche. Adner (2010) showed how effectively this strategy worked for dot matrix printers with the advent of lasers, mechanical watches with the advent of quartz watches, and calculators with the advent of PCs. The questions to assess the viability of a bold retreat are:

- What elements or valued attributes of your app does the post-envelopment platform leave unaddressed?
- Which of the platform's (not the app's) end-users care about these attributes?
- If you focused on this segment of end-users, would that result in a sustainable business?
- How would product and pricing have to change? Sometimes, increasing pricing becomes viable after a bold retreat. For example, the average price of a new, well-engineered mechanical watch increased after the advent of quartz watches. Similarly, the prices of fountain pens increased about tenfold after ballpoint pens largely replaced them in the 1960s.
- How would your pool of rivals be different after a bold retreat? Remember that smaller niches can support fewer competitors, so early moves are important.

11.7.2 Enhancing app durability

An app's durability is its capacity to survive in the face of rival apps in a platform ecosystem. Like for platforms, we are more interested in changes—increases and decreases—in app durability over time. An app's durability is always relative to rival apps within the same platform. A brilliant idea can put an app on the map, but only unrelenting evolution keeps you there. An app will endure only if it continues to provide a stronger value proposition to its end-users relative to rival apps. The resource litmus test of value, rarity, inimitability, and nonsubstitutability again provides a simple but powerful framework to assess app durability. An app initially gains traction if it provides its end-users the ability to accomplish tasks that are valuable but that they cannot accomplish using other apps or the platform's native functionality (i.e., it is rare). But to sustain this initial advantage, such functionality must also be hard for rival apps to copy (the inimitability criterion) and have no readily available substitutes (the nonsubstitutability criterion). An app that continues to meet the inimitability and nonsubstitutability criteria can viably command a price premia, which the market will bear. (Such price premia need not be money charged directly to end-users and can instead be charged to a third side of the market such as advertisers.) An app's initial advantage is often short-lived because imitation by rival apps replicates valuable technological features and destroys their rarity. The app developer must then resort to the same strategies that platform owners use to bolster platform durability: (1) adding valuable new functionality faster than rival apps and (2) accumulating nonsubstitutable assets such as app-specific network effects that are independent of the platform. The techniques described in the preceding discussion on app plasticity to identify valuable new functionality to add to an app directly contribute to enhancing app durability as well.

However, apps are not victimized by architectural decay with age to the same extent as platforms. Unlike a platform that cannot be scrapped and rebuilt due to ecosystem-wide dependencies, an app can be. Nevertheless, app developers must remain cognizant that as a platform ages, platform owners are more likely to grow more controlling and intrusive in how an app is implemented. (As explained in the previous chapter, this is often motivated by the architectural decay that accompanies an aging platform.) Apps are also less constrained than a platform in their ability to build on new generations of technology and software services from outside the ecosystem. Being able to build on these can make an app more valuable to the platform, as it can compensate for the platform's own weaknesses.

11.7.2.1 Tempering expectations

App developers must, however, shape their expectations of how widely an app will be adopted and the profit margins that they can expect the market to bear. This depends primarily on whether the app's end-users: (1) strongly value network effects in how they use the app and (2) whether their needs are relatively homogenous. If both these conditions are simultaneously met, the app's market will be a winner-takes-most market and one (or few) apps will dominate its category. If even one of these conditions is not met, multiple rival apps will continue to coexist. Unfortunately, this is exactly the kind of market where competition between undifferentiated apps becomes a race to the bottom in terms of pricing. Even when an app is in a market without winner-takes-most dynamics, an app developer can expand an app's installed base by creating multiple variants of an app targeting distinct user segments, as described earlier in this chapter.

11.7.3 **Orchestrating app mutation**

Unlike envelopment, which expands an app's functionality, app mutation creates a distinct derivative app in a different application domain and does not require an overlap in end-users across the existing and mutation target markets. It involves replicating your app's strongest strategic advantage in new markets, contexts, and applications (Courtney, 2001, p. 43). Each mutation move opens up further possibilities of new niches to mutate into. In a real options sense, mutation therefore creates growth options for an app. Just as species can break out of extinction by diversifying, apps can break out of the bloodiest Red Queen races in zero-profit markets by diversifying into different markets where their existing assets give them some advantage.

An app developer must first use the resource litmus test to compare how it would fare using its existing assets against rivals in mutation target markets. Mutation does not require carryover of existing end-users of an app into the new market, although carryover can potentially be valuable where it is viable. Opportunities for app mutation arise primarily from the convergence of previously separate streams of technology. For example, Skype tried but failed to grow into a platform. Yet it managed to successfully mutate into smart televisions (TVs with built-in Internet connectivity using a hardware-embedded version of the app) and use them as a platform to gain a promising position in a completely different market. It also successfully used a carryover strategy, albeit into a small but growing market of smart television owners.

Unlike platform owners who can use app developers as their eyes and ears for spotting mutation opportunities, app developers are on their own. To identify opportunities for mutation, an app developer must look outside its existing markets. The focus should be on identifying either less crowded markets or emerging market domains. The key enabler for platform mutation is governance, particularly the possession of app strategic decision rights by the app developer. The governance structures that enhance app composability and durability are also conducive to app mutation. It also requires a modularized app microarchitecture that can readily be split from the platform and reimplemented if the mutation target is completely outside the original platform ecosystem (as it was in Skype's case).

11.8 **LESSONS LEARNED**

- *App markets are hit-driven markets.* A miniscule number of apps become blockbusters, which encourages more rival entrants. Unlike movie and book markets, entry of rival apps usually expands the pie of the nascent market for everyone.
- *Blockbuster apps often begin with a Eureka moment.* Firsthand insights into real problems, frustrations, and irritations that come only from deep immersion in an app's usage context usually spark an idea that becomes an app.
- *Most apps in nascent markets fail to recognize their real competition.* It is usually not the obvious competitors. Dropbox's was cheap thumb drives, Palm's was paper organizers. Failure to get this reference point right results in overengineering the wrong solutions.
- *Similar apps in the same platform can vary considerably in their architectural properties.* These are shaped by two choices made by app developers: compliance with a platform's interface standards and choice of an app's internal microarchitecture.

- *An app's microarchitecture shapes its evolvability.* An app's microarchitecture has consequences for what an app builds on its own and what it leverages from the platform. It also affects an app's resilience, scalability, processing requirements, and network dependence.
- *Managing app resilience, scalability, and composability.* In the short term, app microarchitecture shapes its resilience; microarchitecture and microarchitecture–governance alignment influences its scalability and composability.
- *Enhancing app stickiness, synergy, and plasticity.* In the medium term, app stickiness, synergy, and plasticity are shaped by an app's microarchitecture–governance alignment.
- *Orchestrating app envelopment, durability, and mutation.* In the long term, envelopment as well as its capacity to rebuff envelopment attacks is influenced by app governance, app durability by an app's microarchitecture–governance alignment, and app durability by app microarchitecture and app governance.

The next chapter recaps the core ideas developed in this book and previews the road ahead for nonplatform product and service businesses as they see their own industries acquire platform-like properties.

The Road Ahead

V

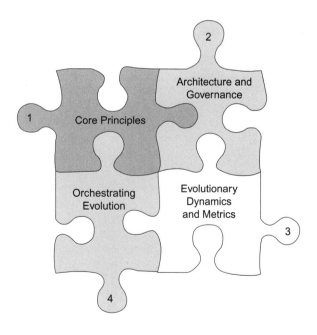

Every Product Is a Platform Waiting to Happen

You can't connect the dots looking forward; you can only connect them looking backwards.
Steve Jobs

IN THIS CHAPTER

- Translating software ecosystem ideas to business ecosystems in nontechnology industries
- Summary of the three key ideas developed in this book:
  - Migration from product and service business models to business ecosystems
  - How ecosystem evolution drives survival
  - How interlocking of ecosystem architecture and governance helps orchestrate ecosystem evolution

Platform thinking predates by almost a century the likes of Amazon, Google, and eBay, which were built natively around the idea. It was instrumental in the rise of General Motors over Ford in the 1920s, Black and Decker's dominance in powered hand tools beginning in the 1930s, and the rise of Komatsu over the market leader Caterpillar in the heavy machinery industry in the 1960s. General Motors, for example, leveraged a common set of base components across multiple models of cars, creating a product platform that could be used as the foundation for cost-effectively creating different cars targeted at different customer segments. This was unlike Ford, whose founder famously said that a customer could have any Ford she wanted as long as it was black. While platform thinking is not new, what is new is that platform-centric business models are becoming the engines of innovation across a variety of unexpected industries such as autos, healthcare, publishing, services, manufacturing, and consumer goods. This chapter describes how managers in just about any industry can actively apply this book's core ideas to their business instead of remaining helpless bystanders in a coming metamorphosis.

In this chapter, we summarize the broader implications of this book's key ideas for firms in industries outside the software industry. Platform-based business models are less an organizing logic and more a biologically inspired way of thinking of the design of economic entities. The emphasis in this chapter is on how managers in traditional, nontechnology industries can use ideas in this book to spot opportunities to reconceive their bread-and-butter businesses as platform businesses. Given the broader focus of this chapter, we therefore refer to business ecosystems rather than just platform ecosystems, complementors rather than app developers, customers rather than end-users, business process architecture, product, and service architecture rather than software architecture, and the ecosystem orchestrator rather than platform owner. Table 12.1 summarizes the broadened application of this book's core themes.

☆"To view the full reference list for the book, click here or see page 283."

Table 12.1 Translating Software Platform Concepts to Broader Business Ecosystems

Focus of This Book	Broader Theme
Software platform ecosystem	Business ecosystem
App developers	Complementors
End-users	Customers
Platform owner	Orchestrator
Software architecture	Business process and product/service architecture

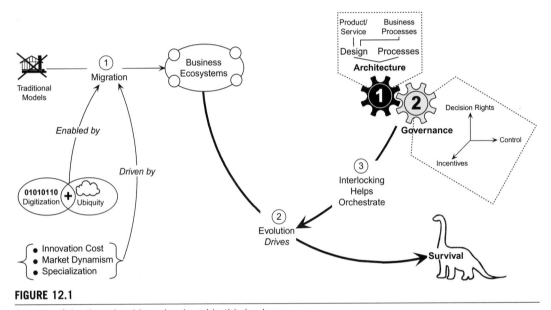

FIGURE 12.1

A recap of the three key ideas developed in this book.

Figure 12.1 summarizes the book's three key ideas extrapolated to business ecosystems. This book's introduction previewed the three ideas on an index card. These are the crux of this book's message and are recapped next in their broader context.

12.1 IDEA 1: MIGRATION TO ECOSYSTEM COMPETITION

The emergence of business ecosystems is changing the first rule of competition that firms compete with rival firms. Competition, in a growing variety of industries, is increasingly migrating to being among rival ecosystems rather than among rival products or services. After this transition, a good product or service without a compelling ecosystem has no shot in the market. The industry-agnostic migration toward business ecosystems is enabled and fueled by the *confluence* of (1) digitization as well as the growing software intensity of products, services, and business processes across industries and

(2) the ubiquity of cheap and fast Internet-based networks. Although these drivers appear to be mere curiosities in isolation, their confluence is creating a perfect storm. Digitization allows products and services to be converted into bits of digital information and ubiquitous connectivity wipes out the costs of acquiring and delivering them from just about any location. This increasingly allows a market offering—product or service—to be pieced together using globally dispersed components and then delivered digitally just about anywhere.

The drivers that are hastening the emergence of business ecosystems are identical to those driving software platforms: the growing costs of innovation coupled with shorter lead times to capitalize on them (a new mass-market prescription drug, for example, costs $900 million in research and development before it hits the shelves), uncertainty in markets composed of demanding customers with diverse needs, pressures to focus on a few core activities that a firm can be really good at, and the rising knowledge content of industries.

12.1.1 Business ecosystems in nontechnology industries

Although the shift toward business ecosystems is most visible in the technology industries, it is a sign across a plethora of nontechnology industries of a looming new blueprint for industrial organization that blends the disciplining power of markets with the partitioning of innovation work among thousands of outside complementors. The key property of business ecosystems is the presence of a central firm—the orchestrator—and a vast network of independent complementors collaboratively creating valuable complements driven by pure self-interest. The pursuit of self-interest by business ecosystem participants is the source of the competitive advantage of business ecosystems. A software system, independent of industry, is often the vehicle that enables large-scale coordination among these ecosystem participants. Even if you are not in the information technology business, it is dangerous to overlook platform thinking; even shoe makers (Nike), retailers (Sears), and sports networks (ESPN) now offer their own APIs.

While this book does not imply that every industry will or should become ecosystem-based, the shift is broader than one might initially realize from casual observation. Industries that have ecosystem potential include telecommunications, publishing, manufacturing, electrical equipment, consumer goods, chemicals, education, healthcare (e.g., health management organizations), textile, credit card businesses, banking, job search services, real estate brokerage, travel, gaming, pharmaceuticals and genetics research, food and beverage, and automotives (including electric vehicles). Consider a few examples of fledgling business ecosystems emerging—but yet to develop into true multisided ecosystems—outside the technology industries. Many of these are examples of crowdsourcing mechanisms and distributed innovation systems that are not yet truly platforms but have the potential to become platforms. (A true platform must have at least two sides (i.e., two distinct groups), such as complementors and consumers, who interact with each other through the platform.)

- *Product and service innovation.* Starbucks uses its MyStarbucksIdea crowdsourcing site to have its customers generate ideas for new products for the company. Several hundred ideas—all generated by Starbucks' customers—have become highly successful products. For example, one customer wanted Starbucks to make ice cubes out of coffee so frozen drinks don't get diluted as they melt. About 10,000 customers agreed. Another customer wanted something to plug the hole on the top of disposable coffee cups to minimize spilling while driving (it is common in the United States to drink coffee while driving). Starbucks introduced a simple "splash stick" suggested by a customer to fix precisely that problem, in turn boosting its drive-through sales of larger-sized drinks that were more prone to spilling in the car. In the Starbucks business ecosystem, customers are the primary source of ideas for new business process innovations, ideas to enhance the in-store experience, and new products. This approach also allows Starbucks to foster a strong sense of ownership of the ideas among its customers, almost guaranteeing their market success. Similar ecosystems have emerged for new product development (e.g., Quirky) and social innovation projects (OpenIDEO).

- *The food and drinks industry.* Atlanta-based Coca Cola Company introduced an innovative 125-flavor Coke FreeStyle soda dispenser in 2009 that centrally collects data on sales of over a hundred individual brands of Coke drinks. The system allows Coke to alter its mix of products multiple times a day at individual stores, by centrally analyzing real-time sales data from thousands of deployments around the United States. A computer embedded in the machine calculates with "surgical precision" the ingredients of over a hundred brands of Coke products, allowing real-time market experiments with dynamic pricing and promotions in even the most staid of industries (Levin, 2013). Coke also uses technology to cultivate direct relationships with its customers and to create a demand-driven supply chain. For example, its MyRewards app has 18 million users in over a hundred countries; it is tweaked and customized to the local markets within each of those countries. This allows Coke to tap into its markets' long-tails.

- *Matching human cognitive and physical labor in markets.* ODesk matches its 3 million workers with expertise in a variety of fields with small employers, who contract by the job. Without ODesk in the middle the buyers and providers of professional services would not have found each other nor would they be able to cost-effectively transact. ODesk therefore lowers search and transaction costs on either side of its business ecosystem. Amazon Mechanical Turk similarly serves as a platform that provides a simpler way to efficiently trade human brain power for white-collar tasks. Similarly, other platforms such as Task Rabbit and Moving Help match buyers and providers of physical labor, contracted by the task. Similar platforms have also emerged specializing in cartographic mapping (Open Street Map), advertising design (Prova), navigation (Waze), and encyclopedia maintenance (Wikipedia and Quora).

- *Production networks.* Hong Kong-based Li & Fung orchestrates a network of over 8000 independent manufacturers in about 40 countries. It aggregates diverse capabilities of an ecosystem of loosely organized partners to produce garments and home goods sold under a variety of major independent and store brands in North America, South America, Europe, and Asia.

- *Innovation and R&D networks.* Proctor and Gamble uses a platform called Connect+Develop to co-create with its customers new product ideas in a variety of personal care and household supplies market segments. Similarly, Eli Lilly uses an open innovation platform called Innocentive to tap into a network of about 300,000 scientists in nearly 200 countries to solve difficult R&D challenges in the biosciences. Similar innovation platforms also have emerged for systems biology (SBV Improver) and genetics research (Merck Gene Index).

- *Finance and venture capital.* Crowd funding platforms such as Kickstarter increasingly provide capital for startups in industries as diverse as music, publishing, game development, and entertainment.

For all enablers in Figure 12.1, it is the injection of software into the value chain of diverse product and service businesses that most opens them up to ecosystem business models that share strong commonalities such as network effects, noncoercive lock-in, increasing returns to scale, and envelopment potential historically found only in the technology industries. More and more businesses and industries are either run on software or deliver some part of their end product as online services. Even the mature auto industry insreasingly relies on software to run engines, control safety features, and navigate cars. The growing digitization of products, services, and business processes coupled with ubiquity pushes the constraint of geography to the backstage. The emerging Internet of Things is only likely to accelerate this trend. Although estimates vary widely, about 20 billion mobile "things"—give or take a few billion—are expected to be connected to the Internet by 2020 (Jacobson et al., 2012, p. 2). So, it is safe to assume that more everyday objects in your own industry will be connected to the Internet. What ones does with them is limited by imagination, not technology. New technology often starts out as a solution in search of a problem. It remains a curiosity until someone figures out a killer *application* for it. This matching of technology with a problem usually comes from deep immersion in a problem domain. This is precisely why managers in the trenches of an industry—not IT professionals—are better positioned to spot ecosystem opportunities. But one must use a platform lens to see them: our lenses determine not only opportunities that we see but also those that we do not see.

But what about physical objects themselves? The doom-and-gloom predictions of the coming demise of manufacturing has been old news for about 200 years. Yet, no amount of digital bytes is going to replace my need for lunch, or a physical automobile, or a brick house. What is going to change eventually is how those physical objects are produced and delivered. Even the constrain of physical form is weakening with the advent of 3D printing (additive manufacturing), which is preparing ground for new models for digitized manufacturing and plausibly a substitute for shipping physical objects just like the MITS Altair and the ZX 81 computers created ground for the subsequent personal computing era. We are in the infancy of 3D printing, perhaps where the Internet was in 1974, but the advances in materials and objects possible to construct (chips, tools, guns, even human organs) appear to be reported with surprising frequency in *The Economist, Business Week, New York Times*, and in various scientific journals. It is important to recognize adoption dynamics for new innovations can vary markedly by industry; telephones took 50 years, cell phones 20 years, and the Internet about 40 years to enter the mainstream. This will make it increasingly unclear where one industry ends and another begins, further blur the boundary between manufacturing and services, and wipe the distinction between patents (which last 20 years) and copyrights (which last 70 years after the death of the creator).

Attempting to predict how fast new innovations such as 3D printing and Internet of Things will mature is likely as reliable as the weatherman's prediction of rain in August in Georgia. It is better to assume that it will rain and accept that we can't be sure just when. Carrying an umbrella just in case is akin to the idea of investing in real options in ecosystems (discussed in Chapter 8). It is also important to assume that digitization-driven convergence will ensure that truly disruptive substitutes in your own industry are more likely to come from nontraditional competitors and colliding ecosystems.

Companies in every industry must assume that a business ecosystem revolution is coming. You don't want to be stuck on the wrong side of this disruption. Watch out for one-sided businesses moving to two sides, for potential "sides" with high search and transaction costs, and for segments of your prospective customer base whose needs are oversupplied or undersupplied by your existing industry business models. Companies that fail to recognize this ongoing shift from products to platforms in their own industries are on an irrecoverable death march. Managers—independent of their industry—should therefore grasp the ideas described in this book to recognize emergent opportunities to introduce business ecosystems in their industries. The Red Queen dynamic inherent in business ecosystems means that firms that get platform thinking will see outsized returns when ecosystems become viable in their industry or in adjacent industries.

12.1.2 Properties unique to business ecosystems

Common business sense and fundamental economics still hold true in business ecosystems, but three less visible properties become more pronounced. First, evolutionary dynamics that historically took 30–40 years can unfold in 5–7 years in platform markets. This requires unprecedented attention to designing ecosystems for evolvability and then orchestrating their evolution. Second, over the past 500 years of modern commerce, major disruptive innovations across every industry have almost always come from industry outsiders, typically new entrants who do not share the assumptions and legacies of industry incumbents. They trigger value erosion by introducing new, more effective, and legacy-free business designs. Every time you open your refrigerator now, I wish you'll remember to curb the reaction of Minnesota's thriving ice harvesters when they first saw the refrigerator—dismissal—when you see such a crude design first emerge in your own industry. Business ecosystems described in this book simply allow such disruption to be harnessed more productively and less destructively, offering opportunities to industry incumbents to earn their keep in the new order in their industries. They also allow incumbent firms to enter adjacent markets through strategies such as envelopment that are more abundant in platform markets. But such silver linings also have a dark cloud: Your competitors can come from unexpected places, and overfocusing on your existing rivals and existing customers can startle you when you face an envelopment attack. Ecosystems' unique properties also expand managers' competitive repertoire. Their multisidedness offers fertile opportunities to create hard-to-break network effects; value-driven, sustainable lock-ins; and the prospects of swallowing adjacent platforms as well as the dangers of being swallowed by one. They also offer a capacity to penetrate long-tail market microsegments typically inaccessible to product and service businesses. Third, the architecture of a business ecosystem is inseparable from how it ought to be governed. Their diversity can be their biggest liability but can become their biggest strength if the two interlock. A misfit between them imposes eventually fatal evolutionary penalties. This requires not just codesigning but also coevolving them as an ecosystem progresses through different stages in its lifecycle.

12.1.3 The three stooges of a business ecosystem

Building an ecosystem is not always an optimal strategy. They offer an advantage only when the effectiveness of the loosely coupled ecosystem exceeds that of a traditional organization. Three distinctive groups—the ecosystem orchestrator, complementors, and consumers—must be better off with a business ecosystem for it to be more attractive than a traditional business model. For ecosystem orchestrators, the value proposition is to innovate faster and cheaper around their core business than rivals, to reach potential untapped market segments, and to focus more deeply on their core competencies. For complementors, the value proposition is a scalable foundation for their own work that allows them to better focus on their own expertise and to reach a vastly expanded market. For consumers, the value proposition is benefiting from faster innovation, increased customization, and lower search and transaction costs.

12.2 IDEA 2: ECOSYSTEM ORCHESTRATION DRIVES EVOLUTIONARY SURVIVAL

The second key idea developed in this book is that the evolution of a business ecosystem determines its prosperity and survival.

12.2.1 The Red Queen race to survive

Business ecosystems that survive evolutionary competition are not the strongest, largest, or the cleverest but the ones that are most adaptive to their environment. Four evolutionary principles must remain center stage: (1) The Red Queen effect (the pressure to keep accelerating ecosystem evolution just to keep up with rival ecosystems, or pay the penalty of irrecoverably falling behind), (2) emergence, (3) the Goldilocks rule of having a just-right degree of modularization in an ecosystem, and (4) the need to deliberately coevolve architecture and governance to maintain their interlocking as an ecosystem ages. Red Queen dynamics require recognizing that adapting to new rivals might require adaptations different from those that worked well against earlier rivals (Barnett and Hansen, 1996).

We used the analogy of a bathtub to describe ecosystem evolution, where the potential basis of competitive advantage is the difference between the inflow of innovations into the ecosystem and those that are copied by rivals (the outflow). This difference—a business ecosystem's stock of innovations— can be increased by either speeding up the inflows or slowing down the outflows. Speed with which new resources are added is therefore the only reliable—but always temporary—source of competitive advantage. But only some resources in a business ecosystem—recognized using a four-part resource litmus test in Chapter 10—foster a competitive advantage. A resource must be valuable and rare to create a competitive advantage and be inimitable and nonsubstitutable to sustain it. Few resources will simultaneously meet all these conditions.

12.2.2 Business ecosystems thrive on orchestration

Business ecosystems can appear to be messy and disorderly. They differ markedly from their market potential, structure, and management approaches from product and service businesses. The constant challenge in business ecosystems is about how to attract and sustain the contributions of outsider complementors, while allowing the orchestrator firm to capture some portion of the new value created. An ecosystem orchestrator's success depends heavily on mobilizing outside resources that are not owned by the firm, organically coordinating the work of complementors with which it does not have authority-based relationships, and learning to compete with rivals for not just customers but also for complementors. Delivering a compelling value proposition to both complementors and end-customers demands orchestration of a business ecosystem, not management, ownership, or control. This paradigm shift is a hard pill for most managers to swallow because it flies in the face of the tenets of ownership and control that have historically been instrumental to the success of traditional business. However, emergent innovation in business ecosystems cannot be planned—only facilitated—by an ecosystem orchestrator. This requires making it cheap and easy for complementors to contribute (the realm of architecture) and creating incentives to motivate them (the realm of governance). Unfortunately, thinking at the architecture–governance nexus does not come naturally to either IT professionals or to managers.

12.2.3 You cannot win the Grand Prix by watching the fuel gauge

Ecosystem evolution is a journey navigated with *evolutionary* metrics. Such metrics can be operational or strategic, and span the short, medium, and long term. They encompass resilience, scalability, and composability in the short term; stickiness, orchestrator synergy, and plasticity in the medium term; and envelopment, durability, and mutation in the long term. Among the nine evolutionary metrics described in this book, you'll find curiously absent those familiar to managers (e.g., return on investment, efficiency, and effectiveness) and to software professionals (e.g., the schedule–budget–quality triad, code quality, and code complexity). We assume those to be necessary for short-term operational performance but insufficient to guide evolutionary survival. Metrics of evolution help steer evolution, separate signals from noise, and help both ecosystem orchestrators and complementors better manage tradeoffs. Three principles guide metrics choices: an outside-in vantage point, focus on the short term without obscuring the long term, and an acceptable cost–benefit balance.

12.2.4 Challenges in business ecosystems evolve over their lifecycle

Strategies that are appropriate for orchestrating ecosystems vary with their stage in their lifecycle. Fledgling business ecosystems must overcome the challenge of getting two sides onboard, each of which will find it attractive to join the ecosystem only when a critical mass already exists on the other side (the chicken-or-egg problem). It must also break the paralyzing dynamic where adopters on one side are waiting for others to join before they commit as well (the penguin problem). Governance fine-tuned to different stages of an ecosystem's lifecycle can help overcome these startup problems. However, a business ecosystem rarely starts out as one; the preceding chapters emphasized that the most ecosystems started out as a product or service that was valuable to one side in and of itself. The silver lining in this observation is that existing products and services that are successful in the market will increasingly encounter opportunities to become a robust foundation for business ecosystems.

Once an ecosystem successfully takes off by overcoming these problems, it enters an evolutionary Red Queen race with rival ecosystems. A different set of challenges then replace the chicken-or-egg and the penguin problem. These include the need to balance complementor autonomy with ecosystem-wide integration (the seesaw problem), need for the work of complementors to be separable from the orchestrator but also to be easy to subsequently reintegrate it with the outputs of other ecosystem participants (the Humpty Dumpty problem), and the need to interlock ecosystem governance with ecosystem architecture (the mirroring principle). Architectures—of business processes and product and service designs—built around modularized, self-organizing principles are key.

12.3 IDEA 3: ORCHESTRATION REQUIRES INTERLOCKING OF ECOSYSTEM ARCHITECTURE AND GOVERNANCE

The third idea developed in this book is that interlocking an ecosystem's architecture with ecosystem governance is key to orchestrating its evolution.

12.3.1 Architecture is an ecosystem's DNA

Conventional coordination and control mechanisms that underpinned the success of many traditional businesses and their value chains can become the albatross of business ecosystems. They fall flat because business ecosystems are rarely conducive to conventional notions of authority-based control, because they have widely fragmented ownership, and because of their sheer scale. Architecture—of business processes, products, and services—is a business ecosystem's DNA that imprints its evolvability, irreversibly preordaining the evolutionary trajectories open and closed to an ecosystem. Architecture instead must provide the blueprint for both partitioning innovation work across the many participants in a business ecosystem and integrating it. For this, architecture must accomplish two things: (1) Partition an ecosystem into an ecosystem core and autonomous complements that use it as a foundation for their own work and (2) allow these moving pieces to be rapidly and inexpensively pieced back together into a coherent product or service offering. Perfect ecosystem architectures—which exist only in theory—are simple, resilient, maintainable, and evolvable.

Tempered modularization endows such properties to architectures. Modularization is accomplished by decoupling the orchestrator's work from its complementors' work and then using stable and explicitly documented interfaces among them. The simple heuristic for partitioning an ecosystem is to keep low-variety, high-reusability functions and business processes with the ecosystem's orchestrator and high-variety, low-reusability ones with the complementors. This distribution must evolve as an ecosystem ages.

Architectural modularization across a business ecosystem also creates the flexibility to cope with an unforeseeable future. It does this by potentially embedding six real options—the flexibility without the obligation to do something in the future—in ways that limit risks while preserving yet-unknown future opportunities. Such flexibility is of value only in the presence of technology and market uncertainty. This flexibility is exercised through five types of discrete evolutionary actions, which we call *modular operators*. A linear representation using modular operators compactly conveys its evolutionary trajectory.

12.3.2 Ecosystem governance is the catalyst for evolution

The old saying that you can drag a horse to the water but you can't make him drink applies astutely well to ecosystems. Architecture, however, only decreases the structural complexity of business ecosystems; decreasing behavioral complexity requires thoughtful governance. Architectures conducive to running an ecosystem provide the means but not the motivation for outside complementors. Even the most thoughtful ecosystem architecture cannot nurture a vibrant ecosystem unless it is governed effectively. A business ecosystem's architecture is useful as a coordination device only when everyone follows the same rules. Motivating complementors through incentives to co-opt them and enforcing compliance with architectural rules are the two key roles of ecosystem governance.

Governance is how the ecosystem orchestrator influences its ecosystem. The ideal governance structure is one that is simple, transparent, realistic, and fair. Governance has three dimensions: (1) who decides what across the ecosystem (decision rights), (2) how an ecosystem orchestrator controls ecosystem complementors (control mechanisms), and (3) pricing policies. Decision rights encompass strategic and implementation decisions about the ecosystem's core and its complements. Control uses a mix of formal (gatekeeping, metrics, and process) control and informal (relational) control mechanisms. Pricing policies involve decisions about whether complementors or end-users are subsidized, for how long, whether the ecosystem orchestrator charges fees, and the pie-splitting structure. Such policies must match an ecosystem's business model, its stage in its lifecycle, and its architecture.

12.3.3 Architecture and governance as the interlocking gears of an ecosystems' evolutionary motor

The interlocking of architecture and governance shapes ecosystem-wide evolution in the short, medium, and long term. These evolutionary effects are manifested in their resilience, scalability, and composability in the short term; stickiness, synergy, and plasticity in the medium term; envelopment, competitive durability, and mutation in the long term. The motor of ecosystem evolution stalls if its two gears—architecture and governance—fall out of alignment. The reward for maintaining alignment is the potential for a Cambrian explosion of innovation across a business ecosystem. Fostering emergent innovations across the business ecosystem requires attention to a different set of evolutionary metrics spanning multiple time horizons and correcting emergent misalignments between ecosystem governance and architecture. Most innovations in business ecosystems emerge from their complementors' selfish pursuit of self-interest and rarely from some grandiose vision of selfless collectivism. The tripartite design of ecosystem governance spanning decision rights allocation, control, and pricing by the orchestrator ensures that such pursuit of self-interest also furthers the interests of its ecosystem.

The fundamental premise of biologically inspired business ecosystems is as old as our species: Encouraging everyone to do what they can do best makes everyone better off.

About the Author

Amrit Tiwana is a professor in the Terry College of Business at the University of Georgia. He has also held joint appointments in computer science and management departments, giving him a unique vantage point to author *Platform Ecosystems*. Professor Tiwana regularly advises in the United States, Europe, and Japan industry consortia, government agencies, and major technology companies such as IBM, UPS, NTT Japan, Fujitsu, Hitachi, Toshiba, Mitsui, Mitsubishi Electric, Sumitomo Steel, Kansai Electric, Sony, Eli Lilly & Company, Japan Electronics and IT Industry Association, and Finland's INFORTE. His ongoing research involves Mozilla and Blackberry developer communities.

Platform Ecosystems builds on recent research developments in information systems, software engineering, and business strategy. Professor Tiwana has been a direct contributor to research in peer-reviewed journals in all three fields. He serves on the editorial boards of leading information systems journals (such as *Information Systems Research*, *Journal of Management Information Systems*, and *IEEE Transactions on Engineering Management*) and business strategy journals (*Strategic Management Journal*). Dr. Tiwana is the best-selling author of *The Knowledge Management Toolkit* (Prentice Hall), which is translated into several foreign languages, widely used in business schools, and has continuously been in print since it first appeared 15 years ago. He received his doctorate from Georgia State University. Home Page: PragmaticTheory.com

References

Adner, R., 2012. The Wide Lens. Portfolio, New York.

Adner, R., Kapoor, R., 2010. Value creation in innovation ecosystems: how the structure of technological inter-dependence affects firm performance in new technology generations. Strateg. Manag. J. 31 (3), 306–333.

Adner, R., Levinthal, D., 2001. Demand heterogeneity and technology evolution: implications for product and process innovation. Manag. Sci. 47 (5), 611–628.

Adner, R., Snow, D., 2010. Bold retreat. Harv. Bus. Rev. 88 (March), 1–7.

Agarwal, R., Bayus, B., 2002. The market evolution and sales takeoff of product innovations. Manag. Sci. 48 (8), 1024–1041.

Anderson, S., Dekker, H., 2005. Management control for market transactions. Manag. Sci. 51 (12), 1734–1752.

Anderson, P., Tushman, M., 1990. Technological discontinuities and dominant designs: a cyclical model of tech-nological change. Adm. Sci. Q. 35, 604–633.

Andreessen, M., 2011. Why software is eating the world. Wall Street J. August 20th. http://online.wsj.com/article/SB10001424053111903480904576512250915629460.html.

Ang, S., Straub, D., 1998. Production and transaction economies and IS outsourcing: a study of the U.S. banking industry. MIS Q. 22 (4), 535–552.

Argyres, N., Bigelow, L., 2010. Innovation, modularity, and vertical deintegration: evidence from the early US auto industry. Organ. Sci. 21 (4), 842–853.

Armstrong, M., 2006. Competition in two-sided markets. RAND J. Econ. 37 (3), 668–691.

Armstrong, M., Wright, J., 2007. Two-sided markets, competitive bottlenecks and exclusive contracts. Econ. Theory. 32 (2), 353–380.

Arthur, B., 2009. The Nature of Technology. Free Press, New York.

Arthur, B., 2011. The second economy. McKinsey Q. (October), 1–9.

Athey, S., Roberts, J., 2001. Organizational design: decision rights and incentive contracts. Am. Econ. Rev. 91 (2), 200–205.

Baldwin, C., 2008. Where do transactions come from? Modularity, transactions, and the boundaries of firms. Ind. Corp. Change. 17 (1), 155–195.

Baldwin, C., Clark, K., 2000. Design Rules: The Power of Modularity. MIT Press, Cambridge, MA.

Baldwin, C., Clark, K., 2006. The architecture of participation: does code architecture mitigate free riding in the open source development model? Manag. Sci. 52 (7), 1116–1127.

Baldwin, C., von Hippel, E., 2011. Modeling a paradigm shift: from producer innovation to user and open collab-orative innovation. Organ. Sci. 22 (6), 1399–1417.

Baldwin, C., Woodard, J., 2009. The architecture of platforms: a unified view. In: Gawer, A. (Ed.), Platforms, Markets and Innovation. Edward Elgar, Cheltenham, UK, pp. 19–44.

Banker, R.D., Kauffman, R.J., Kumar, R., 1992. An empirical test of object-based output measurement metrics in a computer aided software engineering (CASE) environment. J. Manag. Inf. Syst. 8 (3), 127–150.

Banker, R.D., Kauffman, R.J., Wright, C., Zweig, D., 1994. Automating output size and reuse metrics in a repository-based computer-aided software engineering (CASE) environment. IEEE Trans. Softw. Eng. 20 (3), 169–187.

Barnett, W., Hansen, M., 1996. The Red Queen in organizational evolution. Strateg. Manag. J. 17 (1), 139–157.

Bernheim, B., Whinston, M., 1998. Incomplete contracts and strategic ambiguity. Am. Econ. Rev. 88 (4), 902–932.

Bester, H., Krähmer, D., 2008. Delegation and incentives. RAND J. Econ. 39 (3), 664–682.

Bollen, N., 1999. Real options and product life cycles. Manage. Sci. 45 (5), 670–684.

Boudreau, K., 2010. Open platform strategies and innovation: granting access vs. devolving control. Manag. Sci. 56 (10), 1849–1872.

Bradach, J., Eccles, R., 1989. Price, authority, and trust: from ideal types to plural forms. Annu. Rev. Sociol. 15 (1), 97–118.

Brusoni, S., Prencipe, A., 2006. Making design rules: a multidomain perspective. Organ. Sci. 17 (2), 179–189.

Burrows, P., 2011. How apple feeds its army of app makers. BusinessWeek. (June 13–19), 39–40.

Caillaud, B., Jullien, B., 2003. Chicken and egg: competition among intermediation service providers. RAND J. Econ. 34 (2), 309–328.

Cardinal, L.B., 2001. Technological innovation in the pharmaceutical industry: the use of organizational control in managing research and development. Organ. Sci. 12 (1), 19–36.

Chui, M., Loffler, M., Roberts, R., 2010. The Internet of things. McKinsey Q. 2, 1–9.

Coff, R.W., 1999. When competitive advantage doesn't lead to performance: the resource-based view and stakeholder bargaining power. Organ. Sci. 10 (2), 119–133.

Courtney, H., 2001. 20/20 Foresight. Harvard, Boston.

de Weck, O., Roos, D., Magee, C., 2011. Engineering Systems. MIT Press, Cambridge, MA.

Dekleva, S., Drehmer, D., 1997. Measuring software engineering evolution: a Rasch calibration. Inf. Syst. Res. 8 (1), 95–104.

Dhanaraj, C., Parkhe, A., 2006. Orchestrating innovation networks. Acad. Manag. Rev. 31 (3), 659–669.

Dougherty, D., 1992. A practice-centered model of organizational renewal through product innovation. Strateg. Manag. J. 13 (1), 77–92.

Dougherty, D., Dunne, D., 2011. Organizing ecologies of complex innovation. Organ. Sci. 22 (5), 1214–1223.

Economist, 2010a. Bigger and better than Wi-Fi. Economist. www.economist.com/node/17647517 (accessed 9.08.2012).

Economist, 2010b. Power from thin air. Economist. www.economist.com/node/16295708 (accessed 25.10.2012).

Economist, 2012a. Make your own angry birds. Economist. (July 21), 55.

Economist, 2012b. Outsourcing is so last year. Economist. www.economist.com/blogs/babbage/2012/05/future-customer-support (accessed 12/6/2012).

Eick, S., Graves, T., Karr, A., Marron, J., Mockus, A., 2001. Does code decay? Assessing evidence from change management data. IEEE Trans. Softw. Eng. 27 (1), 1–12.

Eisenhardt, K., 1989. Agency theory: an assessment and review. Acad. Manag. Rev. 14 (1), 57–74.

Eisenmann, T., Parker, G., van Alstyne, M., 2006. Strategies for two-sided markets. Harv. Bus. Rev. 84 (10), 1–10.

Eisenmann, T., Parker, G., Van Alstyne, M., 2011. Platform envelopment. Strateg. Manag. J. 32 (12), 1270–1285.

Ethiraj, S., Levinthal, D., 2004a. Bounded rationality and the search for organizational architecture: an evolutionary perspective on the design of organizations and their evolvability. Adm. Sci. Q. 49 (3), 404–437.

Ethiraj, S., Levinthal, D., 2004b. Modularity and innovation in complex systems. Manag. Sci. 50 (2), 159–173.

Ethiraj, S., Levinthal, D., Roy, R., 2008. The dual role of modularity: innovation and imitation. Manag. Sci. 54 (5), 939–955.

Evans, D., Schmalensee, R., 2007. Catalyst Code. Harvard Press, Boston, MA.

Evans, D., Hagiu, A., Schmalensee, R., 2006. Invisible Engines: How Software Platforms Drive Innovation and Transform Industries. MIT Press, Cambridge, MA.

Farrell, J., Saloner, G., 1985. Standardization, compatibility, and innovation. RAND J. Econ. 16 (1), 70–83.

Farrell, J., Saloner, G., 1986. Installed base and compatibility: innovation, product preannouncement, and predation. Am. Econ. Rev. 76, 940–955.

Farrell, J., Saloner, G., 1992. Converters, compatibility, and the control of interfaces. J. Ind. Econ. XL (March), 9–35.

Fenton, N., Neil, M., 1999. Software metrics: successes, failures and new directions. J. Syst. Softw. 47 (3), 149–157.

Fichman, R., 2004. Real options and IT platform adoption: implications for theory and practice. Inf. Syst. Res. 15 (2), 132–154.

Fichman, R., Keil, M., Tiwana, A., 2005. Beyond valuation: real options thinking in IT project management. Calif. Manage. Rev. 47 (2), 74–96.

Fichman, R., Moses, S., 1999. An incremental process for software implementation. Sloan Manage. Rev. (Winter), 39–52.

Gamba, A., Fusari, N., 2009. Valuing modularity as a real option. Manag. Sci. 55 (11), 1877–1896.

Garud, R., Kumaraswamy, A., 1993. Changing competitive dynamics in network industries: an exploration of sun microsystems' open systems strategy. Strateg. Manag. J. 14, 351–369.

Gawer, A., Cusumano, M., 2008. How companies become platform leaders. Sloan Manag. Rev. 49 (2), 28–35.

Gulati, R., Singh, H., 1998. The architecture of cooperation: managing coordination costs and appropriation concerns in strategic alliances. Adm. Sci. Q. 43, 781–814.

Hagui, A., 2006. Pricing and commitment by two-sided platforms. Rand J. Econ. 37 (3), 720–737.

Heller, M., 2008. The Gridlock Economy: How Too Much Ownership Wrecks Markets, Stops Innovation, and Costs Lives. Basic Books, New York.

Henderson, R., Clark, K., 1990. Architectural innovation: the reconfiguration of existing product technologies and the failure of established firms. Adm. Sci. Q. 35, 9–30.

Hibbs, C., Jewett, S., Sullivan, M., 2009. The Art of Lean Software Development. O'Reilly, Sebastopol, CA.

Hilhorst, C., Ribbers, P., van Heck, E., Smits, M., 2008. Using Dempster-Shafer theory and real options theory to assess competing strategies for implementing IT infrastructures: a case study. Decis. Support Syst. 46 (1), 344–355.

Hoetker, G., 2005. How much you know versus how well I know you: selecting a supplier for a technically innovative component. Strateg. Manag. J. 26, 75–96.

Hoetker, G., 2006. Do modular products lead to modular organizations? Strateg. Manag. J. 27 (6), 501–518.

Huchzermeier, A., Loch, C.H., 2001. Project management under risk: using the real options approach to evaluate flexibility in R&D. Manage. Sci. 47 (1), 85–101.

Iansiti, M., Levien, R., 2004. Keystone Advantage: What the New Dynamics of Business Ecosystems Mean for Strategy, Innovation, and Sustainability. Harvard Business Press, Boston, MA.

Jackson, N., 2011. Infographic: the Internet of things. Atlantic. www.theatlantic.com/technology/archive/2011/07/infographic-the-internet-of-things/242073/ (accessed 21.9.2012).

Jacobson, D., Brail, G., Woods, D., 2012. APIs: A Strategy Guide. O'Reilly, Sebastopol, CA.

Jensen, M., Meckling, W., 1992. Specific and general knowledge and organizational structure. In: Werin, L., Wijkander, H. (Eds.), Contract Economics. Blackwell, Oxford, UK, pp. 251–274.

Kamel, R., 1987. Effect of modularity on system evolution. IEEE Softw. (January), 48–54.

Kapoor, R., Adner, R., 2012. What firms make vs. what they know: how firms' production and knowledge boundaries affect competitive advantage in the face of technological change. Organ. Sci. 23 (5), 1227–1248. http://dx.doi.org/10.1287/orsc.1110.0686.

Katz, M., Shapiro, C., 1994. Systems competition and network effects. J. Econ. Perspect. 8 (2), 93–115.

Kim, S., Mcfarland, R., Kwon, S., Son, S., Griffith, D., 2011. Understanding governance decisions in a partially integrated channel: a contingent alignment framework. J. Market. Res. 48 (3), 603–616.

Kirsch, L.J., 1997. Portfolios of control modes and IS project management. Inf. Syst. Res. 8 (3), 215–239.

Langlois, R., 2002. Modularity in technology and organization. J. Econ. Behav. Organ. 49, 19–37.

Langlois, R., Garzarelli, G., 2008. Of hackers and hairdressers: modularity and the organizational economics of open-source collaboration. Ind. Innov. 15 (2), 125–143.

Levin, R., 2013. Driving the top line with technology: an interview with the CIO of Coca-Cola. McKinsey Q. (March), 1–4.

MacCormack, A., Rusnak, J., Baldwin, C., 2006. Exploring the structure of complex software designs: an empirical study of open source and proprietary code. Manag. Sci. 52 (7), 1015–1030.

Macher, J., Boerner, C., 2012. Technological development at the boundaries of the firm: a knowledge-based examination in drug development. Strateg. Manag. J. 33 (9), 1016–1036.

McGrath, R., 1997. A real options logic for initiating technology positioning investments. Acad. Manage. Rev. 22 (4), 974–996.

Meadows, D., 2008. Thinking in Systems. Chelsea Green Publishing, White River Junction, VT.

Messerschmitt, D., Szyperski, C., 2003. Software Ecosystem. MIT Press, Cambridge, MA.

Meyer, M., Selinger, R., 1998. Product platforms in software development. Sloan Manag. Rev. 40 (1), 61–74.

Mezias, J.M., Mezias, S.J., 2000. Resource partitioning, the founding of specialist firms, and innovation: the American feature film industry, 1912–1929. Organ. Sci. 11 (3), 306–322.

Moneverde, K., 1995. Technical dialog as an incentive for vertical integration in the semiconductor industry. Manag. Sci. 41 (10), 1624–1638.

Monteverde, K., Teece, D., 1982. Supplier switching costs and vertical integration in the automobile industry. Bell J. Econ. 13 (1), 206–213.

Nault, B., 1998. Information technology and organization design: locating decisions and information. Manag. Sci. 44 (10), 1321–1335.

Ostrovsky, M., Schwarz, M., 2005. Adoption of standards under uncertainty. RAND J. Econ. 36 (4), 816–832.

Ouchi, W., 1979. A conceptual framework for the design of organizational control mechanisms. Manag. Sci. 25 (9), 833–848.

Ouchi, W., 1980. Markets bureaucracies and clans. Adm. Sci. Q. 25 (1), 129–141.

Parker, G., Van Alstyne, M., 2005. Two-sided network effects: a theory of information product design. Manag. Sci. 51 (10), 1494–1504.

Parnas, D., 1972. On the criteria to be used in decomposing systems into modules. Commun. ACM. 15 (9), 1053–1058.

Parnas, D., 1979. Designing software for ease of extension and contraction. IEEE Trans. Softw. Eng. 5 (2), 128–137.

Parnas, D., Clements, P., Weiss, D., 1985. The modular structure of complex systems. IEEE Trans. Softw. Eng. 11 (3), 259–266.

Penrose, E., 1959. The Theory of the Growth of the Firm. Basil Blackwell, Oxford.

Pil, F., Cohen, C., 2006. Modularity: implications for imitation, innovation, and sustained advantage. Acad. Manag. Rev. 31 (4), 995–1011.

Prentice, C., 2010. The washers and dryers that talk back. BusinessWeek. (August 9), 23–24.

Rochet, J., Tirole, J., 2003. Platform competition in two-sided markets. J. Eur. Econ. Assoc. 1 (4), 990–1029.

Rochet, J., Tirole, J., 2006. Two-sided markets: a progress report. RAND J. Econ. 37 (3), 645–667.

Rogers, E., 1995. Diffusion of Innovations, fourth ed. Free Press, New York.

Rohfls, J., 2003. Bandwagon Effects in High-Technology Industries. MIT Press, Cambridge, MA.

Rysman, M., 2009. The economics of two-sided markets. J. Econ. Perspect. 23 (3), 125–143.

Saloner, G., Shepard, A., 1995. Adoption of technologies with network effects: an empirical examination of the adoption of automated teller machines. RAND J. Econ. 26 (3), 479–501.

Sanchez, R., 1995. Strategic flexibility in product competition. Strateg. Manag. J. 16, 135–159.

Sanchez, R., Mahoney, J., 1996. Modularity, flexibility, and knowledge management in product organization and design. Strateg. Manag. J. 17 (1), 63–76.

Schilling, M., 2000. Toward a general modular systems theory and its application to interfirm product modularity. Acad. Manag. Rev. 25 (2), 312–334.

Schilling, M., 2005. Strategic Management of Technological Innovation. McGraw Hill, Boston, MA.

Schrage, M., 2000. Serious Play. Harvard Business School Press, Boston, MA.

Shy, O., 2001. Economics of Network Industries. Cambridge University Press, Cambridge, UK.

Simon, H., 1962. The architecture of complexity. Proc. Am. Philos. Soc. 106 (6), 467–482.

Simon, H., 1978. Rationality as process and as product of thought. Am. Econ. Rev. 68 (2), 1–16.

Simon, H., 2002. Near decomposability and the speed of evolution. Ind. Corp. Change. 11 (3), 587–599.

Sosa, M., Eppinger, S., Rowles, C., 2004. The misalignment of product architecture and organizational structure in complex product development. Manag. Sci. 50 (12), 1674–1689.

Strietfeld, D., 2012. As boom lures app creators, tough part is making a living. New York Times (November 17). www.nytimes.com/2012/11/18/business/as-boom-lures-app-creators-tough-part-is-making-a-living.html.

Tadelis, S., 2002. Complexity, flexibility, and the make-or-buy decision. Am. Econ. Rev. 92 (1), 433–437.

Thompson, A., 2010. Good morning, this is your coffeemaker calling. BusinessWeek. (September 20), 41–42.

Tiwana, A., 2008a. Does interfirm modularity complement ignorance? A field study of software outsourcing alliances. Strateg. Manag. J. 29 (11), 1241–1252.

Tiwana, A., 2008b. Does technological modularity substitute for control? A study of alliance performance in software outsourcing. Strateg. Manag. J. 29 (7), 769–780.

Tiwana, A., 2009. Governance-knowledge fit in systems development projects. Inf. Syst. Res. 20 (2), 180–197.

Tiwana, A., Bush, A., 2007. A comparison of transaction cost, agency, and knowledge-based predictors of IT outsourcing decisions. J. Manag. Inf. Syst. 24 (1), 263–305.

Tiwana, A., Keil, M., 2007. Does peripheral knowledge complement control? An empirical test in technology outsourcing alliances. Strateg. Manag. J. 28 (6), 623–634.

Tiwana, A., Konsynski, B., 2010. Complementarities between organizational IT architecture and governance structure. Inf. Syst. Res. 21 (2), 288–304.

Tiwana, A., Konsynski, B., Bush, A., 2010. Platform evolution: coevolution of architecture, governance, and environmental dynamics. Inf. Syst. Res. 21 (4), 675–687.

Trigeorgis, L., 1993. The nature of option interactions and the valuation of investments with multiple real options. J. Financ. Quant. Anal. 28 (1), 1–20.

Utterback, J., 1996. Mastering the Dynamics of Innovation. Harvard Press, Boston, MA.

van Schewick, B., 2012. Internet Architecture and Innovation. MIT Press, Cambridge, MA.

Vazquez, X., 2004. Allocating decision rights on the shop floor: a perspective from transaction cost economics and organization theory. Organ. Sci. 15 (4), 463–480.

von Hippel, E., 1986. Lead users: a source of novel product concepts. Manag. Sci. 32 (7), 791–805.

von Hippel, E., 1988. Sources of Innovation. MIT Press, Cambridge, MA.

Wernerfelt, B., 1984. A resource-based view of the firm. Strateg. Manag. J. 5, 171–180.

Williamson, O., 1987. The Economic Institutions of Capitalism. Free Press, New York, NY.

Williamson, O.E., 1991. Comparative economic organization: the analysis of discrete structural alternatives. Adm. Sci. Q. 36 (2), 269–296.

Williamson, O., 1999. Strategy research: governance and competence perspectives. Strateg. Manag. J. 20, 1087–1108.

Williamson, O., 2010. Transaction cost economics: the natural progression. Am. Econ. Rev. 100 (3), 673–690.

Williamson, P., De Meyer, A., 2012. Ecosystem advantage: how to successfully harness the power of partners. Calif. Manag. Rev. 55 (1), 24–46.

Young-Ybarra, C., Wiersema, M., 1999. Strategic flexibility in information technology alliances: the influence of transaction cost economics and social exchange theory. Organ. Sci. 10 (4), 439–459.

Zook, C., Allen, J., 2003. Growth outside the core. Harv. Bus. Rev. 81 (December), 2–9.

Zweben, S.H., Edwards, S.H., Weide, B.W., Hollingsworth, J.E., 1995. The effects of layering and encapsulation on software development cost and quality. IEEE Trans. Softw. Eng. 21 (3), 200–208.

Glossary

App An add-on software subsystem or service that connects to the platform to add functionality. Also referred to as a module, extension, plug-in, or add-on. Apps are downstream complements for platforms; platforms are functionally more desirable when there are a wide variety of complements available to them.

App microarchitecture A description of how an app interacts, communicates, and interoperates with the platform. This does not have a 1:1 mapping with platform architecture because platform architecture is for apps as envisioned by a platform owner; app architecture is the same architecture as realized in the implementation of an individual app by its developer.

App microarchitecture, client-based Where presentation logic, application logic, and data access logic are placed on the client side but data storage logic is placed on the server side.

App microarchitecture, client–server Where the four functional elements of an app between clients and servers are evenly split.

App microarchitecture, cloud Where all four functional elements of an app—presentation logic, application logic, data access logic, and data storage logic—reside on the server side; the client device is a "dumb" terminal that only accepts user inputs and display outputs.

App microarchitecture, internal Where a description of how the functional elements—presentation logic, application logic, data access logic, and data storage logic—are distributed between a client and a server connected by the Internet. The five common app microarchitectures are (1) standalone, (2) cloud, (3) client-based, (4) client–server, and (5) peer-to-peer. Also known as network architecture.

App microarchitecture, peer-to-peer Where each device simultaneously acts as a client and as a server.

App microarchitecture, standalone Where all four functional elements—presentation logic, application logic, data access logic, and data storage logic—are placed on the client device and nothing resides on the server side.

Application logic Functional elements of an app where the core distinctive work that makes it valuable to its end-users is performed.

Application programming interface (API) An interface designed to accept a broad class of apps in ways that allow app developers to use the platform's capabilities without having to concern themselves with how those capabilities are implemented in the platform.

Architectural resilience One malfunctioning app cannot cause the entire ecosystem to malfunction; usually ensured through loosely coupling apps with a platform.

Architectural simplicity When the architecture of a platform is simple enough to be comprehensible by one person at a high level of abstraction.

Architecture A conceptual blueprint that describes how the ecosystem is partitioned into a relatively stable platform and a complementary set of apps that are encouraged to vary, as well as the design rules binding on both.

Augment (evolutionary operator) The addition of a new subsystem to the ecosystem, adding new functionality. The notation for it used in this book is +.

Bathtub model of platform evolution The net difference between innovation inflows and outflows can potentially differentiate it from rival ecosystems. Inflows are innovations that enter an ecosystem, contributed primarily by app developers and the platform owner and to a lesser extent by end-users, upstream suppliers in the platform's value chain, and ideas copied from rival platforms. Outflows are innovations that are copied by rival platforms.

Chicken-or-egg problem The dilemma that neither side will find a two-sided technology solution with potential network effects attractive enough to join without a large presence of the other side.

Coevolution Simultaneously adjusting architecture and governance of a platform or app to maintain alignment between them.

Competitive durability The degree to which the adopters of a technology solution continue to regularly use it long after its initial adoption.

Complements Two products are complements when one increases the attractiveness of the other; think of cookies and milk or a laptop and a Web browser.

Complex system A system comprised of a number of smaller subsystems whose interactions and interdependencies are difficult to predict. A system's complexity is is a function of the number of unique subsystems present in it.

Complexity, behavioral When a platform ecosystem's aggregate behavior is difficult to predict or control.

Complexity, structural When the interconnections between parts of a platform ecosystem are difficult to describe.

Composability Changes can be made with ease within a platform or app without compromising its reintegration with the ecosystem. This can be measured as integration effort by person-hours per change.

Control mechanism The method that platform owners use to implement and enforce rules that reward desirable behavior, punish bad behavior, and promulgate standards of behavior among app developers. Its goal is to ensure coordination between the platform owner and app developers.

Control portfolio The combination of gatekeeping, process, metrics, and relational control mechanisms used by a platform owner over an app developer.

Data access logic Functional elements of an app focused on accessing and retrieving data that an app uses.

Data storage logic Functional elements of an app focused on storing data that an app uses.

Decision rights Who—the platform owner or app developer—makes what decisions. Can be exclusively with the platform owner (which represents centralization) or with an app developer (which represents decentralization), and shared anywhere in between.

Diffusion curve A description of whether a technology solution is in the stage of having attracted the geeks, early majority, early adopters, late majority, or laggards to its user base.

Divide-and-conquer strategy Divvying a platform ecosystem into manageable components—the platform and its many apps—that can be developed independently and subsequently brought together. This is primarily done using a modular architecture.

Dominant design A technology solution that implicitly or explicitly becomes the gold standard among competing designs that defines the design attributes that are widely accepted as meeting users' needs.

Durability A platform or app's endurance over time in a competitive marketplace. Can be measured as the change in the percentage of its initial adopters who remain active users.

Ecosystem The collection of the platform and the apps specific to it.

Emergence The properties of a platform that arise spontaneously as its participants pursue their own interests based on their own expertise but adapt to what other ecosystem participants are doing.

Envelop (evolutionary operator) The addition of the functionality of an adjacent solution with a shared user base to the original ecosystem, swallowing the target's functionality. This is a special case of the augment operator. The notation for it used in this book is $+^e$.

Envelopment Swallowing of a platform or app of the functionality of a solution in an adjacent market with overlapping users. This can be measured as the count of successful envelopment moves made or envelopment attacks rebuffed.

Envelopment, horizontal The most widespread envelopment move through which a platform or app swallows the functionality of a product or service—or even a platform—in an adjacent market.

Envelopment, vertical An envelopment move by a platform or app into adjacent parts of the ecosystem's value chain.

Evolvability The capacity of a platform or app to efficiently change as new requirements, needs, and possibilities emerge.

Fixed costs Baseline costs incurred (e.g., initial development costs, services provisioning costs, operating expenses) even if the platform had zero users on either side. Fixed costs are spread over the number of users, so fixed costs per user decline as the number of users grows.

Gatekeeping control A platform owner uses predefined criteria for judging what apps and app developers are allowed into a platform's ecosystem. The platform owner sets this criteria, not just for *what* is allowed in but also *who* is allowed in.

Gears of evolution Architecture and strategy are the two gears of a platform's evolutionary motor that must interlock and align. Realizing the potential of thoughtfully designed architectures requires ensuring that a platform is governed to take advantage of its architecture. The two can be perfect in isolation but will underdeliver on their potential if one does not align well with the other.

Goldilocks rule The idea that humans gravitate toward the middle over the two extreme choices given any three ordered choices.

Good architecture, properties Simplicity, resilience, maintainability, and evolvability.

Governance Who decides what in a platform's ecosystem. This encompasses partitioning of decision-making authority between platform owners and app developers, control mechanisms, and pricing and pie-sharing structures.

Humpty Dumpty problem When separating an app from the platform makes it difficult to reintegrate them.

Icarus paradox The very reasons that led to a platform's market success eventually hinder its ability to respond to new generations of technology, eventually causing their downfall.

Implementation decision rights Specify how a party (app developer or platform owner) should implement the objectives specified by strategic decision rights. Such technical execution decisions pertain to the choice of features, functionality, design, user interface, and implementation details. They apply to both platforms and apps.

Interface standardization The degree to which an app communicates, interoperates, and exchanges data with the platform using explicitly defined interfaces, protocols, and rules that are not allowed to change.

Interfaces Specifications that describe how the platform and apps interact and exchange information.

Invert (evolutionary operator) The addition of the functionality widely used by other interacting systems to the original ecosystem. Invert potentially demodularizes by converting a modular pair of systems into a monolithic system. This is a special case of the augment operator. The notation for it used in this book is $+^i$.

Leapfrogging Embracing a disruptive technology solution and using it as the foundation for the firm's market offering in lieu of an incumbent solution in the decline phase of its S-curve.

License, perpetual A one-time payment by an end-user that grants nonexpiring rights to use the app. The license can either be an individual license (the buyer can use the app on a limited or unlimited number of instantiations of the platform), a machine license (which allows use only on a particular machine for which it was purchased), or a floating license (which allows the user to use it on any one machine at a time).

License, subscription-based Allows the user to use an app for the duration of an active subscription period, during which it usually includes all future updates to the app.

License, usage-based A utility-oriented licensing model that charges the user based on actual usage using some direct measure, such as number of times used or number of hours used.

Lock-in The ways in which a platform can make it more desirable for existing adopters to stay and not leave for a rival.

Long-tail strategy Going after small, niche markets with highly specialized and uncommon needs than mainstream, mass-market customers that would be economically unfeasible for mass market–oriented companies to economically serve. Think of this book versus a Stephen King horror bestseller and which one a bookstore in an airport would likely carry.

Maintainability To cost-effectively make any changes within the platform without inadvertently breaking apps that depend on it. Conversely, changes in an app should not require parallel tweaking in the platform. Designing for maintainability also increases a platform's composability.

Market volatility Not knowing how potential end-users will respond to a project, how fast they will adopt it, and whether rival platforms or apps will quickly replicate to match the features and capabilities introduced by the project. Market volatility also arises from attempting to target a market where the needs of end-users (and also of app developers in the case of platforms) are diverse.

Metrics-based control A platform owner rewards or penalizes app developers based on the degree to which the outcomes of their work achieves prespecified and objectively measurable performance targets predefined by the platform owner.

Mirroring hypothesis The organizational structure of a platform's ecosystem must mirror its architecture.

Modular operators The five discrete operations that can be performed on a platform or an app, and within the ecosystem to evolve it. Think of them as the alphabet—or baby steps—to precisely describe evolutionary paths in platform ecosystems.

Modularity The degree to which the platform and apps can be designed, implemented, operated, and altered independent of each other.

Modularization Achieved in a platform ecosystem by decoupling a platform from apps and codifying the interface specifications for how an app interacts with a platform. Its two core functions are partitioning and systems integration.

Multihoming When a participant on either side—an end-user or an app developer—participates in more than one platform ecosystem

Multisidedness The need to attract at least two distinct mutually attracted groups (such as app developers and end-users) who can potentially interact more efficiently through a platform than without it.

Mutate (evolutionary operator) The replication of a system to create a distinct derivative system intended for use in a different application domain. The notation used in this book is $\approx$.

Mutation The unanticipated, serendipitous creation of a spinoff platform or app that inherits some of the properties of the parent system but with a different purpose.

Network effects A property of a technology solution where every additional user makes it more valuable to every other user on the same side (same-side network effects) or the other side (cross-side network effects).

Packetization The ability to digitize "something"—an activity, a process, a product, or service—that was previously not digitized. Anything that can be digitized can be broken into Internet data "packets" and transported instantaneously and at near-zero cost across large distances.

Partitioning The decomposition of a platform ecosystem such that each subsystem within it is relatively autonomous from others.

Penguin problem When potential adopters of a platform with potentially strong network effects stall in adopting it because they are unsure whether others will adopt it as well.

Plasticity The degree to which a platform or app can deliver functionality that it was not originally designed to deliver to its primary existing and prospective users. This can be measured as the average count of major features added to it per release over its lifetime.

Platform The extensible codebase of a software-based system that provides core functionality shared by apps that interoperate with it, and the interfaces through which they interoperate.

Platform ecosystem See *Ecosystem*.

Platform lifecycle A multifaceted characterization of whether a technology solution is in its pre or post-dominant design stage, its current stage along the S-curve, and the proportion of the prospective user base that has already adopted it.

Platform owner The lead firm primarily responsible for the platform; sometimes also called an ecosystem's keystone firm or economic catalyst.

Platform synergy The degree to which an app is designed specifically for a particular platform. This can be measured as change in the number of functions called by the app to APIs unique to a platform as an app ages.

Port (evolutionary operator) Replicating the functionality of an app to allow it to function on a platform different from which it was originally implemented. This is a special case of the mutate operator. The notation used in this book is $\approx^P$.

Presentation logic The functional elements of an app where almost all of the interaction—for example, receiving inputs and presenting the application's output—with the end-user occurs.

Process control A platform owner rewards or penalizes app developers based on the degree to which they follow prescribed development methods and procedures that it believes will lead to outcomes desirable from a platform owner's perspective.

Real option The right to do something along a project's evolutionary trajectory—grow, scale, switch ingredients, stage expansion, or kill a project—without the obligation to do it. Many of the six types of real options can realistically be embedded in a project.

Real options thinking A way of thinking that disciplines how platform and app projects can be structured to protect against potential losses while preserving potential gains. It is an approach to position for the upside by hedging against possible futures.

Red Queen effect The increased pressure to adapt faster just to survive is driven by an increase in the evolutionary pace of rival technology solutions.

Relational control A platform owner relies on shared culture, similar set of values, and shared norms to shape their behaviors.

Resilience The capacity of a platform or app to function acceptably in the event of a failure elsewhere within or outside the ecosystem. This can be measured as the recovery time of a platform or app after a failure outside it.

Resource Tangible assets such as a platform's capabilities, functionality, user base, complementing apps, and patents as well as intangible assets such as brand recognition and reputation.

Resource litmus test A resource can help (1) create a competitive advantage if it is valuable and rare and (2) sustain a competitive advantage if it is inimitable and nonsubstitutable.

Risk transfer in platforms Unlike traditional product development where a company must bear most innovation risk, the costs and risks of developing new platform-specific innovations shift from the platform owner to the app developers.

Scalability The degree to which the functional performance and financial viability of a platform or app is size-agnostic. This can be measured as the increase in its latency, responsiveness, or error rates per additional 1,000 users or as direction of the shift in its financial breakeven point per 1,000 fewer users.

S-curve A technology's lifecycle that describes its progression from introduction, ascent, maturity, and decline phases.

Search costs The costs incurred by customers prior to transacting making a purchase, largely from having to decide who to buy from.

Seesaw problem The challenge of managing the delicate balance between app developers' autonomy to freely innovate and ensuring that apps seamlessly interoperate with the platform.

Software embedding Making a business process or activity into software.

Split (evolutionary operator) The subdivision of a monolithic system into two smaller subsystems; modularizes monolithic systems. The notation for it used in this book is $\neq$.

Stickiness The "eyeball time" between a platform or app and its primary users. This can be measured as the change in hours per end-user session over time, the count of end-user sessions per week over time, or in API calls made by an app on average as the platform ages (platform-level only).

Strategic decision rights Decision rights that specify what a party (app developer or platform owner) should accomplish. They apply to both platforms and apps.

Substitute (evolutionary operator) The substitution of one subsystem in the ecosystem with another. The notation used in this book is $\updownarrow$.

Subtract (evolutionary operator) The removal of a subsystem from the ecosystem. The notation for it used in this book is —.

Systems integration costs The effort required by an app developer to manage the dependencies among a platform and apps in an ecosystem. These include costs of integrating an app with the platform and of integrating an app with other potentially interacting apps in the ecosystem.

Technical volatility Immaturity of technology, unpredictability of how it will evolve, the need for integrating a system with other existing systems within and outside a platform ecosystem, and a platform project's sheer complexity.

Tipping The point at which a critical mass of adopters makes positive network effects take off.

Transaction costs The costs incurred by customers during the purchase process.

Ubiquity The property of being present everywhere; refers specifically to Internet-based data networks in this book.

Valuable ignorance When, in doing their own work, app developers need not know how a platform does what it does nor need to understand the intricacies of the platform-native functionalities on which their app draws.

Value chain of ecosystems A platform ecosystem can also be divided into its upstream and downstream parts of a value chain. The upstream part is what goes into producing the platform itself (e.g., component and hardware suppliers, software licensors, manufacturing partners, network connectivity providers). The downstream part includes platform complement producers (primarily app developers), end-users who adopt it, and other intermediaries between the platform owner and end-users.

Variable costs The additional costs besides fixed costs that increase with the number of users (e.g., bandwidth costs, end-user support costs, or storage costs). See also *Fixed costs*.

Index

Note: Page numbers followed by *b* indicate boxes, *f* indicate figures and *t* indicate tables.